INTERNATIONAL ACCLAIM FOR
FROM BOSTON TO BEIJING

Leaders of the Future will have to understand globalization. Nobody can help them more than Nancy Adler!

— Marshall Goldsmith,
Co-Editor, *The Leader of the Future* (U.S.)

An invaluable resource. *From Boston to Beijing* guides you though the complexities of a multicultural world, sharing insights into the ways...cultural diversity can help your business. Adler's advice is simple; recognize cultural differences, understand them, and then use that knowledge to your advantage when building effective multicultural teams. With this book packed, crossing the border will hold few fears for the well prepared manager.

— Steven Wilkinson,
Commissioning Editor, BBC (United Kingdom)

From Boston to Beijing provides practical, meaningful business applications...in the face of global challenges.

— Pri Notowidigdo,
Managing Partner, Amrop International (Indonesia)

FROM BOSTON
TO BEIJING

FROM BOSTON TO BEIJING

Managing with a World View

Nancy J. Adler

SOUTH-WESTERN
™
THOMSON LEARNING

Australia • Canada • Mexico • Singapore • Spain • United Kingdom • United States

First trade edition 2002

Printed in Canada
1 2 3 4 5 04 03 02

For more information contact South-Western, 5101 Madison Road, Cincinnati, Ohio, 45227 or find us on the Internet at http://www.swcollege.com
For permission to use material from this book:
• In the U.S., contact us by telephone: 1-800-730-2214 or by fax: 1-800-730-2215
• Outside the U.S., contact us via the web: http://www.thomsonrights.com

Library of Congress Cataloging-in-Publication Data
Adler, Nancy J.
    International dimensions of organizational behavior / Nancy J. Adler.—4th ed.
        p. cm.
    Includes bibliographical references and index.
    ISBN 0-324-07475-1
    1. Organizational behavior—Cross-cultural studies.   I. Title.
    HD58.7.A33   2000
    658—dc21
                                                                00-046396

To my mother,

LISELOTTE ADLER,

who brought together two worlds and
two very different cultures
in creating the home
in which I grew up.

Contents

Preface

THE WORLD OF ORGANIZATIONS is no longer defined by national boundaries. *From Boston to Beijing* breaks down the conceptual, theoretical, and practical boundaries limiting our ability to understand and work with people in countries around the world. Until recently, much of the published material on leadership and management came primarily from the American experience: American managers and American-trained researchers observed the behavior of people in U.S.–based organizations. From their observations and research, they developed models and theories to explain the behavior of people and organizations. The problem was in their assumption: they implicitly assumed that what was true for Americans working in the United States was also true for people from other countries working worldwide. Both managers and researchers assumed that Americans' work behavior was universal. They were wrong. *From Boston to Beijing* challenges us to go beyond our parochialism and to see the world from a global perspective.

Today, managers no longer have the luxury of reducing global complexity to the simplicity of assumed universality; they no longer have the luxury of assuming that there is only one best way to manage. Luckily, we have learned that global complexity is neither unpredictable nor random. Variations across cultures and their impact on organizations follow systematic, predictable patterns. Starting with a core of traditional, primarily U.S.–based understandings of the behavior of people in organizations, *From Boston to Beijing* becomes a guide for modifying our attitudes, thinking patterns, and behavior. Far from ignoring the historical body of managerial knowledge and experience, *From Boston to Beijing* expands our understanding of people's behavior at work to include the diversity and complexity of today's global environment.

From Boston to Beijing is divided into three sections. The first section, "Culture: A Major Impact on Organizations," describes the ways in which cultures vary, how that variance systematically affects organizations, and how people can recognize, manage, and effectively use cultural variance within their own work environments. The second section, "Leveraging Cultural Diversity," presents an integrated approach to managing in multicultural work environments. Chapter 4 investigates cross-cultural problem solving and organizational development; Chapter 5 presents the dynamics of multicultural teams; Chapter 6 reviews approaches to leading, motivating, and decision making from a global perspective; and Chapter 7 summarizes global approaches to resolving conflict and to negotiating.

The third part, "Managing Global Managers," presents a series of issues that are unique to global management. It addresses the human resource management dilemmas involved in managing one's life and career while moving across international borders. Chapter 8 describes the cross-cultural entry and reentry transitions from the employee's perspective and addresses such questions as: What is cultural shock? How does one adjust to a new culture? How should international employees manage reentry back into their home country and organization? Chapter 9 also presents global transition issues, but from the spouse's perspective. Chapter 10 introduces the challenges of managing global careers. How do the routes to the top of major companies vary from country to country? What do managers see as the most important benefits and drawbacks in pursuing global careers? Given its focus on global managers, this section goes far beyond the scope of domestically oriented books on both management and organizational behavior.

Given the familiarity that most people have with Amercians' approaches to managing, *From Boston to Beijing* often uses the United States as a reference point and as a point of comparison. American readers will recognize the familiar ways in which organizational behavior is usually described and be able to add a more global perspective to that knowledge. Readers from all countries will gain a better understanding of their own culture's practices and ways of conducting business, both relative to traditional U.S.–based descriptions and, more importantly, relative to a wide variety of countries worldwide. No country's system or perspective is any better or worse—any more or less effective—than any other country's; rather, each is distinct and therefore must not be understood as a replica of any other nation.

Cross-cultural management is a new field relative to the traditional practice of management. *From Boston to Beijing* integrates what is known in the field at the beginning of the twenty-first century. Our knowledge will continue to grow far beyond today's understandings. Even though the limits of our understanding at times restrict us, they also define the boundaries and excitement of an important, rapidly expanding field of knowledge. Far from leaving with a sense of knowing all there is to know, it is hoped that readers will finish the book with a sophisticated awareness of the world beyond their own national boundaries, an understanding of the limits of their own knowledge, and a set of questions to guide their management decisions and future inquiry.

ACKNOWLEDGMENTS

The process of understanding the human dynamics in global management has brought together some of the best thinking and insights from executives, managers, consultants, scholars, and researchers worldwide. The process is evolving. What we know today is so much more than what we understood yesterday, and yet so much less than what we will need for tomorrow. The excitement and passion in the search is predicated on our need to understand ourselves in a world in which no part of humanity is very far away, a world in which our success as well as our survival depends on our understanding and respect for each other.

I would like to thank the many people who have contributed to this book, each from his or her unique perspective and expertise. The quality of this book is shared by all, the errors and limitations are mine alone. My thanks to: Liselotte Adler (USA), Arshad Ahmad (Pakistan), Nakiye Boyacigiller (Turkey), Jill deVillafranca (Canada), Joseph J. diStefano (Switzerland), Angela Dowson (Canada), Paul Evans (England), John Graham (USA), Jon Hartwick (Canada), Mary Hess (USA), Maryann Jelinek (USA), André Laurent (France), Phyllis Lefohn (USA), Robert T. Moran (USA), Eileen Newmark (USA), Pri Notowidigdo (Indonesia), France Pepper (Canada), Roger Putzel (USA), Vijit Ramchandani (India), Indrei Ratiu (Britain/Romania), George Renwick (USA), Stephen Rhinesmith (USA), David Ricks (USA), Karlene Roberts (USA), Anita Salustro (USA), Suzanne Sellitto (Canada), Richard Vilas (USA), and Frances Westley (Canada).

A special thank you goes to Troy Anderson for his always helpful research assistance, to Robine Andrau for her excellent editing, to Rola Zoayter for her patient and conscientious typing and organizing, to John Szilagyi of South-Western and Tom Woll of Cross River Publishing Consultants for their professionalism and enthusiasm in managing the entire project, and to Louise Dubreil, without whose help, encouragement, and insight this book would have never become a reality.

Culture: A Major Impact on Organizations

1

Culture and Management

Verité en-deçà des Pyrénées, erreur au-delà.
> (*"There are truths on this side of the Pyrenees which are*
> *falsehoods on the other."*)[1]
>   —BLAISE PASCAL

Capital raised in London in the Eurodollar market by a Belgium-based corporation may finance the acquisition of machinery by a subsidiary located in Australia. A management team from French Renault may take over an American-built automotive complex in the Argentine. Clothing for dolls, sewn in Korea on Japanese-supplied sewing machines according to U.S. specifications, may be shipped to Northern Mexico for assembly with other components into dolls being manufactured by a U.S. firm for sale in New York and London during the Christmas season. A California-manufactured airbus . . . is powered by British . . . engines, while a competing airbus . . . flies on Canadian wing assemblies. A Frenchman is appointed president of [a] U.S. domiciled . . . corporation, while an American establishes . . . a Swiss-based international mutual fund (30:1–2).

MANAGING THE GLOBAL ENTERPRISE and modern business management have become synonymous. The terms international, multinational, transnational, and global can no longer be relegated to a subset of organizations or to a division within the organization. Success now transcends

3

national boundaries. In fact, the very concept of domestic business may have become anachronistic. Today "the modern business enterprise has no place to hide. It has no place to go but everywhere" (57:xiii).

Executives no longer question the increasing importance of global business. As indicated in the *21st Century Report* (38), more than two-thirds of the world's CEOs view foreign competition as a key factor in their firm's business success. Similarly, two-thirds of the world's CEOs expect to generate employment and revenues increasingly from outside their firm's home country (38:30,31). These same executives believe that effectively managing the human system is critical to global success (38:2).

The post–World War II years saw a major expansion of world trade. From 1948 through 1972 world exports grew from $51 billion to $415 billion, representing a sevenfold increase in monetary terms and a fourfold increase in volume (23:23).[2] By 1980 international trade volume exceeded $1 trillion as compared with $800 billion in 1975 (46). In the 1990s, world exports grew from $4.3 trillion in 1990 to $7.1 trillion in 1999, an increase of 66 percent (29). By the 1990s, Coca-Cola, for example, earned higher profits selling soda to the Japanese than to Americans (85:5). Today's world trade dwarfs all prior statistics.

By the mid-1980s, the U.S. Commerce Department estimated that some 70 percent of U.S. firms faced "significant foreign competition" in their domestic markets, up from only 25 percent a decade earlier (69:11). By the end of the 1980s, the chairman of the Foreign Trade Council estimated the figure to be 80 percent. Today, at the beginning of the twenty-first century, global competition is serious, pervasive, and here to stay.

What does the future portend? According to *The Economist*, "Over the next 25 years, the world will see the biggest shift in economic strength in more than a century" (33:3). Emerging economic giants will dwarf developed industrial economies, and "within a generation, China will overtake . . . [the United States] as the world's biggest economy" (33:4). Already in the 1990s, the average annual percentage change in total output in developing countries was more than twice that of advanced economies (5.3% versus only 2.3% [29]). Moreover, many of the top 15 economic performers will be from today's rapidly developing economies, with countries such as Thailand and Taiwan overtaking Britain (33:4). The developing world's share of world exports of manufactured goods has already jumped more than 400 percent in just the last 25 years (33:4).

Will today's economically developed countries continue to prosper or will they lose out to the gains forecast for developing economies?[3] Pessimists argue that with increasing access to advanced technology, jobs will shift from workers in rich countries to cheap, educated labor in economically developing countries. They claim that free trade with developing countries is a recipe for mass unemployment, huge wage inequalities, and a massive migration of firms to low-wage countries. In a dramatic role reversal, economically developing countries that historically were considered victims of multinational exploitation would now be viewed as villains, stealing capital and jobs and, ironically, creating inequities by destroying the wealth of developed economies.

On the surface this pessimistic scenario appears true, especially when comparing the hourly wages of production workers. In the late 1990s, it cost $28 an hour to employ a production worker in Germany, $19 an hour in Japan, and $18 an hour in the United States; but only $5 in Hong Kong, $1.75 in Mexico, and 50 cents in Sri Lanka (95). According to the president of the World Economic Forum, it will soon be possible for countries to have high productivity, advanced technology, and low wages (84). A French consumer electronics group, for example, already employs three times as many highly skilled workers in Asia as in France. Similarly, the Italian sportswear maker Fila produces only 10 percent of its sportswear in Italy; it subcontracts the rest in lower-wage Asian economies.

Optimists, however, predict a different scenario. According to optimists, advanced economies, far from losing out to the growing prosperity of economically developing countries, will benefit from it. Billions of new consumers in the developing world will markedly increase demand for exports from the advanced economies. In just the past decade, for example, exports from high-income to low- and middle-income countries have already more than doubled. In addition, the optimists contend that both advanced and developing economies benefit from increased competition. Greater economies of scale and better allocation of resources resulting from increased competition and financial diversification are improving expected rates of return for all players. Nevertheless, the inflows of foreign direct investment into economically developing countries are impressive, increasing sevenfold from $19 billion to $148 billion in just the last decade (29). Over the same period, the proportion of foreign direct investment into developing countries increased from 12 to 41 percent of the total (97). Far from dramatically losing out, foreign direct investment in the world's richest economies increased from $169 billion to $234 billion over the same period (97).

Although international businesses have existed for centuries, the world has clearly entered an era of unprecedented global economic activity, including worldwide production, distribution, and increasingly large numbers of international joint ventures, multinational mergers and acquisitions, and global strategic alliances. Examples of new global operations and alliances abound, with most major firms earning more from their international than from their domestic operations. Global companies such as Asea Brown Bovari, Honda, British Petroleum, Siemens, Motorola, and Eastman Kodak each do business in more than 50 countries (51:3). The 1992 economic integration of the European Union and the 1999 introduction of the common European currency, the Euro, focused the world's attention on transborder business activity and the importance of trading blocs. Although the U.S. and Canadian economies have been inextricably linked to the world economy for years, the signing of the North American Free Trade Agreement refocused Canadian, Mexican, and U.S. attention on global business.

As Professor Ian Mitroff observes, "For all practical purposes, all business today is global. Those individual businesses, firms, industries, and whole societies that clearly understand the new rules of doing business in a world economy will prosper; those that do not will perish" (65:ix). Mitroff challenges us to realize that "It is no longer business as usual. Global competition has forced . . . [executives] to recognize that if they and their organizations are to survive, let alone prosper, they will have to learn to manage and to think very differently" (65:x).

GLOBAL STRATEGY AND CULTURE[4]

To succeed, corporations must develop global strategies (98). The final decades of the twentieth century made the importance of such recognition commonplace, at least among leading firms and management scholars; the twenty-first century has made it imperative. Incorporating today's global realities, new time- and quality-sensitive approaches to managing research and development, production, marketing, and finance have evolved rapidly. Yet, only in the last decade has an equivalent evolution in understanding international organizational behavior and managing global human resource systems developed. Although other functional areas increasingly use global strategies that were largely unheard of—or would have been deemed inappropriate—only one or two decades ago, many firms continued to conduct the worldwide management of people as if neither the strategic challenges presented by the external economic and technological environment nor the internal structure and organization of the firm had changed.

Focusing on global strategies and management approaches from the perspective of people and culture allows us to understand the influence of national and ethnic cultures on organizational functioning. Rather than becoming trapped within the most commonly asked, although unfortunately misleading, question of *whether* organizational dynamics are universal or culturally specific, this book focuses on the crucially important questions of *when* and *how* to be most effectively sensitive to culture.

PHASES OF DEVELOPMENT

As we investigate the influence of cultural diversity on multinational and global firms, it becomes clear that national cultural differences are important but that their relative impact depends on the stage of development of the firm, industry, and world economy. Using the model shown in Table 1-1, which traces the development of global enterprises, we can trace distinct variations in the relative importance of cultural diversity and, consequently, equally distinct variations in the most appropriate approaches to managing people worldwide (4;5;96). Whereas historically the order of the phases has varied, primarily depending on the company's age and origin as an Asian, European, or North American firm, the order presented here reflects the most common evolution for North American firms. Today, as transnational dynamics increasingly define global business competitiveness, firms frequently skip specific phases in order to position themselves to more rapidly maximize their global competitive advantage within a particular industry.

Domestic Phase

As shown in Tables 1-1 and 1-2, historically, most firms initially operated from a domestic, or ethnocentric, perspective. Firms produced unique products and services that they offered almost exclusively to their own home, domestic market. The uniqueness of the product or service and the lack of international competition negated the firm's need to demonstrate sensitivity to national cultural differences. When firms exported products, they often did so without altering them for foreign consumption. Foreign buyers, rather than the home country product-design, manufacturing, or marketing teams, absorbed the inconvenience of inherent cultural differences. In some ways the implicit message sent to foreigners was "We will allow you to buy our product"; and, of course, the assumption was that foreigners would want to buy. During this initial

TABLE 1-1 Multinational Corporate Evolution

	Domestic Phase	Multidomestic Phase	Multinational Phase	Global Phase
Competitive strategy	Domestic	Multidomestic	Multinational	Global
Importance of world business	Marginal	Important	Extremely important	Dominant
Primary orientation	Product/Service	Market	Price/Cost	Strategy
Product/service	New, unique	More standardized	Completely standardized (commodity)	Mass-customized
Type of development emphasized	Product engineering	Process engineering	Engineering not emphasized	Product and process engineering
Technology	Proprietary	Limited sharing	Widely shared	Almost instantly and extensively shared
R&D/Sales	High	Decreasing	Very low	Very high
Profit margin	High	Decreasing	Very low	High, yet immediately decreasing
Competitors	None	Few	Many	Significant (few or many)
Market	Small and domestic	Large and multidomestic	Larger and multinational	Largest and global
Production location	Domestic	Domestic and primary foreign markets	Multinational, based on least cost	Global, least cost
Exports	None	Growing, high potential	Large, saturated	Imports, exports, and "transports"
Structure	Functional divisions	Functional with international division	Multinational lines of business	Global alliances, "heterarchy"
	Centralized	Decentralized	Centralized	Coordinated and decentralized

SOURCE: © 2002 Nancy J. Adler. See Adler and Ghadar (5). Phases I–III are based on Vernon (96).

TABLE 1-2 Corporate Cross-Cultural Evolution

	Domestic Phase	Multidomestic Phase	Multinational Phase	Global Phase
Strategy	Domestic	Multidomestic	Multinational	Global
Primary orientation	Product/ Service	Market	Price/Cost	Strategy
Perspective	Ethnocentric	Polycentric or Regiocentric	Multinational	Global/Multicentric
Cultural sensitivity	Marginally important	Very important	Somewhat important	Critically important
With whom	No one	Clients	Employees	Employees and clients
Level	No one	Workers and clients	Managers	Executives
Strategic assumption	"One way" or "One best way"	"Many good ways" Equifinality	"One least-cost way" Simultaneously	"Many good ways"

SOURCE: © 2002 Nancy J. Adler. See Adler and Ghadar (5).

phase, people, assumptions, and strategies from the headquarters' country dominated management: firms in the domestic phase regarded cross-cultural management and global human resource systems as largely irrelevant.

Multidomestic Phase

Domestic competition ushered in the second phase, and with it the initial need to market and produce abroad. Irrelevant during the initial domestic phase, sensitivity to cultural differences became critical to implementing effective corporate strategy in the multidomestic phase. The domestic phase's product orientation shifted to a market orientation, with companies now needing to address each foreign market separately and differently.

Whereas the unique technology of the domestic phase's products and services fit well with an ethnocentric "one-best-way" approach, during the multidomestic phase firms began to assume there were "many good ways" to manage, each dependent on the particular country involved.

Successful companies no longer expected foreigners to absorb cultural mismatches between buyers and sellers. Rather, home-country representatives modified their style to fit with that of their clients and colleagues in foreign markets. Although cultural differences became important in the design and marketing of culturally appropriate products and services, they became *critical* in worldwide production. Managers had to learn culturally appropriate approaches to managing people in each country in which the company operated.

Multinational Phase

By the 1980s many industries had entered the multinational phase. The competitive environment for these industries had changed again, giving rise to demands for culturally sensitive management practices. In multinational industries, a number of companies produce almost indifferentiable products (practically commodities), with a lower price offering each company its only potentially significant competitive advantage. From this global price-sensitive—and therefore cost-sensitive—perspective, cultural awareness declines in importance. Price competition among almost identical products and services produced by various multinational companies negates the importance of most cultural differences and almost all advantages gained by cultural sensitivity.

As shown in Table 1-2, the primary product design and marketing assumption is no longer the domestic phase's "one best way" or even the multidomestic phase's "many good ways" but rather "one least-cost way." The primary market becomes global, with almost no geography-based market segmentation. Firms can gain competitive advantage only through process engineering, sourcing critical factors on a worldwide basis, and benefiting from economies of scale. Price competition significantly reduces the perceived influence of cultural differences.

Global, or Transnational, Phase

Many managers believed that the multinational phase would be the ultimate phase for all industries. Their assumption proved to be false. Although a number of industries today continue to operate under the norms of the multinational phase, a fourth phase has emerged for firms in the most globally competitive industries. In this phase, top quality, least-possible-cost products become the baseline, the minimally acceptable standard. Competitive advantage comes from strategic thinking, mass customization, and outlearning one's competitors. Product and service ideas are drawn from worldwide sources, as are the factors and locations of production. Companies, however, tailor final products and services and their marketing to discrete market niches. Critical components of this market segmentation are nationality and ethnicity. Culture, once again, becomes a factor critical to competitive success.

Successful global firms competing under transnational dynamics need to understand their potential clients' needs, no matter where in the world the clients live. They need to be able to quickly translate these worldwide client needs into products and services, produce those products and services on a timely and least-cost basis, and then deliver them to clients in a culturally acceptable fashion for each of the national and ethnic communities involved.

By this global phase, the exclusive product, sales, or price orientation of past phases almost completely disappears. Companies replace these individual orientations with a culturally responsive design orientation, accompanied by a rapid, worldwide, least-cost production function. Needless to say, culture is critically important to this most advanced stage. Similarly, the ability to manage cross-cultural interaction, multinational teams, and global alliances becomes fundamental to overall business success. Whereas effective global human resource strategies varied in past phases from being irrelevant to being helpful, by the global phase they become essential, a minimum requirement for organizational survival and success.

CROSS-CULTURAL MANAGEMENT

The importance of world business has created a demand for managers sophisticated in global management and skilled at working with people from other countries (83). Cross-cultural management helps managers understand the behavior of people in organizations around the world and work with employees and clients from many different cultures (26; 41;73). Cross-cultural management *describes* the behavior of people within countries and cultures; *compares* the behavior of people across countries and cultures; and, perhaps most important, seeks to improve the *interaction* among colleagues, managers, executives, clients, suppliers, and alliance partners from countries and cultures around the world. Cross-cultural management thus expands the scope of domestic managerial practice to encompass multicultural and global dynamics. Rather than cross-cultural and global management being seen as a subset of traditional domestic management, domestic management is now recognized as a limited subset of global and cross-cultural management.

Parochialism

Parochialism means viewing the world solely through one's own eyes and perspective. A person with a parochial perspective neither recognizes other people's different ways of living and working nor appreciates that such differences can offer significant opportunities or create serious consequences. People in all cultures are, to a certain extent, parochial. For example, journalists, politicians, and managers alike have frequently decried Americans' parochialism.[5] Americans speak fewer foreign languages, demonstrate less interest in other cultures, and are more naïve in global business situations than the majority of their trading partners. In *The Tongue-Tied American* (86), U.S. Congressman Paul Simon deplored the shocking state of foreign language illiteracy in the United States and emphasized the heavy price Americans pay for it diplomatically, commercially, economically, and culturally. His message was a "shocking indictment of the complacent, potentially catastrophic monolingual arrogance of . . . [Americans], from top government leaders to the . . . [person] in the street" (91). Echoing Simon's sentiments in reference to South America, former U.S. Congressman James Symington explained the problem as Americans'

> fundamental, dogged, appalling ignorance of the Latin mind and culture. Foreign students and statesmen refresh their perceptions of the United States by reading our poets, essayists, novelists and humorists. But our approach is like that of the man who, when asked which hurts most, ignorance or apathy, replied, "I don't know and I don't care." Such indifference cannot be justified by our otherwise commendable concern for what people do rather than what they think. . . . Preoccupied with acting, we seldom miss opportunities to ignore thought. [Perhaps, in the future] . . . diplomats—possibly even presidents—might know something of the cultural lessons that stir our neighbors' hearts (87).

Fortune magazine reports that "A 'Copernican revolution' must take place in the attitudes of American CEOs as the international economy no longer revolves around the U.S., and the world market is shared by many strong players" (54:157). Lester Thurow, former dean of MIT's Sloan School of Management, asserts that CEOs "must have an understanding of how to manage in an international environment. . . . To be trained as an *American* manager is to be trained for a world that is no longer there"

(34:50). Similarly, Harvard management professor Rosabeth Moss Kanter asserts that "Global thinking is what's important for companies today, not [simply] international operations (49; also see 8;9;10; 36;58;66;72;76; 77;78). "The task is not to build a sophisticated structure, but to build a matrix in the minds of managers (8:212). Many business leaders predict that the next generation of top executives will have to have multiple global assignments to reach the top (14:B18;20). Royal Dutch Shell, for example, requires four global expatriate assignments before it considers a manager for promotion into the executive ranks. Yet, in the United States such global exposure and experience has neither been the norm in the past nor, unfortunately, is it common today (12).

Two decades ago a *Dun & Bradstreet* survey found that only a handful of the 87 chairmen and presidents of the 50 largest U.S. multinational corporations could be considered career internationalists. Of the 87 top executives, 80 percent had had no international experience at all, except for inspection tours (27). Today, executive recognition of the importance of global experience has increased, but not as rapidly as one might have predicted. For example, whereas almost two-thirds of today's U.S. executives see "emphasizing an international outlook" as very important for twenty-first century CEOs, only a third consider experience outside of the United States as very important, and fewer than one in five consider foreign language training as very important (54:158). By comparison, more than eighty percent of non-U.S. executives consider an international outlook as very important for future CEOs, twice as many (70% versus 35%) consider experience outside of their home country as very important, and more than three times as many (64% versus 19%) consider foreign language training as very important (38;54:158).

Why have many Americans ignored the need to think and to act globally? Americans' historic parochialism is understandable and at the same time unfortunate. Because the United States has such a large domestic market (over 274 million people) and English became the world's business language, many Americans continue to assume that they neither need to speak other languages nor to go to other countries to succeed in business. Few young Brazilians, Israelis, Swedes, or Thais remain trapped in this parochial assumption.

Historical U.S. political and technological dominance also led many Americans to believe that they could conduct business strictly from an American perspective. In many fields in which for years U.S. technology was the only advanced technology available, potential clients and trading partners from around the world had no option but to "buy American." Global business expertise was unnecessary because the product sold itself (domestic phase). In the public sector, projects transferring technology from the United States to economically developing countries further encouraged Americans to view the world from an American perspective (multidomestic phase). An Indonesian's comments describing how some Americans' views of people from economically developing countries capture this technologically based parochialism:

> The questions Americans ask me are sometimes very embarrassing, like whether I have ever seen a camera. Most of them consider themselves the most highly civilized people. Why? Because they are accustomed to technical inventions? Consequently, they think that people living in bamboo houses or having customs different from their own are primitive and backward (82).

The academic community further reinforced U.S. managers' tendency toward parochialism. Most management schools are in the United States, the vast majority of management professors and researchers are U.S. educated, and the majority of management research has focused on U.S. companies. Out of more than 11,000 articles published in 24 management journals, approximately 80 percent described studies focusing on U.S. companies conducted by American researchers (1). Fewer than 5 percent of articles describing the behavior of people in organizations include the concept of culture (1). Fewer than 1 percent focus on people from two or more cultures working together, a crucial area to understand for global business success (1). The number of cross-cultural management articles is increasing much more slowly than the rate at which business has gone global (35;59;61;68).

Even in the last decade, only 6.5 percent of organizational behavior and human resource management (HRM) articles published in leading U.S. management journals were international; however, almost three times as many (17.5%) published in leading management journals outside of North America were international (4). Among these international articles, almost every reported study (96%) found that culture had a significant impact on managerial styles and organizational success (4). The manager about to negotiate a major contract with a national from another country, the executive about to become director of Asian, European, or Latin American operations, and the newly promoted vice president for global marketing all receive less guidance than they need from the available management literature.

The United States will continue to have a large domestic market, English will continue to be the language of global business, and technological excellence will continue to typify many U.S. companies. Nonetheless, the domain of business has rapidly moved beyond national boundaries; the limitations of monolingualism have become more apparent; and sustained technological superiority in many industries has become a cherished memory. Intense global competition in the last decade has rendered parochialism self-defeating. No nation can afford to act as if it is alone in the world (parochialism) or as if it is superior to other nations (ethnocentrism). The U.S. economy, like that of all other countries, is inextricably linked to the health of the world economies. Like businesspeople the world over, Americans must now compete and contribute based on world-class standards and on a global scale.

Global Versus Domestic Organizations

Global organizations differ from their domestic counterparts. They are more geographically dispersed and more multicultural. The term *geographic dispersion* refers to the scope of global organizations' operations over vast distances worldwide (50). Whether organizations produce in multiple countries or only export to them, whether employees work as expatriates or only travel abroad, whether legal ownership involves joint ventures, wholly owned subsidiaries, or strategic alliances, global firms must manage despite the added complexity of working in many countries simultaneously. Geographic dispersion confronts organizations with fluctuations in exchange rates, substantial transportation and communication costs, varying customs regulations, and many other complexities determined by greater distances and national borders.

Multiculturalism, the second fundamental dimension of global firms, means that people from many cultures (and frequently many countries) interact regularly. Domestic firms can be multicultural if their employees or clients come from more than one culture. Many organizations in Quebec, Canada, for example, employ Anglophones (English speakers) and Francophones (French speakers) to work within the same organization, as do many companies in California that hire Hispanic and Asian as well as Anglo-Saxon employees."[6] Multiculturalism adds to the complexity of global firms by increasing the number of perspectives, approaches, and business methods represented within the organization.

To successfully manage the geographical dispersion and multiculturalism of multinational organizations, managers must develop a global mindset (8;10;17;18;36;53;58;66;76;89). In fact, it is the mindsets of key managers that shape business strategy and ultimately determine the success of the firm. Managers with a global mindset address strategic business decisions as cosmopolitans, always considering the broader world picture rather than just the local situation (10 based on 64;42). Similarly, using their highly developed cognitive complexity, managers with global mindsets simultaneously consider the multiple complex multicultural situations facing the firm, and consistently make appropriate trade-offs and decisions among competing multinational options (10).

Whereas most books on global management have focused on understanding and managing geographical dispersion, this book focuses primarily on managing multiculturalism and raises such questions as: How do people vary across cultures? How do cultural differences affect organizations? When do global managers recognize cultural differences? What are the best strategies for managing corporate multiculturalism?

WHAT IS CULTURE?

To understand the differences between domestic and global management, it is necessary to understand the primary ways in which cultures around the world vary. Anthropology has produced a literature rich in descriptions of a full range of cultural systems, containing profound implications for managers working outside their native country. After cataloging more than 100 different definitions of culture, anthropologists Kroeber and Kluckhohn (55:181) offered one of the most comprehensive and generally accepted descriptions of culture:

> Culture consists of patterns, explicit and implicit, of and for behavior acquired and transmitted by symbols, constituting the distinctive achievement of human groups, including their embodiment in artifacts; the essential core of culture consists of traditional (i.e., historically derived and selected) ideas and especially their attached values; culture systems may, on the one hand, be considered as products of action, on the other, as conditioning elements of future action.

Culture is therefore something (15:19)

- Shared by all or almost all members of some social group
- Older members of a group try to pass on to younger members
- Shaping behavior, or . . . structuring one's perception of the world (as in the case of morals, laws, and customs)

Managers frequently see culture as "the collective programming of the mind which distinguishes the members of one human group from another . . . the interactive aggregate of common characteristics that influence a human group's response to its environment" (45:25). In general, we see people as being from different cultures if their ways of life as a group differ significantly.

Cultural Orientations

The cultural orientation of a society reflects the complex interaction of values, attitudes, and behaviors displayed by its members (43). As shown in Figure 1-1, individuals express their culture and its normative qualities through the values they hold about life and the world around them. These values in turn affect their attitudes about the form of behavior con-

FIGURE 1-1 Culture Influences Behavior and
Behavior Influences Culture

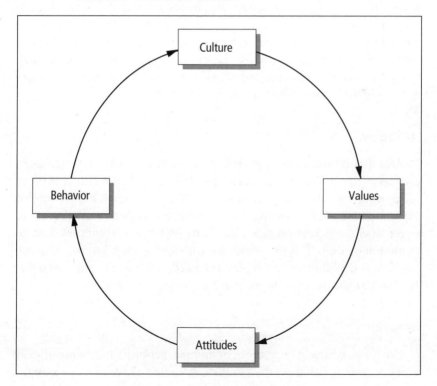

sidered most appropriate and effective in any given situation. The continually changing patterns of individual and group behavior eventually influence the society's culture, and the cycle begins again. What are the differences among values, attitudes, and behavior?

Values

Values differentiate what is, and is not, desirable to individuals and groups within society. Values therefore influence people's selection from available modes, means, and ends of action. Values can be both consciously and unconsciously held (52). Values therefore reflect relatively general beliefs that either define what is right and wrong or specify general preferences (15:23). Research has shown that personal values affect corporate strategy (13;32;37;39;44;75;77;81;93) and that managerial values affect all forms of organizational behavior (8;31;70;71), including selection and reward systems (15); superior/subordinate relationships (62); and team dynamics, communication, leadership, and conflict management styles (57). Latin American managers, for example, consider loyalty to the family to be highly important—a value that leads them to hire members of their own family whenever possible. U.S. managers strongly believe in individual achievement—a value that leads them to emphasize a candidate's personal track record and performance on qualifying exams rather than membership in a particular family. In both cases a strongly held value influences managerial behavior.

Attitudes

Attitudes express values and predispose a person to act or to react in certain ways toward particular situations. Attitudes often reflect a person's relationship to a given product or service. Market research has shown that French Canadians, for example, have a positive attitude toward pleasant or sweet smells, whereas English Canadians prefer smells with efficient or clean connotations. Advertisements for Irish Spring soap directed at French Canadians therefore stress the pleasant smell, whereas the ads directed at English Canadians stress the inclusion of effective deodorants.[7]

Behavior

Behavior, which is any form of human action, varies dramatically across cultures. Based on their culture, Middle Easterners, for example, stand closer together (a behavior) than do North Americans, whereas Japanese stand farther apart than do either North Americans or Middle Easterners. Latin Americans touch each other more frequently during business negotiations than do North Americans, and both touch more frequently than do Japanese. Culture defines people's behavior.

Cultural Diversity

Diversity exists both within and among cultures; however, within a single culture certain behaviors are favored and others repressed. The norm for a society is the most common and most generally accepted pattern of values, attitudes, and behavior. In global business, for example, a man wearing a dark gray business suit reflects the norm through a favored behavior, whereas a man wearing a green business suit would violate the same norm. A society's cultural orientation describes the attitudes of most people most of the time, never of all the people all of the time. Accurate stereotypes reflect societal or cultural norms.

Societies enforce norms by communicating disapproval toward transgressors—people who engage in prohibited behavior. Society strongly enforces some norms, such as laws, while more weakly enforcing other norms, such as customs and habits. You can assess a norm's importance by observing how severely society condemns those who violate it. In the United States, for example, an important norm proscribes bribery. Companies caught using bribery to increase their business are publicly prosecuted and fined, both punishments reflecting severe cultural sanctions. A less important norm in the United States is the custom of saying "Good morning" when greeting colleagues at the beginning of the day. If one day I fail to say "Good morning," it is unlikely that society will severely punish me. At worst, my colleagues may assume that I am preoccupied or perhaps tired.

Anthropologists Kluckhohn and Strodbeck (52) discuss a set of assumptions that allows us to understand the cultural orientations of a society without doing an injustice to the diversity within the society.[8] The six assumptions (75) are as follows:

1. "There are a limited number of common human problems for which all peoples at all times must find some solutions." Each society, for example, must decide how to clothe, feed, and house its people. Each society must decide on systems of justice, communication, education, health, commerce, transportation, and government.
2. "There are a limited number of alternatives which exist for dealing

with these problems." People, for example, may house themselves in tents, caves, igloos, single-family dwellings, or apartment buildings, but they cannot survive the winter without some form of housing.

3. "All alternatives are present in all societies at all times, but some are preferred over others."

4. "Each society has a dominant profile or values orientation and, in addition, has numerous variations or alternative profiles." People may cure disease, for example, with chemotherapy, surgery, acupuncture, acupressure, prayer, or nutrition. The Chinese tend to prefer acupressure and acupuncture; the British prefer chemotherapy and surgery; and Christian Scientists prefer prayer.

5. "In both the dominant profile and the variations, there is a rank ordering of preference for alternatives."

6. "In societies undergoing change, the ordering of preferences will not be clearcut." As information-technology revolutionizes society, for example, organizations' preferences to communicate using the Internet, fax, telephone, e-mail, or postal system become unclear; different organizations make different choices.

These assumptions emphasize that cultural descriptions always refer to the norm or stereotype; they never refer to the behavior of all people in the culture, nor do they predict the behavior of any particular person.

HOW DO CULTURES VARY?

As shown in Table 1-3, six basic cultural dimensions describe the orientations of societies. (52;57). The six dimensions answer the questions: Who am I? How do I see the world? How do I relate to other people? What do I do? How do I use space and time? Each orientation reflects a value with behavioral and attitudinal implications. As summarized in Table 1-4, this section presents the six values dimensions with management implications for each. Examples are given highlighting differences between cultural orientations in the United States and those in a range of other countries.

How Do People See Themselves?

How do societies see the individual: as good or as evil? Americans traditionally see people as a mixture of good and evil, but capable of choosing one over the other. They believe in the possibility of improvement through change. Some other cultures see people as basically evil—

TABLE 1-3 How Cultures Vary: Values Dimensions

Perception of	Dimensions		
Individual *Who am I?*	Good	Good and evil	Evil
World *How do I see the world?*	Dominant	Harmony	Subjugation
Human Relations *How do I relate to* *other people?*	Individual	Laterally extended groups	Hierarchical groups
Activity *What do I do?*	Doing	Controlling	Being
Time *How do I place myself* *in time?*	Future	Present	Past
Space *How do I relate to space?*	Private	Mixed	Public

SOURCE: Based on Kluckhohn and Strodbeck (52), as adapted by Lane and diStefano (57).

as reflected in the Puritans' orientation. Others see people as basically good—as reflected in utopian societies throughout the ages. Societies that believe people to be good tend to trust them a great deal, whereas societies that consider people to be evil tend to mistrust them. In high-trust societies, for example, people leave doors unlocked and do not fear being

TABLE 1-4 Does Culture Affect Management? Yes!—
Cultural Dimensions and Management

Cultural Dimensions	U.S. Cultural Orientation	Contrasting Cultural Orientation
What is the nature of people?	Mixture of good and evil Change is possible.	Good (Evil) Change is impossible.
Managerial Implication:	Emphasize training and development; give people the opportunity to learn on the job.	Emphasize selection and fit; select the right person for the job; do not expect employees to change once hired.

continued on next page ■

■ continued from previous page

TABLE 1-4 Does Culture Affect Management? Yes!—
Cultural Dimensions and Management

Cultural Dimension	U.S. Cultural Orientation	Contrasting Cultural Orientation
What is a person's relationship to the external environment?-	People dominant over nature and other aspects of the external environment.	Harmony (Subjugation)
Managerial Implication:	Policy decisions made to alter nature to fulfill people's needs—i.e., building dams or drilling for oil in wildlife areas.	Policy decisions made to protect nature while meeting people needs.
What is a person's relationship to other people?	Individualistic	Group (Hierarchical or Lateral)
Managerial Implication:	Executive reviews academic and employment history for each candidate in order to select the best person for the job.	Personnel director selects the closest relative of the chief executive as the best person for the job.
Managerial Implication:	Individuals make decisions	Groups make decisions
What is the primary mode of activity?	Doing	Being (Controlling)
Managerial Implication:	Employees work hard to achieve goals; they maximize their time at work.	Employees work only as much as needed to earn a living; they minimize their time at work.

continued on next page ■

robbed or assaulted. In low-trust societies, people bolt their doors. After making a purchase, people in high-trust societies expect to receive the merchandise and correct change; they do not expect the salesperson to cheat them. In low-trust societies, *caveat emptor* ("let the buyer beware") rules the marketplace; one can only trust oneself. In many countries people are more trusting in rural communities than in urban centers. Today's web-mediated e-business challenges buyers to trust unseen sellers, and sellers to assess their confidence levels in unseen buyers.

Today many Americans and Canadians lament that their fellow citizens cannot be trusted the way they used to be. A Toronto hotel, for

■ *continued from previous page*

TABLE 1-4 Does Culture Affect Management? Yes!—
Cultural Dimensions and Management

Cultural Dimension	U.S. Cultural Orientation	Contrasting Cultural Orientation
How do people see space?	Private	Public
Managerial Implication:	Executives hold important meetings in large offices behind closed doors with secretary screening interruptions.	Executives hold important meetings in moderate-sized offices or in open areas, with open doors and many interruptions from employees and visitors.
What is a person's relationship to time?	Future/Present	Past (Present)
Managerial Implication:	Mission statement refers to 5- and 10-year goals while focus is kept on this year's bottom line and quarterly reports; emphasize the innovation and flexibility needed to meet a dynamic and. changing future	Mission statement this year reflects policy statements of 10 years ago; the company strives to maintain tradition, stability, and continuity in order to perform in the future as it has in the past.

SOURCE: Adapted by Adler, 2002 from Adler (3:41), based on Kluckhohn and Strodbeck (52) and diStefano (25); also see Lane and diStefano (57).

example, posts a sign reminding guests that "Love is leaving the towels." Los Angeles gas stations, to assure that motorists will not drive away without paying, require them to pay twenty dollars or sign a credit card slip before filling their gas tanks. A Minneapolis firm, National Credential Verification Service, makes a profitable business of exploiting the lack of trust among corporate recruiters and job candidates by exposing résumé fraud. Out of 233 personnel officers responding to a survey of *Fortune 500* companies, only one said that deception by applicants for executive positions was diminishing (60:85). To add to this mistrust, many people find it more difficult to trust foreigners than citizens of their own country.

Managers in the People's Republic of China describe their approach as combining the extremes of good (Confucian tradition) with evil (the tra-

ARE PEOPLE GOOD OR EVIL? CAN THEY BE TRUSTED?[9]

Can a Bosnian Trust a Canadian Working in Sweden?

A young Canadian in Sweden found summer employment working in a restaurant owned by Bosnians. As the Canadian explained, "I arrived at the restaurant and was greeted by an effusive Bosnian man who set me to work at once washing dishes and preparing the restaurant for the June opening.

"At the end of the first day, I was brought to the back room. The owner took an old cash box out of a large desk. The Bosnian owner counted out my wages for the day and was about to return the box to the desk when his private phone rang in the front room. The owner hesitated: should he leave me sitting in the room with the money or take it with him? Quite simply, could he trust me?

"After a moment, the man got up to answer the phone, leaving me with the open money box. I sat there in amazement: how could he trust me, someone he had known for less than a day, a person whose last name and address he didn't even know?"

This incident contrasts perceptions of individuals as good or evil. The Bosnian manager believed individuals to be good and inherently trustworthy. For this reason, he could leave his new employee alone with the money without worrying that the Canadian would steal it. The Canadian employee's surprise that this stranger trusted him with the money is a reflection of the North American's values orientation. Believing that people are capable of both good and evil, North Americans would proceed more cautiously than did the Bosnian. If the Canadian had been in the owner's shoes, he probably would have taken the cash box with him to the other room to answer the telephone, rather than risk trusting his new employee not to steal.

dition of Lao Tzu)—a marriage of opposites. They also described their belief that peasants are good while rich people are not so good, as reflected in a story told among people living in Tianjin, the fourth largest city in the People's Republic of China:

At the Franco-Chinese joint venture wine factory in Tianjin between France's Remy Martin and China's Dynasty, a French director left his wallet filled with French francs in a ped-a-cab. The ped-a-cab driver, a peasant, waited all day outside the factory to return the Frenchman's wallet.

Perhaps because people fear the unknown, they frequently tend to assume that evil intentions motivate foreigners' behavior. Canadian government officials, for example, thought the Inuits, a native people, were evil when they burned down the doors in their Canadian-built public housing projects. The officials misinterpreted the Inuits' behavior as vandalism and therefore judged it to be evil, whereas the Inuits had actually altered the houses to fit their normal—doorless—lifestyle. The Canadian government condemns the destruction of property, whereas the Inuits condemn closed doors that separate people from family members and neighbors.

Apart from believing in people's inherent goodness or tendency toward evil, do people believe that adults can improve themselves? Societies and organizations vary widely in the degree to which they believe that adults are capable of change. Organizations that believe people can change, for example, emphasize training and development, whereas organizations that believe people are set in their ways emphasize selection systems. With today's e-revolution, some organizations choose to replace many of their current administrative-support personnel and to hire e-technology and information systems experts in their place. Other companies attempt to retrain their current employees to use the new state-of-the-art technology. The first strategy—primarily hiring new employees—assumes that change is not possible, whereas the second strategy of training present employees assumes that change is possible. North Americans' emphasis on MBA education and executive development seminars strongly reflects their belief that change is possible. The Chinese saying that the "Chinese . . . strive to become better and, when better, to become perfect" also reflects a strong belief in the ability of adults to change. As one Shanghai executive exclaimed, applying the belief to his own career path, "I was trained as an engineer and now I am an export/import manager. I changed!"

How Do People See Their Relationship to the World?

What is a person's relationship to the world? Are people dominant over their environment, in harmony with it, or subjugated by it? North Americans generally see themselves as dominant over nature. Other societies, such as the Chinese and Navaho, attempt to live in harmony with nature. They see no real separation between people and their natural environment, and their beliefs allow them to live at peace with the environment. In contrast to both of these orientations, a few remote tribal societies see people as subjugated by nature. People in these cultures accept and honor, rather than interfere with, the inevitable forces of nature.

How does a company see its environment? Are its relevant external environments—cultural, economic, legal, political, social, and technological—seen as stable and predictable or as turbulent, chaotic, and unpredictable? Do companies assume that they can control their competitive environment, that they must be in harmony with it, or that they will be dominated by it?

North Americans' approach to agriculture exemplifies the dominance orientation. By assuming, for instance, that people can and ethically should modify nature to enhance their own well-being, dominance-oriented agribusiness executives use fertilizers, pesticides, and genetically modified seeds to increase crop yields. By contrast, harmony-oriented farmers attempt only to plant the "right" crops in the "right" places at the "right" time of the year in order to maintain the soil in good condition. Farmers subjugated by nature hope that sufficient rain will fall, but they do not construct irrigation systems to assure sufficient water for their crops. Although they hope or pray that pests will not attack their crops, they refuse to use chemical insecticides.

Other examples of North Americans' dominance orientation include astronauts' conquest (dominance) of space, economists' structuring of markets, sales representatives' attempts to influence buyers' decisions, and, perhaps most controversial today, biotechnology and genetic engineering's attempt to alter life itself. The contrasting relationships become clearer in the sayings of three societies:

Saying	Culture	Meaning
Ayorama: *"It can't be helped"*	Inuit—Canada	Reflects subjugation
En Shah Allah: *"If God is willing"*	Moslem—Arab	Reflects harmony with nature and submission to God
Can Do: *"I will do it"*	American—U.S.	Reflects dominance

HOW DO I RELATE TO THE WORLD? DOMINANCE VERSUS HARMONY[10]

Feng Shui

When the Hong Kong branch of a North American bank moved to a new location, the expatriate executive had to choose between two offices. He selected the one that was larger, regularly shaped, and adjacent to the vice president's office. His Chinese clients, however, became uncomfortable visiting him in his new office. One client with whom he was particularly friendly explained why: "The room has bad feng shui." Feng Shui, or "wind water," are earth forces, which the Chinese believe can cause success or failure. Feng shui reflects the belief that the layout and orientation of people's workplaces and homes affects them and their activites. The goal of feng shui is to be in harmony with the environment.

The expatriate executive faced a dilemma. Reflecting power and status in North America, he had chosen his new office for its size and proximity to the seat of power. In contrast, the Chinese clients believed the office had bad feng shui, and predicted little business success unless he changed offices.

Ultimately, on the recommendation of his Chinese clients, the executive moved into a smaller office, where the space was awkwardly cut up by a pillar. On the advice of his Chinese clients, he placed a mirror on the pillar to overcome this drawback. There were no dire consequences or business failures; his clients were comfortable with the new office and chose to continue to do business with him. North American and Chinese perceptions of the world clearly differ.

North Americans want to control nature, whereas the Chinese want to be in harmony with it. The expatriate executive had originally chosen his office based on reasons that appeared rational from his cultural perspective of dominance—and he wanted to maximize his status and influence through office size and proximity. But to the Chinese, his decision was not rational; the room was unlucky because it lacked harmony with nature. The expatriate was sensitive to Chinese cultural values and changed offices.

A society's orientation toward the world is pervasive. In news reporting, when Sir Edmund Hillary reached the top of Mt. Everest, for example, the Western dominance-oriented press reported the story as "Man conquers mountain"; in contrast, the Chinese harmony-oriented press reported the same story as "Man befriends mountain." Religious writings similarly reflect a people's cultural orientation. The *Bible*, for example, states in Genesis, "Let them have dominion over the earth"; whereas the *Tao Te Ching* states, "Those who would take over the earth and shape it to their will, I notice, never succeed"—a dominance orientation contrasting with one of harmony.

How Do People Relate to Other People? Individualism versus Collectivism[11]

Americans are individualists; they use personal characteristics and achievements to define themselves, and they value individual welfare over that of the group. By contrast, in group-oriented societies people define themselves as members of clans or communities and consider common goals and the group's welfare most important. The relevant group may be lateral or hierarchical. Lateral groups include all those with members of a particular family, community, or organization; hierarchical groups include members from multiple generations.

The United States is strongly individualistic and weak on its loyalty to groups, teams, and communities. Americans, for example, praise their sports heroes by singling out individual excellence: "Mark Smith and the team trounced the opposition." They praise corporate performance by singling out and rewarding the chief executive officer (CEO). General Electric's outstanding financial performance is often attributed to CEO Jack Welch, as in the subtitle of the book *How Jack Welch Is Making General Electric the World's Most Competitive Company (90)*.

Compared with people in more group-oriented societies, Americans are more geographically mobile and their relationships, especially with co-workers, are less permanent. Due to its individualism, the United States has been described as a temporary society with temporary systems, uprootedness, disconnectedness, nonpermanent relationships, and high mobility (11). More group-oriented societies, such as Japan, China, and the Israeli kibbutzim, emphasize group harmony, unity, and loyalty. Individuals in these societies frequently fear being personally ostracized or bringing shame to their family or group for behavior that deviates from the norm.

Personnel policies also follow either individual or group orientations. Individual-oriented personnel directors tend to hire those best qualified to do the job based on personal skills and expertise. Individualistic applicants will therefore submit résumés listing personal, educational, and professional achievements. Group-oriented personnel directors also tend to hire those most qualified, but the prime qualifications they seek are trustworthiness, loyalty, and compatibility with co-workers. They hire people who are well known to them, including friends and relatives of people already working for the organization. Therefore, rather than sending well-prepared résumés listing individual achievements, applicants seek introductions to the personnel director through a mutual friend or relative; and initial discussions center on mutual friends, family, or community members. The managing director of one group-oriented company in Ghana expressed his belief that only people who are known by other employees in the company can possibly be trusted to act responsibly.

The personnel managers' actions can appear biased, illogical, and unfair when viewed from the perspective of a contrasting culture. Many individualistic North Americans see group-oriented hiring practices as nepotism because they see these practices only from their own culture's perspective. Many more group-oriented Latin Americans question the ethics of North American managers, who choose not to be loyal to their friends and family (93).

The organization of firms in individualistic and collective societies differs. In individualistic societies, such as those of Canada and the United States, organization charts generally specify individual positions, each with a detailed job description listing formal duties and responsibilities. By contrast, organization charts in more group-oriented societies, such as Hong Kong, Indonesia, and Malaysia, tend to specify only sections, departments, and divisions, except for the top one or two positions (74). Group-oriented societies describe assignments, responsibilities, and reporting relationships in collective terms.

The individual versus group orientation also influences decision making. In North America, individuals make decisions. North Americans, therefore, make decisions relatively quickly, although implementation frequently gets delayed while the decision maker explains the decision and gains concurrence from other members of the organization. By contrast, in Japan, a group-oriented culture, many people make the decision rather than just one. The process of group decision making is less flexible and more time-consuming than the individualistic system because concurrence must be achieved prior to making the decision. However, be-

---

PERSONAL RELATIONSHIPS: INDIVIDUALISM VERSUS COLLECTIVISM[12]

The German Won't Hire the Serbian's Daughter

Rade, an engineer who had immigrated to Western Germany from the former Yugoslavia, worked for a highly respected German engineering firm. His daughter Lana had recently graduated from a prestigious German university. Rade considered it his duty to find his daughter a job, and he wanted his German boss to hire Lana. Although the boss felt Lana was extremely well qualified for the open position, he refused to have a father and daughter working in the same office. The very suggestion of hiring family members was repugnant to him. Rade believed that his boss was acting unfairly—he saw no problem in his daughter working with him in the same office.

The unfortunate outcome was that Lana was neither considered nor hired; the boss lost respect for Rade; and Rade became so upset that he requested a transfer to a new department. Neither Rade nor his boss understood that the conflict was caused by the fundamentally different values orientations in the two cultures.

---

cause all parties already understand and concur, the Japanese can implement a decision almost immediately after it is made.

Activity: Doing or Being

Americans' dominant mode of activity is *doing*, or action. They stress achieving outcomes that they can measure by objective standards; that is, standards believed to be external to the particular individual and capable of being consistently applied to other situations and outcomes. Managers in doing-oriented cultures motivate employees with promises of promotions, raises, bonuses, and other forms of public recognition. The contrasting orientations are being and *controlling*. In the *being* orientation, people, events, and ideas flow spontaneously; people stress release, indulgence of existing desires, and living and working for the moment. If managers in *being*-oriented cultures do not enjoy their colleagues and current projects, they quit; they will not work strictly for future rewards. People in *control*-oriented societies restrain their personal desires by detaching themselves from the objects they might desire; such control, they believe, allows each individual to develop as a more integrated person. The doer is more active; the person focused on being is more relaxed. The doer actively tries to achieve the most in life; the person focused on being wants to experience life as it is.

The doing and being orientations affect planning quite differently.

ACTIVITY: DOING VERSUS BEING[13]

Kashmir Versus Sweden

In the 1980s the United Nations appointed a Swedish army officer as an observer in Kashmir. His job was to travel around the turbulent province situated between Pakistan and India looking for troop movements on each side. The officer and his family moved into a houseboat on the river in Sringar, the capital of the province. As has been customary for Europeans working in Kashmir, the family employed a "boy"— a servant—to perform all the family's household services during their stay. The servant was always very polite and pleasant, cooked delicious meals, and kept the houseboat neat and clean.

The family was very pleased with his work, and after a short time decided to give him a raise. Surprisingly, the servant did not turn up for work the next day, and his little brother arrived in his place. On his new higher salary, the servant had employed his younger brother to work for the family. With the raise he could maintain his own desired standard of living and help his younger brother without personally having to work.

Because the Kashmiri servant was a Hindu, he did not believe he could improve his standard of living in this lifetime. So by being good and not disturbing the harmony of his circumstances (i.e., by simply *being*), he believed he could be reincarnated into a higher position in his next life. This natural tendency to accept life with no expectations for either improvement or material goods contrasts sharply with the Swedish family's notion of working hard to achieve personal goals and improve one's material lot in this life (i.e., their *doing* orientation). The Swede's surprise at seeing the younger Kashmiri brother arrive for work reflects this contrast.

Being-oriented managers view time as generational, and therefore believe that planning should allow for the extended time needed for true change to occur. Major projects often need a generation, or certainly a decade, to achieve significant results. Managers focused on being, allow change to occur at its own, often slow, pace. They do not push or rush things to achieve short-term results. By contrast, doers believe that planning can speed up the change process if plans are carefully thought out, specific target dates set, and progress frequently reported (79). Be-ers believe that this type of planning is possible but unwise, because it rarely works immediately and is fruitless in the long run.

The activity orientation also explains why people work. To achieve goals, doers maximize work; to live fully, be-ers minimize work. Increasing the salaries of doers and be-ers has opposite effects. Salary increases motivate most doers to work more hours because the rewards are greater; they motivate most be-ers to work fewer hours because they can earn enough money in less time and still enjoy life. U.S. expatriate managers (doers), using salary as a motivational tool, made a severe mistake when they raised the salaries of a group of rural Mexican workers (be-ers), only to discover that by doing so they had decreased the total hours that these particular Mexicans wanted to work. Similarly, Canadians working in Malaysia found that workers were more interested in spending extra time with their family and friends than in earning overtime pay bonuses.

Time: Past, Present, or Future

What is the temporal focus of human life? What relationship does a given society have toward time? Is the society oriented toward the past, present, or future? Past-oriented cultures believe that plans should be evaluated in terms of their respect for the customs, traditions, and the wisdom of society and that innovation and change are justified only to the extent that they respect past experience. By contrast, future-oriented cultures believe that they should evaluate plans in terms of the projected future benefits to be gained. Future-oriented managers justify innovation and change more in terms of future economic benefits and have less regard for past social, cultural or organizational customs and traditions.

In contrast with most North Americans, many Europeans show more respect for the past. Many Europeans believe that preserving history and conserving past traditions remain important, whereas North Americans give tradition less importance. North American businesspeople focus on the present and near future; they may talk about achieving five- or 10-year

TIME: PAST, PRESENT, OR FUTURE[14]

Bus Schedules in the Bahamas

In the Bahamas, bus service is managed similarly to many taxi systems. Each driver owns his own bus and collects passenger fares for his income. There is no set schedule nor a set time when the bus will run or arrive at a particular location. Everything depends on the driver.

Bus drivers in the Bahamas are present-oriented; what they feel like doing on a particular day at a particular hour dictates what they will actually do. If the bus driver feels hungry, for example, he will go home to eat lunch without waiting for a preset lunch hour. Drivers see no need to repeat yesterday's actions today nor to set tomorrow's schedule according to the needs and patterns of yesterday.

This present orientation contrasts sharply with the behavior of bus drivers in London, New York City, Paris, Toronto, and most other urban centers in the Western world. Drivers in these cities have planned schedules that they follow to the best of their ability. Present-oriented behavior has the advantage of flexibility, whereas more future- or past-oriented behavior has the advantage of predictability.

plans, but they work toward achieving this quarter's results. North American employment practices also reflect a short-term orientation. Employees who do not perform well during their first year with an organization are fired or at best not promoted. U.S. companies do not give them 10 years to demonstrate their worth. Japan by contrast, has traditionally had a long-term, future-oriented time horizon. When large Japanese firms hired employees, both parties made a commitment for life. Major Japanese firms invested in years of training for each employee because they could expect the employee to work with the firm for 30 to 40 years. North American firms invested far less in training because a lifetime commitment between the company and the employee was neither given nor expected.

Societies use different standards of temporal precision. What defines when people arrive late and when they are on time for work, meetings, or business lunches? How much variation is acceptable? How long do managers expect scheduled appointments to last—five minutes or two hours? What is the typical length of a project assignment—one week or three

TIME: THE LONG TERM VERSUS THE SHORT TERM[15]

A Question of Contracts

The directors of a Japanese firm and a Canadian firm met in Vancouver to negotiate the sale of coal shipments from British Columbia to Japan. The companies reached a stalemate over the length of the contract. The Japanese, ostensibly to reduce the uncertainty in their coal supply and to assure continuous, stable production in Japan, wanted the Canadians to sign a 10-year contract. The Canadians, on the other hand, did not wish to commit themselves to such a lengthy agreement in the event that they could find a more lucrative offer in the interim. Whereas the Japanese wanted to reduce the level of risk in their coal supply, the Canadians expressed their willingness to assume the additional risk of losing a steady buyer for the potential benefits of a more profitable future buyer.

The negotiations had hit a snag. Unless the culturally based time frame of the contract could be resolved, no contract would be signed. A deal that would benefit both parties had a distinct possibility of remaining unconsummated.

TIME: A PAST ORIENTATION

The People's Republic of China

Whereas odysseys to outer space lure more future-oriented Americans to movie houses, historical dramas have traditionally led box-office sales in China, and the more ancient the story, the better. Chinese children, so far, have no space-age superman to emulate. Even at play, they pretend to be the Monkey King, the supernatural hero of a famous medieval epic (63:12).

Similarly, Chinese scientists look to the past for inspiration. In the national archives, teams of Chinese meteorologists comb voluminous weather records of the last 300 years in an effort to discover patterns that might help them predict the droughts and floods that still plague the country. Seismologists in charge of improving China's earthquake prediction methods use similar long-term, past-oriented approaches (63).

years? A U.S. engineer working in Bahrain expressed surprise at his Arab client's response to his apologetic explanation that, "Unfortunately, due to unforeseen delays, the new plant would not come on-line until six months after the originally planned date." The Bahrainian responded, "We have lived for thousands of years without this plant; we easily can wait another six months or a year. This is no problem."

Diversity exists within societies as well as between societies. Past-, present-, and future-oriented people exist within every society. Comparing lawyers and economists in the United States highlights this temporal diversity. U.S. lawyers use a past orientation in citing precedent to adjudicate the outcome of cases, whereas economists use a future orientation in conducting cost-benefit analyses to predict the possible outcomes of alternative corporate and governmental strategies over the next five to 10 years.

Space: Public or Private

How do people use physical space? Is a conference room, an office, or a building seen as public or private space? When can I enter an office directly, and when must I wait outside until granted permission to enter? The public versus private dimension defines the arrangement of organizational space. North Americans give private offices to more important employees, and even separate open-offices with partitions between desks. They hold important meetings behind closed doors, usually in the executive's large, private office, and generally with minimal interruptions.

The Japanese, by contrast, use no partitions to divide desks; bosses often sit together with their employees in the same large room. Middle Easterners often have numerous people present during important meetings—some related, and some not related, to the issues being discussed. Both Middle Easterners and Japanese have a more public orientation than do most North Americans. By contrast, the Germans and British typically exhibit an even more private orientation than do most North Americans. When visitors meet a German manager for the first time, the German's secretary must generally announce the guests before the German manager's closed office door will be opened to admit them.

SUMMARY

Cultures vary in distinct, significant, and predictable ways. Our ways of thinking, feeling, and behaving as human beings are neither random nor haphazard but rather are profoundly influenced by our cultural heritage.

Until we leave our own community, we often remain oblivious to the dynamics of our shared culture. As we come in contact with people from other cultures, we become aware of our uniqueness and begin to appreciate our differences. In interacting with foreigners, we learn to recognize and value our fundamental humanity—our cultural similarities and dissimilarities. For years people chose to believe that organizational functioning was beyond the influence of culture; they operated as if organizational outcomes were determined only by task and technology. Today we know that work is not simply a mechanistic outgrowth of either technology or task. At every level, culture profoundly influences the behavior of organizations as well as the behavior of people within organizations.

FILM NOTE

The British Broadcasting Corporation video program *World Without Borders* documents the evolution of a multinational firm, Cable and Wireless, from its domestic origins in the United Kingdom through the multidomestic stage, and into its current multinational and planned transnational strategies. European and North American professors comment on Cable and Wireless's strategy and competitive environment, while presenting frameworks for understanding and managing the evolution of global firms.

To order the BBC video programs, please contact:

CANADA	UNITED STATES	WORLDWIDE
BBC Worldwide Americas	BBC Worldwide Americas	British Broadcasting Corporation
65 Heward Avenue	747 Third Avenue	Open University Production Centre
Toronto, Ontario	6th and 7th Floors	Walton Hall, Milton Keynes
Canada M4M 2T5	New York, NY 10017 USA	England MK7 68H
Tel: 416-469-1505	Tel: 212-705-9300	Tel: 44-1908-665-228
Fax: 416-469-0642	Fax: 212-888-0576	Fax: 44-1908-655-300
		email: stephen.wilkinson@bbc.co.uk

2

How Do Cultural Differences Affect the Way We Work?

Deep cultural undercurrents structure life in subtle but highly consistent ways that are not consciously formulated. Like the invisible jet streams in the skies that determine the course of a storm, these currents shape our lives; yet their influence is only beginning to be identified.   — EDWARD T. HALL (7:12)

PEOPLE DRESS DIFFERENTLY, eat different foods, and celebrate different holidays in countries around the world. But do those differences affect the ways people work together? Do people organize, manage, and work differently from culture to culture?

WORK BEHAVIOR VARIES ACROSS CULTURES

In which ways does the behavior of people in organizations vary across cultures? Managers and researchers have observed systematic and culturally based differences in people's work-related values, attitudes, and behaviors.

Each of us has a set of attitudes and beliefs—filters through which we see management situations. As shown in Figure 2-1, managers' beliefs, attitudes, and values cause both vicious and benevolent cycles of behavior. Douglas McGregor, an early American management theorist, gave us prototypical examples of this pattern in his classical "Theory X" and "Theory Y" managerial styles (16). According to McGregor, Theory X

FIGURE 2-1 Influence of Managers' Attitudes on Employee Behavior: A Self-Fulfilling Prophecy

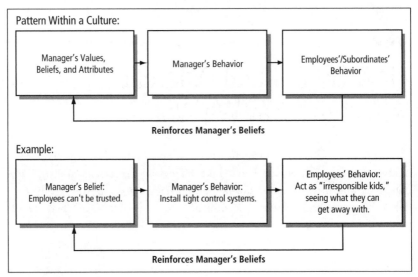

SOURCE: Adapted by Adler, 2002. Based on Douglas McGregor, *The Human Side of Enterprise*, 25th anniversary edition, McGraw-Hill, New York, 1985.

managers do not trust their subordinates. They believe that employees will not do a good job unless closely supervised. These managers establish tight control systems—such as time clocks and frequent employee observation—to assure themselves that employees are working. The employees, realizing that management does not trust them, start behaving irresponsibly—they arrive on time only when the time clock is working and only work when the manager is watching. The manager, observing this behavior, becomes more distrustful of the employees and installs even tighter control systems. According to McGregor, the manager's belief that employees cannot be trusted leads to the employees' irresponsible behavior, which in turn reinforces the manager's belief that employees cannot be trusted—a vicious cycle and a counterproductive, yet self-fulfilling, prophecy.

McGregor's Theory Y describes a more benevolent cycle. Managers who trust their employees give them overall goals and tasks without instituting tight control systems or close supervision. The employees, believing that management trusts them, do their best work whether or

---

MANAGEMENT: TRUSTING OR NAIVE[1]

Canadian Employees and Filipino Management

A Canadian bank employee described his Filipino boss's low-trust approach to management.

While working at the Royal Bank, I had a most unbearable and suspicious manager who had authority over all administrative employees, including me. The problem was that he seemed to totally distrust his subordinates. He constantly looked over our shoulders, checking our work, attitudes, and punctuality. Although most of his employees resented this treatment, they recognized that he was an extremely conscientious supervisor who honestly believed in what he called "old-style" management. He really thought that employees are lazy by nature. He therefore believed that he must pressure them into working. As the manager, he felt justified in treating his employees severely.

I found his attitude condescending and counterproductive. As a group, the employees thought of themselves as basically trustworthy. However, we decided that since our boss showed no respect for us, we would give him the same treatment in return. This resulted in a work environment filled with mistrust and hostility. The atmosphere affected everyone's work: employees became less and less willing to work, and the manager increasingly believed that his employees were lazy and that he needed to be severe with them. Luckily, the situation caught the eye of the boss, who resolved it after lengthy discussions. Only then did it become clear that we were not seeing the situation in the same way. From the manager's perspective, he was simply showing his caring and involvement with his subordinates. As he explained, Filipino employees who were not treated like this might have felt neglected and unimportant. Unfortunately, we were not Filipinos and, as Canadians, did not respond as many Filipinos might have responded.

---

not their manager is watching them. The manager, seeing that the employees are working, becomes more convinced that they can be trusted. Managers' attitudes influence their own behavior, which in turn influences their employees' attitudes and behavior, which then reinforce the managers' original attitudes and behavior.

Managers communicate respect for and trust in their employees in different ways, depending on their cultural background. Managers from more *specific cultures* tend to focus only on behavior that takes place at work, whereas managers from more *diffused cultures* focus on a wider range of behavior, including behavior taking place in employees' private lives. As a part of a major cross-cultural management study, Fons Trompenaars and Charles Hampden-Turner (20), a world-renowned Dutch and British management research and consulting team, asked managers from around the world if their companies should provide employees with housing. Whereas most managers from such diffused cultures as the former Yugoslavia (89%), Hungary (83%), China (82%), and Russia (78%) believe that the company should provide housing, managers from more specific cultures reject the idea as interfering with employees' private lives (20:86). Less than 20 percent of managers from such specific cultures as Australia, Denmark, France, the Netherlands, Sweden, Switzerland, the United Kingdom, and the United States believe that company-provided housing was a good idea (20:86). Managers from diffused cultures communicate their respect by showing concern for an employee's whole life. By contrast, managers from specific cultures demonstrate their respect by not intruding in employees' private lives. It is easy to see how misunderstanding and mistrust can grow between managers from one culture and employees from another culture.

Worldwide Differences in Managerial Style

André Laurent (14), a highly acclaimed professor at INSEAD, a leading international management school located in France, studied the philosophies and behaviors of managers in three Asian countries (Indonesia, Japan, and the People's Republic of China), nine Western European countries, and the United States. Laurent asked managers from each country to describe their approach to more than 60 common work situations. He found distinctly different patterns for managers in each of the countries.

Task and Relationship

In response to the statement, "The main reason for a hierarchical structure is so that everybody knows who has authority over whom," for example, managers from some countries strongly agreed, whereas managers from other countries strongly disagreed. As shown in Table 2-1, most U.S. managers disagree with the statement; they believe that the

TABLE 2-1 "The Main Reason for a Hierarchical Structure Is So That Everybody Knows Who Has Authority Over Whom."

More Task Oriented   More Relationship Oriented

Agreement Rate Across Countries

United States	Germany	Sweden	Nether-lands	Great Britain	Spain	Italy	France	Japan	P.R.C.	Indonesia
17%	26%	30%	31%	34%	34%	42%	43%	50%	70%	83%

NOTE: P.R.C. refers to the People's Republic of China.
SOURCE: From André Laurent, "The Cultural Diversity of Western Conceptions of Management," in *International Studies of Management and Organization*, vol. 13, no. 1–2 (Spring–Summer 1983), pp. 75–96. Reprinted by permission of M. E. Sharpe, Inc., Armonk, NY. Updated and expanded, 1993.

main reason for a hierarchical structure is to organize tasks and facilitate problem solving around those tasks. Coming from an extremely task-oriented culture, many Americans believe that a flat organization with few hierarchical levels—in which most employees work as colleagues rather than bosses and subordinates—can function effectively. They believe that such minimal hierarchy is possible if tasks and roles are clearly defined and the organization is not too large.

By contrast, many managers from more relationship-oriented cultures, such as most Asians, Latin Americans, Middle Easterners, and Southern Europeans, strongly agree with Laurent's statement. Eighty-three percent of Indonesian managers reported that the main reason for a hierarchical structure was to have everyone know who has authority over whom. They did not believe that even a small organization could exist, let alone succeed, without a formal hierarchy.

Perhaps these different beliefs explain some potential problems that occur when Americans work with Indonesians. Americans, for example, typically approach a project by outlining the overall goal, designating each of the major steps, and then addressing staffing needs. Their approach goes from task to people. Indonesians, on the other hand, first want to know who will manage the project and who will work on it. Once they know who the leader will be and the hierarchy of people involved, they can assess the project's feasibility. The Indonesians' approach goes from people to task. Both cultures need to understand the project's goals and staffing arrangements, but the importance of each is reversed. An American would rarely discuss candidates for project director before at least broadly defining the project, whereas Indonesians would rarely discuss project feasibility before knowing who they would select as leader.

Similarly, in response to the statement, "In order to have efficient work relationships it is often necessary to bypass the hierarchical line," Laurent found large and consistent differences across cultures. As shown in Table 2-2, Swedish managers see the least problem with bypassing. They are task oriented and value getting the job done; to Swedes, solving problems means going directly to the person most likely to have the needed information and expertise, and not necessarily to their boss. Most Swedish managers believe that a perfect hierarchy—in which their boss would know everything—is impossible; they therefore view bypassing as a natural, logical, and appropriate way for employees to work efficiently in today's complex and rapidly changing organizations.

By contrast, most Italians, being more relationship oriented than the Swedes, consider bypassing the boss an act of insubordination. Most Italian managers believe that frequent bypassing indicates a poorly designed organization. Italians therefore respond to bypassing by reprimanding the employee or redesigning the hierarchical reporting structure. Imagine the frustration and potential for failure when Swedes form joint ventures and strategic alliances with Italians. When Swedish employees begin working in a typical Italian organization, they will attempt to accomplish their work goals responsibly by continually bypassing hierarchical lines and going directly to the people in the organization whom they believe

TABLE 2-2 "In Order to Have Efficient Work Relationships, It Is Often Necessary to Bypass the Hierarchical Line."

More Task Oriented									More Relationship Oriented
Disagreement Rate Across Countries									
Sweden	United States	Great Britain	France	Netherlands	Germany	Indonesia	Italy	P.R.C.	Spain
26%	32%	35%	43%	44%	45%	51%	56%	59%	74%

NOTE: P.R.C. refers to the People's Republic of China.

SOURCE: From André Laurent, "The Cultural Diversity of Western Conceptions of Management," in *International Studies of Management and Organization*, vol. 13, no. 1–2 (Spring–Summer 1983), pp. 75–96. Reprinted by permission of M. E. Sharpe, Inc., Armonk, NY. Updated and expanded, 1993.

have the needed information and expertise. Because the Swedes do not consult their new Italian boss, the Italian will assume that the Swedes are insubordinate and hence a threat to both the alliance and the project. In the reverse situation, the Swedish boss, frustrated with the Italian subordinates' constant communication and requests for information and permission, will assume that Italian employees lack initiative and are unwilling both to use their personal judgment and to take risks. Why else, asks the Swedish manager, would the Italians always consult me, the boss, before acting on matters for which the boss need not be consulted? Is either side right? No, they just differ.

Should Managers Be Experts or Problem Solvers?

Laurent found little agreement across national borders on the nature of the manager's role. As shown in Figure 2-2, more than four times as many Indonesian and Japanese managers as U.S. managers agreed with

FIGURE 2-2 Should Managers Be Experts? It All Depends on Where You Live?

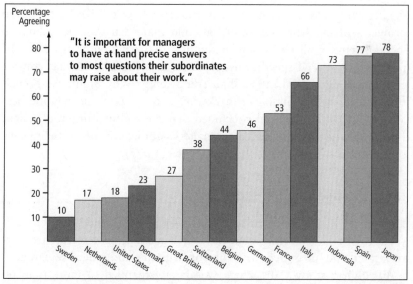

SOURCE: Adapted by Adler, 2002. From André Laurent, "The Cultural Diversity of Western Conceptions of Management," in *International Studies of Management and Organization*, vol. 13, no. 1–2 (Spring–Summer 1983), pp. 75–96. Reprinted by permission of M. E. Sharpe, Inc., Armonk, NY. Expanded, 1993.

the statement, "It is important for managers to have at hand precise answers to most questions their subordinates may raise about their work." Most U.S. managers believe that the role of the manager is to be a problem solver: managers should help their employees discover ways to solve problems, rather than simply answering their questions directly. Furthermore, U.S. managers believe that merely providing answers discourages subordinates' initiative and creativity and ultimately diminishes their productivity. By contrast, the French generally see the manager as an expert. Most French managers believe that they should give precise answers to subordinates' questions in order to maintain their credibility as experts and managers. They believe that their subordinates' sense of security depends on receiving precise answers. Most French believe that people should not hold managerial positions unless they can give precise answers to most work-related questions. (See page 79, the Iranian's view, for another example of the expert perspective.)

Is a manager primarily an expert or a problem solver? Again, the question has no single right answer because organizations from different cultures maintain different beliefs. Problems, however, arise when managers from one culture interact with managers and employees from other cultures. When an American manager tells French employees, "I don't know the answer, but maybe if you talk to Simon in marketing he will know," the French employees do not assume that they have received appropriate problem-solving help but rather assume that their American boss is incompetent. Similarly misunderstanding the situation, American employees who receive specific answers from their French boss may consider the boss egotistical rather than competent: "Why didn't the French boss tell them that Simon in marketing is the expert and has the best answer?" Overall, Laurent concluded that the national origin of Asian, European, and North American managers significantly affects their views on how effective managers should manage (14:77).

Dimensions of Difference

Differences in work-related attitudes exist across a wide range of cultures. Geert Hofstede, an eminent Dutch management researcher, corroborated and integrated the results of Laurent's and others' research. In a 40-country study (10), which was later expanded to more than 60 countries, including both Oriental and Occidental cultures (5;9;11;12), 160,000 managers and employees working for a U.S. multinational corporation were surveyed twice. Hofstede, like Laurent, found highly significant differences in the behavior and attitudes of employees and managers from each country even though they worked within the same multi-national corporation—differences that did not change over time. Hofstede found that national culture explained more of the differences in work-related values and attitudes than did position within the organization, profession, age, or gender. In summarizing the most important differences, Hofstede initially found that managers and employees vary on four primary dimensions: individualism/collectivism, power distance, uncertainty avoidance, and career success/quality of life.[2] Later, Hofstede and his colleagues identified a fifth dimension, Confucian dynamism (5;12).

Individualism and Collectivism

A culture is *individualistic* when people see themselves primarily as separate individuals and make their main commitments to themselves. Individualistic cultures form loosely knit social networks in which people focus primarily on taking care of themselves and their immediate families. *Collective* cultures are characterized by tight social networks in which people strongly distinguish between their own group (in-groups, including relatives, or clans or organization members) and all other groups. Collectivist members of the same group hold common goals and objectives, not individual goals that focus primarily on self-interest. People in collective cultures expect members of their particular in-groups to look after them, protect them, and give them security in exchange for their loyalty to the group. Two-thirds of all surveyed Arab executives, for example, thought employee loyalty was more important than efficiency (17). This dimension reflects similar values to those of the individual/group values orientation discussed in Chapter 1 on pages 28–30 (6).

Determinism characterizes such collectivist cultures as the Japanese, where people believe that the will of the group should determine members' beliefs and behavior. This belief is reflected in the Japanese saying, "The nail that sticks out will be pounded down." By contrast, free will and self-determination characterize individualistic cultures such as that of the United States, where individuals believe that each person should determine his or her own beliefs and behavior. In each nation, cultural beliefs become self-fulfilling. People from individualistic cultures also tend to believe that certain universal values should be shared by all. People from collectivist cultures, on the other hand, accept that different groups hold different values. Being individualistic, most North Americans believe that democracy—especially North American–style democracy—ideally should be shared by all. Many people from collectivist cultures find such a view hard to understand.

Collectivist cultures control their members more through external societal pressure (shame) whereas individualistic cultures control their members more through internal pressure (guilt). Members of collectivist cultures place more importance on fitting in harmoniously and saving face.

FIGURE 2-3 Countries Differ on Power Distance and Individualism/Collectivism

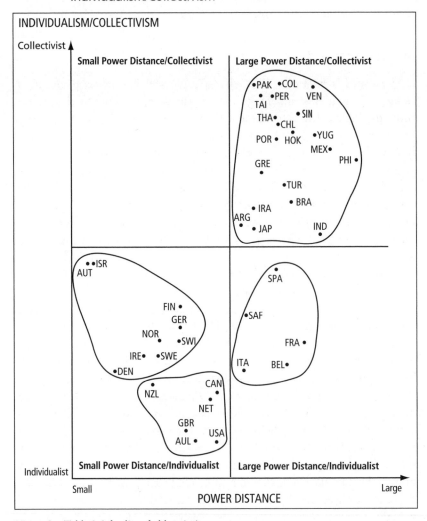

NOTE: See Table 2-3 for list of abbreviations.

SOURCE: From Geert Hofstede, "Motivation, Leadership, and Organization: Do American Theories Apply Abroad?" in Organizational Dynamics, Summer 1980. Copyright © Geert Hofstede.

Members of individualistic cultures place more emphasis on individual self-respect. In many ways the two orientations trade off individual freedom against collective protection: Do I do what is best for me or what is best for the group? Do I take care only of myself or does the group take care of me? Do I expect the boss to hire me because I have the right education and work experience (individual) or because I come from the right family or social class (group)? Do I expect to be promoted on the basis of my performance in the company or on the basis of my seniority with the company? In times of economic recession, do I expect the least productive workers to be laid off or every employee to take a pay cut? Figure 2-3 shows the ranking of countries on the individualism/collectivism dimension and Table 2-3 shows the abbreviations used in Figures 2-3, 2-4, and 2-5.

The Dutch-British management research team of Fons Trompenaars and Charles Hampden-Turner also found that managers worldwide vary markedly in their orientation toward individualism and collectivism (20). Among other questions, they asked managers which of the following two options would be most likely to improve the quality of life (20:47):

1. Giving individuals the maximum opportunity to develop themselves
2. Having individuals continuously taking care of their fellow human beings

The vast majority of American (79%), Canadian (79%), and Norwegian managers (76%), for example, selected the first option stressing individual-freedom, whereas most managers in Nepal (69%), Kuwait (61%), Egypt (59%), and Eastern Germany (55%) selected the second option stressing collective responsibility (20:48).

Which is better, individualism or collectivism? The answer is neither and both. As Trompenaars and Hampden-Turner point out, in complex societies, forming a synthesis between opposites has become increasingly necessary (8). Individualism and collectivism are complements of each other, with their relationship being "essentially circular with two starting points" (20:55). Individualistic and collectivist cultures

go through . . . [the same] cycles, but starting at different points [with each reversing what the other considers to be ends and means]. The individualistic culture sees the individual as "the end" and improvements to collective arrangements as the means to achieve it. The collectivist culture sees the group as its end and improvements to individual capacities as a means to that end (20:55).

TABLE 2-3 Country Abbreviations as Used in Figures 2-3, 2-4, and 2-5

ARG	Argentina	FRA	France	JAP	Japan	SIN	Singapore
AUL	Australia	GBR	Great Britain	MEX	Mexico	SPA	Spain
AUT	Austria	GER	Germany	NET	Netherlands	SWE	Sweden
BEL	Belgium	GRE	Greece	NOR	Norway	SWI	Switzerland
BRA	Brazil	HOK	Hong Kong	NZL	New Zealand	TAI	Taiwan
CAN	Canada	IND	India	PAK	Pakistan	THA	Thailand
CHL	Chile	IRA	Iran	PER	Peru	TUR	Turkey
COL	Colombia	IRE	Ireland	PHI	Philippines	USA	United States
DEN	Denmark	ISR	Israel	POR	Portugal	VEN	Venezuela
FIN	Finland	ITA	Italy	SAF	South Africa	YUG	Yugoslavia

SOURCE: From Geert Hofstede, "Motivation, Leadership, and Organization: Do American Theories Apply Abroad?" in Organizational Dynamics, Summer 1980. Copyright © Geert Hofstede.

Power Distance

The second dimension, power distance, reflects the extent to which less powerful members of organizations accept an unequal distribution of power. How willingly do employees accept that their boss has more power than they have? Is the boss right because he or she is the boss (high power distance) or only when he or she knows the correct answer (low power distance)? Do employees do their work in a particular way because the boss wants it done that way (high power distance) or because they personally believe that it is the best way to do it (low power distance)?

In high power-distance countries, such as India, the Philippines, Poland, and Venezuela, managers and employees consider bypassing to be insubordination; whereas in low power-distance countries, such as Israel and Denmark, employees expect to bypass their boss frequently in order to get their work done (18). When negotiating in high power-distance countries, companies find it important to send representatives with titles equivalent to or higher than those of their counterparts from the other organization. Titles, status, and formality command less importance in low power-distance countries. As shown in Figures 2-3 and 2-4, the United States ranks relatively low on power distance.

Uncertainty Avoidance

The third dimension, uncertainty avoidance, reflects the extent to which people in a society feel threatened by ambiguity and therefore try to avoid ambiguous situations by providing greater certainty and pre-

INDIVIDUALISM AND COLLECTIVISM[3]

The Pacific Area Travel Association

A global market research firm in Tokyo conducted a survey of travel market potential for the Pacific Area Travel Association (PATA), an organization of national tourist offices from various Pacific Rim nations. Although they conducted the survey through a standard questionnaire, each nation was invited to submit a few of its own open-ended questions.

All countries responded promptly. Of the ten countries surveyed, the U.S. Department of Commerce was the first to send in questions. Individual names were always attached to each letter and fax from the United States.

Shortly after completing the PATA survey, the company received a contract for a similar study for the Association of Southeast Asian Nations (ASEAN). Due to the similar content, the researchers conducted the ASEAN study in an almost identical fashion to the PATA survey. They requested open-ended questions from the national tourism offices of Indonesia, Malaysia, the Philippines, Singapore, and Thailand. Because they had completed the collection of questions in a little over a month for PATA, the company assumed six weeks would be more than sufficient for the ASEAN nations. They guessed wrong! The ASEAN nations required considerably more time than did the PATA countries. The market research firm had to exchange many letters and faxes between the Philippines and Tokyo before it received their final responses. Moreover, every communication from the Philippines included a different individual's name on it as its sender.

In thinking over these responses, the survey researchers concluded that the contrast between the Americans' and the Filipinos' responses to the same task stemmed from the relative emphasis on the individual versus the group. Whereas the U.S. office gave sole responsibility to an individual, the more group-oriented Filipinos delegated the task to a whole department. Since the Philippines office involved everyone in the task, it naturally took longer.

dictability. Organizations reduce uncertainty by establishing more formal rules, rejecting deviant ideas and behavior, accepting the possibility of identifying absolute truths and attaining unquestionable expertise, and providing their employees with greater career stability. Offering lifetime employment, for example, is more common in high uncertainty-avoidance countries such as Greece, Japan, and Portugal; whereas high job mobility occurs more commonly in low uncertainty-avoidance countries such as Denmark and Singapore. The United States, with its very high job mobility, ranks relatively low on uncertainty avoidance.

As shown in Figure 2-4, common images of organizations vary markedly depending on a country's orientation on power distance and uncertainty avoidance. People in countries such as Denmark that rank low on both dimensions see organizations as resembling *village markets*: the organizations have little hierarchy, everyone talks with everyone else, and risk taking is both expected and encouraged.

Employees in high power-distance and low uncertainty-avoidance countries such as Singapore and the Philippines tend to view their organizations as *traditional families*. As the traditional head of the family, the father protects family members physically and economically. In exchange, the family expects loyalty from its members. Reflecting the same dynamics, bosses in Singapore expect to take care of their employees in exchange for employees' loyalty.

POWER DISTANCE[4]

An American Executive in London

An American executive moved to London to manage his company's British headquarters. Although the initial few weeks passed relatively uneventfully, it bothered the executive that visitors were never sent directly to his office. A visitor first had to speak with the receptionist, then the secretary, and then the office manager. Finally the office manager would escort the visitor to see the American executive. The American became annoyed with this practice, which he considered a total waste of time. When he finally spoke with his British employees and urged them to be less formal and to send visitors directly to him, they were chagrined.

After a number of delicate conversations, the American executive began to understand the greater emphasis on formality and hierarchy in England. He slowly learned to ignore his impatience when the British greeted guests using their more formal, multistep approach. Visitors to the British headquarters continued to see the receptionist, secretary, and office manager before being sent to meet the American.

FIGURE 2-4 Countries Vary on Power Distance and
Uncertainty Avoidance

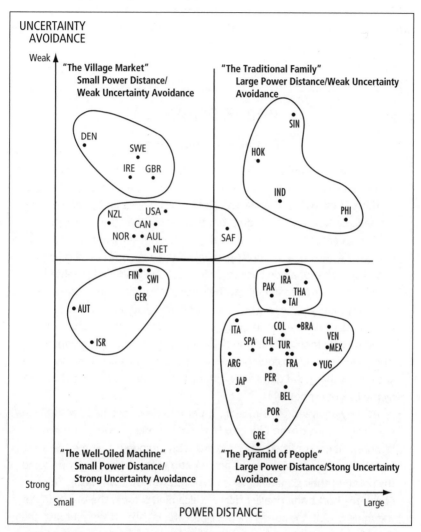

NOTE: See Table 2-3 for list of abbreviations.

SOURCE: From Geert Hofstede, "Motivation, Leadership, and Organization: Do American Theories
Apply Abroad?" in *Organizational Dynamics*, Summer 1980. Copyright © Geert Hofstede.

Employees in countries such as the former Yugoslavia and Mexico, which are high on both dimensions, tend to view their organizations as *pyramids of people* rather than traditional families. Everyone in the organization knows who reports to whom, and formal lines of communi-

---

POWER DISTANCE[5]

The Chinese Dinner Party

One of Canada's leading banks invited a Chinese delegation for dinner. The senior Canadian chose to share his hosting responsibilities with a colleague.

The dinner was not a success. Both the Chinese and Canadians remained relatively uneasy throughout the meal. During the dinner, no welcoming speeches or toasts to mutual good health were made. At the end of the meal, the Chinese stood up, thanked the bank officials, declined the Canadians' offer of a ride back to their hotel, and left feeling slighted.

The Canadians also felt upset. They found the departure of the Chinese to be very rude, yet they did not know what they had done wrong to cause the Chinese to leave so abruptly. Despite planning the menu carefully (avoiding such foods as beef and dairy products), providing excellent translation services, and extending normal Canadian courtesies, the Canadians knew something had gone wrong; they felt worried and somewhat hurt by the lack of rapport.

As they analyzed the situation, it became clear they had not fulfilled the expectations of the Chinese. First, having two people share hosting responsibilities confused the hierarchically minded Chinese. Second, because the Chinese view age as an indication of seniority, they considered the youth of their Canadian hosts as a slight to their own status. Third, in China, the host traditionally offers a welcoming toast at the beginning of the meal, which the guests then reciprocate; by not offering a toast, the Canadians insulted the Chinese. The specific incident that upset the Canadians—the abrupt departure of the Chinese following the banquet—was, in fact, neither unusual nor a problem: the Chinese retire early and it was getting late.

The Canadians' lack of understanding of the hierarchical nature of Chinese society and the Chinese ways of communicating respect clearly cost them in their business dealings with the visiting delegation.

cation run vertically, never horizontally, up and down the organization. In pyramid organizations, which operate vertically, management reduces uncertainty by emphasizing who has authority over whom. Pyramid organizations resemble a fire department: not only is it clear who is chief, but the fire chief's word becomes law (high power distance). The department clearly defines all procedures and tolerates little or no questioning or deviance—little or no ambiguity. When the alarm rings, firefighters do not stop to discuss who will drive the pumper or who will ride on the hook and ladder, because management has previously clearly defined each role and task.

In high uncertainty-avoidance and low power-distance countries such as Israel and Austria, organizations tend to resemble *well-oiled machines*: they operate highly predictably without needing a strong hierarchy. Most North American post offices provide excellent examples of this type of organization: they reduce uncertainty by clearly defining roles and procedures.

Career Success and Quality of Life[6]

The fourth dimension contrasts societies focused more narrowly on career success with those more broadly emphasizing quality of life. Career-success societies emphasize assertiveness and the acquisition of money and things (materialism), while not showing particular concern for people. By contrast, *quality-of-life* societies emphasize relationships among people, concern for others, and the overall quality of life.

Societies that stress career success usually define women's and men's roles more rigidly and narrowly than do quality-of-life societies. For example, women may drive trucks or practice law and men may become preschool teachers, nurses, or house husbands more easily in societies emphasizing quality of life than in those stressing traditional career success. As shown in Figure 2-5, the Scandinavian countries strongly emphasize quality of life, the United States emphasizes career success more than quality of life, and Japan and Austria strongly emphasize career success. Japanese and Austrians generally expect women to stay home and to care for children without following a career outside the home. The United States encourages women to work, but offers them only a limited amount of support for company-sponsored maternity leaves and child care. The Swedes expect women to work; Sweden offers parents the option of paternity or maternity leave to take care of newborn children and the state provides day-mothers to care for older children.

The career-success/quality-of-life dimension strongly affects work-

FIGURE 2-5 Countries Vary on Uncertainty Avoidance
and Career Success/Quality of Life

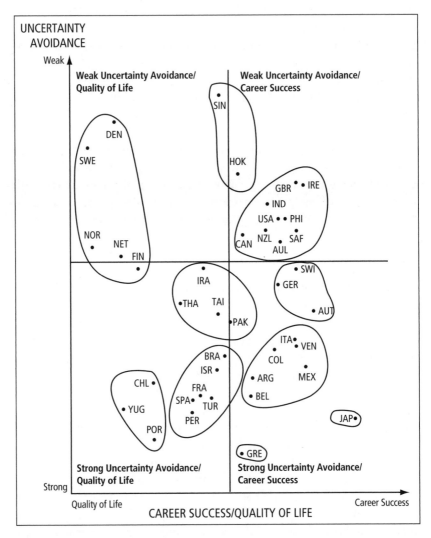

NOTE: See Table 2-3 for list of abbreviations.

SOURCE: From Geert Hofstede, "Motivation, Leadership, and Organization: Do American Theories Apply Abroad?" in *Organizational Dynamics*, Summer 1980. Copyright © Geert Hofstede.

CAREER SUCCESS AND QUALITY OF LIFE[7]

Do Swedish Managers' Have an "Inadequate" Commitment to Business?

Swedish policy encourages parents to take paternity or maternity leave at their discretion. When Sweden first initiated the policy, the managing director of the Swedish Postal Service created an uproar by announcing his intention to take paternity leave for a number of months to stay home with his newborn child. At a press conference, he explained that executives do not differ from other employees: everyone wants and needs to balance work with family life. He also explained that he believed that any organization that cannot function for a period of time without its managing director had no *raison d'être*.

Swedish expatriate managers often do not have the opportunity to explain their desire for balancing their professional and private life to their colleagues from other countries. Swedes frequently surprise their international clients when they end the work week on Friday at 5 p.m. or announce their intention to fly home at the end of the day because they want to spend more time with their families. Swedish business-people describe many of their international colleagues, especially Americans, as willing to work all evening and all weekend just to finish an important project. Americans, on the other hand, frequently resent the Swedes' behavior, judging it to reflect an inadequate commitment to work. In actuality, the Swedes' choices simply demonstrate their strong commitment to quality of life, whereas the Americans and other similar foreigners behave according to their equally strong commitment to the particular project (career success orientation).

place motivation. Japanese *quality circles*, for example, primarily strive to achieve maximum quality (career success/high uncertainty avoidance); whereas the innovative Swedish work groups—originally used at Volvo—attempt to enhance job satisfaction and flexibility (high quality of life/low uncertainty avoidance). Because societies emphasizing quality of life also often create high-tax environments, extra income frequently fails to strongly motivate employees (in Sweden, for example). Conversely, societies emphasizing career success often develop into lower-tax environments in which extra income and other visible signs of career success effectively reward achievement (Mexico and the United States, for example).

Confucian Dynamism

After identifying the first four dimensions, Hofstede and his Hong Kong-based colleague, the eminent cross-cultural psychologist Michael Bond, conducted the first global management survey ever developed with Chinese managers and employees. Based on this survey, Hofstede and Bond identified a fifth dimension, *Confucian dynamism*, which measures employees' devotion to the work ethic and their respect for tradition (5;12). Many observers attribute the rapid economic growth in the 1990s of Asia's "Four Tigers"—Hong Kong, Singapore, South Korea, and Taiwan—to their extremely strong work ethic and commitment to traditional Confucian values (12).

Rules Versus Relationships: Which Determine Our Behavior?

Building on the work of Laurent and Hofstede, Trompenaars and Hampden-Turner (20) conducted a major survey of more than 15,000 managers in 40 countries. In addition to results that corroborate those of their colleagues, they went beyond the prior work to document additional dimensions and to highlight some of the ethical issues posed by managers misinterpreting conflicting cultural signals.

Trompenaars and Hampden-Turner (20:34), for example, asked managers from around the world to consider what they would do in the following situation:

> You are riding in a car driven by a close friend. He hits a pedestrian. You know he was going at least 35 miles per hour in an area of the city where the maximum allowed speed is 20 miles per hour. There are no witnesses. His lawyer says that if you testify under oath that he was only driving 20 miles per hour it may save him from serious consequences. What right has your friend to expect you to protect him?
>
> a. My friend has a definite right as a friend to expect me to testify to the lower figure.
> b. He has some right as a friend to expect me to testify to the lower figure.

c. He has no right as a friend to expect me to testify to the lower figure.
What do you think you would do in view of the obligations of a sworn witness and the obligation to your friend?

d. Testify that he was going 20 miles an hour.

e. Not testify that he was going 20 miles an hour.

In response to this situation, managers expressed a wide range of opinions. More than 90 percent of managers in Canada (96%), the United States (95%), Switzerland (94%), Australia (93%), Sweden (93%), Norway (93%), and Western Germany (91%) said that society's rules were made for everyone and that, therefore, their friend had no right to expect them to testify falsely (20:35). They consequently would not testify that their friend was driving at 20 miles per hour when the truth was that he was driving faster (20:35). By contrast, fewer than half the managers in South Korea (26%), Venezuela (34%), Russia (42%), Indonesia (47%), and China (48%) would refuse to support their friend; each would therefore testify in his favor (20:35).

Why do such extreme differences characterize the managers' responses? The underlying dimension separating those who would and would not testify is whether the society believes more in universalism or particularism. Managers who refuse to testify adhere to more universalistic values. Universalistic societies, such as Canada and the United States, believe that laws apply to everyone and they therefore must be upheld by everyone at all times. The general (or universalistic) principle of what is legal, or illegal, takes precedence over the particular details of who is involved in the specific situation. By contrast, in particularist societies, such as South Korea and Venezuela, the nature of the relationship determines how someone will act in a particular situation. To a person from a particularist culture, it makes a difference if someone is a best friend or family member. For a person from a universalistic culture, it makes no difference what my relationship is to a particular person; rules are seen as applying equally to everyone. Ask yourself what you would do in the situation. Then ask yourself, if it had been your mother or daughter driving the car, would you be more or less likely to testify than you would be for a friend? How much difference does relationship make for you? When is loyalty more important than truth? When is truth more important than loyalty?

Although firms tend to become more universalistic as they operate more globally, clashes between universalistic and particularistic cultures remain legendary. Universalistic cultures, for example, rely on extensive and specific contracts to document the "rules" of doing business together, whereas particularistic cultures use much more loosely written agreements and rely on the strength of their personal relationships to maintain the commitment. Particularists view detailed contracts, and especially penalty clauses, as a sign that they are not trusted and that therefore no relationship exists. They consequently feel little need to adhere to the contract. Interestingly, as many Asian, Middle Eastern, and Latin cultures have shown, personal relationships can, at times, be more durable than contracts, as well as more flexible.

Clearly, joint ventures, strategic alliances, and overall business negotiations between universalists and particularists raise ethical questions, from both cultures' perspectives:

> Businesspeople from both societies . . . tend to think [of] each other [as] corrupt. A universalist will say of particularists, "they cannot be trusted because they will always help their friends"; a particularist, conversely, will say of universalists, "you cannot trust them: they would not even help a friend" (20:32).

Coming from a particularistic culture, a team of Brazilian negotiators explained to us that they only tell the truth once they have gotten to know the other party; that is, once they have developed a personal relationship. They described American and Canadian negotiators, who often accused Brazilians of lying, as naïve for not understanding how negotiating really works. The Americans, for whom truth is an absolute—a "universal" that is unrelated to the particular negotiation or the particular people involved—accused Brazilians of acting deceitfully. Americans tell the same "truth" to everyone, without regard for the nature or depth of the relationship. Brazilians tailor their comments, their "truth," to the particular individuals involved. Both sides consider truth and relationship to be important, however the relative emphasis on truth telling versus loyalty causes marked differences in behavior.

ARE ORGANIZATIONS BECOMING MORE SIMILAR?

Are organizations becoming more similar worldwide or are they maintaining their cultural dissimilarities? Is the world gradually creating one way to conduct business or is the world maintaining a set of distinct markets defined by equally distinct national boundaries, each with its own culturally distinct approach to business?

The question of convergence versus divergence has puzzled global managers for years. If people around the world are becoming more similar, then understanding cross-cultural differences should become less important. If people are remaining dissimilar, then understanding cross-cultural differences in organizations will become increasingly important.

To clarify this dilemma, John Child (4), a leading British management scholar, compared research on organizations across cultures. Reviewing a myriad of cross-cultural studies, he found one group of highly reputable management scholars repeatedly concluding that the world is becoming more similar and another equally reputable group of scholars concluding the opposite—that the world's organizations are maintaining their dissimilarity. Looking more closely, Child discovered that most studies concluding convergence focused on macrolevel issues—such as the organization's structure and its technology—whereas most studies concluding divergence focus on microlevel issues—in particular, the behavior of people within organizations. We can therefore conclude that organizations worldwide are growing more similar, while the behavior of people within them is maintaining its cultural uniqueness. Organizational structures and strategies in Canada and Germany may look increasingly similar from the outside, but Canadians and Germans continue to behave in their own culturally distinct fashion within each organization. Although both Germans and Canadians, for example, install robots in their factories, each culture interacts differently with the robots.

DOES ORGANIZATIONAL CULTURE ERACE NATIONAL CULTURE?

Over the last decade, managers and researchers have increasingly recognized the importance of organizational culture as a socializing influence and climate creator (2;3;13;21). Unfortunately, rather than enhancing our understanding of national cultures (1;19), our understanding of organizational culture has often tended to limit it. Many managers believe that organizational culture moderates or erases the influence of national culture. They assume that employees working for the same organization—even if they come from different countries— will behave more similarly than differently. They implicitly believe that national cultural differences only become important in working with foreign clients, not in working with international colleagues within their own organization.

Does organizational culture erase or at least diminish national culture? Surprisingly, the answer is no (15). Employees and managers bring their cultural background and ethnicity to the workplace. As described earlier,

FIGURE 2-6 Organization Culture Magnifies Cross-Cultural Differences

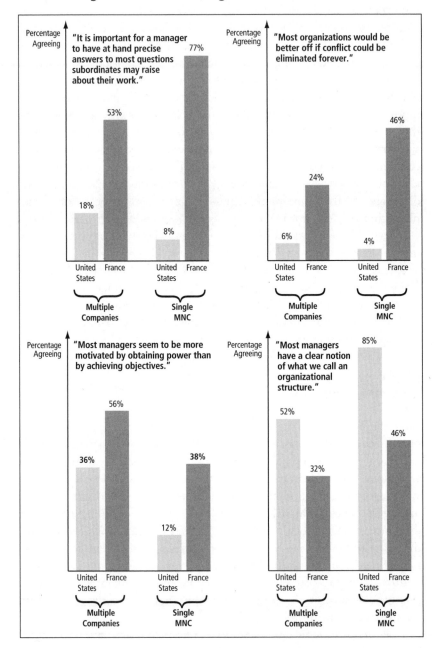

Source: Adapted by Adler, 2002. From André Laurent, INSEAD. Fontainebleau, France, 1981.

Hofstede found striking cultural differences within a single multinational corporation. In his study, national culture explained 50 percent of the differences in employees' attitudes and behaviors worldwide. National culture explained more of the differences than did professional role, age, gender, or race (10).

Even more strikingly, Laurent found more pronounced cultural differences among employees from around the world working within the same multinational company than among those working for organizations in their native lands. After observing managers from nine Western European countries and the United States who were working for companies in their native countries (e.g., Swedish managers working for Swedish companies, Italian managers working for Italian companies), Laurent replicated his research in a single multinational corporation with subsidiaries in each of the ten original countries. He assumed that managers working for the same multinational corporation would behave more similarly than their domestically employed colleagues. Instead, as shown in Figure 2-6, he discovered that the managers employed by the multinational were maintaining or even strengthening their cultural differences. The cultural differences were significantly greater among managers working within the same multinational corporation than they were among managers working for companies in their own native country. When working for multinational companies, Germans seemingly became more German, Americans more American, Swedes more Swedish, and so on. Surprised by these results, Laurent replicated his research in two additional multinational corporations, each with subsidiaries in the same nine Western European countries and the United States. Similar to the results from the first company, corporate culture did not reduce or eliminate national differences in the second and third corporations. Far from reducing national differences, organizational culture maintains and enhances them.

Why might organizational culture enhance national cultural differences? Neither managers nor researchers know the answer with certainty. Perhaps pressure to conform to the organization culture of a foreign-owned company brings out employees' resistance, causing them to cling more firmly to their own national identities. Perhaps our ethnic culture is so deeply ingrained in us by the time we reach adulthood that the company's organizational culture cannot erase it. Perhaps other as-yet-unexplained forces are operating. The unambiguous conclusion remains, however, that employees maintain or enhance their culturally specific ways of working even when employed by multinational or global organizations.

SUMMARY

Laurent's research documents a wide range of cultural differences in work-related values, attitudes, and behavior. Hofstede's five dimensions—individualism/collectivism, power distance, uncertainty avoidance, career success/quality of life, and Confucian dynamism—along with Trompenaars and Hampden-Turner's additional dimensions, highlight the most important cultural differences influencing organizations. To manage effectively in either a global or a domestic-multicultural environment, we must recognize which differences are operating and learn to use them to our advantage, rather than either attempting to ignore the differences or simply allowing them to cause problems. Chapter 3 presents various ways in which we perceive, describe, interpret, and evaluate cultural differences. Chapter 4 then explores approaches organizations can take to benefit from the diversity of cultural backgrounds among their employees. The myth that organizations can operate "beyond nationality" remains, in fact, a myth.

3

But Do They Understand?
Communicating Across Cultures

If we seek to understand a people, we have to try to put ourselves, as far as we can, in that particular historical and cultural background. . . .It is not easy for a person of one country to enter into the background of another country. So there is great irritation, because one fact that seems obvious to us is not immediately accepted by the other party or does not seem obvious to him at all. . . . But that extreme irritation will go when we think . . . that he is just differently conditioned and simply can't get out of that condition. One has to recognize that whatever the future may hold, countries and people differ . . . in their approach to life and their ways of living and thinking. In order to understand them, we have to understand their way of life and approach. If we wish to convince them, we have to use their language as far as we can, not language in the narrow sense of the word, but the language of the mind. That is one necessity. Something that goes even further than that is not the appeal to logic and reason, but some kind of emotional awareness of other people.

—JAWAHARLAL NEHRU, *Visit to America*

ALL BUSINESS ACTIVITY involves communicating. Within global businesses, activities such as leading, motivating, negotiating, decision making, and problem solving, are all based on the ability of managers from one culture to communicate successfully with colleagues, clients, and suppliers from other cultures. Communicating effectively challenges managers even when working domestically with a culturally homoge-

63

neous workforce. When colleagues speak a variety of languages and come from an array of cultural backgrounds, communicating effectively becomes considerably more difficult (12:3–5,121–128;15:1).

SUCCESSFUL CROSS-CULTURAL COMMUNICATION

Communicating involves exchanging meaning: it is my attempt to let you know what I mean. Communication is any behavior another person perceives and interprets: it is your understanding of what I mean. Communication includes sending both verbal messages (words) and nonverbal messages (tone of voice, facial expression, behavior, physical setting, etc.). It includes consciously sent messages as well as messages that the sender is totally unaware of having sent. Whatever I say and do, I cannot *not* communicate. Communication therefore involves a complex multilayered, dynamic process through which we exchange meaning.

Every communication involves a message sender and a message receiver. As diagrammed in Figure 3-1, the sent message is never identical to the

FIGURE 3-1 Communicating Across Cultures

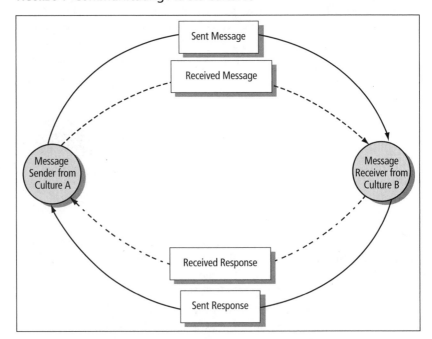

received message. Why? Communication is not direct, but rather indirect; it is a symbolic behavior. I cannot communicate my ideas, feelings, or information directly; rather, I must externalize or symbolize them before they can be communicated. *Encoding* is the process of producing a symbol message. *Decoding* is the process of receiving meaning from a symbol message. Message senders must encode their meaning into a form that the receiver will recognize, that is, into words and behavior. Receivers must then decode the words and behavior—the symbols—back into messages that have meaning for them.

For example, because the Cantonese word for *eight* sounds like *faat*, which means prosperity, a Hong Kong textile manufacturer Lau Ting-Pong paid $5 million in for car registration number 8. A year later, a European millionaire paid $4.8 million at Hong Kong's Lunar New Year auction for vehicle registration number 7, a decision that mystified the Chinese, since the number 7 has little significance in the Chinese calculation of fortune (19).

Similarly, the members of Hong Kong's prestigious Legislative Council refrained from using numbers ending in 4 to identify their newly installed lockers. Some Chinese consider numbers ending with the digit 4 to be jinxed, because the sound of the Cantonese word *sei* the is same for *four* and *death*. The number 24, for instance, sounds like *yee sei*, or *death-prone* in Cantonese (11).

The process of translating meanings into words and behaviors, that is, into symbols, and back again into meanings is based on a person's cultural background. The greater the difference between senders' and receivers' backgrounds, the greater difference is in the meanings they attach to particular words and behaviors. For example:

> A British boss asked a new, young American employee if he would like to take an early lunch at 11 A.M. each day. The employee answered, "Yeah, that would be great!" The boss, hearing the word *yeah* instead of the word *yes*, assumed that the employee was rude, ill-mannered, and disrespectful. The boss responded curtly, "With that kind of attitude, you may as well forget about lunch!" The employee was bewildered. What had gone wrong? In the process of encoding agreement (his meaning) into *yeah* (a word symbol) and decoding the *yeah* spoken by a new employee to the boss (a word, behavior, and content symbol), the boss received a message entirely different from the message the employee had meant to send. Unfortunately, as is the case in most miscommunication, neither the sender nor the receiver was fully aware of what had gone wrong and why.

Cross-cultural communication occurs when a person from one culture sends a message to a person from another culture. Cross-cultural miscommunication occurs when the person from the second culture does not receive the sender's intended message. The greater the difference between the sender's and the receiver's cultures, the greater is the chance for cross-cultural miscommunication. For example:

A Japanese businessman wants to signal his Norwegian client that he is uninterested in a particular sale. To be polite, the Japanese says, "That will be very difficult." The Norwegian interprets the statement to mean that unresolved problems remain, not that the deal is off. The Norwegian responds by asking how her company can help solve the problems. The Japanese, believing he has sent the message indicating no sale, is mystified by the Norwegian's response.

CULTURALLY "BIZARRE" BEHAVIOR[1]

Only in the Eyes of the Beholder

While in Bangkok's notorious traffic, a Canadian executive's car was hit by a Thai motorist who had crossed over the double line while passing another vehicle. After failing to establish that the fault lay with the Thai driver, the Canadian flagged down a policeman. After several minutes of seemingly futile discussion, the Canadian pointed to the double line in the middle of the road and asked the policeman directly, "What do these lines signify?" The policeman replied, "They indicate the center of the road and are there so I can establish just how far from the center the accident occurred." The startled Canadian became silent. It had never occurred to him that the double line might not mean "no passing allowed."

Unwritten rules reflect a culture's interpretation of its surroundings. A foreign columnist for the English-language Bangkok Post once proclaimed that the unwritten traffic rule in Thailand is: "When there are more than three cars in front of you at a stop sign or intersection, start your own line!" This contravenes the Western stay-in-line ethic, of course, but it effectively portrays, albeit in slightly exaggerated fashion, a fairly consistent form of behavior at intersections in Thailand. And it drives non-Thais crazy!

Communication does not necessarily result in understanding. Cross-cultural communication continually involves misunderstanding caused by misperception, misinterpretation, and misevaluation. When the sender of a message comes from one culture and the receiver from another, the chances of accurately transmitting a message are reduced. People from different countries see, interpret, and evaluate events differently, and consequently act upon them differently. In approaching cross-cultural situations, effective businesspeople therefore assume difference until similarity is proven. They recognize that all behavior makes sense from the perspective of the person behaving and that logic and rationale are culturally relative. In cross-cultural business situations, labeling others' behavior as bizarre usually reflects culturally based misperception, misinterpretation, or misevaluation; rarely does it reflect intentional malice or pathologically motivated behavior.

CROSS-CULTURAL MISPERCEPTION: WHY CAN'T THEY SEE IT MY WAY?

Do the French and the Chinese see the world in the same way? No. Do Venezuelans and Ghanaians see the world in the same way? Again, no. No two national groups *see* the world in exactly the same way. Perception is the process by which individuals select, organize, and evaluate stimuli from the external environment to provide meaningful experiences for themselves (3;13;15;17). When Mexican children, for example, simultaneously view tachistoscopic pictures of a bullfight and a baseball game, they generally only remember seeing the bullfight. Looking through the same tachistoscope, American children only remembered seeing the baseball game (4). Similarly, when researchers show adult card players artificially altered cards, they fail to see that the hearts are black and the clubs are red.

Why do the children not see both pictures? Why do the adults fail to correctly see the unexpected playing card colors? The answer lies in the nature of perception. Perceptual patterns are neither innate nor absolute. They are selective, learned, culturally determined, consistent, and inaccurate.

- Perception is *selective*. At all times the environment contains too many stimuli for us to observe everything. We therefore screen out most of what we see, hear, taste, and feel. We screen out the overload and allow only selected information through our perceptual filter to our conscious mind (5).

- Perceptual patterns are *learned*. We are not born seeing the world in a particular way; rather, experience teaches us to perceive the world in specific ways.
- Perception is *culturally determined*. We learn to see the world in a particular way based on our cultural background.
- Perception is *consistent*. Once we see something in a particular way, we tend to continue to see it that way.
- Perception is *inaccurate*. We see things that do not exist and do not see things that do exist. Our background, values, interests, and culture act as filters and lead us to distort, block, and even create what we choose to see and to hear. We perceive what we expect to perceive. We perceive things according to what we have been trained to see, according to our cultural map.

For example, read the following sentence and quickly count the number of *F*s:

> FINISHED FILES ARE THE RESULT OF YEARS OF SCIENTIFIC STUDY COMBINED WITH THE EXPERIENCE OF YEARS.

Most people who do not speak English immediately see all six *F*s. By contrast, many English speakers only see three *F*s; they do not see the *F*s in the word *of*. Why? Because people automatically revert to their habitual and natural behavior; that is, they do what they always do. People who can read English will automatically *read* the sentence (a natural behavior), even when asked to *count* the *F*s (an unusual behavior). Because the word *of* is not important for understanding the sentence's meaning, they simply do not see either the *of*s or the *F*s in *of*. We selectively see those words that are important according to our cultural conditioning (in this case, our linguistic conditioning). Once we see a phenomenon in a particular way, we usually continue to see it in that way. Once we stop seeing *of*s, we do not see them again (even when we look for them); we do not see things that do exist. One particularly astute manager at Canadian National Railways makes daily use of perceptual filters to her firm's advantage. She gives reports written in English to bilingual Francophones to proofread and those written in French to bilingual Anglophones. She uses the fact that the native English-speakers "see" more errors—especially small errors—in French and native French-speakers "see" more errors in English.

The distorting impact of perceptual filters causes us to see things that do not exist. In an executive development program, for example, U.S.

FIGURE 3-2 Perceptual Filters Change the Story

SOURCE: From the Rumor Clinic of the Anti-Defamation League. Reprinted by permission.

executives were asked to study the picture shown in Figure 3-2 and then to describe it to a second colleague who had not seen the picture.[2] The second colleague then attempted to describe the picture to a third colleague who had not seen the picture, and so on. Finally, the fifth colleague described his perception of the picture to the group of executives and compared it with the original picture. Among the numerous distortions, the executives, similar to other groups, consistently described the black and the white man as fighting; the knife as being in the hand of the black man; the white man as wearing a business suit; and the black man as wearing laborer's overalls. Clearly the inaccurate stereotype of blacks (as poorer, working class, and more likely to commit crimes) and of whites (as richer, upper class, and less likely to perpetrate violent crime) altered the observers' perceptions, thus totally changing the meaning of the picture (2). The executives' personal and cultural experiences, and therefore their perceptual filters, allowed them to see things that did not exist and to miss seeing things that did exist.

CROSS-CULTURAL MISINTERPRETATION: WHY DON'T THEY UNDERSTAND US?

Interpretation occurs when an individual gives meaning to observations and their relationships; it is the process of making sense out of perceptions. Interpretation organizes our experience to guide our behavior. Based on our experience, we make assumptions about what we perceive so we will not have to rediscover meanings each time we encounter similar situations. We make assumptions, for example, about how doors work, based on our experience of entering and leaving rooms; thus we do not have to relearn how to open a door each time we encounter a new door. Similarly, when we smell smoke, we generally assume it is the result of a fire. We do not have to stop and wonder if the smoke indicates a fire or a flood. Consistent patterns of interpretation help us to act appropriately and quickly within our day-to-day world.

Categories: Simplifying Reality

Because we are constantly bombarded with more stimuli than we can absorb and more perceptions than we can keep distinct or interpret, we only perceive those images that may be meaningful to us. We group perceived images into familiar categories that help us to simplify our environment, become the basis for our interpretations, and allow us to function in an otherwise overly complex world. As a driver approaching an intersection, for example, I may or may not notice the number of children in the back seat of the car next to me, but I will notice whether the traffic light is red or green (selective perception). If the light is red, I automatically place it in the category of all red traffic signals (categorization). This time, like prior times, I stop (behavior based on interpretation). Although people are capable of distinguishing thousands of subtly different colors, I do not take time to notice if the red light in Istanbul is brighter or duller than the one in Singapore or more orange or purple than the one in Nairobi; I simply stop. Categorizing helps me to distinguish what is most important in my environment and to behave accordingly.

Categories become counterproductive when we place people and things in the wrong groups. Cross-cultural miscategorization occurs when I use home-country categories to make sense of situations abroad. A Korean businessman, for example, entered a client's office in Stockholm and encountered a woman sitting behind the desk. Assuming she was a secretary, he announced he wanted to see Mr. Silferbrand. The woman responded by saying the secretary would be happy to help him. The Korean became confused. In assuming that most women work as secretaries rather than managers, he misinterpreted the situation and acted inappropriately. His categorization made sense to him because most women in Korean offices are secretaries, but it proved inaccurate and counterproductive in Sweden, because this particular Swedish woman was an executive, not a secretary.

Stereotypes: Helpful or Harmful?

Stereotyping involves a form of categorization that organizes our experience and guides our behavior toward various groups within society. Stereotypes never accurately describe individual behavior; rather, they describe the behavioral norm for members of a particular group (1;7). The Paris-based Intercultural Management Associates, for example, describes stereotypes of English and French businesspeople as follows:

> We have found that for every set of negative stereotypes distinguishing the British and French there corresponds a particular values divergence that, when recognized, can prove an extraordinary resource. To illustrate: The French, in describing the British as "perfidious," "hypocritical," and "vague," are in fact describing English . . . [managers'] typical lack of a general model or theory and . . . their preference for a more pragmatic, evolutionary approach. This fact is hard for the French . . . to believe, let alone accept as a viable alternative, until, working alongside one another, the French . . . come to see that there is usually no ulterior motive behind . . . English . . . [managers'] vagueness but rather a capacity to think aloud and adapt to circumstances. For [their] part, the English . . . come to see that, far from being "distant," "superior," or "out of touch with reality," . . . [French managers'] concern for a general model or theory is what lends vision, focus, and cohesion to an enterprise or project, as well as leadership and much needed authority (8).

Stereotypes, like other forms of categories, can be helpful or harmful depending on how we use them. Effective stereotyping allows people to understand and act appropriately in new situations. A stereotype becomes helpful when it is

- *Consciously held.* People should be aware they are describing a group norm rather than the characteristics of a specific individual.

- *Descriptive rather than evaluative.* The stereotype should describe what people from this group will probably be like and not evaluate the people as good or bad.
- *Accurate.* The stereotype should accurately describe the norm for the group to which the person belongs.
- *The first best guess* about a group prior to acquiring information about the specific person or persons involved.
- *Modified,* based on further observation and experience with the actual people and situations.

Because we believe stereotypes reflect reality, subconsciously held stereotypes are difficult to modify or discard even after we acquire real information about a person. If a subconscious stereotype also inaccurately evaluates a person or situation, we are likely to maintain an inappropriate, ineffective, and frequently harmful guide to reality. Assume for example, that I subconsciously hold the stereotype that Anglophone Québecois[3] refuse to learn French and therefore believe they should have no rights within the province (an inaccurate, evaluative stereotype). I then meet a monolingual Anglophone and say, "See, I told you that Anglophones aren't willing to speak French! They don't deserve to have rights here." I next meet a bilingual Anglophone and conclude, "He must be an American because Canadian Anglophones always refuse to learn French." Instead of questioning, modifying, or discarding my stereotype ("Some Anglophone Canadians speak French"), I alter reality to fit the stereotype ("He must be American"). Stereotypes increase effectiveness only when used as a first best guess about a person or situation prior to acquiring direct information. Stereotypes never help when adhered to rigidly.

Indrei Ratiu (16), in his work with INSEAD, a leading international business school in France, and the London Business School, found managers identified as "most internationally effective" by their colleagues altered their stereotypes to fit the actual people involved, whereas managers identified as "least internationally effective" maintained their stereotypes even in the face of contradictory information. For example, internationally effective managers, prior to their first visit to Germany, might consciously stereotype Germans as being extremely task oriented. Upon arriving and meeting a very friendly and lazy Herr Schmidt, they would alter their description to say that most Germans appear extremely task oriented, but Herr Schmidt seems friendly and lazy. Months later, the most internationally effective managers are only able to say that some Germans appear very task oriented, whereas others seem quite relationship oriented (friendly); it all depends on the person and the situation. In this instance, the highly effective managers use the stereotype as a first best guess about the group's behavior prior to meeting any individuals from the group. As time goes on, they modify or discard the stereotype entirely; information about a particular individual always supersedes the group stereotype. By contrast, the least internationally effective managers maintain their stereotypes. They would assume, for example, that the contradictory evidence in Herr Schmidt's case represents an exception, and would continue to believe that Germans are highly task oriented. In drawing conclusions too quickly on the basis of insufficient information—premature closure (13)—their stereotypes become self-fulfilling (18).

Canadian psychologist Donald Taylor (5;20) found that most people maintain their stereotypes even in the face of contradictory evidence. Taylor asked English and French Canadians to listen to one of three tape recordings of a French Canadian describing himself. In the first version, the French Canadian used the Francophone stereotype and described himself as religious, proud, sensitive, and expressive. In the second version, he used neutral terms to describe himself. In the third version, he used terms to describe himself that contradicted the stereotype, such as not religious, humble, unexpressive, and conservative. After having listened to one of the three versions, each person was asked to describe the Francophone on the tape (not Francophones in general). Surprisingly, people who listened to each of the three versions used the same stereotypic terms—religious, proud, sensitive, and expressive—even when the voice on the tape had conveyed the opposite information. People evidently maintain stereotypes even in the face of contradictory evidence.

Given that stereotyping is useful as an initial guide to reality, why do people malign it? Why do parents and teachers admonish children not to stereotype? Why do sophisticated managers rarely admit to stereotyping, even though each of us stereotypes every day? The answer is that we have failed to accept stereotyping as a natural process and have consequently failed to learn to use it to our advantage. For years we have viewed stereotyping as a form of primitive thinking, as an unnecessary simplification of reality. We have also viewed stereotyping as unethical: stereotypes can be inappropriate judgments of individuals based on inaccurate descriptions of groups. It is true that labeling people from a certain ethnic group as "bad" is not ethical, but grouping individuals into categories is neither good nor bad—it is simply the human process of reducing complexity to manageable proportions. Negative views of stereotyping simply cloud our ability to understand people's actual behavior and impair our awareness of our own stereotypes. *Everyone* stereotypes. Rather than pretending not to stereotype, effective global managers need to become aware of their cultural stereotypes and learn to set them aside when faced with contradictory evidence.

In conclusion, some people stereotype effectively and others do not. Stereotyping becomes counterproductive when we:

- Place people in the wrong group,
- Incorrectly describe group norms,
- Evaluate the group rather than simply describing it,
- Confuse the stereotype with the description of a particular individual,
- Fail to modify the stereotype based on our actual observations and experience.

Causes of Misinterpretation: Going from Error to Understanding

Perceiving a person or situation inaccurately causes misinterpretation. Misinterpretation results from inaccurately interpreting what is seen; that is, by using my meanings to make sense out of your reality. The following encounter between an Austrian and a North American businessperson reflects a case of misinterpretation, a type of misattribution that is all too typical of many global business situations.

> I meet an Austrian client for the sixth time in as many months. He greets me as Herr Smith. Using my North American perspective, I interpret his very formal greeting as a warning that he either dislikes me or is uninterested in developing a closer business relationship with me. I have, however, misinterpreted the situation. I have inappropriately used the norms for North American business behavior, which include more informal and demonstrative business behaviors (by the sixth meeting, I would say "Good morning, Fritz," not "Good morning, Herr Ranschburg") to interpret the Austrian's more formal behavior ("Good morning, Herr Smith"). Using North American interpretations, a businessperson would only maintain formal behavior after the first few meetings if he either disliked or distrusted their associates. Such misinterpretation could jeopardize both the business transaction and the ongoing relationship.

Culture strongly influences, and in many situations determines, how we interpret situations. Our cultural background determines both the categories we use and the meanings we attach to them. Sources of cross-cultural misinterpretation include subconscious cultural blinders, a lack of cultural self-awareness, projected similarity, and parochialism.

Causing Problems: Subconscious Cultural Blinders

Because most interpretation goes on at a subconscious level, we are often unaware of the assumptions we make and their cultural basis. Our home-culture reality never forces us to examine our assumptions or the extent to which they are culturally based, because we share them with most other citizens from our country. All we know is that things do not work as smoothly or logically when we work outside our own culture as when we work with people more similar to ourselves. For example:

> Canadians conducting business in Kuwait were surprised when their meeting with a high-ranking official was not held in a closed office and was constantly interrupted. Using Canadian-based cultural assumptions—that important people have large private offices with secretaries monitoring the flow of people into the office, and that important business is not interrupted because it takes precedence over less important business—the Canadians interpreted the Kuwaiti's open office and constant interruptions to mean that the official was neither as high ranking nor as interested in conducting business with them as they had previously believed. The Canadians' misinterpretation of the Kuwaiti's office environment unfortunately led them to lose interest in working with the Kuwaiti.

The problem is that the Canadians' interpretation derives from their own North American cultural norms, not from the norms of Middle Eastern culture. The Kuwaiti may well have been a high-ranking official who was very interested in doing business. The Canadians will never know.

Cases of subconscious cross-cultural misinterpretation occur frequently. In the 1980s, for example, a Soviet Russian poet, after lecturing at U.S. universities for two months, observed that "Attempts to please an American audience are doomed in advance, because out of twenty listeners five may hold one point of view, seven another, and eight may have none at all" (1). The Soviet poet confused Americans' freedom of thought and speech with his ability to please them. He assumed that one can only please an audience if all members hold the same opinion. Another example of well-meant misinterpretation comes from the U.S. Office of Education's advice to U.S. teachers working with newly arrived Vietnamese refugee students (21):

> Students' participation was discouraged in Vietnamese schools by liberal doses of corporal punishment, and students were conditioned to sit rigidly and speak out only when spoken to. This background . . . makes speaking freely in class hard for a Vietnamese student. Therefore, don't mistake shyness for apathy.

Perhaps the extent to which this interpretation is culturally based becomes clearer when we imagine the opposite advice that the Vietnamese Ministry of Education might have given to Vietnamese teachers planning to instruct American children for the first time.

> Students' proper respect for teachers was discouraged by a loose order and students were conditioned to chat all the time and to behave in other disorderly ways. This background makes proper and respectful behavior in class hard for American students. Therefore, do not mistake rudeness for lack of reverence.

Causing Problems: A Lack of Cultural Self-Awareness

Although we may think that the biggest obstacle to conducting business around the world is understanding people from other cultures, the greater difficulty actually involves becoming aware of our own cultural conditioning. As anthropologist Edward Hall explains, "What is known least well, and is therefore in the poorest position to be studied, is what is closest to oneself" (10:45). We are generally least aware of our own cultural characteristics and express surprise when we hear foreigners describe us. Many Americans, for example, are surprised to discover that people from other cultures see them as hurried, overly law-abiding, very hard working, extremely explicit, and overly inquisitive (see the box "Cross-Cultural Awareness: Americans as Others See Them"). Many American businesspeople were equally surprised by a *Newsweek* survey reporting the characteristics most and least frequently associated with them (see Table 3-1). Asking people from other cultures to describe businesspeople from your own country is a powerful way to see yourself as others are likely to see you.

Another revealing way to understand the norms and values of a culture is to listen to their common sayings and proverbs. What does a society encourage, and what does it prohibit? The box on page 80, "Revealing North American Values: Proverbs," lists some common North American proverbs and the values each teaches.

To the extent that we are able to see ourselves through the eyes of people from other cultures, we can modify our behavior, emphasizing our

TABLE 3-1 Seeing Ourselves through Others' Eyes:
How People from Other Cultures See Americans

Characteristics Most Commonly Associated with Americans*					
Brazil	France	Great Britain	Japan	Mexico	Western Germany
Intelligent	Nationalistic	Friendly	Nationalistic	Industrious	Energetic
Inventive	Energetic	Self-indulgent	Friendly	Intelligent	Inventive
Energetic	Inventive	Energetic	Decisive	Inventive	Friendly
Industrious	Decisive	Industrious	Rude	Decisive	Sophisticated
Nationalistic	Friendly	Nationalistic	Self-indulgent	Greedy	Intelligent

Characteristics Least Commonly Associated with Americans*					
Brazil	France	Great Britain	Japan	Mexico	Western Germany
Lazy	Lazy	Lazy	Industrious	Lazy	Lazy
Self-indulgent	Rude	Sophisticated	Lazy	Honest	Sexy
Sexy	Honest	Sexy	Honest	Rude	Greedy
Sophisticated	Sophisticated	Decisive	Sexy	Sexy	Rude

*From a list of 14 characteristics.
SOURCE: Adapted by Adler, 2002. From *Newsweek*, July 11, 1983. Copyright © 1983 by Newsweek, Inc. All rights reserved. Reprinted by permission.

most appropriate and effective characteristics and minimizing those least helpful in the particular situation. The more culturally self-aware we become, the more able we will be to predict the effect our behavior will have on others.

Handicapping Effectiveness: Projected Similarity

Projected similarity refers to the assumption that people are more similar to you than they actually are, or that another person's situation is more similar to your own situation than it in fact is. Projecting similarity is both a natural and a common process. Managers from 14 countries, for example, described the work and life goals of a foreign colleague in their work team (6). As shown in Figure 3-3, in every case the managers

FIGURE 3-3 Projecting Similarity: People from Other Cultures Seem More Similar to Me Than They Are

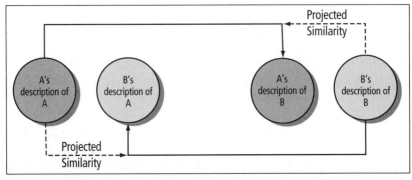

assumed their foreign colleagues were more like themselves than they actually were. Projected similarity involves imagining, assuming, and actually perceiving similarity when differences exist. Projected similarity particularly handicaps people in cross-cultural situations. As a South African, I assume that my Greek colleague is more South African than he actually is. As an Egyptian, I assume that my Chilean colleague behaves more similarly to me than she actually does. When I act based on this assumed similarity, I often find that I have acted inappropriately and thus ineffectively.

With the accelerated use of global communication tools—such as the Internet, e-mail, and all forms of e-commerce—the probability of inappropriately projecting similarity has increased markedly (9). Why? Because the chances of people from different cultures who do not know each other communicating with one another is higher, while the amount of contextual information they have about each other is much lower than in face-to-face meetings. Parties contacting each other electronically simply do not notice that they need to adjust their ways of communicating and interpreting meaning to fit the cultures involved.

Underlying projected similarity is subconscious parochialism. I assume that the only one way to be is my way. I assume that the only way to see the world is my way. I therefore view other people in reference to me and to my way of viewing the world. People may fall into an

illusion of understanding while being unaware of . . . [their] misunderstandings. "I understand you perfectly but you don't understand me" is an expression typ-

AMERICANS AS PEOPLE FROM OTHER CULTURES SEE THEM[4]

People from many countries often become puzzled and intrigued by the intricacies and enigmas of American culture. The following quotations report actual observations made by people from around the world who visited the United States. As you read their observations, ask yourself in each case why the observer, whether accurate or not, saw Americans in this way. How would you explain the trait in question?

India. "Americans seem to be in a perpetual hurry. Just watch the way they walk down the street. They never allow themselves the leisure to enjoy life; there are always too many things for them to do."

Kenya. "Americans appear to us rather distant. They are not really as close to other people—even fellow Americans—as Americans overseas tend to portray. It's almost as if an American says, 'I won't let you get too close to me.' It's like building a wall."

Turkey. "Once we were out in a rural area in the middle of nowhere and saw an American come to a stop sign. Though he could see in both directions for miles and no traffic was coming, he still stopped!"

Colombia. "The tendency in the United States to think that life is only work hits you in the face. Work seems to be their one . . . motivation."

Indonesia. "In the United States, everything has to be talked about and analyzed. Even the littlest thing has to be 'Why, Why, Why?' I get a headache from such persistent questions."

Ethiopia. "Americans are very explicit; . . . [they] want a 'yes' or 'no.' If someone tries to speak figuratively, Americans become confused."

Iran. "The first time . . . my [American] professor told me, 'I don't know the answer, I will have to look it up,' I was shocked. I asked myself, 'Why is he teaching me?' In my country a professor would give the wrong answer rather than ever admitting ignorance."

ical of such situations. Or all communicating parties may fall into a collective illusion of mutual understanding. In such situations, each party may wonder later why other parties do not live up to the "agreement" they had reached (14:3).

Most global managers do not think of themselves as parochial. They believe that as world travelers they appreciate foreigners' perspectives,

REVEALING NORTH AMERICAN VALUES: PROVERBS[5]

North Americans have heard the proverb "Don't cry over spilt milk" hundreds of times, and it has made its point. Why? Because it is much more powerful in teaching practicality to say "Don't cry over spilt milk" than to say "You'd better learn to be practical." Consider the following North American proverbs and the values each teaches.

PROVERB	VALUE
Cleanliness is next to godliness.	Cleanliness
A penny saved is a penny earned.	Thriftiness
Time is money.	Efficiency
Don't cry over spilt milk.	Practicality
Waste not; want not.	Frugality
Early to bed, early to rise, makes a person healthy, wealthy, and wise.	Diligence; Work ethic
God helps those who help themselves.	Initiative
It's not whether you win or lose, but how you play the game.	Good sportsmanship
A person's home is his castle.	Privacy, Value of personal property
No rest for the wicked.	Guilt, Work ethic
You've made your bed, now sleep in it.	Responsibility
Don't count your chickens before they're hatched.	Practicality
A bird in the hand is worth two in the bush.	Practicality
The squeaky wheel gets the grease.	Assertiveness
Might makes right.	Superiority of physical power
There's more than one way to skin a cat.	Originality, Determination
A stitch in time saves nine.	Planning; Preparation
All that glitters is not gold.	Caution; Wariness
If at first you don't succeed, try, try again.	Persistence, Work ethic
Take care of today, and tomorrow will take care of itself.	Preparation for future
Laugh, and the world laughs with you; weep and you weep alone.	Pleasant outward appearance

which is not always true. The following are two examples of managers' projected similarity and their consequent culturally based misinterpretation:

> Danish managers working with a Saudi executive reacted with concern when the Saudi explained that the plant they were constructing would be completed on time, "En shah allah" ("If God was willing"). The Danes didn't believe that God's will would influence the progress of construction. They continued to see the world from their own parochial Danish perspective and assumed that "En shah allah" was either an excuse for not getting the work done, or was altogether meaningless.
>
> Similarly, when Balinese workers' families refused to use birth control methods offered by their global company's health officer, explaining that it would break the cycle of reincarnation, few Western managers considered the possibility that they too might be reborn a number of times. Instead, they pejoratively assumed that the Balinese either were superstitious, or simply did not understand, or feared Western medical practices.

While it is important to understand and respect the other cultures' points of view, it is not necessary to either accept or adopt them. Understanding and respect do not imply acceptance. Rigid adherence to one's own belief system, however, reflects parochialism, and parochialism underlies projected similarity.

One of the best exercises for developing empathy and reducing both parochialism and projected similarity is role reversal (see the box "How Well Do You Know Your International Colleagues?"). Imagine, for example, that you are a businessperson from a culture other than your own. Imagine the type of family you would have come from, the number of brothers and sisters you have, the social and economic conditions you grew up with, the type of education you received, the ways in which you chose your profession and position, the manner in which you were introduced to your spouse, your goals in working for your organization, and your life goals. Asking these questions forces you to see other people as they really are, and not as mere reflections of yourself. It forces you to see both the similarities and differences, and not simply to imagine similarities when differences actually exist. Moreover, role reversal encourages highly task-oriented businesspeople, such as Americans, to see their colleagues from other cultures as whole people rather than merely as someone with a position and a set of skills needed to succeed on the current project.

HOW WELL DO YOU KNOW YOUR INTERNATIONAL COLLEAGUES?

Think about a colleague from another culture with whom you are currently working or have worked in the past. See how many of the following questions about him or her you can answer, how many you think you know the answer to but are not certain of (and therefore run a risk of *projected-similarity error*), and how many you do not know at all (and therefore run a high risk of *selective-perception error*). If you are still in contact with the colleague, you may want to check the accuracy of your perceptions with him or her after having completed your personal review. Note that questions are written as if your colleague is a woman. If your colleague is a man, just imagine the following questions are about him (instead of *her*).

Family Background

- How large a family does she come from? How many brothers and sisters does she have? Is she the oldest? Youngest?
- From what socioeconomic status is her family? Is the family among the richest in the country? The poorest? Did her parents earn the family wealth or was it inherited? Is the family highly respected in the community? Why? Why not?
- What religion is she? How important is religion to her? Can you ask her about her religion? Does she want to tell you about her spiritual beliefs? How does her religion or spiritual beliefs affect the way she works? How do they affect the way she works with you?
- What type of education did she receive? Did she attend private school? Public school? Religious school? What proportion of people in her country have attained the same level of education? Did she gain entrance into the highest levels of education primarily through performance (tests), money, or personal connections? Did she receive all of her education in her home country? Does she consider her education to be superior or inferior to your own education?
- Is she married? Whom did she marry? Was it an arranged marriage? Does her husband's family influence where she works? Is her closest relationship with her husband? Her mother? Her children?

continued on next page ■

■ *continued from previous page*

- Does she have children? How many? What type of relationship does she have with her children? How much time does she spend with her children each day? Would she consider sending her children away to boarding school? What does she see as her responsibility to her children?
- What type of home does she live in? Is it in an elite neighborhood? Is she satisfied with it? Does she live with her extended family (parents, grandparents, aunts, uncles) or her nuclear family?
- As a person, what is most important to her? What are some of her most deeply held values?

Career Background

- Why did she choose the career or profession she did? Is it what her father or mother did? Is it considered a high-status profession?
- Why does she work? For the money? Prestige? Loyalty? Responsibility? Personal satisfaction? Does she have to work to survive economically? Does she come from a culture that "works to live" or "lives to work"?
- What does she need to do to get ahead in her career? How important to her career is the success of her work with you?
- In her culture, how are people viewed who work with foreigners? Who travel internationally? Who have foreigners as friends?
- Do high-potential managers in her company (and culture) or just average performers usually get sent abroad to work?

Culture

- What does she think about your culture? What does she see as your culture's strengths? What would she like to learn from your culture? What does she want to learn from you?
- What totally annoys her about your culture? What does she see as your culture's weaknesses? How does she see your culture as getting in the way of working with you?
- In which ways does she see your culture as being ahead of her culture? In which ways does she see her culture as being ahead of your culture? Does she believe in cultural synergy; that is, that your two cultures can be combined to develop new and innovative approaches to business, including to managerial and organizational challenges?

CROSS-CULTURAL MISEVALUATION: WHY DO WE BELIEVE THERY'RE WRONG?

Even more than perception and interpretation, cultural conditioning strongly affects evaluation. Evaluation involves judging whether someone or something is good or bad. Cross-culturally, we use our own culture as the standard, judging that which is like our own culture as normal and good and that which is different as abnormal and bad. Our own culture becomes a self-reference criterion: because no other culture is identical to our own, we tend to judge all other cultures as inferior. Evaluating others' behavior rarely helps in trying to understand, communicate with, or conduct business with people from another culture. The following example highlights the potentially negative consequences of misevaluation:

> A Swiss executive waits more than an hour past the appointed time for his Spanish colleague to arrive and to sign a major supply contract. In his impatience he concludes that the Spaniard must be lazy and totally unconcerned about business. The Swiss executive has misevaluated his colleague by negatively comparing the colleague's behavior to his own culture's standards for business punctuality. Implicitly, he has labeled his own culture's behavior as good ("The Swiss arrive on time, especially for important meetings, and that is good") and the other culture's behavior as bad ("The Spanish do not arrive on time and that is bad").

COMMUNICATING CROSS-CULTURALLY: GETTING THEIR MEANING, NOT JUST THEIR WORDS

Communicating effectively across cultures is possible; however, global managers cannot approach communication in the same way as domestic managers. First, effective global managers "know that they don't know." They assume difference until similarity is proven rather than assuming similarity until difference is proven.

Second, in attempting to understand their colleagues from other cultures, effective global managers emphasize description; they observe what is actually being said and done, rather than interpreting or evaluating it. Describing a situation is the most accurate way to gather information about it. Interpretation and evaluation, unlike description, are based more on the observer's own culture and background than on the observed situation. My interpretations and evaluations therefore tell me more about myself than about the actual situation. Although managers, as decision makers, must continually evaluate people (e.g., performance appraisal) and situations (e.g., project evaluation) based on their organization's standards and objectives, effective global managers delay making judgments until they have taken sufficient time to observe and interpret the people and situation from the perspectives of all cultures involved.

Third, when attempting to understand or interpret a cross-cultural situation, effective global managers try to see it through the eyes of their colleagues worldwide. This role reversal reduces the myopia of viewing situations strictly from one's own perspective.

Fourth, once effective global managers develop an explanation for a situation, they treat the explanation as a guess (as a hypothesis to be tested) and not as a certainty. They systematically check with colleagues from home and abroad to make certain that their guesses—their initial interpretations—are plausible. This checking process allows them to converge meanings—to delay accepting their interpretations of the situation until they have confirmed them with others.

Increasing Understanding: Converging Meanings

Global managers use a variety of methods to increase the chances of accurately understanding businesspeople from other cultures. The box "What Do I Do If They Do Not Speak My Language?" suggests what to do to increase effectiveness when business colleagues are not native speakers of your language. Each approach is based on presenting the message through multiple channels (for example, stating your position and showing a graph to summarize the same position), paraphrasing to check that colleagues from other cultures have understood your meaning (and not just your words), and converging meanings (always double-checking with the other person to verify that you have communicated what you had intended to communicate).

Standing Back from Yourself

Perhaps the most difficult skill in effectively communicating across cultures involves standing back from yourself; becoming aware that you do not know everything, that certain situations may not make sense, that your guesses may be wrong, and that the heightened ambiguity will probably continue. In this sense the ancient Roman dictum "knowledge is power" is true. In knowing yourself, you gain power over your perceptions and reactions; you can control your own behavior and your reactions to others' behavior. Cross-cultural awareness complements

WHAT DO I DO IF THEY DO NOT SPEAK MY LANGUAGE?[6]

Verbal Behavior

- *Speak slowly & clearly.* Enunciate each word. Do not use colloquial expressions.
- *Repeat.* Repeat each important idea using different words to explain the same concept.
- *Use simple sentences.* Avoid compound, long sentences.
- *Use active verbs.* Avoid passive verbs.

Nonverbal Behavior

- *Restate ideas visually.* Use as many visual restatements as possible, such as pictures, graphs, tables, and slides.
- *Use appropriate gestures.* Use appropriate facial and hand gestures to emphasize the meaning of words.
- *Demonstrate themes.* Act out as many themes as possible.
- *Pause frequently.*
- *Summarize.* Distribute written summaries of your verbal presentation.

Accurate Interpretation

- *Guard the silences.* When the other person is silent, wait. Do not jump in to fill the silence. The other person is probably just thinking more slowly in the nonnative language or translating.
- *Assume they're intelligent.* Do not equate poor grammar and mis-pronunciation with lack of intelligence; it is usually a sign of non-native language use.
- *Assume difference.* If unsure, assume difference, not similarity.

Understanding

- *Don't assume they understand.* Unless proven otherwise, assume they do not understand.
- *Check for comprehension.* Ask colleagues to paraphrase their under-standing of your presentation. Do not simply ask whether they understand. Let them explain what they understood.

Design

- *Take breaks.* Take more frequent breaks. Second language compre-hension is exhausting.

continued on next page ■

■ *continued from previous page*

- **Design small modules.** Divide the material you are presenting into smaller, shorter modules.
- **Allocate extra time.** Allocate more time for each module than you usually need for presenting the same material to native speakers of your language.

Motivation

- **Encourage them.** Verbally and nonverbally encourage nonnative language speakers to participate.
- **Draw people into meeting.** Encourage marginal and passive participants to contribute.
- **Reinforce.** Do not embarrass novice speakers; reinforce their attempts to speak you language.

---

in-depth self-awareness. A lack of self-awareness negates the usefulness of cross-cultural awareness.

One of the most poignant examples of the powerful interplay between description, interpretation, evaluation, and empathy involved a Scottish businessman's relationship with a Japanese colleague. The box "Communicating Across Cultures: Japanese Pickles and Mattresses, Incorporated" recounts the Scottish businessman's experience.

COMMUNICATING ACROSS CULTURES: JAPANESE PICKLES AND MATTRESSES, INCORPORATED[7]

It was my first visit to Japan. As a gastronomic adventurer, and because I believe cuisine is one route that is freely available and highly effective as a first step towards a closer understanding of another country, I felt disappointed on my first evening when the Japanese offered me a Western meal.

continued on next page ■

■ *continued from previous page*

As tactfully as possible, I suggested that sometime during my stay I would like to try a Japanese menu, if it could be arranged without inconvenience. The small reluctance evident on the part of my hosts was due, I assumed, to their thought that I was just being polite asking for Japanese food, but I didn't really like it. So to be good hosts, the Japanese had to politely find a way to not serve it to me! But eventually, by an elegantly progressive route starting with Western food with a slightly Japanese bias through to genuine Japanese food, my hosts were convinced that I really wanted to eat Japanese style and was not simply "posing."

From then on they became progressively more enthusiastic in suggesting the more exotic Japanese dishes, and I guess I graduated when, after an excellent meal one night (apart from the Japanese pickles) on which I had lavished praise, they said, "Do you like Japanese pickles?" To this, without preamble, I said, "No!" With great laughter all around, they responded, "Nor do we!"

During this gastronomic getting-together week, I had also been trying to persuade them that I really did wish to stay in traditional Japanese hotels rather than the very Westernized ones my hosts had selected because they thought I would prefer my "normal" lifestyle. I should add that, at this time, traditional Japanese hotels were still available and often cheaper than, say, the Osaka Hilton.

Anyway, after the pickles joke, it was suddenly announced that Japanese hotels could be arranged. For my remaining two weeks in Japan, as I toured the major cities, on most occasions a traditional Japanese hotel was substituted for the Western one on my original itinerary.

As you know, a traditional Japanese room has no furniture except a low table and a flower arrangement. The "bed" is a mattress produced from a concealed cupboard just before you retire, accompanied by a cereal-packed pillow.

One memorable evening my host and I had finished our meal together in my room. I was expecting him to shortly say goodnight and retire to his own room, as he had been doing all week.

However, he stayed unusually long and was obviously in some sort of emotional crisis. Finally, he blurted out, with great embarrassment, "Can I sleep with you?!"

continued on next page ■

■ *continued from previous page*

As they say in the novels, at this point I went very still! My mind was racing through all the sexual taboos and prejudices my own upbringing had instilled, and I can still very clearly recall how I analyzed: "I'm bigger than he is so I can fight him off, but then he's probably an expert in the martial arts, but on the other hand he has shown no signs of being gay up until now and he is my host and there is a lot of business at risk and there's no such thing as rape, et cetera . . . !"

It seemed a hundred years, though it was only a few seconds, before I said, feeling as if I was pulling the trigger in Russian roulette, "Yes, sure."

Who said that the Orientals are inscrutable? The look of relief that followed my reply was obvious. Then he looked worried and concerned again, and said, "Are you sure?"

I reassured him and he called in the maid, who fetched his mattress from his room and laid it on the floor alongside mine. We both went to bed and slept all night without any physical interaction.

Later I learned that for traditional Japanese one of the greatest compliments you can be paid is for your host to ask, "Can I sleep with you?" This goes back to the ancient feudal times, when life was cheap, and what the invitation was really saying was, "I trust you with my life. I do not think that you will kill me while I sleep. You are my true friend."

To have said "No" to the invitation would have been an insult—"I don't trust you not to kill me while I sleep"—or, at the very least, my host would have been acutely embarrassed because he had taken the initiative. If I refused because I had failed to perceive the invitation as a compliment, he would have been out of countenance on two grounds: the insult to him in the traditional context and the embarrassment he would have caused me by "forcing" a negative, uncomprehending response from me.

As it turned out, the outcome was superb. He and I were now "blood brothers," as it were. His assessment of me as being "ready for Japanization" had been correct and his obligations under ancient Japanese custom had been fulfilled. Through my own cultural conditioning, I had initially totally misinterpreted his intentions. It was sheer luck, or luck plus a gut feeling that I'd gotten it wrong, that caused me to respond correctly to his extremely complimentary and committed invitation.

SUMMARY

Communicating across cultures confronts us with our limited ability to perceive, interpret, and evaluate people and situations. Our culturally based perspectives render everything relative and slightly uncertain. Entering a culture that is foreign to us is tantamount to knowing the words without knowing the music, or knowing the music without knowing the dance. Our natural tendencies lead us back to our prior experience: our default option becomes the familiarity of our own culture, thus precluding our accurate understanding of others' cultures.

Strategies to overcome our natural parochial tendencies exist. With care, we can avoid our ethnocentric default options. We can learn to see, understand, and transcend our cultural conditioning. When working in other cultures, we can emphasize description rather than interpretation or evaluation, and thus minimize self-fulfilling stereotypes and premature judgments. We can recognize and use our initial stereotypes as guides rather than rejecting them as unsophisticated simplifications. Effectively communicating across cultures presupposes the interplay of alternative realities. It rejects the actual or potential domination of one reality over another.

PART TWO

Leveraging Cultural Diversity

4

Creating Cultural Synergy

Bhinneka Tunggal Ika *("Unity Through Diversity")*
— NATIONAL MOTTO OF INDONESIA
E Pluribus Unum *("Out of Many One")*
— MOTTO ON ALL COINS IN THE UNITED STATES OF AMERICA

IS CULTURE VISIBLE? Does cultural diversity have an impact on organizations? If so, is its impact positive or negative, helpful or harmful to organizations? How should businesspeople manage cultural diversity? Should they ignore it, minimize it, or leverage it? This chapter investigates the invisibility of culture and our own cultural blindness. It describes the advantages and disadvantages of working in culturally diverse environments, and presents alternative strategies for managing and potentially benefitting from cultural diversity and its outcomes.

CULTURAL INVISIBILITY: STRATEGIES FOR RECOGNIZING CULTURE

Cultural Invisibility

Do managers see culture? No. Few managers believe that culture significantly affects the day-to-day operations of organizations. Global managers often see themselves as beyond passport, and their organizations as beyond nationality.

To better understand the impact of cultural diversity on organizations, we conducted a series of studies (5). We selected Montreal as an ideal location to study cultural diversity because it has the largest English-speaking population in the predominantly French-Canadian province of Quebec. In the study, 60 organizational development consultants described the positive and negative impacts of cultural diversity on their organizations and work. Two-thirds said they saw no impact whatsoever. Of the remaining one-third, only one consultant reported observing a positive impact. Interestingly, although television, radio, Internet, and newspaper reports daily attest to Montrealers' recognition of the influence of bilingualism and biculturalism on the social, political, and economic environment of Quebec, most organizational development consultants reported seeing no influence of culture on the world of work.

The consultants are not alone. Management scholars also demonstrate an equivalent cultural blindness (2;6;7;9;10). In the 1970s, less than 5 percent of management research published in the most prominent academic and professional journals considered either international or domestic multiculturalism (2). Given the dramatic increase in global business activity over the last few decades, one would expect a significant increase in the proportion of international and multicultural articles published (6:552). Trends similar to those in the 1970s, however, continued in the 1980s (13;18;20). Not until the 1990s did the number of international and multicultural articles begin to increase, and even then the proportion remained less than 10 percent (6). American scholars have conducted the vast majority of management studies, with most focusing on U.S. organizations, and yet they continue to assume their findings apply universally (7;9;10). Given that the United States is culturally distinct on a number of dimensions—most prominently, Americans' extreme individualism—this overgeneralization is particularly misleading. Management researchers, perhaps to an even greater extent than their business colleagues, have ignored the influence of culture on organizations.

Cultural Blindness: Why Is Seeing Culture Illegitimate?

Cultural diversity, whether international or domestic, does exist and does affect the ways in which we behave in organizations (for example, see Chapters 1 and 2 and references 15, 16, and 24 among many others). As one Swiss executive recognized, "Local culture affects virtually every aspect of our business." Yet according to two South African executives, "Interest in cultural differences is offensive" (21).

In many instances people associate recognizing cultural differences with simplistic, primitive, and sometimes even immoral ways of thinking. They label managers who recognize the diversity within their organizations as prejudiced, racist, sexist, ethnocentric, and unprofessional. North American cultural norms, for example, encourage managers to blind themselves to gender, race, and ethnicity; that is, to attempt to see people only as individuals and therefore to judge them based solely on their professional skills. This culture-blind approach causes problems by confusing the recognition of culturally based differences with the judging of those same differences. Managers recognize cultural differences when they realize that people from different cultures behave differently and that those differences affect the ways in which their organizations function. Recognition, however, is not the same as judging people from one culture to be better or worse than those from other cultures; it is simply an acknowledgment that they differ. No cultural group inherently manages any better or worse than any other group. Ignoring cultural differences is unproductive. Judging colleagues and clients based on their membership in particular groups fosters prejudice—a prejudgment based on group, rather than individual, characteristics—not productivity. Far from increasing organizational effectiveness, judging cultural differences as good or bad usually leads to inappropriate, offensive, racist, sexist, and ethnocentric attitudes and behaviors. Recognizing differences has the opposite effect. *Cultural blindness*—choosing not to see cultural differences—reduces our perception of people to less than who they are, and limits the ability of organizations to benefit from diversity; that is, it precludes organizations' ability to minimize the problems caused by cultural diversity and to maximize the potential advantages it offers.

When we blind ourselves to cultural diversity, people from other cultures become mere projections of ourselves. As described in Chapter 3, we frequently see similarity even when difference exists; we project similarity. As one Canadian manager inaccurately observed, "It is very easy to work with people from other cultures. People are basically the same and have the same needs and aspirations" (8). Although people are not the same, we inaccurately perceive them to be the same—to have the same needs and aspirations. Cultural blindness is therefore both perceptual and conceptual: we neither see nor want to see differences. To effectively manage cross-culturally, a concerted effort must be made to recognize cultural diversity without judging it—to see difference where difference exists.

Diversity Causes Problems

Culture is generally invisible and, when visible, managers usually see it as causing problems. Managers rarely believe cultural diversity benefits organizations. Global executives attending management seminars at INSEAD, the leading international management school in France, for example, described the advantages and disadvantages of cultural diversity to their companies. Whereas every executive could describe disadvantages, fewer than a third could list an advantage (8;17). As a French executive summarized, "I have been involved in many situations over the years, but I can't think of one made easier because it involved more than one culture." His Danish colleague agreed, "I can think of no situation in my experience where managing ordinary business became easier or more effective because it involved people from more than one culture."

In the Montreal study described earlier (5), only one of the 60 organizational development consultants mentioned an advantage to the organization from cultural diversity. Similarly, the 52 corporate and academic experts from around the world who participated in the McGill International Symposium on Cross-Cultural Management had a considerably harder time identifying the benefits to be gained from diversity than the problems it causes (1). Every executive and academic present at the Symposium could identify a series of diversity-related problems (1).

What types of problems does diversity cause? As shown in Table 4-1, diversity most frequently causes problems in convergent processes; it causes problems when the organization needs employees to think or to act in similar ways. Diversity renders communication (converging on similar meanings) and integration (converging on similar actions) more difficult. People from different cultures fail to understand one another; they do not work in the same ways or at the same pace. The potential for increased ambiguity, complexity, and confusion becomes highest when organizations or projects require decisions and clarity—convergence.

Diversity causes problems when managers and employees overgeneralize organizational practices and processes from one culture to other dissimilar countries and cultures. Problems result, for example, when managers export marketing campaigns developed in one country without adapting them to the new target countries:

Africa/United States

[An American multinational] tried to sell baby food in an African nation by using its regular label showing a smiling baby and stating the type of baby food in the jar. Unfortunately, the local population took one look at the labels and interpreted them to mean the jars contained ground-up babies! Sales, of course, were terrible (22:31).

Cultural diversity causes problems when a culturally diverse team must reach a single agreement, whether formal or informal:

Japan/Switzerland

Settlement of a licensing agreement between a Japanese and a Swiss company became much more difficult due to large differences in the two countries' decision-making and legal systems, the inability of the Swiss to understand

TABLE 4-1 Recognizing Potential Advantages and Disadvantages from Diversity

ADVANTAGES	DISADVANTAGES
Synergistic Advantages: **Organizational Benefits Derived from Cultural Diversity**	**Cross-Cultural Disadvantages:** **Organizational Costs Caused by Cultural Diversity**

Expanding meanings
  Greater openness to new ideas
  Multiple perspectives
  Multiple interpretations
	Diversity increases
	  Ambiguity
	  Complexity
	  Confusion

Expanding alternatives
  Increasing creativity
  Increasing flexibility
  Increasing problem-solving skills
	Difficulty converging meanings
	  Miscommunication
	  Harder to reach agreement
	Difficulty converging actions
	  Harder to agree on specific actions

Culture-Specific Advantages: **Benefits from Working with a Particular Culture**	**Culture-Specific Disadvantages:** **Costs Inherent in Working with a Particular Culture**

Increased understanding of local
  political, social, legal, economic,
  and cultural environment
Better understanding of local employees
Better able to work effectively with
  local clients
Better able to market effectively to
  local customers
	Overgeneralizing
	  Organizational policies
	  Organizational strategies
	  Organizational practices
	  Organizational procedures
	
	Ethnocentrism

the Japanese language, the long distances and time differences, and the lack of spontaneity. In one's own country, these difficulties would not exist or could easily be overcome (13).

Cultural diversity increases complexity and difficulty in developing company-wide policies procedures:

Personnel Records in Europe

In line with the American parent company's policies, European subsidiaries attempted to design a common system for developing historical medical records on all employees. Human resource managers from Germany, Italy, Luxembourg, the Netherlands, Spain, Sweden, and the United Kingdom convened a meeting to agree on what could be accomplished and how. Despite procedures that worked well in the United States, the American parent company found the variety of national legislation, cultural concerns, and requirements to consult with work councils and trade unions prior to reaching agreement imposed severe limitations on the scope of usable information. In a domestic setting, the variety of constraints would have been lower and those remaining clearly understood by all people developing the system. An effective medical records system would have been much easier to develop if only one country had been involved (8).

Diversity Makes Potential Advantages Possible

Whereas diversity causes the most problems in convergent processes, it leads to the most potential advantages in divergent processes. Diversity becomes most advantageous when the organization wants to expand its perspective, strategy, tactics, or approach. Diversity can become an advantage in attempting to reposition the organization, reposition strategy from a bricks-and-mortar to an e-commerce environment, launch a new project, create a new idea, develop a new marketing plan, design a new operation, or assess emerging trends from a new perspective.

If diversity is well managed, organizations can benefit from both synergistic and culture-specific advantages, including enhanced creativity, flexibility, and problem-solving skills, especially on complex problems involving many qualitative factors, improved effectiveness in working with culturally distinct clients and colleagues, and an improved understanding of the dynamics and communication patterns within the organization (14;25). As outlined in Table 4-1, some managers focus on the synergistic advantages of multicultural organizations, in particular on their ability to operate more flexibly and to stay open to new ideas. They note the advantages that multiple perspectives bring to problem solving and to avoiding *groupthink*.[1] Others stress culture-specific advantages, including the ability of multicultural organizations to better understand customers' needs worldwide; for example, in tailoring their marketing campaigns to the national and cultural preferences of clients in each country.

When managers use cultural diversity as a resource, rather than treating it as a liability, they benefit from its potential advantages to the organization. Global managers reap the benefits of cultural diversity in strategic alliances, joint ventures, global projects, and all types of multinational business. Executives describe the following benefits to their companies from diversity (8):

New Product Development

A U.S. pharmaceutical firm developed a new, lucrative anticancer drug by combining an initial discovery made in their Italian subsidiary with research conducted in conjunction with the U.S.-based National Cancer Institute (the best-equipped institute for therapeutical research in the world), new Swedish creativity techniques, new Japanese and Chinese therapy indications, and major financing from Germany and the United States.

Accepting New Ideas

New ideas that seem threatening or absurd when mentioned by someone from one's own country are often easier to "hear" when suggested by colleagues from another culture. During the energy crisis, for example, American and British workers initially complained that the low thermostat settings were restrictive. When a British team then went to Korea to design the Pony car, they were amazed that the Koreans had to break ice before they could wash their products. Thereafter, the low thermostat settings no longer seemed so restrictive.

New Perspectives, Better Communication, and Cooperation

A European firm involved all its European subsidiaries in creating a Technical and Field Support Center. By including all countries in defining the "where, how, and why" of operations, the Center avoided any one nation's dictatorial decisions, which, in the past, had caused continuous conflicts between countries.

New Perspectives

A Franco-American joint venture required an outside audit of their Algerian subsidiary. The American partner unsuccessfully proposed an American accounting firm. The French partner, with a similar lack of success, proposed a French accounting firm, but failed to gain agreement from the American partner. The two finally agreed on a French-affiliated office of an American accounting firm that agreed to assign two French-speaking British citizens to do the job. Everybody was happy.

Benefiting from Diversity

Culture is not one of the concepts easily recognized or readily used by managers to explain the behavior of individuals, teams, or organizations. Unless given an explicit model indicating the impact of cultural diversity, managers often fail to consider it as a possible explanation for variations in organizational functioning. They see factors other than culture influencing individual and organizational behavior. The follow-up to the Montreal organizational development study highlighted the value of giving managers a model demonstrating cultural diversity's ability both to generate advantages and to cause problems for organizations (5). The value of the model became evident when the follow-up study did not replicate the results of the original interviews. Following the initial 60 interviews in the original study, a similar group of 75 Canadian organizational development consultants received questionnaires asking them to describe the positive and negative impacts of cultural diversity on their organizations. Unlike the open-ended interviews, the structured questionnaire specifically gave the consultants a model highlighting the potentially positive and negative consequences of cultural diversity. Most consultants responding to the questionnaire, unlike their interviewed counterparts, reported seeing an impact of cultural diversity on their organization, with almost half identifying positive influences.

As shown in Figure 4-1, the original interviewees had viewed the impact of cultural diversity in one of three ways. Most had considered it nonexistent, as having no impact whatsoever. Some had seen it as being primarily negative. Only a very few had viewed the impact of cultural diversity as being potentially either negative or positive, but not both. In the interviews, the consultants had failed to see the possibility of cultural diversity simultaneously offering advantages and disadvantages to the organization. By contrast, most questionnaire respondents recognized the possibility of cultural diversity leading simultaneously to both highly positive and highly negative outcomes within the same organization. They did not see positive impacts (advantages) as necessarily related to the lack of negative impacts (problems) (5).

The two parts of the study differed in that the first group, the interviewees, were not given either the concept of culture or a model suggesting its possible positive and negative impacts, whereas the second group—those responding

FIGURE 4-1 How Does Cultural Diversity Impact Organizations?
Positively? Negatively? Both? Neither?

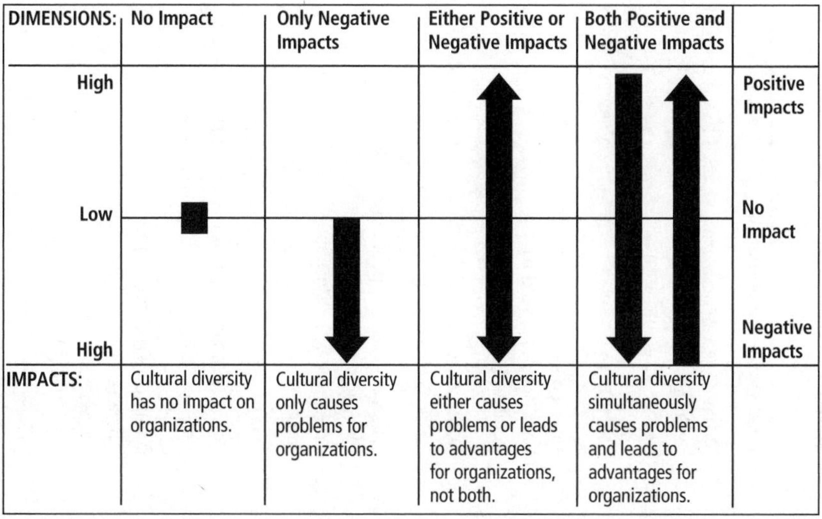

DIMENSIONS:	No Impact	Only Negative Impacts	Either Positive or Negative Impacts	Both Positive and Negative Impacts	
High					Positive Impacts
Low	■				No Impact
High					Negative Impacts
IMPACTS:	Cultural diversity has no impact on organizations.	Cultural diversity only causes problems for organizations.	Cultural diversity either causes problems or leads to advantages for organizations, not both.	Cultural diversity simultaneously causes problems and leads to advantages for organizations.	

Source: Adapted by Adler, 2002. Reprinted with permission from *Journal of Applied Behavioral Science*, "Organizational Development in a Multicultural Environment," by Nancy J. Adler, vol. 19, no. 3 pp. 349–365, copyright © 1983 by NTL Institute.

to the questionnaire—were explicitly given both. Although they rarely do so naturally, managers are able to "see" cultural diversity and appreciate its positive and negative impacts when given a model. If culture is not explicitly pointed out, managers unfortunately often remain culture blind.

Strategies for Managing Cultural Diversity

Managers' ability to recognize cultural diversity and its potential advantages and disadvantages defines an organization's approach to managing diversity (5). As shown in Table 4-2, managers' most common response to cultural diversity is *parochial*—they choose not to recognize cultural diversity or its impact on the organization. In parochial organizations, managers believe that "our way is the only way" to organize and manage. The second most common response is *ethnocentric*—managers recognize diversity, but only as a source of problems. In ethnocentric organizations, managers believe that "our way is the best way" to organize and work; they view all other ways as inferior. Only when managers

TABLE 4-2 Which Organizations Benefit from Cultural Diversity?

Type of Organization	Perception	Strategy	Most Likely Consequences	Frequency
	What is the perceived impact of cultural diversity on organizations?	How should the impact of cultural diversity on organizations be managed?	What consequences can managers expect with this perception and strategy?	How common are these perceptions and strategies?
PAROCHIAL Our way is the only way.	NO IMPACT: Cultural diversity has no impact on organizations.	IGNORE DIFFERENCES: Ignore the impact of cultural diversity on organizations.	PROBLEMS: Problems occur but they are not attributed to cultural diversity.	VERY COMMON
ETHNOCENTRIC Our way is best.	NEGATIVE IMPACT: Cultural diversity causes problems for organizations.	MINIMIZE DIFFERENCES: Minimize the sources and impact of cultural diversity on organizations. If possible, select a unicultural workforce.	SOME PROBLEMS AND FEW ADVANTAGES: Managers reduce problems by reducing diversity; they ignore or eliminate potential advantages.	COMMON
SYNERGISTIC Leveraging our ways and their ways may work best.	POTENTIAL NEGATIVE AND POSITIVE IMPACTS: Cultural diversity leads to both advantages and problems for organizations.	MANAGE DIFFERENCES: Train managers to recognize and use cultural differences to create advantages for the organization.	SOME PROBLEMS AND MANY ADVANTAGES: Managers recognize and benefit from the many advantages resulting from cultural diversity. Some problems continue to occur and need to be managed.	LESS COMMON

SOURCE: Adapted in 2002 from Nancy J. Adler, "Organizational Development in a Multicultural Environment," in *Journal of Applied Behavioral Science*, vol. 19, no. 3, Summer 1983. Copyright © 1983 NTL Institute.

explicitly recognize the concept of culture can the response to cultural diversity be *synergistic*—seeing cultural diversity as leading to both advantages and disadvantages. Employees and managers using synergistic approaches believe that "our way and their way differ, but neither is inherently superior to the other." They believe that creative combinations of our way and their way produce the best approaches to organizing and working.

Each of the various assumptions and perceptions produces different implications for organizations' approaches to managing diversity. If managers assume the impact of cultural diversity is negligible, as is the case in parochial organizations, they will select strategies that ignores diversity. As one parochial manager described, "Cultural diversity is just not important enough to consider; it is irrelevant." This strategy precludes the possibility of effectively managing diversity. It precludes the possibility of enhancing positive impacts and minimizing negative impacts.

Alternatively, if managers assume that the only impacts of cultural diversity are negative, as is the case in ethnocentric organizations, then they will select strategies that minimizes the sources and impacts of cultural diversity within the organization. Ethnocentric managers implement minimizing strategies in one of two ways: either by attempting to select a culturally homogeneous workforce, or by attempting to socialize all employees into the behavioral patterns of the dominant culture. Ethnocentric organizations, by minimizing diversity, preclude all possibility of benefiting from the many cultures of their employees and clients.

Managers who see the impacts of cultural diversity as potentially both positive and negative attempt to *manage the impacts of cultural diversity rather than manage the diversity itself*. Managers using this synergistic approach minimize potential problems by managing the impacts of cultural diversity, rather than by attempting to minimize the diversity itself. Similarly, they maximize potential advantages by managing the impacts of diversity, rather than by ignoring them. Organizations using a synergistic approach train their members to recognize cultural differences and to leverage them to create advantages for the organization.

The first two strategies—ignoring and minimizing cultural differences—occur naturally and are therefore quite common. Only when managers recognize both the existence of cultural diversity and its potential advantages to the organization does it become probable that they will choose to manage the diversity rather than attempting to ignore or minimize it. Cultural diversity has both potential advantageous and disadvantageous consequences; the organization's approach to diversity, and not the diversity itself, determines its ultimate costs and benefits.

CULTURAL SYNERGY

According to Buckminster Fuller, synergy involves "a new way of thinking . . . which helps to free one from outdated patterns and can break the shell of permitted ignorance" (12). Synergy is "the behavior of whole systems that cannot be predicted by the behavior of any parts taken separately. . . . In order to really understand what is going on, we have to abandon starting with parts, and we must work instead from whole to particular" (12). The book *Managing Cultural Synergy* emphasizes that "the very differences in the world's people can lead to mutual growth and accomplishment that is more than the single contribution of each party to the intercultural transaction" (19). It suggests that we can

> go beyond awareness of our own cultural heritage to produce something greater by cooperation and collaboration. Cultural synergy builds upon similarities and fuses differences resulting in more effective human activities and systems. The very diversity of people can be utilized to enhance problem solving by combined action. Those in international management have unique opportunities to foster synergy on a global basis (19).

Cultural synergy, as an approach to managing the impact of cultural diversity, involves a process in which managers form organizational policies, strategies, structures, and practices based on, but not limited to, the cultural patterns of individual organization members and clients. Culturally synergistic organizations create new forms of management and organization that transcend the distinct cultures of their members (3:172). This approach recognizes both the similarities and differences among the cultures that compose a global organization and suggests that we neither ignore nor minimize cultural diversity, but rather view it as a resource in designing and developing organizational systems (3:172). From a synergistic perspective, cultural diversity is a key resource in all global learning organizations.

As summarized in Table 4-3, a set of assumptions that differs from those most commonly held about cross-cultural interaction within work settings forms the basis of the cultural synergy approach (4). The first commonly held, and yet misleading, assumption is *homogeneity*, the belief that all people are basically the same. Believing a culture is homogeneous is the most common assumption—especially in the United States, where it forms the basis of the "melting pot" myth. Cultural synergy, by contrast, assumes *heterogeneity*. Synergy is based on the assump-

TABLE 4-3 Misleading versus More Appropriate Cultural Assumptions

Common, but Misleading, Assumptions		Less Common, but More Appropriate, Assumptions	
HOMOGENEITY	*Melting pot myth:* We are all the same.	HETEROGENEITY	*Cultural pluralism:* We are not all the same; groups within society differ.
SIMILARITY	*Similarity myth:* "They" are all just like me.	SIMILARITY AND DIFFERENCE	*They are not just like me:* Many people differ from me culturally. Most people exhibit both cultural similarities and differences when compared to me.
PAROCHIALISM	*Only-one-way myth:* Our way is the only way. We do not recognize any other way of living or working.	EQUIFINALITY	*Multiple ways:* Many culturally distinct ways of living one's life, working, and reaching one's goals exist.
ETHNOCENTRISM	*One-best-way myth:* Our way is the best way; all other approaches are inferior.	CULTURAL CONTINGENCY	*Our way is one possible way:* Many different and equally good ways can be used to reach the same goal. The best way depends on the cultures of the people involved.

SOURCE: Adapted in 2002. From Nancy J. Adler, "Domestic Multiculturalism: Cross-Cultural Management in the Public Sector," in William Eddy, ed., *Handbook of Organization Management.* Copyright © 1983 Marcel Dekker, Inc., New York, NY.

tion that we are not all the same—that the various groups within society differ, with each maintaining its cultural distinctness. Appreciating a pluralistic, rather than a homogeneous, society underlies the synergy approach. In addition, rather than assuming that the similarities among people are most important, cultural synergy assumes that similarities and differences share equal importance. Moreover, whereas the most commonly held assumption posits that "our way is the only way" of living, working, and reaching business goals (parochialism), cultural synergy assumes *equifinality*—that many equivalent ways (*equi*) to live, to work, and to reach goals (*finality*) exist, and that no culture's way is inherently superior. Furthermore, whereas most people are, to some extent, *ethnocentric* (believing that theirs is the best way to live and to work), the synergy approach assumes *cultural contingency*—that the best way depends on the particular cultures of the people involved.

In a survey of 145 executives from around the world, 83 percent preferred the synergy approach, yet only a third described their organizations as using a synergistic approach for multinational and multicultural problem solving (8). Although global managers clearly recognize the value of approaching problem solving from a synergistic perspective, they also appreciate that the approach is neither easy nor traditional. The following section describes a three-step process for creating synergistic solutions to dilemmas faced by culturally diverse organizations.

Culturally Synergistic Problem Solving

Culturally synergistic organizations reflect the best aspects of all members' cultures in their strategy, structure, and process without violating the norms of any single culture. Managers in synergistic organizations regularly use diversity as a key resource in solving problems. As outlined in Figure 4-2, the process of developing culturally synergistic solutions to organizational problems involves describing the situation from each culture's perspective, culturally interpreting the situation, and developing new culturally creative solutions (3:173).

Step 1: Describing the Situation

What cross-cultural dilemmas does the organization face? What cross-cultural conflicts are managers confronting? Going beyond their own perspective, can managers describe conflicts from the perspectives of each of the various cultures involved? Describing the situation involves one of the most difficult and critical steps in finding solutions to complex

FIGURE 4-2 Creating Cultural Synergy

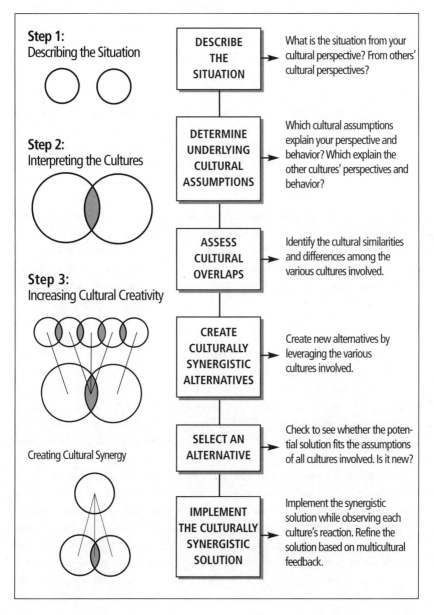

Source: Adapted in 2002 from N. J. Adler, "Cultural Synergy: The Management of Cross-Cultural Organizations," in *Trends and Issues in OD: Current Theory and Practice* by W. W. Burke and L. D. Goodstein, eds., 1980 by Pfeiffer & Company. Reprinted with permission.

multicultural problems. Across cultures, people's divergent values, perceptions, attitudes, and behaviors magnify the challenges faced in understanding and resolving organizational problems. In each of the following examples, conflict arises because each culture views the situation exclusively from its own perspective (3:178):

Japan

An American sales manager expressed his growing frustration with his Japanese employees: "I'm an 'open-door manager.' I expect my employees to come to me when they have a problem. But these Japanese never come until there's a crisis . . . until it's too late to do anything." When questioned later about his behavior, the Japanese sales representatives explained that "Americans see everything as a problem!" In analyzing the situation, it becomes clear that people's cultural perspectives determine when they see a situation as a problem. Westerners often see life as a series of problems to be resolved, whereas non-Westerners frequently view life as a series of situations to be accepted (23). Americans, therefore, define more situations as problems than do the Japanese. Americans also define situations as problems much earlier than do the Japanese (3:178).

Egypt

An Egyptian executive, after entertaining his Canadian guest, offered him joint partnership in a new business venture. The Canadian, delighted with the offer, suggested that they meet again the next morning with their respective lawyers to finalize the details. The Egyptian never showed up. The surprised and disappointed Canadian tried to understand what had gone wrong: Did Egyptians lack punctuality? Was the Egyptian expecting a counteroffer? Were lawyers unavailable in Cairo? None of these explanations proved to be correct; rather, the problem was caused by the different meaning Canadians and Egyptians attach to inviting lawyers. The Canadian foresaw the lawyers' presence as facilitating the successful completion of the negotiation; the Egyptian interpreted it as signaling the Canadian's mistrust of his verbal commitment (3:178). Canadians often use the impersonal formality of a lawyer's services to finalize agreements. Egyptians, by contrast, more frequently depend on the personal relationship between bargaining partners to accomplish the same purpose.

The first step in the process of creating cultural synergy involves recognizing that a problem situation exists. Global managers recognize that a conflict may develop even when it does not make sense from their own cultural perspective (3:178). They then describe the situation from each culture's perspective (not just from their own perspective), while refraining from interpreting or evaluating the situation from any culture's point of view.

Step 2: Culturally Interpreting the Situation

Why do members of different cultures think, feel, and act the way they do? What historical and cultural assumptions must we make to understand the present situation? Once global managers recognize that a problem exists, they can use the synergy approach to analyze it from each culture's perspective. The second step in the process of creating cultural synergy, therefore, involves identifying and interpreting the similarities and differences in thoughts, feelings, and actions among the cultures involved (3:178). All behavior is rational and understandable from the perspective of the person behaving; however, our culturally based perspectives and biases often lead us to misunderstand the logic of other cultures' behavioral patterns (3:179). Whereas a single-culture perspective limits managers' flexibility in global situations, multiple perspectives enhance their understanding and options.

Changing perspectives is achieved through role reversal. During cultural interpretation, managers from each culture attempt to understand the underlying assumptions that lead people from other cultures to behave as they do. During this process, managers identify similarities and differences between their own culture's assumptions and behaviors and those of other cultures. The following example illustrates Americans' and Iranians' misinterpretations of each other's culture:

Iran

An American engineer who was teaching Persians to use a particularly complex technology became disappointed in the progress of his trainees and therefore decided to give them poor performance reviews. One Persian came to the American and queried, "But I thought you were my friend. Why don't you give me a better review?" The American became furious. Only later, in analyzing and interpreting the underlying cultural assumptions, did the American come to understand the importance Persians place on friendship relative to task accomplishment. Similarly, the Persian came to recognize that Americans base their system of equity solely on competence rather than on competence and relationship (23;24). Both cultures value friendship and achievement; they simply differ in the relative importance they attach to each (3:179).

Step 3: Increasing Cultural Creativity

Organizations create synergistic alternatives by searching for culturally appropriate ways to solve problems involving people from multiple cultures. The initial question—"What can people from one culture learn from people of another culture to enhance their effectiveness and productivity?"—focuses on learning transfer. The second, and more important, question—"How can we combine and leverage our various cultures' ways of working?"—focuses on synergy. The answer should be compatible with the assumptions of all represented cultures. Culturally synergistic solutions are novel and transcend the behavioral patterns of each individual culture (3:179). Selecting the best solution only becomes possible after the situation has been adequately described and interpreted from a cross-cultural perspective (see Chapter 3). The box "Creating Cultural Synergy: Uruguay and the Philippines" presents an example of the process of creating cultural synergy.

Implementation

Organizations must plan the implementation of culturally synergistic solutions carefully. Before organization members will understand the need for changes based on synergistic problem solving, they must develop cultural self-awareness (an understanding of their own cultural assumptions and patterns of behavior) as well as cross-cultural awareness (an understanding of other cultures' assumptions and patterns of behavior). Without some understanding of the cultural dynamics involved, proposed changes often appear absurd; with cultural understanding, the organization can solve its problems and implement the changes needed to foster high-quality client service, employee effectiveness, and job satisfaction (3:180). The box "Creating Cultural Synergy: Japanese and American Scheduling" highlights a synergistic scheduling plan implemented by an American air freight company for its routes between Japan and the United States.

Strategies That Include Synergy

Which strategies do the most effective managers use when working with global strategic alliance and joint venture partners? Which approaches work most effectively in negotiating across national borders and in work-

CREATING CULTURAL SYNERGY

Uruguay and the Philippines

Situation Description

A Uruguayan doctor on staff at a major California medical center expressed concern upon realizing that a Filipino nurse was improperly using a particular machine to treat a patient. He instructed the nurse on the proper procedure and asked if she understood. She said she did. Two hours later the patient's condition deteriorated because the nurse had continued to administer the treatment improperly. The doctor more sharply queried the nurse, and she again affirmed her understanding of the procedure. What went wrong?

Interpretation

In analyzing the situation, the doctor came to understand that many Filipinos will not contradict people in respected positions. To the Filipino nurse, the doctor's status was clearly above hers. He was older; she was younger. He was a doctor; she was a nurse. He was a man; she was a woman. Based on her cultural assumptions, she could not tell the doctor that she did not understand without implying that he had given her poor instructions and thus causing him to lose face. The doctor, based on his cultural assumptions, expected "open communication"; he expected the nurse to say whether she understood his instructions and to ask questions if she did not. He considered it a sign of incompetence to assume responsibility for a patient's care without fully understanding the manner of treatment.

Synergistic Solution

After analyzing the situation, the medical center administrator suggested a culturally synergistic solution. Upon giving his initial instructions, the doctor was to ask the nurse to describe the procedure that she would follow. As the doctor listened, he could assess the accuracy of the nurse's understanding and identify areas that needed further explanation. The nurse, never having been asked directly if she understood, would not be forced to say "no" to a superior. The medical center administrator solved the problem without violating either cultures' assumptions (3:179–180). The medical center could achieve its goal—the delivery of excellent medical care—without violating the norms of either culture.

continued on next page ∎

■ continued from previous page

Japanese and American Scheduling[2]

Describing the Situation

American sales representatives of a U.S.–based air freight company with extensive Asian operations generally promised customers specific dates and hours for flight arrivals of freight shipments. Shipments, however, often arrived late. American customers would usually expect, understand, and forgive such delays if given an adequate explanation, whereas Japanese customers expected the company to keep its promises and lost faith in the company when it failed to adhere to the promised arrival times. Unlike the Americans, the Japanese sales representatives often refused to promise delivery times until, as one American sarcastically explained, "the plane had arrived on the runway" or, as the Japanese explained, "they could be certain that their promises would be kept." The Japanese sales representatives' lack of promising, however, did not work with American clients, who expected definite timetables; when they were not given scheduled arrival times, the American clients began to distrust the company's ability to perform its services.

Interpreting the Situation

The air freight company needed to design a uniform "promising" system that would be culturally appropriate for both American and Japanese employees and clients. From the American perspective, the system had to be definite enough to engender credibility with American customers. From the Japanese perspective, the promises to customers had to conform to reality sufficiently so that no one would lose face.

Creating a Synergistic Solution

After analyzing the underlying cultural dynamics in both systems, the sales representatives agreed that they should begin promising delivery within a range of time, rather than at specific times. For instance, they would promise clients delivery "late morning Thursday," rather than at 11:05 a.m. (scheduled flight arrival time). Thus Americans could continue to make promises and the Japanese would rarely find themselves promising something the company could not deliver.

This solution recognizes the values of both cultures without undermining either culture's management practices. As a synergistic solution, it is new and appropriate to both cultures (3:180–181).

FIGURE 4-3 Global Strategy: What Are Your Options?

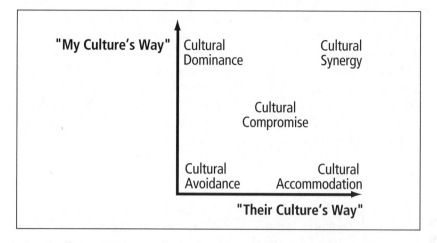

ing with global project teams? Do the most highly effective global managers always use synergy? No.

As shown in Figure 4-3, managers have five basic options to choose from in selecting their approach to managing multicultural situations. In all cross-cultural situations, managers must create a balance between continuing to work in their own way—that is, the way they manage at home—and adapting to the ways of other cultures. Exhibiting maximum flexibility and sensitivity, the most highly effective global managers use all five strategic options, selecting a specific option based on the particular situation and people involved.

Cultural Dominance

The first option is cultural dominance: continuing to use the approaches you use at home. Historically, companies having considerably more power than their counterparts—based on their larger size, more advanced technology, or more significant financial resources—have often used a dominance approach. Individual managers often choose to use a cultural dominance approach when they believe strongly their way is the only right way, especially in situations involving fundamental ethical issues. One Swedish manager, for example, refused to lower the safety standards on his company's products, even though the lower standards were legally acceptable in the potential buyer's country. The Swede lost the contract because his bid, which included the higher safety standards, came in too high. Similarly, an American manager refused to accept a small, personal gift from a Korean client because his company, based on American practices, believed that gift giving represented a form of bribery. To the Korean, gift giving represented a form of relationship building. The American's behavior mystified the Korean—"How could a small personal gift be considered a bribe?" In both cases, home-culture-based personal ethics determined the manager's behavior; in both cases, it compromised the business relationship.

Cultural Accommodation

The second approach, cultural accommodation, is the opposite of cultural dominance. Rather than attempting to maintain one's own home-country practices when working with colleagues from another culture, managers attempt to imitate the practices of their international colleagues. When working abroad, they attempt to blend into the local culture. They follow the maxim "When in Rome, do as the Romans do." Managers who consistently use cultural accommodation are often accused by their home-country colleagues of having "gone native," with executives from the home country fearing that they will no longer fully represent either the home country's or the home organization's interests.

A German executive attempted to use cultural accommodation in Japan to get his first contract with a particularly important potential Japanese client. The German spent the first two weeks in Kobe and Osaka dining and playing golf with the Japanese, without scheduling any formal business meetings or product discussions. Although the German manager's boss in Munich became increasingly annoyed, thinking his colleague had confused a business trip with a vacation, the German executive was accommodating perfectly to the Japanese style of doing business: he was allowing the Japanese to get to know him (relationship building) before focusing on the details of the contract (task focus). The German got the contract.

Managers who learn the local language of countries in which they work are using a cultural accommodation strategy. Similarly, managers who denominate contracts in the local currency are using cultural accommodation. Their accommodation approach allows local managers to continue using their normal, comfortable ways of doing business.

Cultural Compromise

The third approach, cultural compromise, combines the first and second approaches. Using cultural compromise implies that both sides concede something in order to work more successfully together. For example, French and Russian potential joint venture partners held initial meetings alternately in Moscow and Paris. Each had to travel to half the meetings, but neither experienced the inconvenience of traveling and working away from their own headquarters every time.

In compromise solutions, the more powerful partner often gives up less than the weaker partner. Both sides, however, make concessions for the business relationship to succeed. Home-country colleagues often label managers who give up too much as weak and sometimes even accuse them of "caving in."

Cultural Avoidance

The fourth approach, cultural avoidance, is the choice to act as if no differences nor any potential conflicts exist. This approach, used more frequently by Asian managers than by their Western counterparts, usually emphasizes "saving face" in lieu of openly and explicitly confronting the potentially conflictual details inherent in the business relationship. Managers use cultural avoidance most commonly when the unresolved issue is less important than maintaining the long-term business relationship or contract.

In negotiating the final details of a major construction contract in Eastern Malaysia, for example, the American human resource manager thought he had resolved all potential disagreements regarding salaries and benefits. He therefore reacted with surprise when he saw that the Malaysian version of the benefits package included dental care for workers and their families, including the children of second, third, and fourth wives.[3] Even though the Americans had never considered including dental care, or any other benefits, for the families of workers' second, third, or fourth wives, and they knew that such benefits had never been discussed or promised, they chose not to confront the Malaysians. Perhaps the Malaysians, based on their cultural tradition, had assumed that "family" meant "all wives' families," whereas it had never occurred to the Americans that "family" might mean anything other than one wife's (or husband's) family. Rather than upsetting a project that would be good for both the Americans and Malaysians, the Americans chose "not to notice" the additional expense for benefits included in the contract.

Cultural Synergy

As discussed in this chapter, the fifth approach, cultural synergy, develops new solutions to problems that leverage the cultural differences among all cultures involved while respecting each culture's uniqueness. Culturally synergistic solutions always go beyond what would be needed in a purely domestic situation. The use of foreign languages provides an excellent example. When businesspeople meet, they have to use language to communicate. If they speak different native languages, they must choose in which language to communicate. When a British company insists on working in English with its Swedish alliance partner, it is using cultural dominance. If the Swedes immediately agree, they are choosing to employ cultural accommodation. If each side chooses to speak in its own language and use interpreters, they are employing a compromise approach. However, when Norwegian and Austrian business partners choose to communicate in English, they are using synergy. Global businesspeople in both Norway and Austria often speak English, the international business language; however, neither speaks English as a native language. English allows both cultures to conduct business without either side capitulating and becoming disadvantaged by speaking the other's language. Similarly, denominating contracts in a basket of currencies—rather than in one of the currencies of the countries involved—is a synergistic approach to managing the risk of future exchange-rate fluctuations.

SUMMARY

In *Fortune's* cover story on "What the Leaders of Tomorrow See," Corning's CEO asserted, "Future leaders will have to learn how to manage cultural diversity" (11:59). Cultural synergy is a powerful approach to managing the impact of cultural differences that encourages organizations to leverage their diversity, rather than ignoring or minimizing it. Synergistic solutions create new forms of managing by recognizing and transcending the array of unique ethnic cultures of employees and customers. Synergy, far from ignoring the presence of cultural diversity within the organization, recognizes both its potentially positive and negative impacts. Unlike the more commonly used cultural dominance and accommodation approaches, synergy emphasizes managing the impacts of diversity, rather than attempting to eliminate the diversity itself.

The synergy approach to problem solving involves three fundamental steps: cross-cultural situation description, cultural interpretation, and cultural creativity. Global managers first define problems from the perspectives of all cultures involved. They then analyze the patterns that make each culture's behavior logical from within its own perspective. Only then can they create solutions that foster the organization's effectiveness and productivity without violating the norms of any culture involved.

The synergy approach creates organizational solutions to problems by using cultural diversity as a resource and an advantage to the organization. Synergy is most useful in resolving important issues in which cross-cultural interaction among employees and clients occurs daily. Organizations should not, however, consider synergy to be the only approach.

Introducing culturally synergistic problem solving to an organization for the first time involves managing change. The most fundamental change is one of perspective: executives must guide their organizations toward a more inclusive and more global world view. Many organizations find it helpful to begin the cultural synergy process by providing opportunities for managers to become more culturally self-aware (enhancing their recognition and understanding of their own culture's ways of doing business) and more cross-culturally aware (enhancing their recognition and understanding of the culturally based work styles of customers and colleagues from other cultures). With heightened and more broadly based awareness of cultural dynamics, organizations can begin to address the culturally based conflict situations inherent in global management. Whereas managers often initially address problems explicitly, formally, and slowly, later synergistic problem-solving sessions become more informal, implicit, and considerably less time-consuming. Learning acquired during initial sessions becomes part of the organization's increasingly global perspective and cross-cultural competence.

Cultural synergy is *an* approach, not *the* approach; it is one of five options that highly effective global managers use regularly. The synergistic problem-solving process is not a quick fix. It is a systematic process for increasing the options open to executives, managers, and employees working in increasingly global business environments. The synergy approach works equally effectively for competing successfully in multicultural domestic environments.

5

Succeeding in Multicultural Teams

It was once said that the sun never set on the British Empire. Today the sun does set on the British Empire, but not on the scores of global corporate empires including those of IBM, Unilever, Volkswagen, and Hitachi.
— LESTER BROWN, *President of Worldwatch Institute* (76:320)

GLOBAL BUSINESS USED to be a minor component of industrial activity; now it dominates. Global management used to involve simply sending one of "our" managers "over there" to sell products to foreign clients; now people from many countries work within the same companies, and in many cases, "we" have become the foreigners. Global management used to involve sending a few expatriates to direct operations abroad; now members of corporate boards, executives, and employees represent every nationality. Today hundreds of thousands of firms headquartered in high-technology, countries have operations outside their home nations (see 76:320).

In the 1990s, global business brought contact with foreign cultures home to every business. Today, with e-commerce, managers may work for foreign-owned firms without leaving their own communities, sell primarily to nonnative clients, and negotiate with component suppliers worldwide, all while regularly attending video conferences and web-based meetings with colleagues from around the world. Globally distanced design teams routinely develop revolutionary new products in e-meetings among experts on five continents, none of whom ever have to leave home to participate in the telephone, e-mail, and web-based discussions. Cross-cultural dialogue has become the foundation on which global business succeeds or fails.

MANAGING THE MULTICULTURAL WORKFORCE

Both domestically and globally, the multicultural workforce has become a reality (51). The impact of multiculturalism, however, varies significantly with the type of competitive environment and the firm's overall strategy. As shown in Figure 5-1, prior to the last decade, global cultural diversity had a minimal impact on domestic firms, even while domestic multiculturalism was strongly influencing business outcomes. Sophisticated managers in U.S. firms, for example, coached their colleagues to appreciate and to effectively manage a workforce composed of African-American, Asian-American, Hispanic, and Native American women and men. Assuming the domestic workforce was homogeneous or defined by white male norms was never appropriate and is no longer effective.

In multidomestic firms (those that only export or operate fairly autonomous operations abroad), the impact of culture becomes highly significant. Multidomestic firms must adapt their strategies, as well as their products and services, to the local culture in each country in which they operate. In multinational firms, by contrast, the impact of cultural differences lessens slightly because price and cost dominate all other considerations.

FIGURE 5-1 How Important is Cultural Diversity?

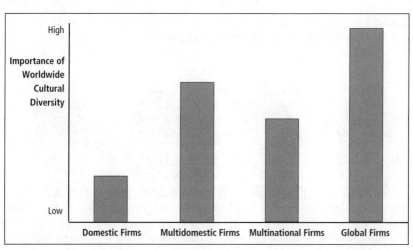

By the time firms adopt global strategies, the impact of cultural diversity increases dramatically in importance. Global firms must understand cross-cultural dynamics to formulate their business strategies, to locate production facilities and suppliers worldwide, and to design and market culturally appropriate products and services, all while managing cross-cultural interaction throughout the organization, from the most senior executive committees to the shop floor. As more firms move from domestic, multidomestic, and multinational strategies to operating as truly global companies and alliances, the importance and impact of cultural diversity increase markedly. In global firms, the impact of cultural diversity, which once was merely "nice to understand," becomes imperative for survival, let alone success (3). (See Chapter 1 for a review of each strategy.)

Similar to the increasing importance of cultural diversity, the location of its impact varies with changes in the firm's competitive business environment and strategy. As shown in Figure 5-2, worldwide cultural diversity traditionally has not affected domestic firms' internal organizational culture or their external relationships with clients. Domestic firms work domestically; only domestic multiculturalism—and not global cultural diversity—directly impacts the internal dynamics of domestic firms and their relationship with the external environment. Today no major firms operate in purely domestic environments; they no longer have the luxury of operating in a simple, domestic environment free from global complexities.

In multidomestic firms, which focus primarily on exporting and pro-

FIGURE 5-2 Global Cross-Cultural Interaction: When Is It Internal to the Organization? When Is It External?

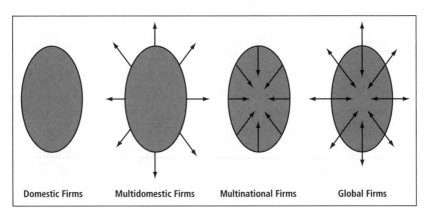

Domestic Firms   Multidomestic Firms   Multinational Firms   Global Firms

ducing abroad, cultural diversity strongly affects relationships external to the firm, especially those with potential buyers and workers in other countries. By contrast, multinational firms place less emphasis on managing cultural differences external to the firm, but increasingly need to manage the growing multinational diversity within the firm. Whereas multidomestic firms primarily use expatriate managers to sell and work abroad, multinational firms hire people from around the world as employees and managers. In multidomestic firms, only expatriates have a high need for developing cultural sensitivity and cross-cultural management skills. By contrast, in multinational firms, because cultural diversity strongly affects the internal organizational culture, many more employees and managers use cross-cultural management skills on a daily basis.

Global firms must continually manage cultural diversity both within the company and between the company and its external environment. To work effectively, everyone from the CEO to the lowest level worker must use cross-cultural skills. This progression from culture's relative lack of importance to its critical importance, with respect to the firm's external environment as well as its internal organizational culture, underlies the general recognition that executives and managers must know how to work effectively in multinational and multicultural teams if they wish to succeed (3).

How do we manage people who differ from us? Research has shown that styles of leading, motivating, communicating, decision making, planning, organizing, and staffing vary among countries of the world (see Chapter 6). What happens when people from dissimilar cultures work together on a day-to-day basis within the same organization? How should organizations manage a multinational workforce?

This chapter investigates approaches to managing cultural diversity within organizations. It begins by reviewing domestic multiculturalism, an important source of multicultural dynamics in teams. It then focuses on cross-cultural interaction within teams: What types of problems does diversity most often cause within global teams? From what potential advantages do well-managed, culturally diverse teams benefit? How can leaders create world-class teams (51)? And, most important, how can management maximize the potential benefits and minimize the potential problems caused by diversity? How can leaders create world-class teams (51)?

DOMESTIC MULTICULTURALISM

You do not have to go abroad to meet people with cultural backgrounds different from your own. With increasing immigration, a growing number of people working abroad, and the presence of indigenous and ethnic communities, managers who never leave home often face a multicultural workforce in local companies and organizations.

Multiple culturally distinct populations live in all countries of the world. Singapore, for example, has four cultural and linguistic groups: Chinese, Eurasian, Indian, and Malay. Belgium includes two linguistic groups, Flemish and French. Switzerland has four distinct ethnic communities: French, German, Italian, and Romansh. Canada, a multicultural country by national policy, uses two official languages, English and French. Many countries, including Israel and the United States, have developed historically as havens for immigrants from around the world.

Each population exhibits a culturally unique lifestyle. Most of us are familiar with the typical foods of major ethnic groups: no one thinks spaghetti is Russian, tortillas are Chinese, or sushi is Senegalese. But many of us remain unaware of how extensively other cultures' lifestyles differ from our own. Even if we consider ourselves internationally sophisticated, many of us fail to recognize the culturally distinct attitudes and behaviors that our fellow citizens bring with them to the workplace (2).

The city of Los Angeles highlights the pervasiveness of domestic multiculturalism and its impact on the workplace. Since 1970 more than two million foreign immigrants have settled in Los Angeles (8:17). Of Los Angeles' 550,000 school children, 117,000 speak one of 104 languages more fluently than English, including 35 fluent only in Gujarati, a language of western India (8:18). Los Angeles no longer has a majority population but constantly "adjusts to the quirky, polyglot rhythms of 60,000 Samoans and 30,000 Thais, 200,000 Salvadorans and 175,000 Armenians" (8:18). Los Angeles is the second largest Mexican agglomeration after Mexico City (37:52), more Samoans live in Los Angeles than on the island of Samoa 4,000 miles away (70:1), and more Israelis live there than in any other city outside of Israel (78). A former lieutenant governor of California recognized his state's central, inevitable reality already two decades ago: "If the present trends continue, the emerging ethnic groups will constitute more than half the population of California by 1990, and . . . [California] will become the country's first Third World state" (42:35). His prediction was absolutely accurate.

Other cities and states in the United States reflect the same pattern. Of the 700,000 largely middle-class Cubans who left Cuba by 1978, more than 60 percent settled in Dade County, Florida (37:51). More than 1.3 million Puerto Ricans live in the greater New York City area (37:55). Hawaii has become a domestic microcosm of Eastern and Western cultures. These diverse communities have seen a resurgence of ethnic self-identity, both among new immigrants and among European populations that seemed all but assimilated (64). Based on these and dozens of other similar statistics, multiculturalism has emerged as a dominant fact of domestic life. Even if they wanted to, citizens of most countries can neither forget multiculturalism nor relegate it to the domain of global managers or diplomats.

Perhaps William Somerset Maugham best captured the essence of domestic multiculturalism in *The Trembling Leaf* when he described Hawaii, a state whose 900,000 residents represent 29 percent Caucasian, 27.5 percent Japanese, 18 percent Hawaiian and part Hawaiian, 10 percent Filipino, 4.5 percent Chinese, 1 percent each Korean, Samoan, and black, and 8 percent mixed or miscellaneous (33:97):

> It is a meeting place of East and West, the very new rubs shoulders with the immeasurably old . . . you have come upon something singularly intriguing. All these strange people live close to each other, with different languages and different thoughts; they believe in different gods and they have different values; two passions alone they share, love and hunger. And somehow as you watch them, you have an impression of extraordinary vitality.

TEAMS: THE ORGANIZATION IN MICROCOSM

Organizations consist of teams, and teams form the basic structure of organizations. Companies organize employees into many forms of temporary and permanent work teams, including departments, offices, task forces, subcommittees, committees, commissions, and boards. The quality of performance of such teams varies from poor to excellent, from totally unproductive to highly productive. Teams can espouse values and goals that society views as either desirable or destructive. Teams can accomplish much that is good, or they can cause great harm. From the organization's perspective, teams can be highly effective or totally ineffective. There is nothing implicitly good or bad, effective or ineffective, about a team (50).

The productivity of a work team depends on its task, the resources available to it, and its process. The team's goal defines its task. This task can involve a decision or recommendation, a project or report, or an action or series of actions. The team's resources include the people, information, materials, time, money, and energy available for accomplishing the particular task. A task force, for example, may have three or five people available; it may have one week or four months allocated to it; it may have a large budget or no budget at all; it may have very limited or completely unlimited computer access, e-business, and web-based skills.

The team's process consists of the actual steps taken by individuals or the team when confronting a task. The team's process includes all the intrapersonal and interpersonal actions used by people to transform their resources into products and services, along with all nonproductive actions prompted by competing motivations, frustration, and inadequate understanding (75:8).

A team's actual productivity therefore results from its potential productivity minus its losses due to faulty process (75:9):

**Actual productivity = Potential productivity –
Losses due to faulty process**

Actual productivity depends on how well a team works together and uses its resources to accomplish its task.

TYPES OF DIVERSITY IN TEAMS

Team members can have very similar or quite different backgrounds, perspectives, and experience (9). Although diversity can refer to many characteristics, including gender, race, profession, nationality, age, and ethnicity, this chapter focuses on culture-based diversity (83). Homogeneous teams are those with all members coming from the same culture; multicultural teams are those with members coming from more than one culture (84). Multicultural teams can be divided into three types: token teams having a single member from another culture, bicultural teams having members from two cultures, and multicultural teams having members from three or more cultures.

Homogeneous Teams

In homogeneous teams, all members share a similar background. People working in a homogeneous team generally perceive, interpret, and evaluate the world more similarly than do members of heterogeneous teams. A team of male Finnish bankers, for example, is homogeneous, based on gender, culture, and profession. A team of Mexican and Panamanian stockbrokers is professionally, but not culturally, homogeneous.

Token Teams

In token teams all but one member comes from the same background. In a team of Australian lawyers with one Turkish attorney, for example, the Turkish attorney would be the token member. In such a token team, the Turkish attorney would probably see and understand situations somewhat differently from his Australian colleagues. In the last decade, predominantly male management teams began to pay considerable attention to the few, often token, female members. Today many corporations focus significantly more attention on leveraging the potential contributions of their token members of various ethnic groups.

Bicultural Teams

In bicultural teams, two or more members represent each of two distinct cultures; for example, a fifty–fifty partnership between Peruvians and Bolivians, or a task force composed of Saudi Arabian and Jordanian managers, or a committee of seven Spanish and three Portuguese executives. Bicultural teams must continually recognize and integrate the perspectives of both represented cultures. If the team has an unequal number of members from each culture, the culture of the group with the most representatives is likely to dominate.

Multicultural Teams

In multicultural teams, members represent three or more ethnic backgrounds. United Nations agencies offer good examples of multicultural organizational structures, as do the committees of the European Union (EU) and the Association of Southeast Asian Nations (ASEAN). Today, an increasing number of corporate task forces are globally distanced teams—that is, teams composed of members from around the world who meet electronically. The economic and political power structure of the represented members moderates the team's dynamics and, therefore, its effectiveness. To perform most effectively, multicultural teams need to recognize and integrate all represented cultures.

Although few studies describe cross-cultural interaction within management teams (13;56;57;58;74), considerable research exists on the conditions for effective team functioning within the United States (23; 27;29;30;38;40;48;52;55;75;82). A growing literature describing team behavior in countries around the world, often with American comparisons, also exists (56;57;58;72). Researchers have studied such diverse peoples as black and white Americans (69), Arabs (14), the British (54), Canadians (73), Hispanics (18), Hong Kong and American Chinese (60), Indians (6;59), Japanese (17;62), Lebanese (20), New Zealanders (7), and South Africans, Nigerians, and Filipinos (28). Research conclusively demonstrates that the behavior of people in work teams varies across cultures. Among other differences, researchers have found that team members from more collectivist cultures—such as those in China and the Middle East—work more cooperatively with each other, seem less likely to "free ride," and enjoy working together more than most of their counterparts in more individualist cultures—such as those in Australia, Canada, and the United States (15;16;21;22).

CULTURAL DIVERSITY'S IMPACT ON TEAMS: POSITIVE OR NEGATIVE?

Cultural diversity can have positive and negative impacts on teams' productivity (45;56;57;58;61;80;81). Diversity augments potential productivity while greatly increasing the complexity of processes members must manage for teams to realize their full potential (75:107). Multicultural teams have the potential to achieve higher productivity than their homogeneous counterparts, but they also risk experiencing greater losses due to faulty process. As shown in the following model, actual productivity of multicultural teams can therefore be higher, lower, or the same as that of single-culture teams:

($\downarrow$ or $\uparrow$)	**Actual** productivity	= ($\uparrow$)	**Potential** productivity	− ($\uparrow$)	**Losses due to** faulty process

Multicultural teams, for example, can have multiple perspectives on any given situation, thus potentially increasing their insight and, consequently, their productivity (53). Multicultural teams, however, also frequently experience greater difficulty than their homogeneous counterparts in integrating and evaluating these perspectives, thus causing losses in productivity due to faulty process.

Productivity Losses Due to Faulty Process

Diversity makes team functioning more challenging because team members find it more difficult to see, understand, and act on situations in similar ways. Diversity makes reaching agreement more difficult. Team members from similar cultures find it easier to communicate clearly with one another and trust one another more readily. In culturally diverse teams, misperception, miscommunication, misinterpretation, and misevaluation abound (see Chapter 3). Because members of multicultural teams more frequently disagree on expectations, the appropriateness of relevant information, and the need for particular decisions, they generally experience higher levels of stress than do homogeneous teams. Diversity increases the ambiguity, complexity, and inherent confusion in team processes (see Chapter 4, Table 4-1). Process losses diminish productivity (43;45).

Cohesiveness is the ability of team members to act as one. Team members' ability, when necessary, to perceive, interpret, and act on situations in similar or mutually agreed upon ways determines the team's level of cohesiveness. Due to their lower level of similarity, multicultural teams initially exhibit less cohesion than most homogeneous teams.

As shown in Table 5-1, multicultural teams' higher levels of mistrust, miscommunication, and stress diminish their cohesion (66). More important, these attitudinal and perceptual communication problems also frequently diminish productivity. The following section discusses the main process problems experienced by multicultural teams.

Attitudinal Problems: Dislike and Mistrust

Members of culturally diverse teams express higher levels of mistrust than do their more homogeneous counterparts. Team members often find themselves more attracted to people from their own culture than to people from other cultures (77). Researchers in Belgium, for example, found that Walloon and Flemish individuals speak most frequently to colleagues from their own culture (68). Mistrust, another common problem in multicultural teams, results primarily from inadvertent cross-cultural misinterpretation rather than actual dislike. Many Indian team members, for example, look down when acknowledging authority, a behavior many European and North American managers misinterpret as signaling a lack of trustworthiness. As a result, European and North American team leaders often fail to develop sufficient trust in their Indian colleagues to delegate or share more than trivial responsibilities.

Perceptual Problems: Stereotyping

Team members often inappropriately stereotype colleagues from other cultures rather than accurately seeing and assessing their skills and potential contributions (24). For instance, team members generally talk more to colleagues from higher status cultures than to those from lower status cultures. They assume, usually subconsciously, that national stereotypes apply to individual team members. Thus, in initial meetings, team members often inappropriately judge their colleagues from the most economically developed countries the most favorably (24). A team of engineers, for example, assumed their American colleagues had more technological expertise than did their Moroccan colleagues simply because Morocco is less economically and technologically advanced than the United States. In a parallel situation, an Indian manager described the lack of respect granted him by many of his British colleagues who, he believed, "assume that I am underdeveloped simply because I come from an economically underdeveloped country." Both the initial stereotype and the Indian's

TABLE 5-1 Diversity in Multicultural Teams: Advantages and Disadvantages

ADVANTAGES	DISADVANTAGES
Diversity permits increased creativity	**Diversity causes a lack of cohesion**
Wider range of perspectives	*Mistrust*
More and better ideas	Lower interpersonal attractiveness
Less groupthink	Inaccurate stereotyping
	More within-culture conversations
Diversity forces enhanced	*Miscommunication*
concentration to understand others'	Slower speech among nonnative
Ideas	speakers and translation problems
Perspectives	Less accuracy
Meanings	*Stress*
Arguments	More counterproductive behavior
	Less disagreement on content
	Tension
Increased creativity can lead to	**The diverse team's lack of cohesion**
generating	**causes an inability to**
Better problem definitions	Validate ideas and people
More alternatives	Agree when agreement is needed
Better solutions	Gain consensus on decisions
Better decisions	Take concerted action
Teams can become	**Teams can become**
More effective	Less efficient
More productive	Less effective
	Less productive

resulting frustration interfered with the team's process and diminished the team's productivity.

Communication Problems:
Inaccuracy, Misunderstanding, and Inefficiency

Diversity causes problems by disrupting communication (75). When all members do not fluently speak the team's working language, communication is slowed down (31). In linguistically diverse groups, some members must speak a foreign language or use an interpreter. Both diminish communication speed and increase the chances for errors (31).

Team members from diverse cultures often disagree over the meaning of important issues, such as the cause of particular events, how to determine admissible evidence, how to assess the relevance of specific information, and the possible conclusions that can be drawn (31). On many teams, disagreement remains implicit and, therefore, hidden; members assume they interpret situations similarly when in fact the opposite is true. The following incident between an Indian and his Austrian task force leader highlights such an implicit misinterpretation:

> When asked if his department could complete a project by a given date, the Indian department head said "yes" even though he knew he could not complete the project within the suggested time frame, because he believed that the Austrian task force leader wanted "yes" for an answer. When the completion date arrived and the Indian had not finished the project, the Austrian showed dismay. The Indian's desire to act politely—to say what he thought the task force leader wanted to hear—seemed more important to him than accurately reporting his actual prediction of the completion date. Unfortunately, the Austrian valued accurate information more highly than politeness. Cross-cultural miscommunication disrupted the smooth functioning of work.[1]

Physical Problems: Stress

Tension and stress levels in culturally diverse teams often exceed those in single-culture teams, due primarily to communication inaccuracies and a lack of trust (77). The deductive, analytical discussion style of the French, for example, often causes stress for the more inductive, pragmatic North Americans: the French continually want to discuss principles and historical precedent, whereas North Americans focus on specific details of the immediate situation.[2] Multicultural teams often exhibit symptoms of considerable social stress, including bickering, apathy, single-party (or single-culture) domination of discussions, stubbornness, and reprimanding (31). Multicultural teams frequently show "a quiet climate of politeness and gradually increasing friendliness" (68); however, these rituals of politeness often merely reflect the team's superficial defense against weak cohesiveness (68). Ritual politeness leaves team members frustrated and usually becomes yet another hindrance blocking their realization of high productivity.

Organizational Problems: Decreased Effectiveness

As is evident in the previous examples, cultural diversity diminishes effective team functioning in numerous serious ways. Studies show that members of multicultural teams use "more of their time and effort in creating cohesion and solidarity than [do] members of homogeneous groups" (41;67;68). If unmanaged, cultural differences can paralyze a team's ability to act. For example, as described by one European manager,

> In attempting to plan a new project, a three-person team composed of a British, French, and Swiss manager failed to reach agreement. To the French and Swiss managers, their British colleague seemed unable to embrace a systematic approach; he seemingly insisted on discussing every potential problem before even beginning to make a decision. Whereas the French and Swiss managers agreed to examine everything before making a decision, they disagreed on the sequence and scheduling of operations. The Swiss, being the most pessimistic in his planning, allocated more time for each suboperation than did his French colleague. The result of all these differences in planning style was that a project everyone had initially agreed upon was never initiated. If three French, three Swiss, or three British managers had discussed the project, the team would easily have made the needed decisions. The project would not have stalled for lack of agreement.[3]

Productivity Gains: Potential Advantages from Culturally Diverse Teams

Although encountering more process problems than do homogeneous teams, culturally diverse teams also have the potential to achieve higher productivity, primarily because their greater diversity allows them to function more creatively. Effective teams need to perceive, interpret, and evaluate situations in numerous ways and then agree on the best options and directions. Multicultural teams generate alternatives easily because the team's diversity results in diverging ideas. Leaders of all teams must constantly balance divergence with convergence; that is, generating new ideas (divergence) with gaining agreement on particular decisions and actions (convergence). Balancing creativity (divergence) and cohesion (convergence), however, is particularly challenging for leaders of multicultural teams.

As summarized in Table 5-1, multicultural teams have the potential to invent more options and create more solutions than do single-culture teams. Diversity makes it easier for teams to create more and better ideas (46). It allows them to avoid the trap of *groupthink* (39). It often forces members to pay closer attention to the contributions of their colleagues. Each of these advantages is discussed in the following sections (also see Table 4-1).

Generating More and Better Ideas

Due to the varied backgrounds present in multicultural teams, members create more ideas, alternatives, and potential problem solutions than do homogeneous teams (35;47). Heterogeneous teams also propose more inventive alternatives (34;67) and higher quality solutions to problems (35). Heterogeneous teams, however, only realize their potential when they adequately manage the process problems associated with diversity. In the following example, a Swedish manager describes some of the advantages his pharmaceutical firm benefitted from in moving from a single-culture to multicultural product design team:

> We traditionally carried out product design at our Stockholm headquarters. Once, by accident or design, we brought in an international team to discuss the design of a new allergy product. Due to extreme differences in opinion on what constitutes good medical practice, the team designed the new product with maximum flexibility to suit the requirements of each country. We later discovered that the greater flexibility was a huge advantage in developing and marketing a wide range of internationally competitive products.[4]

Limiting Groupthink

Groupthink describes "a mode of thinking people engage in when they are deeply involved in a cohesive in-group, when [team] members' striving for unanimity overrides their motivation to realistically appraise alternative courses of action. . . . Groupthink refers to a deterioration of mental efficiency, reality testing, and moral judgment that results from in-group pressures" (39:9). Groupthink is a major source of ineffectiveness in teams.

The three major symptoms of groupthink are overestimating the team's power and morality, closed-mindedness, and pressures toward uniformity (39). Compared with their single-culture counterparts, multicultural teams are less likely to prematurely agree on a decision. They are also less likely to engage in the following counterproductive groupthink behaviors (39:175):

1. *Self-censoring* deviations from the apparent team consensus caused by each member's inclination to minimize to themselves the importance of their doubts and counterarguments.
2. *Sharing an illusion of unanimity*; Assuming judgments conform to the majority view, often resulting from self-censoring of deviations, augmented by the false assumption that silence means consent.
3. *Directly pressuring* any member who expresses strong arguments against the team's stereotypes, illusions, or commitments, making clear this type of dissent is contrary to what the team expects from all loyal members.
4. The emergence of *self-appointed mindguards*, or members who protect the team from adverse information that might shatter their shared complacency about their effectiveness and the morality of their decisions.

The consequences of groupthink include incompletely surveying objectives and alternatives, failing to examine the risks inherent in preferred choices, failing to reappraise initially rejected alternatives, conducting poor information searches, introducing selective biases in processing available information, and failing to work out contingency plans (39:175). Multicultural teams are less susceptible to groupthink because they are less likely to subconsciously limit the range of perspectives, ideas, conclusions, and decisions they consider to those of the majority or team leadership.

WHAT'S NEEDED FOR MULTICULTURAL TEAMS TO SUCCEED?

Multicultural teams can potentially become the most effective and productive teams in an organization. Unfortunately, they frequently become the least productive. Figure 5-3 shows the relative productivity of a series

FIGURE 5-3 Team Effectiveness

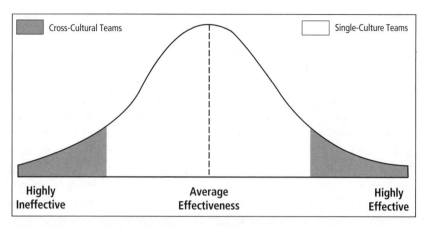

SOURCE: Based on Dr. Carol Kovach's research conducted at the Graduate School of Management, University of California, Los Angeles (UCLA).

of four- to six-member problem-solving teams. Culturally diverse teams often perform either much more or much less effectively than their single-culture counterparts (44). What differentiates the most effective from the least effective teams? Why are culturally diverse teams usually either much more or much less effective than single-culture teams but rarely equally effective?

Highly productive and less-productive teams differ in how they manage their diversity, not, as is commonly believed, in the presence or absence of diversity in the team. When well managed, diversity becomes an asset—a productive resource for the team (6;25;35;45;56;57;63;79). When ignored, diversity causes process problems that diminish the team's productivity. Because diversity is more frequently ignored than well managed (see Chapter 4), culturally diverse teams often perform below expectations and below organizational norms.

As shown in Table 5-2, multicultural teams' productivity depends on their task, stage of development, and the ways in which they manage their diversity. Diversity becomes most valuable when the need for the team to reach agreement (cohesion) remains low relative to the need to invent creative solutions. Diversity functions as an advantage only if the team recognizes when to leverage and when to minimize its diversity, and how creativity and agreement can be balanced. The team leader must accurately assess each situation and emphasize those aspects that best fit the team's overall goals and objectives, as well as its current task.

Is the Task Innovative or Routine?

Whether and how much diversity is desirable depends on the nature of the team's task. When a task requires team members to perform highly specialized roles, it is usually more advantageous to use a diverse team. When everyone must do the same thing, work generally progresses more smoothly if members think and behave similarly (75:106). Corporate consulting teams, for example, generally work most effectively when they include a range of specialists—finance, marketing, production, and strategy experts. Teams assembling radios, on the other hand, generally perform better when all members have similar levels of manual dexterity and coordination.

For some tasks, the ability of the most or the least competent member determines the team's potential productivity. For other tasks, the combination of abilities of all members determines the team's potential productivity. Reward schemes can alter members' performance. When managers reward employees with bonuses based on the best employee's performance, teams focus on helping their best member perform outstandingly. Olympic teams often work in this way: a country receives the gold medal for an individual event based on the performance of its top member. Alternatively, when managers reward an entire department based on the performance of the least productive employee (for example, based on the least productive member exceeding a certain minimal level), teams attempt to increase the

Table 5-2 Effectively Managing Team Diversity

	EFFECTIVE	INEFFECTIVE
	Diversity can be most effective when:	Diversity is least effective when:
TASK	Innovative	Routine
STAGE	Divergence (earlier)	Convergence (later)
CONDITIONS	Differences recognized	Differences ignored
	Members selected for task-related abilities	Member selected on basis of ethnicity
	Mutual respect	Ethnocentrism
	Equal power	Cultural dominance
	Superordinate goal	Individual goals
	External feedback	No feedback (autonomy)

productivity of their weakest member, often by coaching him or her. This approach reflects the philosophy behind the saying "A chain is only as strong as its weakest link." Using another approach, a manager might choose to give all employees a bonus based on the department's average productivity. Under this option, all department members individually and collectively strive to perform as well as possible. Firms often assess managers using this average scheme: managers' performance appraisals depend on their department's overall (or average) productivity. In some firms, managers allow employees to collectively select a reward system. In this case members in each department assess the task and range of abilities within the department and select a reward scheme accordingly.

Cultural diversity provides the biggest potential benefit to teams with challenging tasks that require creativity and innovation. Diversity becomes less helpful when team members work on simpler tasks involving repetitive or routine procedures. With the advent of robots and computer-aided manufacturing processes to do the more routine tasks, people now face a much higher proportion of challenging and nonroutine tasks, almost all of which benefit from well-managed diversity. The more senior the team members, the more likely they are to be involved in challenging, innovative projects and, therefore, the more likely they are to benefit from well-managed diversity. Well-managed diversity has therefore become extremely valuable for senior executive teams both within and across organizations.

At What Stage Is the Team?: Entry, Work, and Action

Work teams progress through three basic stages: entry, work, and action. Early in its life, a team must develop cohesiveness. Members need to begin to know and to trust each other. After this initial entry stage, creativity becomes more important. Teams must create ways of defining their objectives, gathering and analyzing information, and developing alternative forms of action. Although tending to hinder teams' initial development, diversity is highly valuable during the work stage. The team needs creativity (facilitated by divergence) to succeed. During the third and final stage, convergence again becomes important. Teams need to agree, or converge, on which decisions and actions to take. Cohesion, not creativity, fosters agreement. Whereas diversity is generally valuable during the work phase for planning and developing projects, it becomes much less helpful during this final implementation or "action" phase. Table 5-3 summarizes some of the advantages and disadvantages caused by diversity at each stage of the team's development.

TABLE 5-3 Managing Diversity Based on the Team's Stage of Development

Stage	Process	Diversity Makes the Process	Process Based On
ENTRY: Initial team formation	Trust building (developing cohesion)	More difficult	Using similarities and understanding differences
WORK: Problem description and analysis	Ideation (creating ideas)	Easier	Using differences
ACTION: Decision making and implementation	Consensus building (agreeing and acting)	More difficult	Recognizing and creating similarities

Entry: Initially Forming the Team

In the initial stage, team members need to develop relationships and build trust. Team members from more task-oriented cultures, such as Germany, Switzerland, and the United States, spend relatively little time getting to know each other. Members from more relationship-oriented cultures, such as those in Latin America, the Middle East, and Southern Europe, generally spend considerably more time getting to know their teammates. When people from task- and relationship-oriented cultures join the same team, problems in this initial stage can result. While the task-oriented members become impatient to get down to business, their more relationship-oriented colleagues feel rushed and distrustful of their more hurried team members.

On first meeting, team members generally feel drawn to people who are most similar to themselves. They initially trust those people to whom they feel most attracted. Similarity therefore facilitates initial group formation, while visible differences hinder it. Not surprisingly, multicultural teams often find building initial relationships and trust more difficult and time-consuming than do their single-culture counterparts. To counteract this tendency, experienced leaders often focus initially on team members' complementary professional qualifications and equivalent status rather than on the dissimilarities in their cultural backgrounds. Once members have established professional similarity and respect, they can acknowledge their cultural diversity as a potential resource to the team rather than an imminent threat.

Work: Describing and Analyzing Problems

After initially forming the team, members define their work goals and objectives and assess the team's problem-solving potential. During this work stage, teams can use their diversity to generate new perspectives and ideas and thus enhance their ability to create innovative problem definitions and solutions. Although diversity often hinders the team's initial ability to build trust, well-managed diversity can enhance this second, work phase. As discussed previously, diverse teams generally are more able to see situations from multiple perspectives, interpret their perceptions within a wider variety of contexts, and create more numerous alternatives than are single-culture teams. Multicultural teams rarely succumb to groupthink; that is, to members blindly accepting a single definition of any situation.

Action: Making and Implementing Decisions

In the third stage, teams decide what to do and how to do it. Members agree on which alternatives appear best and which action plans appear most effective. Teams reach agreement by building consensus around a particular perspective. Similar to decision making, implementation also depends on consensus: teams must agree on the best way to proceed. These convergent processes—consensus building, agreement, concerted action, and implementation—usually prove easier for single-culture teams than for their multicultural counterparts. The very diversity that makes creating new ideas easier during the second stage renders building consensus and achieving agreement more difficult during the third stage.

MANAGING CULTURALLY DIVERSE TEAMS

Why are only some multicultural teams productive? And why are token teams (those with only one member from another culture) among the least productive (23)? The answer is that the most productive multicultural teams learn to use their diversity when it enhances performance and to minimize the impact of diversity when it diminishes performance. Multicultural teams that are able to create a synergistic culture outperform those that fail to integrate the cultures of individual members into a cohesive team culture. Token teams often fail to create a culturally synergistic culture that integrates the perspective of the one, different token member into the whole. The leader must learn to help the team to integrate its diversity if the team is to function productively (1;36;56;57;82). "By integrating and building on the diverse perspectives of the various members of a team, solutions and strategies can be developed that produce greater results and are more innovative than the simple addition of each contribution alone" (56:5). Diversity leads to "higher performance only when members . . . [are] able to understand each other, [and to] combine and build on each others' ideas" (57:537); that is, when they communicate effectively with each other. Recent research suggests that all teams need the following communication skills to function effectively. They must be able to see situations from another person's perspective, create a shared social reality, explain problems appropriately, and establish agreed-upon norms for interacting. They must also be motivated to communicate, and have confidence that other team members are skilled enough to work effectively together (57 based on 10;11). Multicultural teams face substantially greater challenges than do single-culture teams in developing sufficient communication skills to achieve the prerequisite levels of integration needed for superior performance. Guidelines for increasing productivity and minimizing diversity-related productivity losses due to faulty process follow.

Managing Cultural Diversity

Selecting Members Based on Task Criteria

While acknowledging the team's diverse cultural background, leaders should not select members solely based on their ethnicity but rather primarily for their task-related abilities (65). "To maximize team effectiveness, members should be selected to be homogeneous in ability levels (thus facilitating accurate communication) and heterogeneous in attitudes (thus ensuring a wide range of potential solutions to problems)" (77).

Recognizing Differences

Teams should not ignore or minimize cultural differences: "Many barriers to cross-cultural communication are due to ignorance of cultural differences rather than a rejection of those differences" (19). Teams, therefore, cannot begin to enhance communication without first recognizing and then understanding and respecting cross-cultural differences (12). Research indicates that "culturally trained leader[s], regardless of leadership style . . . achieve . . . high[er] levels of performance and rapport than do non-trained leaders" (26). To enhance the recognition of differences, team members should first describe each culture present without either interpreting or evaluating it. Before beginning to increase understanding and respect, team members must become aware of their own stereotypes and the ways in which they might inadvertently limit the expectations of fellow team members from other cultures. Once members begin to recognize actual differences—that is, once they can differentiate their stereotypes from the actual personalities and behavior of team members (cultural description)—they can begin to understand why members from other cultures think, feel, and act the way they do (cultural interpretation). Subsequently, they can ask what members from each culture can contribute and how their contributions complement those of other members (cultural creativity). In this way, creating effective multicultural teams follows the same process as creating cultural synergy (see Chapter 4).

Establishing a Vision or Superordinate Goal

Members of diverse teams generally have more difficulty agreeing on their purpose and task than do members of homogeneous teams. Global alliances often become troubled because partners from different countries do not clearly understand each other's intent—their purpose, goals, and strategy—because they are initially unable to communicate with each other (32). This misunderstanding happens in part because teams set their overall purpose during the initial stage of team development, the stage during which individual differences tend to dominate and often interfere with creating team cohesion. To maximize effectiveness, leaders need to help teams agree on their vision or superordinate goal, a goal that transcends individual differences. Superordinate goals are often defined broadly, thus giving general direction and focus to the team's subsequent activities. Superordinate goals that require collaboration and cooperation usually decrease prejudice and increase mutual respect (71). This is particularly true when team members require the continued support of their colleagues to achieve results important to all cultures, as well as to the overall organization.

Equalizing Power

Teams generally produce more and better ideas if all members participate. Cultural dominance (disproportionate power vested in members of one culture over those from other cultures) is therefore counterproductive because it stifles nondominant team members' contributions. In multinational teams, leaders must guard against vesting disproportionate power in host-country members, members of the same nationality as the employing organization, members from the most technologically advanced or economically developed countries, or members with ideologies most consonant with their own. Team leaders should manage the distribution of power according to each member's ability to contribute to the task, not according to some preconceived gradient of relative cultural superiority.

Creating Mutual Respect

Ethnocentrism reflects a "view of things in which one's own group is the center of everything and all others are scaled and rated with reference to it" (49:8). Prejudice refers to judging other groups as inferior to one's own. Equal status, close contact, and cooperative efforts toward a common goal decrease prejudice (4;5). "The greater the opportunity for interethnic contacts, the less prejudiced and more frequent the development of cross-ethnic acceptance and friendship" (77:110). For most teams to work effectively, members must respect each other. Team leaders can enhance mutual respect by selecting members of equal ability, making prior accomplishments and task-related skills known to all team members, and minimizing early judgments based on ethnic stereotypes.

Giving Feedback

Given the different perspectives present, culturally diverse teams have more trouble than do single-culture teams in agreeing collectively on what constitutes a good or bad idea or decision. Whereas single-culture teams rapidly develop judgment criteria based on members' similar values, multicultural teams usually experience difficulty and delay before eventually reaching agreement. To encourage effective functioning, managers should give team members positive feedback on their process and output—both as individuals and as a team—early in the team's life. Positive external feedback (given by the team leader or a senior manager who is not on the team) generally aids the team in viewing itself as a team, while additionally serving to teach team members to value the group's diversity, recognize contributions made by each member, and trust the team's collective judgment.

SUMMARY

The potential for superior productivity of culturally diverse teams is high; they possess the breadth of resources, insights, perspectives, and experiences that facilitate the creation of new and better ideas. Regrettably, culturally diverse teams rarely achieve their full potential. Process losses due to mistrust, misunderstanding, miscommunication, stress, and a lack of cohesion often negate the potential benefits of diversity to the team. Only if diversity is well managed can multicultural teams hope to achieve their full potential.

To function effectively, multicultural teams must therefore use their diversity to generate multiple perspectives, problem definitions, ideas, action alternatives, and solutions; learn to achieve consensus, including agreeing on specific decisions and directions, despite the diversity; and balance the simultaneous needs for creativity (divergence) and cohesion (convergence). If multicultural teams fail to generate many new ideas, they become no more effective than individuals working alone. If they fail to achieve consensus, their diversity paralyzes them. If multicultural teams fail to balance creativity and cohesion, they become awkwardly inefficient structures adding little value to the organization.

FILM NOTE

The two-part British Broadcasting Corporation video program, *It's a Jungle Out There* and *The Survival Guide,* presents the issues faced by multinational teams in learning how to function more effectively. The first video, *It's a Jungle Out There,* presents the experiences of an eight-member, five-nationality multinational team of women and men from the team's initial meeting in England through its various experiences on a three-country project in Africa. In the second video, *The Survival Guide,* Professor Nancy J. Adler assesses areas in which the team functions well and those in which it functions poorly. Adler's commentary is based on *International Dimensions of Organizational Behavior,* including material presented in Chapter 5. (Director: Steve Wilkinson, The British Broadcasting Corporation, Open University Production Centre, Walton Hall, Milton Keynes, England MK7 68H; Tel: 44-1908-655-343; Fax: 44-1908-655-300) For additional video programs, see Notes 1 and 2.

6

Global Leadership, Motivation, and Decision Making

For all practical purposes, all business today is global. Those individual businesses, firms, industries, and whole societies that clearly understand the new rules of doing business in a world economy will prosper; those that do not will perish.   — IAN MITROFF (111:ix)

ORGANIZATIONS WORLDWIDE STRIVE to fulfill their organizational and societal missions. They select leaders who articulate a vision that guides them toward achieving long-term goals and short-term objectives. They expect their leaders to motivate the employees in consistent and effective ways. Leaders continually make decisions that influence the success of entire operations.

This chapter reviews the ways in which corporate vision and leadership vary across cultures, how culture influences motivation, and how cross-cultural dynamics impact managerial decision making. Although some principles of leadership, motivation, and decision making apply almost everywhere, the ways in which leaders adapt them to local conditions and work situations determine their success or failure (73). Although approaches to leadership, motivation, and decision making are highly interrelated, each will be discussed separately.

Until recently, most organization theories were "Made in the U.S.A." and therefore shaped by the political, economic, and cultural context of the United States in the twentieth century (33). Although some research exists explaining how American-based management theories can be altered to apply more broadly around the world, and, perhaps more importantly, how management theories indigenous to countries around the world operate, not enough is yet known to fully understand global organizational dynamics (2;12;13;14;15;32).[1] Until such knowledge becomes more widely available, it remains best to resist the temptation of assuming that any particular theory applies everywhere. As cross-cultural psychologist Harry Triandis (146:139) astutely observed, culture's

> influence for organizational behavior is that it operates at such a deep level that people are not aware of its influences. It results in unexamined patterns of thought that seem so natural that most theorists of social behavior fail to take them into account. As a result, many aspects of organizational theories produced in one culture may be inadequate in other cultures.

Prudent leaders assume that current American-based theories apply to the United States, not, as is so tempting, to the world at large.

GLOBAL LEADERSHIP

To act comes from the Latin verb *agere* meaning "to set into motion" (87). The Anglo-Saxon origins of the verb *to lead* come from *laedere*, meaning "people on a journey" (31). Today's meaning of the word *leader*, therefore, denotes someone who sets ideas, people, organizations, and societies in motion; someone who takes the worlds of ideas, people, commerce, organizations, and societies on a journey. To lead such a journey requires vision, courage, and influence.

Leading with Vision

Leaders help to shape the organization's vision, the meaning within which others work and live. Managers, by contrast, act competently within a vision (26;27). What is our vision of success? What do we want our society to look like? How do we ideally want our organizations to function? Who do we want to lead us? Leadership and vision remain fundamental to the understanding of a people and their institutions. The questions involved are universal; the answers are often culturally specific. *The Way of Lao Tzu*, for example, captures a traditional Chinese vision of leadership from the sixth century b.c. (149:214):

I have three treasures. Guard and keep them.
The first is deep love,
The second is frugality,
And the third is not to dare to be ahead of the world.
Because of deep love, one is courageous.
Because of frugality, one is generous.
Because of not daring to be ahead of the world,
   one becomes the leader of the world.

American Arthur Schlesinger expresses a very different leadership vision in *A Thousand Days*, the vision of former U.S. President John F. Kennedy from the 1960s (126):

Above all . . . [President Kennedy] gave the world for an imperishable moment a vision of a leader who greatly understood the terror and the hope, the diversity and the possibility, of life on this planet and who made people look beyond nation and race to the future of humanity.

Britain's Anita Roddick, founder and CEO of the highly successful global firm, The Body Shop, describes her contemporary vision of "corporate idealism" (123:126):

Leaders in the business world should aspire to be true planetary citizens. They have global responsibilities since their decisions affect not just the world of business, but world problems of poverty, national security and the environment. Many, sad to say, duck these responsibilities, because their vision is material rather than moral (123:226).

Although these visions reflect different cultures and centuries, each one expresses the tension between one's immediate national and organizational concerns and the broader interests of humanity and the future. Research suggests that managers' perceptions of what they believe they should be doing varies more than their descriptions of what they actually do (150). It is the tension between the reality of our world today and our aspirations for a better world tomorrow that gives rise to the need for societies to select leaders who can articulate a meaningful vision and guide them toward its realization. In *Beyond National Borders*, Kenichi Ohmae (115) captured a vision for Japan as it moved into the twenty-first century:

Of all the conceivable goals and achievements that Japan might seek to accomplish in . . . [this] century, only one, I believe, is worthy of Japan. It is to prove that without wielding military might, by human strength and resourcefulness alone, a major global power can alleviate the earth's disparities and injustices. . . . Now we must begin to think beyond national borders (115:11).

Traditionally, corporate visions have reflected the values and goals of the society in which they were conceived. Today, with the dominant presence of global firms, corporate visions no longer remain domestic, but are themselves transnational. As witnessed with the economic integration of Europe into the European Union, the founding of the Association of South East Asian Nations (ASEAN) trading block, the increased trade generated by the North American Free Trade Agreement (NAFTA), and the omnipresence of the World Trade Organization (WTO), national borders are vanishing. Whereas historic feuds remain nationally defined from a political perspective, economic pragmatism vanquishes them from a business perspective (54). Business leaders have chosen to transcend national boundaries in ways that remain outside the realm of politicians and government diplomats. As business leaders know, if an idea or action is good for business, it is worth learning and doing no matter where in the world it originated. Global companies, more so than nations, already face the difficult questions involved in integrating visions based on divergent national and cultural values. Their success in defining and implementing transnational visions will determine the future of global companies, and, more importantly, society's potential for success.

Global Leaders: Who Are They and What Do We Know About Them?

Leaders are individuals who significantly affect the thoughts and behaviors of others, without using coercion, but rather, through persuasion (55). Global leadership therefore involves the ability to inspire and influence the thinking, attitudes, and behavior of people worldwide (24;25;26;27;56;94). The very word *leadership*

is a relatively new addition to the English language; it appeared approximately 200 years ago in writings about political influence in the British Parliament. However, from Egyptian hieroglyphics, we know that symbols for "leader" existed as early as 5,000 years ago. Simply put, leaders have existed in all cultures throughout history (44:270).

In the past many people assumed that leaders were born, not made, and they attempted to identify the traits of great leaders. Although every society has had its great leaders, researchers found no consistent set of traits differentiating leaders from other people (142). North Americans, for example, value charisma in their leaders and identify such business and political leaders as Lee Iacocca, former CEO of Chrysler Corporation (82), and Bill Clinton, former president of the United States, as charismatic (40;41). By contrast, Germans do not value charisma in their contemporary leaders, because they associate it with the evil Hitler perpetrated during World War II, in part through his negative charisma. More generally, while the term *leader* evokes a positive image in the United States, for people in many parts of the world it evokes a quite negative image (44:271). For some Europeans, for example, ". . . everything seems to indicate that leadership is an unintended and undesirable consequence of democracy, or a 'perverse effect' as [is said] . . . in France" (61:241–242).

Going beyond the search for leaders' innate traits, researchers tried to identify the types of behaviors outstanding leaders display. They found that the culture in which leaders grow up strongly influences their attitudes and behaviors (99:190–191):

> Consider the implications for leadership of individual attitudes and expectations towards power. As a result of extended experiences with people who have wielded power over them when they were children, adults have expectations about how they should relate to others who have power and how they should behave in return. These attitudes are somewhat modified as a consequence of experiences with teachers, ministers, scout leaders, and other authority figures, but fundamental attitudes toward power are derived from the earliest and most intense experiences with authority figures. . . .
>
> In spite of individual differences, however, these experiences reflect a strong common element in any given culture. As a result, there are generalized expectations about how authority is to be wielded, how the more powerful people should act toward the weaker, and what kinds of behavior the latter might expect from the former. It is expected that one will use social strength according to culturally established norms. Therefore, when acquiring control over others, one also incurs the effects of these expectations about power figures. In short, in a particular culture a person who becomes authoritative in direct relationship to others is expected to act in much the same way as a parent acts in the family. It means that as people develop their expectations of power and attitudes toward it based on their earliest experiences with it, they

will tend to work from these attitudes in every encounter. A superior who fails to conform to these expectations will be seen as an inadequate, unfair, or unjust leader.

Douglas McGregor's classic leadership theory described two different sets of assumptions about the nature of human beings and what they want from their work environment (105) (also see Chapter 2). According to McGregor, some leaders believe they must direct, control, and coerce people in order to motivate them to work. Such leaders assume that the more basic needs for safety, security, and certainty motivate people. By contrast, other leaders believe that they must provide people with freedom, autonomy, and responsibility in order to motivate them to work. These leaders assume that higher-order needs for achievement and self-actualization fundamentally motivate people. According to Anita Roddick, CEO of The Body Shop:

> [People] . . . are looking for leadership that has vision. If you have a company with itsy-bitsy vision, you have an itsy-bitsy company. . . . If you employ people with small thinking and small ideas, you become a company of dwarves (123:223, 225).

Leaders from different cultures vary in the assumptions they make about what motivates most people. In the United States, for example, many leaders assume that people's basic physiological needs for safety and security have been met and that therefore only opportunities to satisfy higher-order needs will motivate most people. They believe that denying these opportunities leads to alienation, lower productivity, and ultimately, high levels of turnover. Most leaders in the United States believe that the majority of the people who work for them want to develop interpersonal relationships characterized by trust and open communication. They therefore assume that people produce more when the workplace is most democratic.

Leaders in the People's Republic of China act similarly, but for very different reasons (128). According to historical explanations (114), the pre-1949 Chinese regarded satisfying lower-order needs as the main objective of the masses, with higher-order needs going unrecognized for all but the upper class. After the revolution two types of managers emerged: The first type, experts who possessed extensive technical expertise, tended to use a more controlling approach to get things done. The second type, leaders who possessed more political and ideological expertise and who were more skilled in managing people, tended to use a more inclusive approach.

This second, more political, group of leaders believed that their leadership approach was closely tied to the philosophy of Chairman Mao. They strongly advocated a more egalitarian workplace in which all employees could improve their lot together, both economically and culturally. They strongly believed that leaders had to give workers' welfare prominence over production, and that material incentives that promoted self-interest and competition had to be discouraged. These leaders encouraged collaboration and broad participation in decision making by replacing individual rewards with collective rewards, and emphasizing democracy and decentralization. Both American and Chinese leaders agree, but for very different reasons, that democratic organizations can perform efficiently and productively; that is, that global competitiveness without dehumanization is possible.

The primary assumption behind most contemporary leadership theories, such as employee-empowerment models, is that people are basically good and trustworthy.[2] Leaders can therefore delegate tasks, allow employees to structure their own work, and feel no need either to closely supervise or to directly control the work flow. Modern leaders often combine a strong concern for task with an equally strong concern for the people they supervise. The best leaders balance the extent to which they initiate structure and the consideration they show their people based on the nature of the task, the environment, and the skills of the particular people involved. Needless to say, culture is a critical aspect of both the environment and the people.

Cultural Contingency: What Works in Brussels May Not Work in Beijing

Some researchers suggest that American approaches to leadership apply abroad (90;114). Most leaders, however, believe that they must adapt their style to the cultures of employees and clients; that is, they believe that leadership is culturally contingent (46). In their groundbreaking research, Haire, Ghiselli, and Porter (63) found that, although the 14 countries they studied showed more similarities than differences, the countries clustered along cultural rather than industrial lines. Dutch scholar Geert Hofstede (86;90) later concluded that participative leadership approaches, which were strongly encouraged by American theorists and managers, were not suitable for all cultures. Employees in high power-distance cultures, for example, expect managers to act as strong leaders; they become uncomfortable with leaders delegating discretionary decisions. Some cultures want their leaders to act as decisive, directive experts; others want leaders to act as participative problem solvers (see Figure 2-4). Laurent

(96:75–76), for example, describes his difficulty explaining matrix management to French managers:

> The idea of reporting to two bosses was so alien to [French] managers that mere consideration of such an organizing principle was an impossible, useless exercise. What was needed first was a thorough examination and probing of the holy principle of the single chain of command and the managers' recognition that this was a strong element of their own belief system rather than a constant element in nature.

"Americans' extreme individualism, combined with their highly participative managerial climate, may render U.S. management practices unique; that is, differentiated from the approaches in most areas of the world" (44:292;45;71). This conclusion is supported by recent research on leadership that found the United States unique in several respects among all of the Eastern and Western cultures studied (78).

Even in countries culturally well suited to more participative leadership (such as England, Sweden, and the United States), organizations must adapt the form of participation to the local culture (53). Although studies vary in the extent to which they see appropriate leadership styles as similar to those most acceptable in the United States (see, for example, descriptions of managers in Europe [113], Germany [95;148], India [88], and Israel [151]), the consensus today is that global managers must be flexible enough to alter their approach when crossing national borders and working with people from other cultures.[3]

Global Leadership Competencies

As organizations disperse globally, they have come to realize that leadership is a skill that most people need, not just a requirement of a few people at the top. In searching for the most important leadership competencies, companies learned that emotional intelligence, not cognitive abilities, explains 90 percent of the difference between average and star performers (59:94). Asian, European, and U.S. companies headed by leaders with strong emotional intelligence outperform the yearly earnings goals of their competitors by up to 20 percent (59:95). Globally, a company's success is clearly linked to the emotional intelligence of its leaders.

What is emotional intelligence? According to psychologist Daniel Goleman, it is a set of five individual and social competencies, including self-awareness, self-regulation, motivation, empathy, and social skills (58;59). Each competency is critical to effective leadership.

Self-awareness is "the ability to recognize and understand your moods, emotions, and drives, as well as their effects on" other people (59:95). Leaders with a high level of self-awareness exhibit self-confidence, a realistic self-assessment, and a self-deprecating sense of humor.

Self-regulation, the second competency, is "the ability to control or redirect disruptive impulses and moods" along with "the propensity to suspend judgment—to think before acting" (59:95). Leaders with a high level of self-regulation exhibit trustworthiness, integrity, comfort with ambiguity, and openness to change.

Motivation, the third emotional-intelligence competency, is reflected in "a passion to work for reasons that go beyond money or status" and "a propensity to pursue goals with energy and persistence" (59:95). Leaders with a high level of motivation show a strong drive to achieve, optimism (even in the face of failure), and organizational commitment.

The fourth emotional-intelligence competency is *empathy*, "the ability to understand the emotional makeup of other people" and "skill in treating people according to their emotional reactions" (59:95). Leaders with a high level of empathy demonstrate an ability to build and retain talent in their organization, show cross-cultural sensitivity, and become known for offering great service to clients and customers.

The fifth emotional-intelligence competency is *social skill*, a "proficiency in managing relationships and building networks" along with an "ability to find common ground and to build rapport" (59:95). Leaders with a high level of social skill are effective at leading change, show a superior ability to build and lead teams, and become known for their persuasiveness.

Global Leadership: Going Beyond the Ordinary

As former U.S. Secretary of State Madeleine Albright challenges us, "We have a responsibility in our time, as others have had in theirs, not to be prisoners of history, but to shape history" (18). Yet historically, leadership "that goes beyond the nation-state and seeks to address all human beings" has been "the most important, but rarest and most elusive, variety of leadership" (55:20). Today's global business environment demands that we seek to go beyond the ordinary leadership of prior centuries. Harvard professor Howard Gardner studied women and men whom society recognizes as extraordinary leaders. He discovered that extraordinary leaders become their organization's and society's chief storytellers; that is, they "achieve their influence through the kinds of narratives or stories they tell about themselves, their society, and the people with whom they are dealing" (55). Without deeply understanding themselves, their organization, and global society, they would be incapable of crafting and telling profoundly meaningful stories. Gardner discovered that extraordinary leaders worldwide possess three competencies that are similar to those Goleman recognized as emotional intelligence. According to Gardner, extraordinary leaders are better at reflecting, leveraging, and framing than are most people. First, extraordinary leaders spend a lot of time reflecting; they think about what they are trying to achieve, review how they are doing, and correct course when things are not going well (55). Second, extraordinary leaders are particularly good at leveraging (55). Because no leader is equally good at everything, extraordinary leaders find out what they are particularly good at and push this competitive advantage as hard as they can (55). Unlike ordinary leaders, they do not worry about activities that they are not good at (55). Perhaps the most surprising of the three competencies is framing. Extraordinary leaders take more risks than average leaders and are particularly good at learning from their failures. It is not that they fail less frequently than ordinary leaders; on the contrary, they fail more frequently. However, they learn more from their failures than do their more ordinary colleagues. Today's challenge is not just to be a leader, but rather to become a global leader who can meet the challenges of the twenty-first century—a leader who can rise to the challenge of shaping history.

Global Leadership: No Longer Men Alone

As Carly Fiorina, CEO of Hewlett Packard and the first woman to lead a Fortune top-20 firm, recognizes, "Anytime you have a fiercely competitive, change-oriented business where results count and merit matters, women will rise to the top" (52). A major shift is taking place in who is leading major companies and countries. Whereas the majority of senior leaders in the twentieth century were men, leadership is now shifting to include both women and men. As Harvard professor Rosabeth Moss Kanter (89:89) emphasizes, in a global economy, "Meritocracy—letting talent rise to the top regardless of where it is found and whether it is male or female—has become essential to business success."

Careful observation reveals a rapidly increasing number of countries and companies moving away, for the first time, from their historic men-only pattern of senior leadership. Of the 47 women who have served in their country's highest political leadership position—either as president or prime minister—more than two-thirds have come into office in just the last decade, and all but seven are the first woman their country has ever selected (3;5;9;10). Similarly, among the current women CEOs leading major global companies, almost all are the first woman whom their particular company has ever selected (4;5;6;8;11). The question is no longer, "Is the pattern changing?" but rather, "Which companies will take advantage of the trend and which will fall behind?" (7;16;17). Which companies and countries will lead in recognizing and understanding the talents women bring to leadership, and which will limit their potential by clinging to historic men-only patterns? Given the recency of women assuming global leadership positions, it is important to recognize that almost all research conducted on senior leaders has, in fact, been conducted on men. Only now, in the twenty-first century, are we beginning to understand women's unique patterns of leadership and accomplishment.

MOTIVATION WORLDWIDE

Beyond culturally appropriate leadership, what causes high productivity and job satisfaction? What energizes members of an organization to produce high-quality work? What directs and channels their behavior to accomplish organizational goals? How do organizations maintain desired behavior? What influences in employees and their environment encourage, or discourage, them from out-performing the competition (139;140)?

One global high-technology firm based in the Silicon Valley in California thought it had the answer. The firm created the "Dragon Slayer Campaign" with posters encouraging employees to "Slay the Dragon." Unfortunately, the American management had not realized that dragons symbolize good luck to the Chinese and that their campaign was not encouraging Chinese employees to beat the competition but rather to destroy their good luck. Understandably, Chinese employees took down the posters and forced the firm to end the campaign.

Numerous motivation theories address these questions and, like the majority of leadership theories, most have been developed in the United States (64). Each attempts to explain why human beings behave in the ways they do and what managers can do to encourage certain types of behavior while discouraging others. Let's look at a few of the historically well recognized motivation theories and determine whether they are universal or culture bound.

Hierarchies of Needs

Psychologist Abraham Maslow (106;107;108) suggested that human beings' five basic needs form a hierarchy: from physiological, to safety, to social, to esteem, to self-actualization needs. According to this theory, higher-order needs (i.e., esteem and self-actualization) only become activated, and thus motivate behavior, after lower-order needs have been satisfied.

Does Maslow's theory, which he based on Americans, hold for employees outside the United States?[4] Hofstede (73) and Trompenaars (147) have shown that it does not (see Chapter 2). For instance, in countries higher on uncertainty avoidance (such as Greece and Japan) as compared with those lower on uncertainty avoidance (such as the United States), security motivates employees more strongly than does self-actualization. Employees in high-uncertainty-avoidance countries often consider job security and lifetime employment more important than holding a more interesting or challenging job. Also contrasting with the American pattern, social needs often dominate the motivation of workers in countries such as Denmark, Norway, and Sweden that stress the quality of life (Hofstede's quality-of-life dimension) over materialism and productivity (Hofstede's career success dimension).[5] People in more collectivist countries, such as Pakistan, tend to stress social needs over the more individualistic ego and self-actualization needs stressed in countries such as the United States. Given the conflicting patterns of motivation of people in individual versus group-oriented cultures, managers using Americans' highly individualist motivation theories must ask:

> In what cultural and historical context does the greatest good involve being able to break apart from one's collective base to stand alone, self-sufficient and self-contained? In the context of an individualistic society in which individualism and self-containment is the ideal, the person who most separates . . . [himself or herself] from the group is thereby seen as embodying that ideal most strongly; the person who remains wedded to a group is not . . . [the] esteemed ideal (125:776).

Economically developing countries, in contrast to the United States and most advanced economies, exhibit relatively high uncertainty avoidance, low individualism, high power distance, and a relatively low emphasis on career success (14;71;72;73;84). Community dominates individualism, for example, in most East African nations. The community dominates all aspects of African thought. Dances are communal and worship is communal. Property was held communally before the colonial era and there are attempts today to reinstate that practice. This inbuilt bias toward the community means that individualism is always seen as a deviance (112:35).

The African norm most clearly valued ". . . is traditional communal responsibility, revealed partly in the condemnation of self-seeking individualism" (127:358). Clearly the motivation of employees from more collective-oriented cultures differs from that of their more individualistic American counterparts.

Numerous research studies testing the hierarchies of needs in different cultures demonstrate similar, but not identical, rank ordering in such diverse cultures as Argentina (79), Anglophone and Francophone Canada (86), Chile (79), India (79;85), Japan (120), Korea (39;93), Liberia (79), Libya (35) Mexico (120;121), the Middle East (14;22;23), Peru (141;154), Russia (50), South Africa (79), Thailand (120), Turkey (120), Venezuela (120), and the former Yugoslavia (120). Although the conflicting patterns of research findings fail to offer definitive conclusions, they strongly indicate that we should not assume that the rank ordering of motivation holds universally (73;30). In summary,

> Studies have found that an individual's frame of reference will determine the order of importance of his needs. It has also been found that his frame of reference is in part determined by his culture. Therefore, it can be said that an individual's needs are partially bound by culture (116).

Human needs may well include fundamental or universal aspects, but their importance and the ways in which they express themselves vary across cultures.

Three Motives: Achievement, Power, and Affiliation

David McClelland, another classic American theorist, suggested that three important motives drive people: the needs for achievement, power, and affiliation (103). Although McClelland has focused more recently on executives' needs for power (104), he initially emphasized the need for achievement as fundamental in explaining why some societies produce more than others (102). In his famous studies in India, for example, he found that entrepreneurs trained in the need for achievement performed better than did untrained entrepreneurs (also see 80).

Comparative research has shown achievement motivation to be rela-

---

WHAT MOTIVATES A PERSON?
A NEW HOTEL IN TAHITI

A major hotel chain chose to develop a new hotel in Tahiti. The developer contracted with a Tahitian skilled in carving large wooden totems. The hotel desired a number of these totems to provide the site with local island atmosphere. The Tahitian quoted a price for carving the first totem and then higher and higher prices for each succeeding totem. This, of course, astonished the hotel developer, who asserted that this was no way to do business. Didn't the Tahitian understand about quantity discounts? The Tahitian artisan, equally mystified, also tried to explain: "No, it is you who doesn't understand. Carving the first totem is fun. Carving each additional totem becomes less fun" (110:134).

---

tively robust across cultures (124). Managers in New Zealand, for example, follow the same pattern observed in the United States (69). Hofstede, however, questions how universal the needs for achievement, power, and affiliation really are (73). Hofstede begins by pointing out that the word *achievement* itself is hardly translatable into any language other than English (73:55). Based on his analysis, Hofstede found that countries with a high need for achievement also have a high need to produce (Hofstede's career success dimension) and a strong willingness to accept risk (Hofstede's weak uncertainty avoidance). As shown in Figure 2-6, Anglo-American countries such as the Canada, Great Britain, and the United States (weak uncertainty avoidance combined with a strong commitment to career success) follow the high achievement motivation pattern, and countries such as Chile and Portugal (strong uncertainty avoidance combined with an equally strong commitment to quality of life) follow the low achievement motivation pattern. Although helpful in explaining human behavior, the needs for achievement, power, and affiliation have not been shown to be universal (see the box "What Motivates a Person? A New Hotel in Tahiti").

External Versus Internal Motivation: The Two-Factor Theory

Frederick Herzberg (66;67) suggested that certain extrinsic factors (those associated with the environment surrounding a job) have only the power to demotivate employees, whereas intrinsic factors (those associated with the job itself) have the power to energize, or motivate, people. The extrinsic and potentially demotivating factors largely correspond to the lower-order physiological and safety needs on the need hierarchy. They include factors associated with job dissatisfaction such as poor working conditions, supervision, relations with coworkers, salary, company policy, and administration. Intrinsic factors, or motivators, which correspond to the higher-order needs on the need hierarchy, include the work itself, responsibility, recognition for work well done, achievement, and advancement.

More recent research has questioned Herzberg's two factors. Research has shown, for example, that people sometimes continue a particular course of action because they have made a prior public commitment to it and not because it continues to be rewarding (138). Similarly, some people, who gain intrinsic satisfaction from a particular activity, switch to explaining their motivation in extrinsic terms after having received an extrinsic reward (retrospective sense-making [see 138, among others]). Others indicate that some behavior is random and neither as goal oriented nor as rational as many American motivation theories would suggest (118).

Hofstede (73) again points out that culture influences factors that motivate and demotivate behavior. According to his dimensions, it is not surprising that the highly individualistic, productivity-oriented American culture has focused on job enrichment (the restructuring of individual jobs to increase productivity); whereas the more quality-of-life oriented and slightly more collectivist societies of Sweden and Norway developed sociotechnical systems and new approaches to the quality of working life (such as the restructuring of employees into work groups to achieve the same ends).

When researchers tested Herzberg's two-factor theory outside the United States, they failed to confirm their initial findings (70). Results in New Zealand, for example, failed to replicate those in the United States. In New Zealand, supervision and interpersonal relationships appear to contribute significantly to satisfaction and not merely to reducing dissatisfaction (69). Similarly, in the former Panama Canal Zone, researchers found citizens of Asia, Canada, Europe, Latin America, the Republic of Panama, and the West Indies cited certain extrinsic factors as satisfiers with greater frequency than did their American counterparts (42).

Similar to other motivation theories, the universality of Herzberg's two-factor theory cannot be assumed. In every culture, certain factors act as motivators and others act as demotivators. Specific motivators and their relative importance are unique to each culture and, all too frequently, to each situation. Managers entering a new culture should observe which factors appear important and not assume that their prior experience in other cultures is transferable.

Expectancy Theories: What Do We Believe Produces Results?

Expectancy theories (97;152;153) claim that people are driven by the expectation that their acts will produce certain results. Workers assess both their ability to perform a task and the probable type of reward for successful performance (continued employment, a paycheck, or the ability to support one's family, for example). According to expectancy theories, the likelihood that an action will lead to certain outcomes or goals (E), multiplied by the attractiveness of the outcome (V, its valence) equals motivation ($M = E \times V$) (98). Expectancy theories depend on the extent to which people believe they have control over the outcomes of their efforts as well as on managers' abilities to identify desired rewards, both of which vary across cultures. Although expectancy theories have clearly advanced our understanding of motivation, they equally clearly vary cross-culturally.

A recent review of our understanding of motivation (137:650–651) underscores that "whether the driving force is thought to be prior reinforcement, need fulfillment, or expectancies of future gain, the individual is assumed to be a rational maximizer of personal utility." Unfortunately, this individual, calculative view of motivation has questionable applicability outside the United States and therefore indicates "a fundamental omission in our motivation theories" (137:651; also see 33).

In countries where individualism dominates, for example, employees see their relationship with the organization from a calculative perspective; whereas in collectivist societies, the ties between the individual and the organization rely on a moral component (20;33;113). Clearly people become committed to organizations for very different reasons in individualistic and collectivist societies (138). Employees with collectivist values make organizational commitments because of their personal ties to managers, owners, and coworkers (collectivism) and much less because of the nature of the job or the particular compensation scheme (individualistic incentives [33]). In Brazil, for example, where people's personal and work lives are highly integrated, it is common for major firms

to help employees with personal financial problems. For example, because of a lack of public social services, employees may have an illness in the family which puts them in a precarious financial position. The personnel departments of larger Brazilian firms regularly provide assistance to employees in such a situation, thus mitigating the impact of the employees' problems on the functioning of the firm (84:292).

Given its individualistic orientation, it is not surprising that the United States has a different pattern from Brazil. While Brazilians expect their firms to take care of employees' personal needs, Americans have no such expectations and therefore much less loyalty to their employers. It is not coincidence that the United States (and not Brazil) has the most executive search firms and the highest level of executive and managerial mobility in the world (33).

As discussed in Chapter 1 (see discussion of the dominance-harmony dimension), people in different cultures vary in the amount of control they believe they have over their environment. Most Americans strongly believe that they control the relevant aspects of their environment. American managers believe that they directly influence the world in which they work (that is, they have a high level of internal attribution). Most American managers, for example, believe that "Where there is a will, there is a way." By contrast, many managers in other parts of the world believe that they only partially control their work environment and the outcomes of their own behavior (that is, they attribute the causes of some events to external circumstances). Many Muslim managers, for example, believe that things will happen only if God wills them to happen (external attribution). Many Latin American managers believe that it is important to be from the right family and social class (external attribution). Many Hong Kong Chinese executives believe that there is an element of *joss*, or luck, involved in all transactions (external attribution). By contrast, most American managers believe that effective problem solving and hard work will get the job done (internal attribution). Expectancy theories work best in explaining the motivation of people in cultures that emphasize internal attribution.

The rewards people want from work also vary greatly across cultures. As discussed in reference to the needs hierarchy, security is very important to some people, congenial relationships are paramount for others, and individual status and respect (career success) dominate for others. A classic study investigated the work goals of 19,000 employees in a large multinational electrical equipment manufacturer operating in 46 countries and reported the results for such countries as Argentina, Australia, Austria, Belgium, Brazil, Canada, Chile, Colombia, Denmark, Finland, France, Germany, India, Israel, Japan, Mexico, New Zealand, Norway, Peru, South Africa, Sweden, Switzerland, the United Kingdom, the United States, and

Venezuela (131). In every country, the five most important goals concerned achievement, especially individual achievement. Next in importance were the immediate environment, general features of the organization, and employment conditions such as pay and work hours. Some of the major differences among the cultural groups included the following (131):

1. English-speaking countries ranked higher on individual achievement and lower on the desire for security.
2. French-speaking countries, although similar to the English-speaking countries, gave greater importance to security and somewhat less to challenging work.
3. Northern European countries expressed less interest in "getting ahead" and work recognition goals and put more emphasis on job accomplishment; in addition, they showed more concern for people and less for the organization as a whole (it was important for them that the job not interfere with their personal lives).
4. Latin American and Southern European countries found individual achievement somewhat less important; Southern Europeans placed the highest emphasis on job security, while both groups of countries emphasized fringe benefits.
5. Germany ranked high on security and fringe benefits and among the highest on "getting ahead."
6. Japan, although low on advancement, also ranked second highest on challenge and lowest on autonomy, with a strong emphasis on good working conditions and a friendly working environment (131).

Expectancy theories are universal to the extent that they do not specify the types of rewards that motivate a given group of workers (109). Managers themselves must determine the level and type of rewards most sought after by a particular group. Although this study's conclusions support the idea that basic human needs are similar, they highlight the fact that culture and environment determine how human needs can best be met.

Global human resource systems are replete with examples of over-generalization resulting from over-reliance of American reward structures. For example (as described in Chapter 1), raising the salaries of a particular group of Mexican workers motivated them to work fewer, not more, hours. As the Mexicans explained, "We can now make enough money to live and enjoy life [one of their primary values] in less time than previously. Now we do not have to work so many hours." In another example, an expatriate Canadian manager in Japan decided to promote one of his Japanese sales representatives to manager (a status reward). To the surprise of the Canadian, the promotion diminished the new Japanese manager's performance. Why? Japanese have a high need for harmony—to fit in with their work colleagues. The promotion, an individualistic reward, separated the new manager from his colleagues, embarrassed him, and therefore diminished his motivation to work.

Motivation Is Culture Bound

Most motivation theories in use today were developed in the United States by Americans and about Americans. Of those that were not, many have been strongly influenced by American theories. Americans' strong emphasis on individualism has led to expectancy and equity theories of motivation: theories that emphasize rational, individual thought as the primary basis of human behavior. The emphasis placed on achievement is not surprising given Americans' willingness to accept risk and their high concern for performance. The theories therefore do not offer universal explanations of motivation; rather, they reflect the values system of Americans (73).

Unfortunately, many American as well as non-American managers have treated American theories as the best or only way to understand motivation. They are neither. American motivation theories—too often assumed to reflect universal values—have failed to provide consistently useful explanations for behavior outside the United States. Managers must therefore guard against imposing domestic American management theories on their global business practices (83).

CROSS-CULTURAL DECISION MAKING

"It could be argued that the essence of living is free choice—the process of making decisions. To be deprived of choices is to lose all meaning" (48:59). Decision making plays a central role in managing; for some people decision making *is* managing (130). The higher the level of management, the greater the number and complexity of the decisions made. Leadership involves making decisions that affect whole organizations, divisions within organization, and often, society itself. Motivation, when viewed from the perspective of decision making, simply becomes the series of choices leaders make in order to influence the behavior of their colleagues and subordinates. Similarly, planning can be viewed as making sets of related decisions. The ultimate dilemma faced by all decision makers is that "no amount of sophistication is going to allay the fact that all your knowledge is about the past and all your decisions are about the future." Decision makers will always act on the basis of inadequate and incomplete knowledge. Good decision makers in every culture are those who learn to cope with the ambiguity and uncertainty of reality. In the past, managers could successfully base their decisions primarily on their own experience and culture; today such a domestic perspective no longer works.

Organization theorists have argued for years about how people make decisions. Some believe that managerial decision making reflects a conscious, rational process in which managers select criteria and use them to evaluate alternative solutions to particular problems. In choosing profit maximization as a prime decision-making criterion, for example, managers might assess a range of business opportunities relative to their potential to generate profit. Alternatively, an equally rational decision rule might be *satisficing* (i.e., meeting acceptable standards on several criteria rather than maximizing performance on a single criterion). When satisficing, managers might assess alternatives until they identify at least one projected to generate a certain acceptable profit margin or result. Without further search they would select that alternative.

Contact with other cultures has created new problems for us when we attempt to use these objective, rational processes. As futurist Robert Theobold (145:42) observed, "We are all having increasing problems as we come to understand that different people have profoundly different visions of reality, and that there is no objective way of sorting out which of these visions is correct."

Other theorists, such as the noted psychoanalyst Sigmund Freud, believed that human decision making was irrational—that forces outside of our conscious control drive decision making. Herbert Simon (129;130), in his administrative theory of individual decision making, describes the process managers use to make decisions as "bounded rationality." According to Simon, managers make choices based on simplified rather than real situations. This "subjective rationality" narrows and alters the objective facts. Because managers from different cultures perceive the world differently, their subjective rationalities differ, as do their ways of simplifying complex realities into perceived environments in which they become capable of making choices.

Along this rational/irrational spectrum, some theorists believe that one best way exists to make decisions; others believe that the best way depends on the particular situation. In certain situations, for example, companies should maximize profit, in others they should satisfice, and in still others they should base their decisions on intuition rather than on traditional economic analysis. In this section we will look at some of the ways in which decision making is culturally contingent; that is, the ways in which the best way depends on the values, beliefs, attitudes, and behavioral patterns of the people involved (38). Cultural contingency is, in fact, one more contingency in the "fit" models of decision making; the decision-making style must fit the culture.

Decision making involves five basic steps (43, based on 48;130):

1. Recognizing the problem
2. Searching for information
3. Constructing alternatives
4. Making a choice
5. Implementating the decision

These steps suggest the following cross-cultural questions: Do managers from different cultures perceive problems in similar ways? Do they gather similar types and amounts of information while investigating a problem? Do they construct similar types of solutions? Do they use similar strategies for choosing between alternatives? Do they implement their decisions in similar ways? The answer to each question is no. As illustrated in Table 6-1, at each step culture influences the ways managers make decisions and solve problems.

Recognizing the Problem

When is a problem a problem? When do people from different cultures recognize that a problem exists? Based on differences in a society's orientation to activity—to "getting things done" (see Chapter 1)—some cultures emphasize solving problems while others focus on accepting situations as they are. In certain cultures, such as the United States, managers perceive most situations as problems to be solved, as opportunities for improvement through change. Other cultures, such as the Indonesian, Malay, and Thai cultures, tend to see no need to change most situations but rather attempt to accept life as it is.

If a problem-solving manager receives a notice that a prime supplier will be three months late in delivering needed construction materials, she will immediately attempt to speed up delivery or find an alternate supplier. If, by contrast, a situation-accepting manager receives a similar notice of delay, he might simply accept that the project will be delayed. Situation-accepting managers believe that they neither can nor should alter every situation that confronts them. Problem-solving managers believe that they both can and should change situations to their own benefit. Situation-accepting managers generally believe that fate or God's will intervenes in the production process (external attribution), whereas problem-solving managers are more likely to believe that they are the prime or only influence on the same process (internal attribution). Consequently, while viewing exactly the same situation, American managers might identify a problem long before their Indonesian, Malay, or Thai counterparts would choose to recognize the situation as a problem. Comparative research has demonstrated that managers' perceptions of situations and their definitions of problems vary across cultures.

Searching for Information

After recognizing that a problem exists, where does the manager gather information to solve it? The noted psychoanalyst Carl Jung suggested two primary modes of gathering information (i.e., of perceiving): sensing

TABLE 6-1 Cultural Contingencies of Decision Making

Five Steps in Decision Making	Cultural Variations	
1. RECOGNIZING THE PROBLEM	*Problem Solving* We should improve the situation.	*Situation Acceptance* Some situations should be accepted as they are.
2. SEARCHING FOR INFORMATION	*Gathering "facts"*	*Gathering ideas and possibilities*
3. CONSTRUCTING ALTERNATIVES	*New, future-oriented alternatives* Adults can learn and change.	*Past-, present-, and future-oriented alternatives* Adults cannot change substantially.
4. MAKING A CHOICE	*Individual decision making* Decision-making responsibility is delegated. Decisions are made quickly. Decision rule: Is it true or false?	*Group decision making* Senior managers often make decisions. Decisions are made slowly. Decision rule: Is it good or bad?
5. IMPLEMENTING THE DECISION	*Slow* Managed from the top Responsibility of one person	*Fast* Involves participation of all levels Responsibility of group

and intuition. Sensors primarily use their five senses to gather information and facts about a situation; intuitive people more frequently gather ideas from the past and future in their attempt to understand the situation. Sensors rely on facts and are often more inductive; intuitive people rely more heavily on images and are often more deductive. Cervantes' *Don Quixote*, the archetypal intuitive, symbolically captures the thinking pattern of intuitive people:

> When life itself seems lunatic, who knows where madness lies? Perhaps to be too practical is madness. To surrender dreams—this too may be madness. To seek treasure where there is only trash. Too much sanity may be madness. And the maddest of all, to see life as it is and not as it should be.6

Cultures vary in the extent to which one or the other style of data gathering (of perceiving) dominates. During the Yom Kippur war in the Middle East, for example, the Americans, as typical sensors, assessed the situation pessimistically for the Israelis because 100 million Arabs were at war with fewer than 8 million Israelis. The Americans based their perception of the situation on fact-oriented, empirical evidence. The Israelis, who are typically more intuitive, based their predictions on their image of the future—the continued existence of a free Jewish state—and therefore remained more optimistic. Moreover, the Israelis felt that the number of Arabs and Israelis was relevant in determining how they would fight the war but was irrelevant in influencing their beliefs about who would win the war. In a similar contrast of perceptual styles, many English Canadians—typically sensors—agonized over Quebec's diminished economic base that would result if the province separated from the rest of Canada. They consequently predicted that people would vote to remain a part of Canada. Many French Canadians, more typically using intuitive perceptions, continued to reiterate their vision of a culturally and linguistically distinct Francophone nation. These French Canadians, while recognizing the economic consequences of separation, considered them less relevant in assessing the validity of their overall goal (see 119).

Constructing Alternatives

What types of alternatives do we construct? Are they predominantly new ideas or ideas rooted in the past? Are they ideas that demand large or moderate amounts of change? Based on a culture's underlying values, the types of alternatives vary. People from more future-oriented cultures, such as California, tend to generate more new alternatives. People from more conservative, past-oriented cultures, such as England, tend to search for historical patterns on which to base alternatives. Californians, when attempting to minimize urban congestion, would be more likely to consider "flying cars" and networks of home offices connected through the Internet; the British are more likely to consider improved traffic control mechanisms. Both societies consider both types of alternatives; but, in each, one type is preferred (112:35). For some past-oriented Africans, being educated is equivalent to rejecting the ways of their ancestors and thus contrasts sharply with the view of more future-oriented Californians (112:35) (see time dimension in Chapter 1).

Similarly, some cultures believe that adults can change, whereas other cultures believe that adults basically remain unchangeable (see discussion of how people see themselves in Chapter 2). Cultures that believe in change stress alternatives that include continuous adult learning and on-the-job training; those that believe in permanence stress initial selection. Today a company's orientation toward change is often reflected in its approach to technology: "Can we train our present employees to learn to use each new generation of e-technology (change is possible), or must we hire new, generally younger employees who are already comfortable with e-commerce (change is impossible)?" Given Americans' strong belief in employees' and managers' ability to learn and to change, it is not surprising that the American Society for Training and Development has more than 50,000 members.

Making a Choice

Who makes the decisions for a company? Are decisions made quickly or slowly? Are information and alternatives discussed sequentially or holistically? Based on a culture's view of the relationships among people (see Chapters 1 and 2), either individuals or groups will hold primary decision-making responsibility. In North American business, individuals usually make decisions. The popular expression "the buck stops here" reflects the belief that ultimately a single person holds responsibility for a particular decision. In Japan, groups make decisions; most Japanese would find it inconceivable for an individual to make a decision prior to consulting his or her immediate colleagues and gaining their agreement (49;91;92;117;145).

At what level are decisions made? In more hierarchical cultures (see Hofstede's power distance dimension, Chapter 2), only very senior managers make decisions. Lower-level personnel hold responsibility for implementing decisions. Most lower-level Indian employees, for example, would wonder about the competence of a superior who consulted them on routine decisions. The majority of Indian managers prefer a more directive style, and up to 85 percent of their surveyed subordinates believe they work better under supervision (88). By contrast, most lower-level Swedish employees expect to make most of their own decisions about day-to-day operations. Thus, it is not surprising that Swedes, not Indians, experimented with some of the first autonomous work groups. At Volvo's Kalmar plant, Swedish management gave groups of employees total responsibility for producing cars (62). The group, not senior management, took responsibility for allocating and scheduling tasks as well as for allocating rewards among employees. Senior management could only delegate this amount of discretion to the shop floor in a low-power-distance country.

Are decisions made slowly or quickly? American businesspeople pride themselves in being quick decision makers. In the United States, being called "decisive" is a compliment. By contrast, many other cultures downplay time urgency—some cultures even increase a decision's value based on the length of time spent in making it. When managers from quick-paced cultures, such as the United States, attempt to conduct business with people from more slow-paced cultures, such as Egypt and Pakistan, the mismatched timing causes problems. Americans, for example, typically become frustrated at Egyptians' slow, deliberate pace and begin to believe that their Middle Eastern counterparts lack interest in getting the job done. Egyptians, on the other hand, in observing the Americans' "overly hasty race" to make decisions, typically conclude that Americans' unwillingness to take more time reflects the lack of importance they place on the business relationship and the particular work at hand (see 1). Time (as discussed in Chapter 1) is a crucial dimension in understanding business behavior cross-culturally.

How much risk is too much? As described by Hofstede in Chapter 2, cultures vary in their uncertainty avoidance (73). Managers in some cultures take more risks than those from other cultures. The extent to which managers enjoy experimenting, trying previously untried alternatives, depends on their aversion to risk.

In what order do businesspeople discuss alternatives? When do they eliminate alternatives? When do they select one particular alternative? As will be discussed in Chapter 7, some holistic cultures, such as China and Japan (144), discuss all alternatives before making any decisions; other more sequence-oriented cultures, such as Canada, Germany, and the

United States, usually discuss alternatives in a preplanned sequence and make incremental decisions as each alternative is discussed.

The overall process of decision making can be described in Jungian terms, with some people acting primarily as "thinkers" and others primarily as "feelers." Thinkers generally process data and make decisions by questioning whether an alternative is correct or incorrect, true or false. Feelers, while equally logical, question whether an alternative is good or bad. Thinkers orient themselves around a belief in absolute truth, whereas feelers orient themselves around a model of "fit": Is there a good or bad fit between this alternative and what we are trying to accomplish? In selecting a new manager, the thinker might stress the individual's expertise and track record. The feeler might stress the candidate's ability to use good judgment and fit in with other members of the organization. Both are equally logical and valid systems for decision making, but each leads to very different choices.

Implementing the Decision

If decisions are to have any value, they must be implemented. Again, depending on the culture, implementation can be quick or slow, innovative or disruptive, managed from the top or involve participation from all levels within the organization, and managed by an individual or a group. Some of the most difficult global business decisions involve ethical considerations. In a survey of *Harvard Business Review* readers, almost half agreed that "the American business executive tends not to apply the great ethical laws immediately to work. He is preoccupied chiefly with gain" (34). Only 5 percent listed social responsibility as a factor influencing ethical standards (34). Half of the respondents attributed unethical practices to superiors who were interested in results no matter how they were attained (34). Global business decisions are often even more difficult to make than domestic decisions because the basis of what is believed to be "right" and "wrong" is culturally determined (143).

Ethical Decision Making

British CEO Anita Roddick defines corporate leadership as moral leadership:

> Authority to lead should be founded on a moral vision rather than a desire to create the biggest or the richest company in the world. I don't understand how anybody can be a leader without a clearly defined moral vision. If your ambi-

tions and interests do not extend beyond the role of making money or expanding your business, as far as I am concerned you are morally bankrupt (123:226).

As global leaders, each of us must define our own moral imperatives. Our moral vision guides our personal and organizational behavior, it frames the goals we set, the trade-offs we are willing to consider, and the decisions we make.

Managing across cultures confronts leaders with profound ethical questions as they attempt to adhere to the highest standards of integrity while making and implementing culturally appropriate decisions. Review the following real situation of "Local Justice and Integrity" (see box), both from the perspective of the North American expatriate managing director who made the decision as well as from the perspective of the local authorities who responded to the information provided to them by the expatriate. Imagine that you are on the company's senior management committee, and decide what you would do in the situation. Consider the Questions for Reflection following the case to guide your analysis.

LOCAL JUSTICE AND INTEGRITY

A major North American company operating in Asia discovered one of the local employees stealing company property of minimal value. The senior managers at the location, all of whom are expatriate Americans, had little doubt about the employee's guilt.

Following the company's standard worldwide procedure, the North American managing director reported the case to the local police. Similar to many other North American companies, this company believed that it was best to let officials from the local culture deal with theft and similar violations in whatever way they found most appropriate, rather than imposing the system of justice from their home culture. The local police arrived at the company, arrested the employee, took him to the police station, and interrogated him according to local procedures. The employee confessed. The police then took the employee outside and shot him dead.

continued on next page ■

■ *continued from previous page*

The North American managing director was devastated. For months, he was haunted by the fact that his action, taken because he thought it was culturally appropriate and fair, had led to the murder of an employee.

Questions For Reflection

1. How should employees be treated when they compromise integrity? Does a company's belief in maintaining the highest level of integrity limit its ability to consider culturally based values differences—and more important, their consequences—between the company's culture and local national cultures?

2. Should companies review their policies on the prevention of theft and the promotion of personal honesty in the light of cultural differences? In which situations, if at all, can companies use worldwide standards and procedures? Must companies define integrity issues differently in each country or region of the world?

Senior Management Committee Decision

3. Given the company's belief in maintaining the highest respect for people while maintaining the highest personal integrity, how should it handle future situations such as this one?

4. If you were the North American managing director, what would you personally have done in this situation? Why? Knowing how the situation turned out, what would you recommend that future managing directors do in similar situations?

The box that follows presents four additional business decisions demanding ethical considerations. As you read each, observe the criteria you would use at each stage of the decision-making process: recognizing the problem, searching for information, constructing alternatives, making a choice, and implementing the decision. To what extent are your criteria culturally determined (122;143)? Under what conditions would you be willing to modify your perspective and decision (65)?

ETHICAL DECISION MAKING ACROSS CULTURES[7]

In each of the following situations, first decide what you would do and why. Note what information you would use to investigate the question, what alternatives you would consider, and what criteria you would use to make the decision. After making your initial decision on your own, meet with a group of your colleagues—preferably including people from other cultures—and make a group decision. Again assess the type of information you would consider, the range of alternatives you generate, the criteria you use to decide, and your implementation plan. Next, develop a contrasting-culture decision; that is, make the opposite decision based on assumptions of a culture that is very different from your own. Finally, following the suggestions in Chapter 4 for creating synergistic solutions, develop a decision and implementation plan that both you and members of the contrasting culture could accept and support. The situations are not easy. Each is based on a real event in which at least one manager believed colleagues, clients, or competitors were acting unethically.

Situation 1: Facilitating Decisions in the Middle East

You hold the position of marketing director for a construction company in the Middle East. Your company has bid on a substantial project that it wants very much to get. Yesterday the cousin of the minister who will award the contract suggested that he might be of help. You are reasonably sure that with his help the chances of your company winning the contract would increase substantially. For his assistance the minister expects $200,000. You would have to pay this amount in addition to the standard fees to your agent. If you refuse to make the requested payment, you are certain that the minister will go to your competition (who has won the last three contracts), and they will make the payment (and probably get this contract, too).

Your company has not established a code of conduct yet, although it formed a committee some time ago to consider one. The government of your country recently passed an ethical business practices act. The pertinent paragraph is somewhat vague but implies that this kind of payment would probably be a violation of the act. The person to whom you report, and those above him, do not want to become involved. The decision is yours to make.

continued on next page ■

■ *continued from previous page*

Situation 2: Hazardous Materials in West Africa

For one year you have been the international vice president of a global company that produces and markets chemicals. The minister of agriculture in a small developing country in West Africa has requested a series of large shipments over the next five years of an insecticide that only your company produces. The minister believes that this insecticide is the only chemical that will rid one of his country's most important crops of a new infestation that threatens to destroy it. You know, however, that one other insecticide would probably work equally effectively. The alternative product is produced in another country and has never been allowed in your own country.

The insecticide your company produces, MIM, is highly toxic. After years of debate, your government has just passed a law forbidding its use in your country. Evidence shows that dangerous amounts are easily ingested by humans through the residue it leaves on vegetables, through animals that eat the crops, and through the water supply. After careful consideration, you tell the minister about this evidence. He still insists on using your company's product, arguing that it is necessary and it will be used "intelligently." You are quite sure that, 10 years from now, the insecticide will begin to damage the health of some of his people.

Both the president and executive vice president of your firm feel strongly that your company should fill the order. In addition to questioning their own government's position, they are very concerned about the large inventory of MIM on hand and the serious financial setback its prohibition will cause the company. They have made it clear, however, that the decision is up to you.

Although the company has a code of conduct and your government has an ethical business practices act, neither covers hazardous materials.

Situation 3: The Southeast Asian Advertising Campaign

You are the new marketing manager for a very large, profitable global company that manufactures automobile tires. Your advertising agency has just presented elaborate plans for introducing a new tire into the Southeast Asian market for your approval. The promotional material clearly implies that your product is better than all local products. In fact, it is better than some, but not as good as others. The proposed adver-

continued on next page ■

■ continued from previous page

tising material tries to attract potential buyers by explaining that for six months your product will be sold at a "reduced price." Actually, the price is reduced from a hypothetical high price that the firm established only so they could "reduce it." The advertisement further claims that your company has tested the tire under the "most adverse" conditions. In reality the new tire has not been tested in the prolonged heat and humidity of the tropics. Finally, the proposed advertisement assures buyers that they will be safer in their cars riding on your tires than ever before. The truth is, however, that they would be equally safe using a competitor's tire that has been available for two years.

You know your product is good. You also know the proposed advertising is deceptive. Your superior has never been concerned about such practices, believing that advertisements must present products as distinctive in order to achieve and maintain a competitive edge. Senior management of your company is counting on a very favorable reception for this tire in Southeast Asia. They are counting on you to see that the tire gets this reception.

Whether you go with the proposed advertisement or not is up to you. Your company has a code of conduct and your government has an ethical business practices act, but neither covers advertising practices.

Situation 4: Cultural Conflict in the Middle East

You became quite upset last week when you read a strong editorial in the *New York Times*, written by a prominent journalist, that strongly criticized your company, especially its major project in a conservative Muslim country.

As the international vice president, you hold responsibility for this project, which is to build and run a large steel plant. Based on the figures, this plant makes a lot of sense, both for your company and for the government of the country that approved the project. But as the journalist pointed out, the company plans to build the steel plant in a rural area, which will have a very disruptive effect upon the values and customs of the people in the whole region. The project will have many negative consequences. The young people from other towns will move to work at the plant, thereby breaking up families and eliminating their primary source of financial and personal security. Working the second

continued on next page ■

■ *continued from previous page*

or third shift will further interfere with family responsibilities as well as religious observances. Working year-round will certainly mean that many people will find themselves unable to return home to help with the harvest. As the company pays the young people more and more, they will gain greater influence, thereby overturning centuries-old patterns of authority. And, of course, the westerners whom the company brings in will probably not live up to local moral standards nor show due respect to local women.

The journalist ended by charging your company with "cultural imperialism" and claiming that your plant, if actually built and put into operation, would disrupt the traditional values and relationships that have provided stability for the country through many generations.

You had known that the new steel plant would cause some social changes, but you had not realized how profound they could be. You have now examined other evidence and discovered that a factory built several years ago by another foreign firm in a similar location is causing exactly the type of problems described by the *New York Times* journalist—and more. Widespread concern in the country over these problems has become one reason for the increasing influence of traditionalists and nationalists in the country, who argue for getting rid of all foreign firms and their disruptive priorities and practices.

Your company has a code of conduct and your government has an ethical business practices act, but neither deals with the destruction of traditional values and relationships. You are on your own here. A lot is at stake for the company and for the people of the region into which you had planned to move. The decision is yours.

SUMMARY

Effective styles of management vary among cultures. Whereas managers in all countries must lead, motivate, and make decisions, the ways in which they approach these core managerial behaviors remain, in part, determined by their own cultural background and that of their work environment. Far from learning only one way to lead, motivate, and decide, managers working across cultures must become flexible enough to adapt to each particular situation and country. In moving from domestic to global management, leaders must develop a wider range of thinking patterns and behaviors, along with the ability to select the pattern best suited to each particular situation. Effective global managers must become chameleons capable of acting in many ways, not experts rigidly adhering to one approach.

Most management theories have been developed in the United States by Americans. The questions they raise—How can I lead most effectively? How should I motivate the workforce? How can I make the best decisions?—are universal, but the solutions remain culturally specific. Rather than being applicable worldwide, many traditional models effectively guide thinking and action only within the American context within which they were developed. Based on the cultural context of their operations, global managers must constantly decide to use more directive or democratic styles of leadership, more individual- or group-oriented motivation schemes, more long-term or short-term criteria for decision making. Their decisions, to be most effective and most appropriate, must depend on the particular culture, industry, organization, and individuals involved. Far from being useless, traditional models guide the questions we ask. Only observation and analysis of each culture and situation can guide our answers.

7

Negotiating Successfully Across Cultures

Let us not be blind to our differences—but let us also direct attention to our common interests and the means by which those differences can be resolved.
— JOHN FITZGERALD KENNEDY, *Former President of the United States* (38)

A CRUCIAL ASPECT OF all interorganizational relationships, including strategic alliances, joint ventures, mergers and acquisitions, licensing and distribution agreements, and sales of products and services, involves negotiating. As the proportion of international to domestic trade increases, so does the frequency of business negotiations among people from different countries and cultures. To succeed in such negotiations, businesspeople need to know how to communicate with and influence members of cultures other than their own (3).

A growing literature exists documenting international negotiating styles (44;56;57;65). Descriptions can be found, for example, of the negotiating behavior of Brazilians (22;25), Canadians (2), Chinese (4; 31;34;39;40;43;49;54;60), French (14;48), Japanese (1;8;10;21;24;29; 42;58;59;64), Mexicans (18;67), Middle Eastern Arabs (6;46;72), and Russians (7;9;51), among many others (5;11;28;30;69). Do Russians bargain with the same expectations and approaches as Arabs? No. Are Arab negotiating styles similar to those of Americans? Again, no. Russians, Arabs, and Americans negotiate in notably different ways.

As shown in Table 7-1 (13;20), Russians typically use an axiomatic approach to negotiating—they base their arguments on asserted ideals.

TABLE 7-1 How Do I Persuade Them?
Successful Styles Vary Across Cultures

	Arabs	North Americans	Russians
PRIMARY NEGO-TIATING STYLE AND PROCESS	Affective appeals made to emotions	Factual appeals made to logic	Axiomatic appeals made to ideals
CONFLICT: COUNTERPARTS' ARGUMENTS COUNTERED WITH . . .	Subjective feelings	Objective facts	Asserted ideals
MAKING CONCESSIONS	Concessions made throughout as a part of the bargaining process	Small concessions made early to establish a relationship	Few, if any, concessions made
RESPONSE TO COUNTERPARTS' CONCESSIONS	Almost always reciprocate counterparts' concessions	Usually reciprocate counterparts' concessions	View counterparts' concessions as weakness and almost never reciprocate
RELATIONSHIP	Long term	Short term	No continuing relationship
AUTHORITY	Broad	Broad	Limited
INITIAL POSITION	Extreme	Moderate	Extreme
DEADLINE	Casual	Very important	Ignored

SOURCE: Adapted by Adler, 2002. Reprinted by permission from *International Journal of Intercultural Relations*, vol. 1, no. 3, Fall 1977 and from E. S. Glenn, D. Witmeyer, and K. A. Stevenson, *Cultural Styles of Persuasion*. Reprinted with permission of Pergamon Press, Ltd.

Russians generally do not expect to develop a continuing relationship with their bargaining partners and therefore see little need for relationship building. As a negotiation progresses, Russians make few, if any, concessions and view their counterparts' concessions as signs of weakness. Russians often start with extreme positions, ignore deadlines, and, due to their very limited authority, frequently check back with headquarters.

By contrast, Arabs typically use an affective approach to negotiating (20)—they counter the other side's arguments with emotional appeals based on subjective feelings. Arabs generally want to build long-term relationships with their bargaining partners. Therefore, they are often willing to make concessions throughout the bargaining process and almost always reciprocate their opponents' concessions. Most Arabs do not feel limited by time or authority; they frequently approach deadlines very casually and rarely lack the broad authority necessary to discuss and to agree on all issues pertinent to the negotiation.

Americans differ from both Russians and Arabs. Americans typically use a factual approach to negotiating (20); they attempt to counter the other side's arguments with logical appeals based on objective facts. Americans make small concessions early in the negotiation in an attempt to establish a relationship, and they generally expect their bargaining partners to do likewise. Americans, far from casual about time and authority, generally take deadlines very seriously and have broad authority.

What happens when Russians begin negotiating with Arabs or Americans? Who persuades whom when styles of negotiating differ? Who wins when bargainers from each culture define the process of negotiating, the rules of the game, differently? How can I get what my company and I want from them while maintaining a good relationship? To succeed in global business, negotiators must continually face and solve these dilemmas.

NEGOTIATING GLOBALLY

Negotiation is a process in which at least one individual tries to persuade another individual to change his or her ideas or behavior (12:152). Business negotiations often involve one party attempting to influence another to make a particular decision or sign a contract. Negotiating is the process in which at least two partners with different needs and viewpoints try to reach agreement on matters of mutual interest (12:152). A negotiation becomes cross-cultural when the parties involved belong to different cultures and therefore do not share the same ways of thinking, feeling, and behaving (12:152). All global negotiations are cross-cultural. Some domestic negotiations, in spanning two or more ethnic groups, are also cross-cultural. Therefore, a Singaporian businessperson negotiating a new e-commerce agreement with a Brazilian; a U.N. official negotiating with ambassadors from several countries concerning the agenda for an upcoming world trade summit; Mexican executives considering a potential strategic alliance with Swedes; and French- and Flemish-speaking Belgians determining national language legislation are all negotiating cross-culturally.

TABLE 7-2 Styles of Negotiation Vary Across Cultures

Japanese	Latin American	North American
Emotional sensitivity highly valued	Emotional sensitivity valued	Emotional sensitivity not highly valued
Hide emotions	Emotionally expressive and passionate	Deal straightforwardly or impersonally
Subtle power plays; conciliation	Explicit power plays; use others' weaknesses	Litigation used more than conciliation
Loyal to employer; employer takes care of employees	Loyal to employer (who is often family)	Little commitment to employer; either side can break ties if necessary
Group decision making by consensus	Decisions come down from one individual	Team provides input to decision maker
Face-saving crucial; decisions often made to save someone from embarrassment	Face-saving crucial in decision making to preserve honor and dignity	Decisions based on cost-benefit analysis; face-saving not generally important
Decision makers openly influenced by special interests	Inclusion of special interests of decision maker expected and condoned	Decision makers influenced by special interests, but often not considered ethical
Not argumentative; quiet when right	Argumentative and passionate when right or wrong	Argumentative, but impersonal, when right or wrong
Written statements must be accurate and valid	Impatient with documentation, seen as an obstacle to understanding general principles	Give great importance to documentation as evidential proof
Step-by-step approach to decision making	Impulsive, spontaneous decision making	Methodically organized decision making
Good of group is the ultimate aim	What is good for group is good for the individual	Profit motive or individual benefit is ultimate aim
Cultivate a good emotional climate for decision making; get to know decision makers	Good personal relationships necessary for good decision making	Decision making impersonal; personal involvements seen as conflict of interest and avoided

SOURCE: Adapted by Adler, 2002. From Pierre Casse, *Training for the Multicultural Manager*, reprinted with permission of Intercultural Press, Inc., Yarmouth, ME. Copyright,

Negotiating effectively cross-culturally is one of the single most important global business skills (15;16;36;71). Global negotiations contain all of the complexity of domestic negotiations, with the added dimension of cultural diversity. Global managers spend more than 50 percent of their time in formal and informal negotiations (47). As highlighted in Tables 7-1 and 7-2, negotiating styles vary markedly across cultures. Countries vary on such key aspects as the amount and type of preparation for a negotiation, the relative emphasis on task versus interpersonal relationships, the use of general principles versus specific details, and the number of people present and the extent of their influence.

According to global negotiations experts, negotiating is not always the best approach to doing business (50). Sometimes the best strategy is "take it or leave it," other times it is bargaining, and, on some occasions, negotiations focusing on problem solving are most appropriate and effective (50:6.24). Negotiating, compared with bargaining and the take-it-or-leave-it approach, demands more time. Managers should negotiate when the value of the exchange is high and the relationship is important; as, for example, when forming a global strategic alliance. As summarized in Figure 7-1, negotiating is generally the preferred strategy for creating win-win solutions in global business. Businesspeople should consider negotiating when any of the following conditions exist:

FIGURE 7-1 When Should I Negotiate?

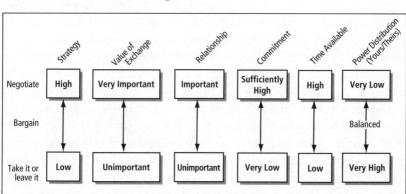

Source: Adapted by Adler, 2002. From Ellen Raider, "Strategy Assessment" in *International Negotiations*, 1982, Situation Management Systems, Plymouth, MA. Reprinted by permission of Ellen Raider International.

- Their power position is low relative to that of their counterpart.
- The trust level among negotiators is high.
- Sufficient time is available to explore each party's multiple needs, resources, and options.
- Commitment, not mere compliance, is important to ensure that all parties carry out the agreement.

In discussing negotiation, this chapter uses the terms *negotiator, bargaining partner, counterpart,* and *opponent* interchangeably.

Cultural diversity makes communicating effectively more difficult (see Chapter 3). Because people from different cultures perceive, interpret, and evaluate the world differently, accurately communicating needs and interests in ways that people from other cultures will understand becomes more challenging, as does fully understanding their words and meanings. Although communicating becomes more difficult across cultures, creating mutually beneficial options often becomes easier. When negotiators overcome communication barriers, identifying win-win solutions—mutually beneficial solutions in which both parties gain—becomes easier. For instance, based on their different perspectives, a seller from one culture may no longer want to keep a particular business, whereas a buyer from another culture may find the same business an especially attractive prospect.

In negotiations between Americans and Japanese, American owners traditionally have concerned themselves more with the viability of the enterprise—with its predicted future revenues and profits. Japanese buyers, on the other hand, have generally shown more interest in market share and in the property and physical plant. A Japanese buyer may find an enterprise particularly valuable for one set of reasons, whereas the American owner may place it on the market for an entirely different set of reasons. Similarly, Vietnamese, with their high unemployment and low wage rates, find producing labor-intensive products a more attractive prospect than do Swiss manufacturers who face high wage rates and negligible unemployment. Differences, rather than similarities, form the basis of mutually beneficial solutions. The probability that negotiators will identify substantial areas of difference, and therefore substantial areas for mutual gain, is greater in multicultural than in single-culture situations.

In some situations, negotiators are able to go beyond mere agreement to create synergistic solutions (see Chapter 4). Whereas mutually beneficial agreements focus on comparative advantage—the exchange of benefits more highly valued by one party than the other—synergy uses differently valued benefits as a resource in creating new options that would never have become possible without the initial differences. Differences, the source of cross-cultural communication complexities and problems, ultimately become the primary resource in creating mutually beneficial, synergistic solutions.

NEGOTIATING SUCCESSFULLY: THE PEOPLE, THE SITUATION, AND THE PROCESS

Each of the three areas on which the success of a negotiation depends—individual characteristics, situational contingencies, and strategic and tactical processes—vary considerably across cultures (17;20;21;26). Although all three affect outcomes, negotiators influence most control over the process: the strategy and tactics. Negotiators can determine the success or failure of a negotiation most directly by managing the negotiating process. This chapter discusses each of the three areas, highlights cultural variations, and recommends the most effective approaches. Effective negotiators base their strategy and tactics on the characteristics of the specific situation and the particular people involved. Although global managers would find it easier if just one best way to negotiate existed, no such consistency nor any guaranteed formula for success exists.

What Qualities Do Good Negotiators Have?

What qualities does a good negotiator possess? According to negotiations expert John Graham's extensive research (21), the answer depends on the cultures involved. As shown in Table 7-3, American managers believe that effective negotiators act highly rationally. Brazilian managers, to the surprise of many Americans, hold an almost identical view, differing only in replacing integrity with competitiveness as one of the seven most important qualities of effective negotiators. By contrast, the opinions of Japanese negotiators differ quite markedly from those of both Americans and Brazilians. Japanese see an interpersonal, rather than a rational, negotiating style as leading to success. Japanese differ from Americans in stressing both verbal expressiveness and listening ability, whereas Americans only emphasize verbal ability. In contrast to Americans, Brazilians, Chinese, and Japanese managers in Taiwan emphasize negotiators' rational skills and, to a lesser extent, their interpersonal skills. To the Chinese, a successful negotiator must be an interesting person and should show persistence and determination, the ability to win respect and confidence, preparation and planning skills, product knowledge, good judgment, and intelligence.

The role that individual qualities play varies across cultures. Favorable

TABLE 7-3 Which Individual Characteristics Do Negotiators See
as Most Important for Negotiating Successfully?
The Answer Varies by Culture

American Negotiators	Brazilian Negotiators	Chinese (Taiwan) Negotiators	Japanese Negotiators
Preparation and planning skill	Preparation and planning skill	Persistence and determination	Dedication to job
Thinking under pressure	Thinking under pressure	Win respect and confidence	Perceive and exploit power
Judgment and intelligence	Judgment and intelligence	Preparation and planning skill	Win respect and confidence
Verbal expressiveness	Verbal expressiveness	Product knowledge	Integrity
Product knowledge	Product knowledge	Interesting	Demonstrate listening skill
Perceive and exploit power	Perceive and exploit power	Judgment and intelligence	Broad perspective
Integrity	Competitiveness		Verbal expressiveness

SOURCE: Professor John Graham, School of Management, University of California at Irvine.

outcomes are most strongly influenced by negotiators' own characteristics in Brazil, opponents' characteristics in the United States, the negotiator's role in Japan (the buyer always does better), and a mixture of the negotiators' and their counterparts' characteristics in Taiwan (21). Specifically, Brazilian negotiators achieve higher profits when they act more deceptively and in their own self-interest, when they express higher self-esteem, and when their bargaining partners act with more honesty. American negotiators achieve greater success when their counterparts are honest, not self-interested, introverted, not particularly interesting as people, and made to feel uncomfortable by the negotiators' actions. By contrast, Japanese buyers always do better than sellers. Both Japanese buyers and sellers can improve their positions by making their bargaining partners feel more comfortable. In Taiwan, negotiators do better when they act deceptively and when their counterparts are neither self-interested nor have particularly attractive personalities.

FIGURE 7-2 How Great an Advantage Does the Buyer Have?
It All Depends on Culture.

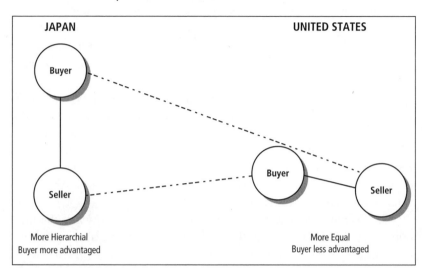

Buyers and Sellers: Who Dominates the Relationship?

The hierarchical relationship between buyers and sellers is crucial in understanding how negotiating styles differ across cultures (22). As shown in Figure 7-2, Japanese buyers and sellers, for example, maintain a vertical, hierarchical relationship; with buyers generally getting most of what they ask for. Sellers, however, expect buyers to take care of them. When the Japanese explain this system to Americans, the Americans frequently ask, "But won't the seller get taken?" The answer is no, because in Japan the group that is higher in the hierarchy takes care of the lower group: management takes care of workers, government takes care of industry, and buyers take care of sellers. *Amae*—indulgent dependence—explains the buyer-seller relationship in Japan.

Buyers and sellers in the United States, by contrast, maintain a less hierarchical, more equal, relationship. The American norm is not amae, but rather independent competition: "May the best person win." Buyers do not expect to take care of sellers, they expect to take care of themselves by getting the best deal possible for their company.

Predictably, problems arise when Japanese and American buyers and sellers negotiate with each other (29:28–29). From the American perspective, being a buyer in Japan is extremely advantageous. According to some Japanese, "Americans ask for the moon!" Many Japanese, in describing their initial negotiations with Americans, say, "When we first came to the United States, we took a beating. As sellers, we gave the American buyers everything they wanted." But because they were working under a different set of expectations, the Americans did not then "take care of" the Japanese sellers. The Japanese thought the Americans took advantage of them, while the Americans believed they had merely driven a hard bargain.

In the reverse situation, American sellers, not trusting Japanese buyers to take care of them, act as equals. They thus fail to behave with appropriate deference to buyers; the Japanese, not surprisingly, perceive the Americans as arrogant. All too frequently, negotiations collapse as a result. Unfortunately, both sides frequently attribute the collapse to unacceptable product or service qualities and price, rather than to the actual cause—cross-cultural differences.

When negotiators bargain with people from many cultures, the most important individual characteristics are good listening skills, an orientation toward people, a willingness to use team assistance, high self-esteem, high aspirations, and an attractive personality, along with credibility and influence within the home organization (27). These individual characteristics, although significant, are not the most important factors determining negotiated outcomes. It is therefore unfortunate that many companies emphasize individual characteristics in selecting members of their negotiating teams rather than training those selected to understand and more skillfully manage the negotiation process.

Negotiating: Which Characteristics of the Situation Lead to Success? Which Lead to Failure?

Situations in which negotiators find themselves vary widely. Effective negotiators recognize and manage the impact of each aspect of the situation on the bargaining process from both their own and their opponents' cultural perspectives. In preparing for global negotiations, they imagine what the situation might look like through the eyes of the other countries' teams: What do they need? What do they want? What is important to them? Who has power? What is at stake? What is their time frame? Where do they draw their personal and organizational bottom line? What is their best alternative to a negotiated solution? Situational factors influence success just as do individual characteristics, but they are rarely as critical to success as the strategy and tactics used.

Location

Should you hold an e-meeting or an inperson meeting? Should you meet at their office, your office, or at a neutral location? Negotiation wisdom generally advises teams to meet in person at their own or a neutral location. Meeting in another country disadvantages negotiators because it reduces their access to information and increases travel-related stress and cost. Meeting at home allows a team to control the situation more easily. A division of Caterpillar of California, for example, increased its control over negotiations by taking international clients out on their yacht. They gained the advantage of removing their clients from interruptions and distractions while limiting their access to information.

Many negotiators select neutral locations. Business entertainment remains a common type of neutral location, used primarily to get to know and improve relations with members of the opposing team. Heavy users of business entertainment, the Japanese spend almost two percent of their GNP on entertaining clients—even more than they spend on national defense (1.5%). Americans generally consider such high business entertainment costs absurd, but perhaps Americans' extraordinarily high legal expenses reflect the cost of insufficient relationship building.

In choosing neutral locations, business negotiators often select resorts geographically located somewhere between each company's headquarters. Asian and North American negotiators, for example, have traditionally selected Hawaii for business meetings; both sides travel, both sides have reduced access to information, and as a consequence, the incentive increases for both sides to conclude the negotiation as quickly as possible. The opportunity cost of executives' time, along with the cost of travel and hotels, usually, but not always, increases pressure to conclude negotiations expeditiously. In one negotiation between an American and a Russian company, negotiators conducted the sessions at a resort in the south of France. The Russian bargainers made it clear that they did not want to end their "vacation" early by concluding the negotiation prematurely.

Physical Arrangements

In traditional American negotiations, the two teams face each other, often sitting on opposite sides of a boardroom table. Unfortunately, this arrangement maximizes competition. By contrast, sitting at right angles facilitates cooperation. If negotiators view the process as a collaborative search for mutually beneficial outcomes (win-win solutions), the physical arrangements should support cooperation, not competition. As an alternative to the boardroom table, negotiators from both teams may choose to sit on the same side of the table, "facing the problem" (18). In this way they compete with the problem, not with the people. The Japanese, in posting all information related to a negotiation on the walls, structure the environment so that all parties involved "face the problem" holistically.

Participants

Who should attend the formal negotiating sessions? Americans tend to want to "go it alone"—they consider extra team members an unnecessary expense. This strategy is usually less effective in global negotiations, where additional team members usually increase the likelihood of success. Why? First, the physical presence of more people communicates greater power and importance—an essential nonverbal message. Second, as discussed earlier, communicating cross-culturally is complex and difficult. Giving some team members primary responsibility for listening to the discussion and observing nonverbal cues while other members focus primarily on conducting substantive negotiations has repeatedly proven to be an extremely effective strategy.

Who should be present at a negotiation? Should the press be present? Will public opinion make it easier or more difficult to develop mutually beneficial solutions? Should the union have direct representation? Should bargainers keep government agencies informed during the negotiation or only present them with the final agreement? The power that government, unions, and public opinion have over business negotiators varies considerably across cultures. Negotiating with government officials from such open democracies as Australia, Canada, and New Zealand, for example, requires broader public debate than is generally necessary in the more tightly controlled governments of Iran and Kenya, or in communist and quasi-communist countries such as Albania, Cuba, and North Korea. Effective global negotiators carefully manage access to the proceedings.

Time Constraints

The duration of a negotiation can vary markedly across cultures. Americans, being particularly impatient, often expect negotiations to take a minimum amount of time. During the Paris Peace Talks, designed to negotiate an end to the Vietnam War, the U.S. team arrived in Paris and made hotel reservations for a week. Their Vietnamese counterparts leased a château for a year. As the negotiations proceeded, timing forced the frustrated Americans to continually renew their weekly reservations to accommodate the more measured pace of the Vietnamese.

Negotiators generally make more concessions as their deadline approaches. Americans' sense of urgency puts them at a disadvantage with respect to their less hurried bargaining partners. Negotiators from outside the United States often recognize Americans' time consciousness, achievement orientation, and impatience. They know that Americans will make more concessions close to their deadline (time consciousness) in order to get a signed contract (achievement orientation). One Brazilian company, for example, invited a group of Americans to Brazil to negotiate a contract the week before Christmas. The Brazilians, aware that the Americans would want to return to the United States by Christmas with a signed contract, knew that they could push hard for concessions and an early agreement. The final agreement definitely favored the Brazilians.

Some negotiators attempt to discover their opponents' deadline and refuse to make major concessions until after that deadline has passed. The local team may determine their opponents' deadlines by checking hotel reservations or politely offering to reconfirm return airline tickets. Effective global negotiators determine the best alternative to not meeting their deadline. If they find the best alternative acceptable, they may choose a less hurried pace than they had originally planned or than they typically use at home.

Status Differences

The United States prides itself on its egalitarian, informal approach to life, in which titles do not seem particularly important and ceremonies are often considered a waste of time. Americans often attempt to minimize status differences during negotiations: for example, they use first names to promote equality and informality. Unfortunately this approach, which succeeds at putting Americans at ease, often makes people from other cultures uncomfortable. Most countries respect hierarchy and formality more than does the United States; and most negotiators from these countries feel more comfortable in formal situations with explicit status differences. The Japanese, for example, must know the other person's company and position before being able to select the grammatically correct form of address. For this reason, the Japanese always exchange business cards—meishi—before a business conversation begins. For similar reasons, German negotiators would almost never address colleagues on their own team, let alone those from another team, by first name. Such informality would severely insult their sense of propriety, hierarchy, and respect.

Age, like title, connotes seniority and demands respect in most countries of the world. Sending a young, albeit brilliant, North American expert to Indonesia to lead a negotiating team is more likely to insult senior Indonesian officials than facilitate a successful exchange of technical information. In almost all cases, North Americans need to increase formality in dress, vocabulary, behavior, and style when working outside of the United States.

THE PROCESS: THE MOST IMPORTANT INFLUENCE ON THE SUCCESS OF A NEGOTIATION

Process is the single most important influence on the success or failure of a negotiation. The process includes managing the negotiation's overall strategy or approach, its stages, and the specific tactics used. As with other aspects of negotiating, the process varies markedly across cultures (30;37;53;61;71). An effective process reflects the situational characteristics and personal backgrounds of the negotiators involved. It balances the position, procedure, timing, and roles of negotiators.

Negotiation Strategy: Succeeding with a Culturally Synergistic Approach

In *Getting to Yes,* based on the work of the Harvard International Negotiation Project, Fisher and Ury (18) propose a principled approach to negotiating. As shown in Table 7-4, this approach includes four steps:

1. Separating the people from the problem
2. Focusing on interests, not on positions
3. Insisting on objective criteria (and never yielding to pressure)
4. Inventing options for mutual gain

Does this principled approach become easier or harder when negotiating globally? Let's analyze the principled approach from a cross-cultural perspective. Cultural differences make communicating more difficult. The first three steps therefore become more difficult: understanding opponents, their interests, and their assessment criteria becomes more complex and

TABLE 7-4 Negotiating Globally: Alternative Approaches

Traditional Approach (Competitive)	Principled Approach (Collaborative/Individual)	Synergistic Approach (Collaborative/Cultural)
Preparation • Define economic issues	*Preparation* • Define interests	*Preparation* • Cross-cultural training • Define interests
Relationship Building • Assess counterpart	*Relationship Building* • Separate the people from the problem	*Relationship Building* • Separate the people from the problem • Accommodate their style and pace
Information Exchange • Exchange task-related information • Clarify positions	*Information Exchange* • Exchange task- and participant-related information • Clarify interests	*Information Exchange* • Exchange task- and participant-related information • Clarify interests and customary approaches
Persuasion	*Inventing Options for Mutual Gain*	*Inventing Options for Mutual Gain Appropriate to All Cultures Involved*
Concessions	*Choice of Best Option* • Insist on using objective criteria • Never yield to pressure	*Choice of Best Option* • Insist on using criteria appropriate to all cultures involved • Never yield to pressure
Agreement	*Agreement*	*Agreement* • Translate and back-translate agreement • If necessary, renegotiate

SOURCE: The traditional approach is based on John L. Graham and Roy A. Herberger, Jr., "Negotiators Abroad—Don't Shoot from the Hip," *Harvard Business Review*, vol. 61, no. 4 (1983), pp. 160–168. The principled approach is based on Roger Fisher and William Ury, *Getting to Yes* (Boston: Houghton Mifflin Company and Penguin Books, 1981). The synergistic approach is based on Nancy J. Adler (see Chapter 4). The table is adapted by Adler (2002) from the work of Dr. George Renwick (unpublished).

fraught with cross-cultural communication pitfalls. By contrast, the fourth step can become easier. Inventing options for mutual gain requires recognizing and using differences. The fewer identical options sought by both negotiating teams, the greater the chances of simultaneously satisfying each teams' needs. If teams recognize, clearly communicate, and understand cross-cultural differences (steps 1, 2, and 3), the differences themselves can become the basis for constructing win-win solutions. Western European countries that import Indonesian batiks, for example, exchange an economically developed market for a labor-intensive good. The Europeans could not afford to hand make batiks in Europe, and the Indonesians could not command as high a price in stable currencies within their own country. This culturally synergistic approach, which uses cultural differences as a resource rather than a hindrance to organizational functioning, allows global negotiators to maximize benefits to all parties. Each step in the principled approach will be discussed as it relates to the four stages of the negotiating process.

Stages of a Negotiation

To prepare for an initial meeting, effective negotiators analyze the situation in terms of their own and their counterparts' needs, goals, and underlying cultural values, determine the limits to their authority, assess power positions and relationships, identify facts to be confirmed, set an agenda, establish overall and alternative concession strategies, and make team assignments. They also determine their *best alternative to a negotiated solution* (18); that is, the most favorable outcome in the event that they fail to reach agreement. This best alternative to a negotiated solution, unlike a conventional *bottom line,* protects negotiators against "accepting terms that are too unfavorable and rejecting terms it would be in . . . [their] interest to accept" (18:104).

Planning

The Huthwaite Research Group conducted a study in the United Kingdom on the behavior of successful negotiators (50). The researchers interviewed and observed successful negotiators in more than 100 negotiations. Negotiators were only considered successful if they were rated as effective by both sides, had a track record of significant success, and had a low incidence of implementation failure. As highlighted in Table 7-5, successful negotiators' planning behavior differed in the following ways from that of their less-skilled colleagues (50):

TABLE 7-5 How Successful Negotiators Plan

Planning Behavior	Skilled Negotiators	Average Negotiators
Planning Time Overall time spent planning	No significant difference	No significant difference
Exploration of Options Number of options and outcomes considered per issue	5.1	2.6
Common Ground Percentage of comments about areas of anticipated common ground	38%	11%
Long Term Percentage of comments about long-term considerations of issues	8.5%	4%
Planned Order: Issues versus Sequences Average planned use of issues versus sequences per session	Issues 2.1	Sequences 4.9
Setting Limits	Range	Fixed-point

SOURCE: Adapted by Adler, 2002. From N. Rackham, *The Behavior of Successful Negotiators*. Copyright © 1976, Huthwaite Research Group, Reston, VA. Reprinted by permission.

- *Planning time.* Both skilled and average negotiators use about the same amount of time for planning. "It is not the amount of planning time that makes the difference, but how the time is used" (50).
- *Exploring options.* Skilled negotiators consider twice as wide a range of action options and outcomes as do their less-skilled colleagues. The greater the number of options, the greater are the chances for success.
- *Establishing common ground.* Although all negotiators focus more on areas of conflict than agreement, skilled negotiators spend over three times as much attention focusing on common ground.
- *Focusing on the long term.* All negotiators spend the vast majority of their time on short-term issues. Skilled negotiators, however, spend more than twice as much time focusing on long-term issues.
- *Setting limits.* Average negotiators set single point objectives, such as requesting $70 per unit. Skilled negotiators set range objectives, such as requesting $50 to $100 per unit. Setting ranges gives skilled negotiators more bargaining flexibility.
- *Using issue versus sequence planning.* Average negotiators use se-

quence planning. They plan to discuss point A, then point B, then point C, and so on. Skilled negotiators, by contrast, use issue planning. They discuss each issue independently, without any predetermined sequence or order.

Following the preparation, formal negotiations proceed through four stages (23;27):

1. Building interpersonal relationship
   (learning about the people)
2. Exchanging task-related information
   (learning about the economic, legal, technical, and logistical issues)
3. Persuading
4. Making concessions and agreements

Countries vary in the emphasis they place on each phase and their style in approaching each phase. As shown in Table 7-4, effective negotiators can use principled strategies to approach each stage:

- to build interpersonal relationships, principled negotiators separate the people from the problem;
- to exchange task-related information, principled negotiators focus on interests, not on positions;
- to effectively persuade the other team, principled negotiators invent options for mutual gain, rather than relying on preconceived positions and high pressure "dirty tricks"; and
- to make appropriate concessions and reach agreement, principled negotiators insist on using objective decision criteria.

Building Interpersonal Relationships

The first phase of a face-to-face negotiation involves getting to know the other people and helping them to feel comfortable. Every negotiation involves the relationship (you and them) and the substance (what you and they want). During relationship building, parties develop respect and trust for members of the other team. Nontask sounding begins the relationship-building process of discovering general areas of similarity and difference in both the relationship and the substance. Similarities become the basis for personal relationships and trust; differences, the basis for mutual exchange. The strategy of separating the people from the problem implies that negotiators can reject their partners' suggestions without rejecting the people themselves, that they can disagree with their counterparts' analysis without labeling them negatively, and that they can enjoy and trust their counterparts as individuals while rejecting their proposals.

Being particularly task- and efficiency-oriented, Americans usually see little need to "waste time" on getting to know people in nontask-related conversations. Americans want to "get down to business"—to discussing and agreeing on task-related issues—almost immediately, often after only five to ten minutes. The U.S. legal system also supports a task-oriented approach. Americans base their transactions on written contracts. Businesspeople in the United States trust the legal system to enforce written agreements (contracts) once all parties involved have signed them. Americans consequently focus on signing contracts rather than developing meaningful relationships with members of the other teams. The American approach and legal system, however, is not replicated in most countries. Many areas of the world have neither strong nor consistently dependable legal systems to enforce contracts. Enforcement mechanisms are personal. People keep commitments to people, not to contracts. People honor contracts if they like and respect the people with whom they are conducting business. They emphasize the personal relationship, not the written agreement.

Americans need to emphasize building relationships with their global partners. They need to discuss broader topics than just business, including the arts, history, culture, and current economic conditions of the countries involved. Effective negotiators view luncheon, dinner, reception, ceremony, and tour invitations as times for interpersonal relationship building and therefore as key to the negotiating process. When American negotiators, often frustrated by seemingly endless formalities, ceremonies, and "small talk," ask how long they must wait before beginning to "do business," the answer is simple: wait until your counterparts bring up business (and they will). Realize that the work of conducting a successful negotiation has already begun, even if business has yet to be mentioned.

Exchanging Task-Related Information

The substance of a negotiation is interests: yours and theirs. Negotiators should therefore focus on presenting their situation and needs, and on understanding their counterparts' situation and needs. Presenting interests—a situation and needs—is not the same as stating a position. A position articulates only one solution for a particular situation from one party's perspective (usually the solution prepared prior to the negotiation). Stating positions limits the ways in which your interests (and by implication, your counterparts' interests) can be met. If, for example, based on an analysis of my personal and family needs (housing, clothing, food, transportation, children's education, health care, and entertainment), I tell my employer that I must have a minimum foreign service salary of $200,000 (a position) to transfer to Hong Kong and she refuses to go above $175,000, we quickly arrive at an impasse. My employer finds $200,000, my one solution to my needs, unacceptable. If, on the other hand, I present my situation and needs, my employer may offer me $175,000 plus company-paid medical insurance, company-owned housing, and use of a company car. Would this offer meet my needs? Perhaps. Would it meet my initial position? No. Focusing on interests rather than positions allows both sides to draw on the widest possible range of mutually agreeable solutions.

In negotiating, cross-cultural miscommunication causes numerous problems. When the Iranians, for example, misinterpreted a bargaining offer presented in English by the United Nations it made the Iranian hostage crisis more difficult to resolve:

> In early 1980, United Nations Secretary General Waldheim flew to Iran to deal with the hostage . . . [crisis]. His efforts were seriously set back when Iranian national radio and television broadcast in Persian a remark he reportedly made on his arrival in Tehran: "I have come as a mediator to work out a compromise." Within an hour of the broadcast, his car was being stoned by angry Iranians (18:34). Why?
>
> In Persian, the word *compromise* . . . lacks the positive meaning it has in English (a "midway solution both sides can live with") and has only a negative meaning ("her virtue was compromised" or "our integrity was compromised"). Similarly, the word *mediator* in Persian suggests "meddler," someone who is barging in uninvited.

A clear understanding of the interests of negotiators from other cultures is difficult. Verbal and nonverbal barriers dramatically influence understanding and outcomes. Misperception, misinterpretation, and misevaluation pervade cross-cultural situations. To begin to understand, effective negotiators try to see the situation from both their own and the other parties' perspectives. Many negotiators use role reversal: they prepare for the negotiation as if they were the other party. Reversing roles forces them to appreciate the situation and issues from the other negotiating team's point of view.

Persuading

In principled, synergistic negotiations, bargainers emphasize creating mutually beneficial options, whereas more traditional negotiators often emphasize persuading the other party to accept a particular option. Creating mutually beneficial options is particularly important for global negotiators. (This chapter reviews the most common methods of persuasion used both domestically and globally in the section on negotiating tactics.)

In successful negotiations, all parties' interests and needs are recognized and satisfied, and therefore all parties win. Effective synergistic negotiators view their counterparts' interests and needs as a part of their own problem. Mutually beneficial options derive from (a) understanding each party's real interests, values, and needs, (b) identifying areas of similarity and difference, and (c) creating new options based primarily on the differences between the parties. Identifying interests more highly valued by one party than the other and using such differences as a resource underlies the creation of mutually beneficial options.

In cross-cultural negotiations, the possibilities for inventing mutually beneficial options exceed those in single-culture situations due to the inherent differences among the parties. If, for example, a company tells its employees that they cannot all take their vacations at the same time, management will probably have a problem in selecting who will receive time off during the holiday season. If all employees are Christian, most will want their vacation during Christmas week. If some employees are Christian and others Jewish, some will be happiest with a Christmas vacation while others will prefer time off during Hanukkah (which rarely coincides with Christmas), Pesah, or the high holidays. Cross-cultural differences, when recognized, facilitate mutually beneficial solutions that are impossible when all employees share similar cultural and religious backgrounds.

Making Concessions and Reaching Agreement

In this fourth stage, principled negotiators insist on using objective criteria in deciding how to make concessions and to reach agreement, rather than resorting to a series of dirty tricks. Although numerous high-pressure tactics exist, such tactics diminish both the relationships and the possibility of developing synergistic solutions. (Specific tactics to avoid will be discussed later.)

Concessions, large or small, can be made at any time during a negotiation. Although the research is not definitive, it appears that negotiators who make early concessions disadvantage themselves in comparison with those making fewer concessions primarily at the end of the bargaining sessions (52). Americans generally negotiate sequentially: they discuss and attempt to agree on one issue at a time. Throughout the bargaining process, Americans make many small concessions, which they expect their counterparts to reciprocate; then they finalize the list of concessions into an overall agreement. In some ways, making small concessions reflects Americans' task-oriented form of relationship building. Negotiators from many other cultures, unlike most Americans, discuss all issues prior to making any concessions. These negotiators view concessions as relative and make them only as they reach a final agreement. This holistic approach to negotiating is particularly evident in Asia.

Similar to many Asians, most Russian negotiators make very few, if any, concessions during a negotiation and rarely reciprocate the other party's concessions. Unlike many of their colleagues, Russian negotiators generally view concessions as signs of weakness, not as gestures of goodwill, flexibility, or trust. In the seven rounds of postwar negotiations between the former Soviet and U.S. governments, for example, the United States made 82 percent of its concessions in the first round, considerably more than did the Russians (35). Mikhail Gorbachev's and Boris Yeltsin's styles in implementing political change in the former Soviet Union highlight the Russian approach to negotiation.

No single approach to concessions has proven to succeed more consistently than has any other in negotiating globally. Effective global negotiators respect their own and their counterparts' domestic styles, and when appropriate, adjust accordingly. The story in the Box on page 197 highlights differences in whom Malaysians and Americans select to negotiate and how negotiators from these two contrasting cultures perform.

NEGOTIATION TACTICS

Negotiating includes both verbal and nonverbal tactics. Whereas most Americans consider verbal tactics most important, many people from other countries do not agree. According to one study, words communicate only 7 percent of meaning, with tone of voice communicating 38

CONTRASTING STYLES:
MALAYS NEGOTIATING WITH AMERICANS[1]

Americans' patterns of negotiating differ depending on the context. Government officials working out a treaty, for example, negotiate somewhat differently from business executives "hammering out" a contract. The pattern portrayed here reflects that of business executives.

American businesspeople usually begin a series of negotiating sessions in a cordial manner, but they express their intent to "get things under way." They are very clear as to what they and their company want, when they want it, and how they will go about getting it; they have planned their strategy carefully. And they have done what they could to "psych out" their counterparts with whom they will be negotiating.

From the outset, American negotiators urge everyone to "dispense with the formalities" and get down to the business at hand. As soon as possible they express their determination, saying something like, "O.K., let's get down to brass tacks."

Americans usually state their position (at least their first position) early and definitively. They plan before long to "really get down to the nitty gritty." They want to "zero in" on the knotty problems and get to the point where "the rubber meets the road" (the point, that is, where "the action" begins). Once the negotiations are "really rolling," Americans usually deal directly with obstacles as they come up, trying to clear them away in quick order, and becoming impatient and frustrated if they cannot.

Most of what Americans want to convey, of course, they put into words: spoken words—often many of them. Their approach, therefore, is highly verbal, quite visible, and thoroughly planned. They outline their alternatives and prepare their counterproposals, contingencies, back-up positions, bluffs, guarantees, and tests of compliance ahead of time; all carefully calculated, and, of course, including lots of numbers. Toward the end of the negotiation, they see that the agreement includes some bail-out provisions, but they usually don't worry too much about them. Making and meeting business commitments "on schedule" is what the American businesspeople's lives are all about— they are not too concerned about getting out of a contract. If they have to get out, then they have to, and they will find a way when the time comes.   *continued on next page* ∎

■ continued from previous page

Americans experience real satisfaction when all the problems have been "worked out," especially if they have been able to get provisions very favorable to their company—and to their own reputation as "tough negotiators." They rest securely when everything is "down in black and white" and the contract is initialed or signed.

Afterwards, Americans enjoy themselves; they relax "over some drinks" and carry on some "small talk" and "joke around" with their own team and their counterparts.

Malay patterns of negotiation, as might be expected, differ markedly from those of the Americans. When they are buying something, Malays bargain with the merchant; and when they are working, they socialize with their boss and coworkers. Their purpose is to develop a sense of relationship with the other person. The relationship then provides the basis, or context, for the exchange. Malays take the same patterns and preferences into their business-negotiating sessions. When all is said and done, it is not the piece of paper they trust, it is the people and their relationships with the people.

Malay negotiators begin to develop the context for negotiating through the interaction routines appropriate to this and similar occasions. These routines are as complicated and subtle as customary American routines; they are cordial but quite formal. Like Americans using their own routines, Malays understand the Malay routines but are seldom consciously aware of them. Neither Malays nor Americans understand very clearly the routines of the other.

To form the preliminary context, it is important to Malays that the proper forms of address be known beforehand and used, and that a variety of topics be talked about that are unrelated to the business to be transacted. This preliminary interaction may continue for quite a while. Malay negotiators want their counterparts to participate comfortably, patiently, and with interest. As in other interactions, it is not the particular words spoken that are of most importance to Malays; rather they listen primarily to the attitudes the words convey, attitudes toward the Malays themselves and toward the matters being negotiated. Attitudes are important to the relationship. At this point and throughout the negotiations, Malays remain concerned as much about the quality of the relationship as the quantity of work accomplished. Motivation is more important to Malays than momentum.

continued on next page ■

■ *continued from previous page*

Malay negotiators, as in other situations, are also aware of feelings—their own and those of their counterparts, and the effects of the exchanges upon both. They are also aware of, and concerned about, how they look in the eyes of their team, how their counterparts look in the eyes of the other team, and how both they and their counterparts will look in the eyes of their respective superiors after the negotiations.

Malays are alert to style, both their own and that of their counterparts. They consider displaying manners as more important than scoring points. Malays value the way one negotiates as well as what one negotiates. Grace and finesse show respect for the other and for the matters under consideration. Negotiating, like other interaction, is something of an art form. Balance and restraint are therefore essential.

The agenda Malays work through in the course of the negotiation usually remains quite flexible. Their strategy is usually rather simple. Malays express their positions in more general terms than do Americans', but hold them no less strongly. They offer their proposals to the other party more than arguing them. Malays do not enjoy sparring. They deeply dislike combat.

In response to a strong assertion, Malay negotiators usually express their respect directly by replying indirectly. The stronger the assertion and the more direct the demands, the more indirect the reply—at least the verbal reply.

Malay teams usually formulate their position gradually and carefully. By the time they present their position, they usually have quite a lot of themselves invested in it. Directly rejecting the position, therefore, is sometimes felt to be a rejection of the people holding the position. Negotiating for Malays is not quite the game that it is for some Americans.

If Malays and their team have arrived at a position from which they and those whom they represent cannot move, they will not move. If it requires a concession from their counterparts, Malays will not try to force the concession. If the counterparts see that a concession is necessary, therefore, and make it, Malays, as polite and considerate people, recognize the move and respect the people who made it. The Malay team usually does not consider a concession as a sign that they can press harder and extract further concessions. Instead, Malays consider a concession by either side as evidence of strength and a basis for subsequent reconciliation and cooperation.

continued on next page ■

■ *continued from previous page*

What about getting out of a contract? Making and meeting business commitments is not what Malays' lives are all about. They have other, often prior, commitments. They therefore enter into contracts cautiously and prefer to have an exit provided.

In addition, Malays are less certain of their control over the future (even their control over their own country) than are Americans. Malays, therefore, often find promising specific kinds of performance in the future by specific dates in a contract, especially in a long-term contract where the stakes are high, difficult. They find promising even more difficult, of course, if they are not certain whether they can trust the people to whom they are making commitments and from whom they are accepting commitments. Malays therefore give a great deal of thought to a contract and to the contracting parties before signing it. And Malays become uneasy if provisions have not been made for a respectable withdrawal should future circumstances make their compliance impossible.

NEGOTIATING FOR OLYMPIC COVERAGE[2]

The Olympic Committee for the Los Angeles Olympics negotiated television broadcasting rights with various countries. From the American Broadcasting Company (ABC), the Olympic Committee received $225 million. From the Japanese, the Committee received $18.5 million. Why did the Japanese pay so much less?

The Japanese originally offered $6 million for the rights and the Olympic Committee countered with $90 million. The Committee's goal was $10 million. The Japanese argued that theirs was a smaller market than that of the United States. Moreover, the Japanese had only one Japanese television station bidding, whereas the Americans had all three major networks bidding up the price (ABC, CBS, and NBC). High expectations (for a low price), convincing arguments (smaller market), and little competition resulted in a final cost to the Japanese network that was twelve times lower than that of its American counterparts.

percent and facial expression 55 percent (45). Both verbal and nonverbal behavior often cause problems cross-culturally. According to global negotiations experts, "It's hard to read the writing on the wall if you don't know the language, much less where to find the wall" (50:3.18). The following section, reviews some of the most common verbal and nonverbal negotiating tactics. Several "dirty tricks" are described, which, although common, do not particularly help in arriving at mutually beneficial agreements.

Verbal Tactics

Negotiators use many verbal tactics. Research (23) has shown that negotiators do better—their profits increase—as (a) the number of questions asked increases; (b) the number of commitments made prior to the final agreement decreases; and (c) the amount of the initial request increases, that is, sellers ask for more and buyers offer less. Consequently, in most cultures, effective negotiators start by having high expectations and making high initial offers (or requests), proceed by asking a lot of questions, and refrain from making many commitments until the final stage of the negotiation.

Initial Offers

The Chinese (43;49) and Russians (32) habitually use extreme initial offers and requests as their opening bargaining strategy. By contrast, Swedes initially request a price close to the one they expect to get. Americans negotiating domestically consistently reach higher and more satisfactory outcomes using extreme rather than moderate opening offers (52). Other research also suggests that bargainers starting with extreme positions have a higher probability of reaching an agreement (40).

Why do extreme initial positions help? Although not yet thoroughly researched cross-culturally, extreme positions are believed by some experts to (a) demonstrate to counterparts that the negotiator will not be exploited (52), (b) allow negotiators to gain more than expected, (c) prolong the negotiating process, thus allowing negotiators to gain more information about their counterparts, (d) modify counterparts' beliefs about the negotiator's preferences, (e) create more room to make subsequent concessions and thus exhibit cooperation, and (f) communicate negotiators' willingness to play the game according to "usual" norms (70:727). Exceptions to the advantages of high initial offers also exist.

TABLE 7-6 Verbal Negotiating Tactics

Tactic	Description	Example
PROMISE	I will do something you want me to do, if you do something I want you to do.	I will lower the price by $50 if you increase the order by 100 units.
THREAT	I will do something you don't want me to do, if you do something I don't want you to do.	I'll walk out of the negotiation if you leak this story to the press.
RECOMMENDATION	If you do something I want you to do, a third party will do something you want.	If you lower your price, more teenagers will be able to buy your product.
WARNING	If you do something I don't want you to do, a third party will do something you don't want.	If you don't settle, the press will spill this whole sordid story on the front page of every newspaper in the country.
REWARD	I will give you something positive (something you want) now, on the spot.	Let's make it easier on you tomorrow and meet closer to your office. I have really appreciated your willingness to meet at my building.
PUNISHMENT	I will give you something negative (something you don't want) now, on the spot.	I refuse to listen to your screaming. I am leaving.
NORMATIVE APPEAL	I appeal to a societal norm.	Everybody else buys our product for $5 per unit.
COMMITMENT	I will do something you want.	I will deliver 100 units by June 15.
SELF-DISCLOSURE	I will tell you something about myself.	We have had to lay off 100 employees this month. We really need to sign a major contract by the end of the year.
QUESTION	I ask you something about yourself.	Can you tell me more about your Brazilian operation?
COMMAND	I order you to do something.	Lower your price.

Japanese diplomats who make extreme opening offers in global negotiations, for example, often have them treated as phony by the other team (1). More importantly, extreme offers appear to discourage synergistic agreements. The following news report highlights the contrasting expectations of American and Japanese negotiators.

Range of Tactics

Some of the more common tactics used in negotiating include promises, threats, recommendations, warnings, rewards, punishments, normative appeals, commitments, self-disclosure, questions, and commands. Table 7-6 describes each briefly. The use and meaning of many of these tactics vary across cultures. As shown in Table 7-7, negotiators from Asia (Japanese), North America (Americans), and South America (Brazilians) use different verbal tactics in negotiating (25). Brazilians, for example, say no nine times more frequently than do Americans, and almost fifteen times more frequently than do the Japanese. Similarly, Brazilians make more initial concessions than do Americans, who in turn make more than the Japanese (25).

The British Huthwaite study, documenting successful negotiators' behavior, analyzed the verbal behavior of skilled and average negotiators (50:6.6–6.13). As shown in Table 7-8, the most skillful British negotiators use fewer irritators, counterproposals, and defend/attack spirals, less argument dilution, and more behavioral labels, active listening, questions, and feeling commentaries. Each of these negotiating tactics is described briefly below.

- *Irritators* refer to words that, although having negligible value in persuading counterparts, cause annoyance. Irritators include such phrases as "generous offer," "fair price," and "reasonable arrangement." Average negotiators use over four times as many irritators as do skilled negotiators.
- *Counterproposals* involve negotiators responding to their counterparts' proposals by simply offering their own proposal. Average negotiators use counterproposals twice as often as skilled negotiators. Skilled negotiators clarify their understanding of counterparts' suggestions before responding with their own proposals.
- *Defend/attack spiral.* Negotiating, by definition, involves conflict. That conflict often leads to heated, value-ladened accusations and defensive statements. Average negotiators frequently respond defen-

TABLE 7-7 Verbal Negotiating Behaviors: How Do Cultures Vary?

Verbal Negotiating Behavior (Tactic)	Average Number of Times Tactic Was Used in Half-Hour Negotiating Sessions		
	BRAZIl	JAPAN	UNITED STATES
Promise	3	7	8
Threat	2	4	4
Recommendation	5	7	4
Warning	1	2	1
Reward	2	1	2
Punishment	3	1	3
Normative appeal	1	4	2
Commitment	8	15	13
Self-disclosure	39	34	36
Question	22	20	20
Command	14	8	6
No's (per 30 minutes)	83	6	9.0
Profit level of first offers (80 max.)	75	62	57.3
Initial concessions	9	7	7.1

SOURCE: Adapted by Adler, 2002. From John Graham, "The Influence of Culture on Business Negotiations," in *Journal of International Business Studies*, vol. 16, no. 1 (1985), pp. 81–96. Reprinted by permission of the Journal of International Business Studies, Newark, NJ.

sively and often attack the other team, first gently and then harder and harder. Skilled negotiators, by contrast, rarely respond defensively. Although they also rarely attack, when they do so, they hit hard and without warning. Average negotiators attack more than three times as frequently as do skilled negotiators.

- *Behavioral labeling* refers to describing what you plan to say before you say it. For example, "Can I ask a question?" and "Can I make a suggestion?" are behavioral labels for asking a question and making a suggestion. Behavioral labels forewarn counterparts. For all behavior except disagreement, skilled negotiators use labeling over five times as often as their average colleagues. Average negotiators label disagreement three times as often as do skilled negotiators.

- *Active listening* involves demonstrating to oneself and one's counterpart that the previous statement has been understood. Active listening does not convey agreement or approval, it strictly reflects understanding. Skilled negotiators use two powerful active listening techniques—testing for understanding and summarizing—more than twice as often as their average colleagues.

TABLE 7-8 How Successful Negotiators Negotiate

Negotiating Behavior	Skilled Negotiators	Average Negotiators
Use of *irritators* per hour of face-to-face negotiating time	2.3	10.8
Frequency of *counterproposals* per hour of face-to-face negotiating time	1.7	3.1
Percent of negotiator's time classified as a *defense/attack spiral*	1.9%	6.3%
Percent of all negotiator's behavior immediately preceded by a *behavioral label*		
Disagreeing	0.4%	1.5%
All behavior except disagreeing	6.4%	1.2%
Percent of negotiator's time spent *actively listening*		
Testing for understanding	9.7%	4.1%
Summarizing	7.5%	4.2%
Questions, as a percent of all negotiating behavior	21.3%	9.6%
Feelings commentary, giving internal information as a percent of all negotiating behavior	12.1%	7.8%
Argument dilution, average number of reasons given by negotiators to back each argument or case they advance	1.8	3.0

SOURCE: Adapted by Adler, 2002. From N. Rackham, *The Behavior of Successful Negotiators*, Copyright © 1976, Huthwaite Research Group, Reston, VA. Reprinted by permission.

- *Questions* are a primary source of gathering information. Skilled negotiators use more than twice as many questions as do average negotiators.
- *Feelings commentary* involves describing what a person feels about a situation. A negotiator might say, "I'm uncertain how to react to what you've just said. If the information you've given me is true, then I would like to accept it; yet I feel some doubts inside me about its accuracy. So part of me feels happy and part feels suspicious. Can you help me resolve this?" Skilled negotiators give almost twice as much feelings commentary as do average negotiators.
- *Argument dilution.* Weak arguments generally dilute strong arguments. Skilled negotiators know that the fewer arguments, the better. Average negotiators use almost twice as many reasons to back each of their positions as do skilled negotiators.

In summary, the Huthwaite group found that skilled British negotiators avoid irritators, counterproposals, defend/attack spirals, and argument dilution. They use behavioral labeling (except for disagreement), active listening, questions, and feelings commentaries. Unfortunately, this important study has not yet been replicated worldwide.

Nonverbal Tactics

Nonverbal behavior refers to what negotiators do rather than what they say. It involves how they say their words, rather than the words themselves. Nonverbal behavior includes the negotiators' tone of voice, facial expressions, body distance, dress, gestures, timing, silences, and symbols. Nonverbal behavior is complex and multifaceted; it sends multiple messages, many of which are responded to subconsciously. Negotiators frequently respond more emotionally and powerfully to the nonverbal than the verbal message, often leading to positive or negative spirals which directly affect the outcome of the negotiation (19).

As with verbal behavior (language), nonverbal behavior varies markedly across cultures. As shown in Table 7-9, the extent to which Americans, Brazilians, and Japanese use silence, conversational overlaps, facial gazing, and touching during a negotiation varies considerably (25).

Silence

Japanese use the most silence, Americans a moderate amount, and Brazilians almost none at all. Americans often respond to silence by

TABLE 7-9 Nonverbal Negotiating Behaviors Vary Across Cultures

Behavior (Tactic)	AMERICANS	BRAZILIANS	JAPANESE
SILENT PERIODS Number of silent periods greater than 10 seconds, per 30 minutes	3.5	0	5.5
CONVERSATIONAL OVERLAPS Number of overlaps per 10 minutes	10.3	28.6	12.6
FACIAL GAZING Minutes of gazing per 10 minutes	3.3	5.2	1.3
TOUCHING Not including handshaking, per 30 minutes	0	4.7	0

SOURCE: From John Graham, "The Influence of Culture on the Negotiation Process," in *Journal of International Business Studies*, vol. 16, no. 1 (1985), pp. 81–96. Reprinted by permission of the *Journal of International Business Studies*, Newark, NJ.

assuming that the other team disagrees or has not accepted their offer. Moreover, they tend to argue and make concessions in response to silence. This response does not cause problems in negotiating with Brazilians, but it severely disadvantages Americans when they negotiate with Japanese. While the Japanese silently consider the Americans' offer, the Americans interpret the silence as rejection and respond by making concessions (e.g., by lowering the price). Similar dynamics occur when nonnative English speakers negotiate in English. As the nonnative English speakers hesitate, to make certain that they fully understand the meaning of the English words, Americans frequently assume that they are rejecting the Americans' position. Again, they tend to misinterpret the silence as rejection and respond by making unnecessary concessions.

Conversational Overlaps

Conversational overlaps are the opposite of silent periods; they occur when more than one person speaks at the same time. As shown in Table 7-9 and Figure 7-3, Brazilian negotiators interrupt each other more than twice as often as do either American or Japanese negotiators (25). Multiple members of the Brazilian team frequently talk simultaneously. By contrast, when Japanese or American negotiators start speaking at the same time, one or the other speaker generally stops talking—thus minimizing the conversational overlap. Cultures, such as the American and Japanese, in which people do not talk while another person is talking, generally interpret conversational overlaps as rude and disrespectful behavior.

Facial Gazing

Facial gazing involves looking directly in the face of one's counterpart. Eye contact is one of the most intense forms of facial gazing. The amount of eye contact and facial gazing often communicates the level of intimacy in a relationship—the more eye contact, the more intimacy. Confusion occurs when the appropriate amount of gazing for one culture communicates too much or too little intimacy for people from another culture. In both cases bargaining partners from the other culture feel uncomfortable. Brazilians use four times as much facial gazing as Japanese, and one and one-half times more than Americans (25).

Touching

Whether negotiators touch each other during bargaining sessions depends on the cultures involved. Not including handshaking, Brazilian negotiators touch each other almost five times every half hour, whereas

FIGURE 7-3 Conversational Overlaps: Who Interrupts Whom?

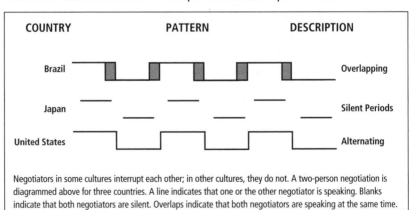

COUNTRY	PATTERN	DESCRIPTION
Brazil		Overlapping
Japan		Silent Periods
United States		Alternating

Negotiators in some cultures interrupt each other; in other cultures, they do not. A two-person negotiation is diagrammed above for three countries. A line indicates that one or the other negotiator is speaking. Blanks indicate that both negotiators are silent. Overlaps indicate that both negotiators are speaking at the same time.

SOURCE: Adapted by Adler, 2002. From John Graham, "The Influence of Culture on the Negotiation Process," in *Journal of International Business Studies*, vol. 16, no. 1 (1985), pp. 81–96. Reprinted by permission of the *Journal of International Business Studies*, Newark, NJ.

there is no physical contact between American or Japanese negotiators (25). Similar to facial gazing, touching communicates intimacy. A hug—*a double abrazo*—in Mexico communicates the development of a trusting relationship, whereas the same gesture offends Germans, for whom it communicates an in-appropriately high level of intimacy.

Dirty Tricks

Neither all domestic nor all global negotiators search for mutually beneficial agreements. In attempting to gain the most for themselves, some negotiators resort to "dirty tricks," tactics designed to pressure opponents into undesirable concessions and agreements. Negotiators can reduce the use of dirty tricks in the following ways (18):

1. Not using dirty tricks themselves
2. Recognizing dirty tricks when their counterparts use them, explicitly pointing them out, and negotiating about their use (i.e., establishing the "rules of the game")
3. Knowing what the cost of walking out is if the other party refuses to use principled negotiation (i.e., knowing what the best alternative is to a negotiated solution)
4. Realizing that tactics that appear "dirty" to people from another culture may seem completely acceptable to members of your team

Avoiding dirty tricks is more complex internationally than domestically. Effective negotiators systematically question their own interpretations of their counterparts' tactics rather than naïvely assuming that others' tactics have the same intended meanings as they would within the negotiator's home culture. Table 7-10 outlines a series of commonly used dirty tricks, including various types of deliberate deception, psychological warfare, and positional pressure tactics (18).

Reviewing the range of dirty tricks from a cross-cultural perspective reveals some of the possible misinterpretations global negotiators face. Brazilians, for example, expect more deception among negotiators who do not know each other than do Americans. Brazilians are therefore more likely to use "phony facts" during the initial stages of a global negotiation than are some of their counterparts (25;62). The recommendation therefore is: "Unless you have good reason to trust someone, don't!" (18).

A negotiating team's discretion (the extent of its authority) varies across cultures. Under communist regimes, Russians and Eastern Euro-

TABLE 7-10 What If They Use Dirty Tricks? Principled Responses to Unprincipled Tactics

Unprincipled Tactics	Examples of Unprincipled Tactics (Ex) and Principled Responses (R)
DELIBERATE DECEPTION	Tactics designed to make you believe something that is not true.
Phony Facts	R: Unless you have good reason to trust some one, don't.
Ambiguous Authority	R: "Alright. We'll treat it as a joint draft to which neither side is committed," or, "Good, you take it to your boss and I'll sleep on it. Then tomorrow either of us can suggest changes."
Dubious Intentions	R: Call their cards and build in a compliance system. Note that less than full disclosure is not the same as deception.
PSYCHOLOGICAL WARFARE	Tactics designed to make you feel uncomfortable, so that you will have a subconscious desire to end the negotiation as soon as possible.
Stressful Situation	Ex: Room too hot or too cold, no private place to talk, their turf, too much touching, etc.
	R: Bring it up and change it.
Personal Attacks	Ex: Opponent comments on your clothes, your appearance ("Were you up all night?"), your status (by interrupting with other business, making you wait), your intelligence (making you repeat things, not listening), refusing to make eye contact.
	R: Recognizing it usually nullifies it. Bringing it up usually ends it.
Good Guy/Bad Guy Routine	Ex: "The price is $4,000" (bad guy). "But, we can offer you $3,800" (good guy).
	R: "Why do you think $4,000 is a reasonable price? What is your principle?" Followed by a warning: "If the price is $4,000, X will happen."
POSITIONAL PRESSURE TACTICS	Bargaining tactics designed to structure a situation so that only one side can effectively make concessions.

continued on next page ■

■ *continued from previous page*

Refuse to Negotiate	R:	Ask why they refuse to negotiate. Will they be seen as weak? Suggest alternatives: negotiate through third parties, negotiate in private, send letters, etc.
Extreme Demands	Ex:	Asking for $100,000 when it is only worth $25,000.
	R:	Ask why they believe it is a reasonable price (demand). Bring tactic to their attention.
Escalating Demands	Ex:	Making one concession and then adding new demands or reopening old demands.
	R:	Call the tactic to their attention and then take a break while you consider which issues you are willing to continue to negotiate on.
Lock-in Tactics	Ex:	Committing to a course of action, usually publicly. Paradoxically, you strengthen your bargaining position as you weaken your control over the situation.
	R:	Don't take lock-in seriously. Resist lock-in on principle: "I understand you are publicly committed to X, but my practice is never to yield to pressure."
Hard-hearted Partner	Ex:	"I would agree, but my partner (i.e., boss) won't."
	R:	Get it in writing and/or negotiate directly with hard-hearted partner.
Calculated Delay	Ex:	Waiting for the 11th hour. (Danger: If the 11th hour arrives, the other side may continue waiting.)
	R:	Make delaying tactic explicit and negotiate about it. Also create objective deadlines (such as starting to negotiate with another firm).
Take It or Leave It	R:	Ignore it. Or, explicitly recognize it, let them know what they have to lose if no agreement is reached, and look for a face-saving way for them to back off.

SOURCE: Adapted by Adler, 2002. Based on R. Fisher and W. Ury, *Getting to Yes*, 1981, Penguin Press, New York, NY.

peans traditionally had very limited authority; they had to check with their superiors if they wanted to deviate at all from the planned agenda. Americans, by contrast, generally have extensive authority; they expect to make the most important decisions at the negotiating table. When the other team has limited authority, experts recommend making all commitments tentative and conditional on the ability of the other party to accept and commit to their side of the deal (20). In cross-cultural business situations, negotiators must remember that the other parties may not be using limited authority as a form of deliberate deception; they may simply come from cultures where the authorities delegate very little discretion to individual team members.

Psychological warfare (tactics designed to make the other person feel uncomfortable) has different meanings in different cultures. A common psychological trick, for example, involves too much touching or too little eye contact. As discussed earlier, both extremes make people uncomfortable; both make them want to get out of the situation quickly (and therefore conclude the negotiation as soon as possible). Problems arise in defining appropriate versus extreme amounts of touching and eye contact across cultures. Latins touch much more than Canadians, who in turn touch more than Swedes. Arabs maintain much greater eye contact than do Americans, who in turn use more than the Japanese. What appears to be a dirty trick from a domestic perspective may, in fact, simply express another culture's typical behavior. As with other potentially inappropriate tactics, negotiators must differentiate intended psychological warfare from unintended expressions of a culture's normal behavior patterns.

CASES FOR REFLECTION

Global firms constantly confront business situations involving cross-cultural negotiating that challenge their notions of effective and ethical behavior. In the following two situations, "Off the Books Payments" and "Extremely High Freight-Forwarding Fees," the senior management team of a major North American–based transnational firm must ethically and effectively manage the immediate situation as well as set a policy to guide managers' behavior in the future. Analyze each situation from both cultures' perspectives before choosing how to manage the immediate situation and recommending a more general corporate policy governing all such situations. Decide whether the parties involved are using dirty tricks or culturally appropriate behavior.

OFF THE BOOKS PAYMENTS

Prestige, a North American-based global firm, sent American Frank Quick to the Middle East to scout out possibilities for increasing the market for a particular Prestige product. Two other global firms compete directly with Prestige for this market, Companies Y and Z.

Frank has spent a year in one Middle Eastern country and has made considerable progress. He has made it quite clear to prospective buyers that Prestige offers a much better product than does the competition. Frank has been working especially hard to obtain a large order from the top officials of a large local company, Ajax, rather than having Ajax place their order with either Company Y or Z.

Ajax presently buys some products from Prestige and some from Companies Y and Z. While admitting that it regards Prestige's products as uniformly superior, Ajax claims it chooses to spread its business among the three suppliers as a hedge against possible failure of supply. Nonetheless, Frank is persisting in his dogged efforts to convince Ajax to choose Prestige as its sole supplier.

Recently, Ajax's vice president of purchasing invited Frank to his office and informed him that Ajax would be willing to gradually taper off business with Companies Y and Z, primarily because Prestige offers a better product. He adds, however, that under-the-table payments are rather common in his country, and proceeds to hint broadly that he accepts substantial payments from both of the other two companies. Subtly, he indicates that if Prestige pays him an amount equal to the combined payments of Companies Y and Z, Prestige will become Ajax's exclusive supplier. If Prestige refuses, however, he will keep Prestige's present contract at its existing level, while expanding Ajax's business with Companies Y and Z, who, he claims, are prepared to make even greater payments than they have made in the past.

Questions for Reflection

1. Under these circumstances, can Prestige continue to conduct any business with Ajax?
2. Does Prestige have an obligation to make public the described under-the-table payments of Companies Y and Z? How much loyalty does Prestige owe to other global firms operating in the host country's business community?

continued on next page ■

■ *continued from previous page*

3. Will making this information public force Companies Y and Z to lose their contracts with Ajax? Will such behavior work to Prestige's advantage or disadvantage?

Senior Management Committee Decisions

1. What should Prestige advise Frank to do? What should Prestige's overall policy on such payments be? Should Prestige walk away from companies or individuals who accept under-the-table payments?
2. Should Prestige expose the other companies? Why? Why not? What moral grounds does a company have to try to change the behavior of other companies?
3. What moral grounds does a company have to try to change the country?
4. What would you do if you were in Frank's position?

EXTREMELY HIGH FREIGHT-FORWARDING FEES

In a certain Asian country the only way companies can get raw materials, parts, and finished products through local customs is to use a local freight-forwarding agent at the airport, seaport, or other point of entry. These agents charge forwarding fees that seem extremely high to many outsiders. The explanation, though hard to pin down, appears to be that the freight-forwarding agents use some of the money that companies pay them to make under-the-table payments to local customs officials. When agents make such payments, shipments appear to clear customs more quickly, thus helping reduce the companies' cycle time.

Business has long been conducted in this way in this country, ostensibly because the government underpays local customs officials and offers them annual raises that do not keep pace with inflation. According to common knowledge, the government assumes that officials will receive part of their income from direct payments from companies and individuals needing customs assistance.

continued on next page ■

■ *continued from previous page*

When Prestige, a North American–based global company, originally entered this country some years ago, it believed that the government did not allow this sort of practice, nor did it take place. In the intervening years, however, the political milieu changed, along with a certain loosening of discipline among civil servants, due in part to surging inflation. Recently, expatriates working in this country for Prestige became increasingly convinced that the situation had become unacceptable, that such payments do not reflect good ethical practice, and that therefore they do not reflect good business practice.

Questions for Reflection

1. Given Prestige's corporate beliefs in the highest level of integrity and the utmost respect for people, what type of respect should Prestige's global managers show to customs and freight-forwarding agents who expect and accept unofficial payments from companies or individuals? How would your behavior change if you knew that typical customs officials in this particular country believe that, far from doing anything unethical, they would be acting unethically, given the inflationary situation, if they failed to accept some additional unofficial payments needed to feed their families and to educate their children? Would knowing the customs agents' appreciation of the situation change your judgment or behavior?

2. Who is to blame? Should Prestige blame the government rather than the individual customs and freight-forwarding agents? Does Prestige have any right to interfere with the procedures of customs and freight-forwarding agents in this, or any other, country?

3. Knowing that such practices exist, what responsibility does Prestige's management have in the host country? Should Prestige make it clear in a quiet but firm way that the company will not participate in such practices? To whom? Are there circumstances under which Prestige should publicly state its position on this issue? What other alternatives does Prestige have?

4. Should an individual Prestige manager who learns about such unofficial payments and reports them to his or her immediate supervisor without apparent effect, report the situation directly to senior management?

continued on next page ■

■ *continued from previous page*
Senior Management Committee Decisions
1. What constitutes ethical behavior in this case?
2. What should Prestige's policy be toward such payments in this country? In all countries?
3. How should Prestige implement this policy?
4. As an individual, what would you be willing to do if you were working in this country? What would you be unwilling to do? Why?

Whose Style to Use?

When should global negotiators continue to use their own cultural style of negotiating and when should they adopt the style of their counterparts? Global negotiations expert Stephen Weiss suggests that negotiators have five options, depending on the nature of the negotiation and the level of cross-cultural knowledge each negotiating team has (63;65;67;68). As outlined in Figure 7-4, if neither team is familiar with the other's culture, it would be best to consider employing agents to represent the teams. If your team has a high knowledge of their culture, but their team has a limited knowledge of your team's culture, you have the option of embracing their cultural approach to negotiating. If the opposite is true, and they have a high knowledge of your culture while you only have a limited knowledge of their culture, you can attempt to induce your counterparts to follow your culture's approach to negotiating. If both teams have a moderate knowledge of their counterparts' culture, both teams can adapt somewhat to each other's style. In the ideal situation, in which both teams have an in-depth knowledge of the other's culture, the two teams can improvise an approach that works for them both, that is, they can create a culturally synergistic approach to the negotiation (see Chapter 4). Although no option guarantees a positive outcome, the higher the cross-cultural knowledge on the part of both negotiating teams, the more options open to them and the greater their chances of reaching a satisfactory agreement.

SUMMARY

"When in Rome, do as the Romans do?" No, when in Rome, or Beijing, or Prague, act like an effective foreigner. Lucian Pye, in his excellent

FIGURE 7-4 When Do I Adapt to Their Style? When Do I Use My Style? Culturally Responsive Negotiating Strategies

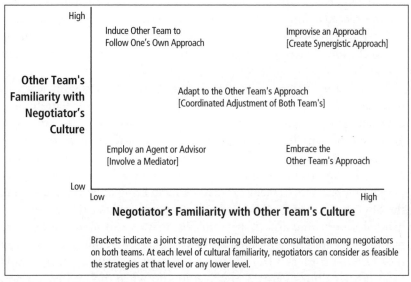

SOURCE: Adapted by Adler, 2002. From Stephen F. Weiss, "Negotiating with Romans—Part 1," in *Sloan Management Review*, Winter 1994, Copyright © *Sloan Management Review*. Reprinted with permission.

book, *Chinese Commercial Negotiating Style,* recommends that foreigners conducting business in the People's Republic of China (49:xii):

(a) practice patience; (b) accept prolonged periods of no movement; (c) control against exaggerated expectations, and discount Chinese rhetoric about future prospects; (d) expect that the Chinese will try to influence by shaming; (e) resist the temptation to believe that difficulties may have been caused by one's own mistakes; and (f) try to understand Chinese cultural traits, but never believe that a foreigner can practice them better than the Chinese.

Pye recommends recognizing and understanding the cultural differences, not trying to become a member of the other culture.

Negotiating styles clearly vary across cultures (3;33;55;58;59;60). Words and behavior that effectively persuade people at home fail to influence businesspeople from other countries. The cultural context of a negotiation significantly influences who should become a member of the negotiating team, where the parties should conduct the negotiation, and which approach—including strategy and tactics—negotiators should use. Negotiating globally requires acute observation skills and a more tentative approach to understanding meaning than its domestic counterpart. Not only does negotiating globally imply "not jumping to conclusions," it rarely allows negotiators to conclude a negotiation definitively.

In preparing to negotiate globally, team members should learn as much as possible about the other cultures—their negotiating patterns and especially their style of negotiating with outsiders (3)—and then approach the actual bargaining sessions with as wide a range of options and alternatives in behavior and substance as possible. In initial meetings, negotiators should emphasize developing a relationship with their bargaining partners (remembering to let them bring up business). During the discussions, negotiators should assume differences exist in negotiating styles until similarity is proven. Negotiators can more easily move from an expectation of difference to an acceptance of similarity than can they recoup their losses from mistakes incurred in acting as if negotiators from other cultures bargain just like you do when in fact they do not. Effective negotiators have high expectations and make high initial offers (or requests), proceed by asking a lot of questions, and refrain from making many commitments until the final stage of the negotiation. When bargaining, effective negotiators use fewer irritators, counterproposals, and defend/attack spirals, less argument dilution, and more behavioral labels, active listening, and feeling commentaries than do less skilled negotiators.

The most effective negotiators approach bargaining sessions searching for synergistic solutions—solutions in which both sides win. The art of negotiating lies in developing creative options and alternatives, not in using persuasive tactics that more often result in giving offense than in gaining agreement.

PART THREE

Managing Global Managers

8

Managing Cross-Cultural Transitions: Expatriate Entry and Reentry

If a man does not keep pace with his companions, perhaps it is because he hears a different drummer. Let him step to the music which he hears, however measured or far away.   — HENRY DAVID THOREAU, *Walden*

GLOBAL ASSIGNMENTS HAVE become an increasingly important, if not essential, part of managers' careers and a source of competitive advantage for global firms (10;14;52;73). However, this has not always been the case. Historically, companies have sent managers to live and work abroad for many reasons, depending primarily on the level of globalization of their industry and the firm's specific business strategy (1;7;19;24;36;54;55;64). As shown in Table 8-1, domestic firms, of course, have no business need to send anyone abroad. Multidomestic firms, by contrast, send people abroad to transfer technology, and, more important from the perspective of the firm, to maintain control over highly autonomous operations in countries around the world. Multi-domestic firms generally select home-country nationals—people who are known and trusted at headquarters—and send them abroad as *expatriates* to get a particular job done. Because the headquarters of multidomestic firms often (although generally erroneously) view international operations as simply replicating what they have already achieved at home, they rarely choose high-potential or top performers for expatriate assignments; rather they settle for average performers. When expatriates

221

TABLE 8-1 What's the Best Type of Global Assignment?
It All Depends on the Company's Business Strategy

Business Strategy	Domestic	Multidomestic	Multinational	Global
GLOBAL ASSIGNMENTS	None	Expatriates	Expatriates and inpatriates	Expatriates, inpatriates, and transpatriates
WHO IS SENT	No One	Home-country nationals sent abroad	Home-country nationals sent abroad and local nationals sent to headquarters	People sent from any country to any other country
	—	Average performers	Good performers	Superior performers: High-potential managers and senior executives
PURPOSE	—	Project (to get the job done abroad)	Project and career development	Project, career, and organizational development
CAREER IMPACT—		Negative for domestic career	Good for global career	Essential for executive suite
PROFESSIONAL REENTRY	—	Extremely difficult	Somewhat difficult	Much easier
GLOBAL ORGANIZATIONAL LEARNING	None	None	Limited	Extensive

from multidomestic firms return home, they often find no job waiting for them, little value given to the international experience they have gained, and receive no benefit to their overall career.

Luckily for expatriates, their experience improves as firms increase their commitment to global business. In contrast to both domestic and multidomestic firms, multinational firms operate highly integrated global lines of business. Multinational firms also send expatriates abroad; but rather than selecting average performers, they choose their best performers—both senior managers who can take responsibility for worldwide lines of business and more junior high-potential managers who need worldwide experience for their career development. Because multinationals are highly integrated, they stay in close contact with their expatriates while the latter are abroad and carefully fit them back into the organization when they return home. Professional reentry is therefore considerably easier for expatriates returning from global assignments in multinational firms than for those returning to multidomestic firms.

In addition to sending expatriates—home-country managers—abroad, multinationals also bring *inpatriates*—managers from various local cultures—into the home country on assignments designed to help them learn about the headquarters' organizational culture and approach to doing business. The headquarters then returns the inpatriates back to their local culture to manage local operations. Unfortunately, corporate learning at this stage is generally one-way: while teaching the inpatriates about the headquarters' culture, multinationals rarely spend any time learning from the inpatriates about their countries' local cultures and business environments.

Expatriate assignments in global firms differ markedly from those in domestic, multidomestic, and multinational firms. Because global firms operate in highly competitive, complexly networked global business environments, they need executives who understand the world and have had experience working on several continents and in numerous countries. Global firms therefore select the best people from anywhere in the world to transfer to anywhere else in the world. Rather than limiting themselves to transfers into and out of headquarters—that is, rather than limiting themselves either to expatriates (home-country nationals sent out to the rest of the world) or inpatriates (managers from throughout the world brought into headquarters)—global firms select *transpatriates*. Transpatriates' prime role is organizational development; they act as the glue that holds globally distributed firms together. For transpatriates to effectively fulfill this role, the organization must stay in close contact with them and actively learn as much as possible from them, both while they work abroad and once they have either returned home or moved on to another global assignment. Unlike their counterparts in domestic, multidomestic, and multinational firms, managers working abroad for global firms find that their experience abroad helps, rather than hinders, their career progress.

Although multidomestic, multinational, and global firms send people abroad for different reasons, in each case the person experiences a predictable series of stages in transferring from a domestic to a global assignment and back home again. As shown in Figure 8-1, companies recruit potential global managers either from within the organization or from other companies. The company then chooses whether to select the

FIGURE 8-1 The Expatriate's Global Career Cycle

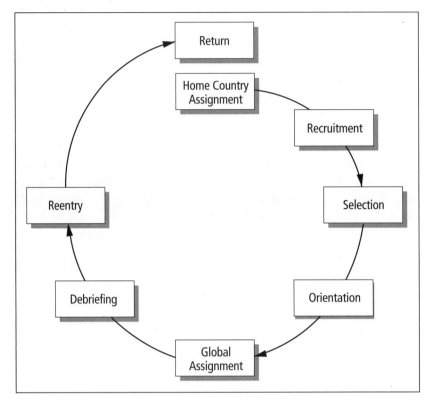

candidate, and the recruit chooses whether to accept the global assignment. Next, many companies provide orientation sessions describing the
global project and local foreign culture as well as the logistical arrangements for moving to a new country (13;15;20;32). Oriented managers,
accompanied by their families, then proceed abroad to accomplish the
assignment. Managers come back to their home country and either
return to positions within the same organization or leave the organization to find positions elsewhere. Few companies conduct reentry or
debriefing sessions. The complete expatriate global career cycle includes
two major international transitions: cross-cultural entry and home-
country reentry. The most successful global companies understand and
manage each phase of the expatriate global career cycle (18;21;33;34;
35;37;38;39;48;58;59;67;71;75;77;78;79;80).

FIGURE 8-2 Culture Shock Cycle: The Highs and The Lows

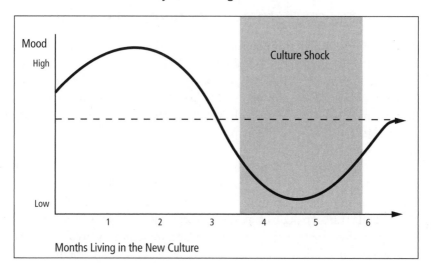

SUCCESSFULLY ENTERING A NEW CULTURE*

Cross-cultural adjustment consists of adjusting to the job, to interacting with host nationals, and to the general nonwork environment (17; also see 16;68). As shown in Figure 8-2, cross-cultural adjustment to a new country can be described as following a U-shaped curve (46). In the initial phase, at the top of the curve, expatriates enjoy a great deal of excitement as they discover the new culture. Business travelers, as compared with expatriates, often have the luxury of remaining at this stage. This initial phase is often followed by a period of disillusionment, during which it is no longer romantic to try to take a cab without knowing where to find the taxi stand; or to wait anxiously on Saturday for the arrival of a letter, only to discover that weekend mail delivery does not exist; or to try to converse intelligently using a severely limited vocabulary. The bottom of the U-shaped curve is marked by *culture shock*—the frustration and confusion that result from being bombarded by too many new and unin-terpretable cues. Following the culture shock phase, expatriates begin adapting to the new culture: they generally begin feeling more positive, working more effectively, and living a more satisfying life. Neither the highs of the initial phase nor the lows of the culture shock phase usually mark this subsequent adjustment phase.

* Note that in the following sections, the word *expatriate* is used to refer to expatriates, inpatriates, and transpatriates.

Experiencing Culture Shock: It Hits the Best the Hardest

Does everyone suffer from culture shock, or does it only afflict globally inexperienced managers and businesspeople moving to significantly different countries? Surprisingly, the most effective global managers often suffer the most severe culture shock (65). By contrast, global managers whom their colleagues evaluate as not particularly effective describe themselves as suffering little or no culture shock. Culture shock is not a disease, but rather a natural response to the stress of immersing oneself in a new environment. Economically and linguistically similar countries can cause culture shock as well as more dissimilar countries. Quebec-based executives experience culture shock arriving in France, as do the Australians transferring to Canada. Severe culture shock is often a positive sign indicating that the expatriate is becoming deeply involved in the new culture instead of remaining isolated in an expatriate ghetto. Experienced expatriates therefore should view culture shock as a sign that they are doing something right, not wrong. For them, the most important question thus becomes how best to manage the stress caused by culture shock, not how to avoid the culture shock itself.

What exactly is culture shock? Culture shock is the expatriate's reaction to a new, unpredictable, and therefore uncertain environment (9). As discussed in Chapter 3, culture shock results from a breakdown in a person's selective perception and interpretive systems. Global managers who have newly arrived in a foreign country ask such questions as "To what should I pay attention?" and "What does it mean?" Millions of sights, sounds, smells, tastes, and feelings bombard global managers, and they find it difficult to know which ones to treat as meaningful and which ones are unimportant and therefore best screened out. Upon entering a new culture, global managers lack an interpretive system based on the local culture and therefore inappropriately and ineffectively use their home culture's interpretive system.

During the initial period in a new culture, global managers often find that other people's behavior does not seem to make sense, and—even more disconcerting—that their own behavior does not produce expected results. They find that the environment makes new demands for which they have neither ready-made answers nor the ability to develop new, culturally appropriate responses. As a North American newly arrived in the Middle East, for example, described:

My third day in Israel, accompanied by a queasy stomach, I ventured forth into the corner market to buy something light and easy to digest. As yet unable to read Hebrew, I decided to pick up what looked like a small yogurt container that was sitting near the cheese. Not being 100 percent sure it contained yogurt, I peered inside; to my delight, it held a thick, white, yogurt-looking substance. I purchased my "yogurt" and went home to eat—soap, liquid soap! How was I to know that soap came in packages resembling yogurt containers, or that market items in Israel were not neatly divided into edible and inedible sections, as I remembered them in the United States. My now "clean" stomach became a bit more fragile and my confidence waned.

Stress

Change causes stress; expatriates face many changes in leaving their home country and organization and transferring to a new country and a new job. Separation from friends, family, children (perhaps for the first time), and parents (perhaps elderly or ill) increases stress. When expatriates arrive in a new country, different perceptions and conflicting values exacerbate the stress. Global managers see situations that they neither understand nor believe to be ethically correct. Many North American expatriates, for example, feel appalled by the poverty in most economically developing countries, especially in contrast to their own relatively luxurious international hotels and expatriate homes.

Stress-related culture shock may take many forms: anger, anxiety, disappointment, embarrassment, frustration, identity confusion, impatience, and physiological responses such as sleeplessness, stomachaches, headaches, and trembling hands. As one executive recalled, "There's some kind of traumatic reaction to it. It evidenced itself in my insomnia. There was something there . . . waking up at 4 A.M. every morning." Because culture shock is a sign that expatriates are beginning to let go of their home culture and engage with the new culture, the appropriate response is not to try to eliminate the culture shock but rather to manage the stress it causes.

Successful expatriates use many highly effective and creative stress management mechanisms for coping with culture shock. The most appropriate method depends on the particular individual and situation involved. Some people participate in regular physical exercise, some practice meditation and relaxation techniques, while others keep a journal ("Yell at the paper, not at the people!"). Many of the most effective global managers create *stability zones* (65). They spend most of their time totally immersed in the new culture, then briefly retreat into an environment—a stability zone—that closely resembles home. Examples of successful stability zones used by executives include checking into a home-country hotel for the weekend, going to an international club and only talking with other compatriots, playing a musical instrument, listening to records, or watching movies in one's native language.

On the job, managers can reduce the stress caused by culture shock by recognizing it and modifying their expectations and behavior accordingly. They can establish priorities and focus their limited energy on only the most important tasks; they can clearly define their responsibilities and educate the home office concerning the cultural and business differences between the new country, headquarters, and other parts of the world; and they can realize that in their new position they will neither work as efficiently nor as effectively, especially initially, as they did previously. The exact nature of the stability zone and stress management mechanisms is less important than global managers' recognition of the highly stressful nature of moving into a new culture and their development of at least one technique to reduce stress that works for them.

Adjusting to Living and Working Abroad

After three to six months, most expatriates escape their culture shock "low" and begin living a more normal life abroad. Little by little, they learn what the new culture considers important and what it considers meaningful. They learn when "yes" means "yes," when it means "maybe," and when it means "no." They learn what to focus on and what to ignore. They learn to differentiate individual behavior from behavior reflecting a cultural pattern. One expatriate, for example, showed his confusion—his inability to differentiate idiosyncratic from culturally patterned behavior—by asking, "Is it that Budi is lazy while most Indonesians work very hard to fulfill their work commitments [idiosyncratic behavior], or is it that most Indonesians work slowly and rarely finish their work [behavior reflecting a cultural pattern]?" Fairly rapidly, the most successful expatriates learn the local language well enough to make themselves understood in day-to-day conversations.

In addition to time (usually at least three to six months), the key to escaping the culture shock low is cross-cultural appreciation and problem solving. Successful expatriates recognize that the foreign environment makes many demands for which they must find or create solutions. In so doing, they realize that blaming others—host nationals, the company, or one's spouse—for their frustrations, no matter how tempting, is not useful. Commonly used ineffective approaches include:

- *Blaming the host nationals.* "These foreigners [who, in fact, are the natives] are stupid; anyone who had any intelligence would never have laid out a city this way! Addresses seem to be scattered randomly down the streets."
- *Blaming the company.* "Why didn't the company tell me that street numbers in Tokyo are not sequential? How do they expect me to find our clients, let alone make sales? The least the company could have done is give me a map and a guide."
- *Blaming one's spouse.* "Here I've been traveling for the last two weeks, eating strange food, trying to get these foreigners to sign the biggest contract that the firm has ever negotiated, and I come home to hear you complaining that the kids can't take a bath because the plumber doesn't speak English. Some help you are!"

Although it is tempting to blame others, it is almost always an unproductive stress management technique and never a good problem-solving approach.

The most successful global managers recognize that they do not fully understand the situation and must find ways to get reliable information and expertise. Their need for immediate decisions versus their lack of sufficient knowledge with which to make those decisions causes both the tension experienced by successful global managers and the large number of inappropriate decisions made by their less effective colleagues. Company-sponsored cross-cultural communication and management programs give expatriates (as well as global business travelers) the skills they need to manage culture shock and work more effectively worldwide.

Experienced expatriates and host nationals who have previously faced and dealt effectively with the same or similar situations can often best empathize with the newcomer's dilemmas.

An Italian colleague of mine described the horror of his first day in Philadelphia. He handed his secretary a stack of letters and manuscripts and told her to type them. Each day he expected her to present him with the finished work and each day he received nothing. Only at the end of a disappointing, frustrating, and unproductive week did an Italian friend of his explain that "In the United States, secretaries have more status than in Italy. You must *ask* them *if* they can do your typing, not *tell* them to do your typing. U.S.

organizations are more egalitarian and less hierarchical than Italian firms."
Sheepishly, my Italian colleague began to *ask*; slowly, he began to receive
typed pages.

Host nationals, although often invaluable as cultural informants, can be
somewhat inarticulate in describing their own culture. People do not
consciously learn the do's and don'ts of their native culture. Rather, as
children, they mimic the behavior of their parents and other adults. Eventually, with maturity, they can perform the behaviors, but they cannot
explain them. A Hungarian businessperson meeting with an Arab, for
example, will not maintain sufficient eye contact. To the Arab, the
Hungarian seems shifty-eyed and not to be trusted. If asked, the Arab
will not be able to describe how often and how long appropriate eye
contact should last. He can do it, but he can't explain it. The frustrated
Hungarian knows that he is doing something wrong but cannot find out
how to behave correctly.

Whatever the source of information, patience and creativity remain
essential. Effective global managers "know that they do not know."
They recognize that they are in a difficult situation and that they will not
act as effectively abroad as they did at home, especially in the initial
stages. They recognize the need for good stress management techniques,
including stability zones, that will not harm their relationship with
colleagues, clients, or family. They also recognize that all members of the
family experience culture shock in adjusting to a new country and that
the transition often affects the spouse more profoundly than the
employee (see Chapter 9). Successful expatriates, and their companies,
therefore view cross-cultural adjustment as a systems issue, not as an
individual problem (60).

MANAGING EXPATRIATES EFFECTIVELY, EQUITABLY, AND ETHICALLY

Managing cross-cultural transitions effectively, equitably, and ethically
presents challenges for even the most sophisticated global firms.
Described in the following boxes are two real situations in which a
company must develop an effective, equitable, and ethical policy both for
the immediate situation and for all such future situations in their worldwide operations. For both cases, "Adjusting to America" and "The
Morality of Having Fun," analyze the situation from both cultural
perspectives before recommending a response to the specific situation
and a more general corporate policy.

ADJUSTING TO AMERICA: WITH OR WITHOUT HELP

T.S. comes from a country that is culturally quite different from the United States and received his education entirely outside the United States. He is a devout member of a profoundly different religious tradition that has only recently gained some prominence among Americans.

Prestige, a North American–based global company, regards T.S. as one of its finest young executives. A year ago Prestige offered T.S. a promotion from his current upper middle management position in his native country to a higher position in the United States. T.S. very much looked forward to the new assignment, both for the additional challenge as well as for the opportunity to advance the good of the company. A number of American Prestige managers who had also wanted the position resisted T.S.'s appointment. However, top management's careful assessment convinced them that T.S. was indeed the most qualified person for the job.

T.S.'s wife and two young children felt happy about his success and were eager to be loyal to him. They expressed uneasiness, however, about moving to the United States, fearing that it would cause considerable cultural and family adjustment.

As feared, the adjustment to America proved extremely difficult, even though T.S. did everything he could to make his family feel at home. Among other issues the lack of servants became a major problem. In their home country, T.S. and his wife lived at a high socioeconomic level, with T.S.'s salary allowing them to employ two servants to do the household chores. Indeed, even as children, both T.S. and his wife had grown up in families sufficiently affluent to afford servants to attend to their needs. (In T.S.'s home country, middle-class citizens can easily afford servants who are not paid a very high wage.)

T.S. and his family now feel a deep need for similar services in the United States. Based on his cultural background, T.S., who ordinarily shuns making waves, is now requesting that Prestige provide him with an extra allowance to hire two servants, explaining to the company that this would "only be fair."

Questions for Reflection

1. Prestige regularly gives American expatriates assigned to T.S.'s home country allowances for servants, along with numerous other benefits such as liberal educational allowances for spouses. Does not a policy

continued on next page ■

■ *continued from previous page*

of the highest respect for people dictate that the company should offer T.S. and his family a lifestyle similar to that which they have grown accustomed since childhood? Is not T.S.'s request reasonable?

2. Should Prestige offer all expatriates transferred to a given country, who hold similar level positions, the same allowances? Should Singaporeans, for example, transferred by Prestige to a country such as China receive the same allowances as those given to American expatriates of the same managerial rank and position?

Senior Management Committee Decisions

1. Should Prestige pay for two servants for T.S.'s family? Why? Why not?

2. When a company transfers managers and executives across borders, does the highest respect for people mean treating everyone the same? Does it mean treating people as they were treated back home? Does it mean treating people as the host country treats its own citizens? On what principle(s) should Prestige base its corporate expatriate policy?

3. Which parts of the expatriate package should be universal? Which parts should be based on accepted practices in the home country? Which parts should be based on the typical practices of the host country?

THE MORALITY OF HAVING FUN

I.M. Urgin, a native of a non-Western country, is a devoted family man with three young children. He recently left his senior management position with a local telecommunications company and joined Prestige, a North American–based global company, receiving a raise commensurate with his new, more senior position. I.M. felt thrilled to work for a truly global company.

The new position required I.M. to leave his native country in order to live and to work in another country in the region that has a religion, values system, and overall culture quite different from his own. For example, I.M.'s home culture does not consider it bad to frequent pros-

continued on next page ■

■ *continued from previous page*

titutes. Some wives even encourage their husbands to go to prostitutes on occasion, as is the case with I.M.'s wife. By contrast, the new host country holds quite different cultural values concerning prostitution. Prostitution is illegal, although the host country officials often overlook the law.

After arriving in the host country, I.M. continues his previous habits, although on a more limited and discrete basis than previously. One of I.M.'s associates at Prestige, a native of the host country, becomes deeply concerned about the legality and morality of I.M.'s actions, and suggests that he stop. I.M. becomes irate. He rigorously defends himself by stating that North American expatriate managers from Prestige living in I.M.'s home country actually form romantic liaisons with local women, including with local Prestige women. I.M. angrily contends that these romantic liaisons create a much more serious problem than going to prostitutes, because the North American men might eventually leave their wives as a result of such relationships. I.M. further argues that in addition to North American culture frowning upon such behavior, it might also upset the local people, with consequent negative effects on the morale of local Prestige workers. I.M. heatedly concludes that "having fun with prostitutes" is much better, and certainly less undesirable, than the North Americans' behavior.

Questions for Reflection

1. Who is to judge the morality here? Must I.M. adhere to the host country's ethics?
2. Does pointing out the new situation by his colleague force I.M. into a new moral context in which formerly innocent acts may now be considered unethical and illegal? What if I.M. comes to think of himself as guilty but remains unable to change his behavior?
3. Even if I.M. thinks he is innocent, does his behavior endanger the integrity of the company? Do the North Americans' "romantic liaisons" in I.M.'s home country endanger the integrity of the company? Does sexual immorality signal a readiness to engage in unethical business practices? How much does an individual's private life impinge on his or her organization and work?
4. Does I.M.'s colleague have any right to report I.M.'s activities to senior management? Does he have a duty to do so?

continued on next page ■

■ *continued from previous page*

Senior Management Committee Decision

1. When is the private life behavior of a manager a concern of the company? When it is illegal? When it is immoral? When it reflects badly on the company from any culture's perspective? Never?
2. Should Prestige ask I.M. to stop going to prostitutes? Should the company require that he stop? Similarly, should the company ask the North Americans in I.M.'s home country to stop forming "romantic liaisons" with locals? Should the company require employees to refrain from such behavior?
3. For you personally, what areas of your private life do you believe are of no concern to the company? The way you raise your children? The way you treat your spouse? The way you treat your parents? The way you treat members of the community? The type of sexual behavior you prefer?

COMING HOME: RETURNING TO ONE'S OWN CULTURE[1]

Cross-cultural reentry is the transition from the foreign country back into one's home country (6;22;47;48;53;74;81). Similar to cross-cultural entry, it involves readjusting to the home-country work and nonwork environments, as well as to interacting again with home-country nationals (13). It involves facing previously familiar surroundings after living and working abroad for a significant period of time. Until the 1980s, companies considered reentry a relatively easy transition, but more recently many began to consider it a major problem (62;63). According to Business International Corporation,

> Repatriating executives from . . . [global] assignments is a top management challenge that goes far beyond the superficial problems and costs of physical relocation. . . . The assumption is that since these individuals are returning home . . . they should have no trouble adapting. . . . However, experience has shown that repatriation is anything but simple (23:74).

Historically, 20 percent of employees who completed global assignments wanted to leave their company when they returned home. According to a *Wall Street Journal* report surveying 34 global companies, "Bosses might quickly become sensitive if they added up the cost to the company of unhappy . . . [returning employees]"(82).

Reentry experiences frequently surprise returnees (22). When transferring abroad, people generally expect new and unfamiliar situations, whereas they do not expect anything unfamiliar when returning home (72). Most returnees expect neither reentry shock nor trauma; they expect to slip easily back into their previous organization, job, and lifestyle.

> I don't expect changes. . . . Because it was only a short stay overseas, I expect to just slip right back into my old mold.

> I expect to have the same friends, the same activities, and the same family connections.

> I do not anticipate culture shock at reentry. . . . I don't expect much trauma.

Returnees come back neither to the world they left nor to the world they are anticipating. While abroad, the expatriate changes, the organization changes, and the country changes. Moreover, during the culture shock phase of adjusting to another country, expatriates often idealize their home country, remembering only the good aspects of home—in essence, creating something to hold on to and to dream about.

> As I shivered in Quebec's −35⁰ winter, I remembered Los Angeles' blue sky and sunshine, driving to the beach on a warm January morning. . . . I didn't remember skies opaque with smog, freeways so clogged with cars that driving anywhere was impossible, nor did I remember my car being broken into while parked at the beach.

When returning home, expatriates face real changes; the gap between the way it was and the way it is, and the gap between their idealized memories and reality. Most feel surprised both at their feelings and by reality. Returnees often describe reentry as an even more difficult transition than their initial entry into the new country.

> Going home is a harder move. The foreign move has the excitement of being new . . . more confusing, but exciting. Reentry is frightening . . . I'll be happy to be home . . . I really wonder if I can adjust back.

Returnees describe stages similar to those of culture shock—first being in a very good mood, quickly plummeting to a very low mood, and then slowly returning to their normal mood. The initial high mood often lasts only a short time, as described by such comments as

> I was pleasantly surprised by our neighbors. They really went overboard to welcome us back.

> It's cleaner . . . and just a reasonable number of people . . . fantastic! . . . freedom of mobility . . . quality of life is higher here and I notice it more.

For most returnees the initial high mood lasts less than a month and many report it lasting only a few hours. The low period therefore begins earlier in reentry than in the entry transition. Returnees' lowest times usually occur during the second and third months back. As American managers returning from assignments in South America describe:

> Some of my friends couldn't even imagine the foreign country. . . . They asked me how it was, but they just wanted to hear "fine."

> In Venezuela, getting things done was a hassle . . . and we said, "In the United States it would be so easy." When we came home, everything was delayed and frustrating. Here in the United States! The U.S. was a continual Venezuela story . . . and we had always said, "This will never happen at home . . . HA!"

> Calling friends, my sister, my mom. . . . Everyone was so busy with their lives that they didn't have time to just talk. They cut me off . . . I understand, but . . .

> I came back with so many stories to share, but my friends and family couldn't understand them. It was as if my years overseas were unshareable.

By the sixth month back home, returnees generally accept their situation and report feeling "average"—neither much better nor much worse than usual.

PROFESSIONAL REENTRY: IT'S NOT AS EASY AS IT SEEMS

Just as the new environment and lifestyle can cause problems when entering another culture, so too can the professional transition back into the home organization (11;12;13;31). Professional reentry has often been more difficult than personal reentry, especially for returnees to multidomestic companies in which global experience is not considered critical to overall corporate success (11;12;13;69). Most managers expect a global assignment to help their career; yet historically they have returned to discover that, at best, it had a neutral effect. Multidomestic companies promote fewer than half of their returning expatriate managers (49:1;82). For many, especially in the short run, the impact of their career is negative. Historically, more than two-thirds of returnees to multi-domestic companies have suffered from the out-of-sight, out-of-mind syndrome (49:1;50). As managers returning to various North American companies commented:

> My colleagues react indifferently to my global assignment. . . . They view me as doing a job I did in the past; they don't see me as having gained anything while overseas.

> The organization has changed . . . work habits, norms, and procedures have changed, and I have lost touch with all that. . . . I'm a beginner again!

> I had no specific reentry job to return to. I wanted to leave international and return to domestic. Working abroad magnifies problems while isolating effects. You deal with more problems, but the home office doesn't know the details of the good or bad effects. Managerially, I'm out of touch.

> I lost time. My career stopped when I left and started again when I returned.

Similarly, many managers complain that their reentry jobs bore them (51). Almost half of surveyed repatriated executives found their reentry position less satisfying than their global assignment (7;49). They describe their positions abroad as offering more excitement and challenge. They miss the greater responsibility, authority, status, decision-making autonomy, and variety of their global assignments. Returnees frequently feel disappointed, discouraged, and angry when they realize that their reentry positions do not live up to their expectations:

> I'm bored at work. . . . I run upstairs to see what [another returning colleague] is doing. He says, "Nothing." Me, too.

> In a lot of ways, the red tape and nonsense that we're experiencing now since we reentered are a lot worse. Maybe I didn't recognize these things before [going abroad] or maybe I'd learned to live with them.

> While overseas, I realized that the home office doesn't do anything right . . . bosses call bosses to get anything done. I had to talk to seven people to get one answer. It's a real bureaucracy.

The transition from one organizational culture to another and from one set of organizational assumptions and behaviors to another can be difficult and stressful. Returnees experience organizational culture shock at the same time as they are experiencing societal culture shock. Luckily for returnees, the evolution of business from less globally integrated multidomestics to today's highly networked and interdependent multinational and global strategies and structures makes professional reentry easier. Due to increasing global competitiveness and integration, expatriates no longer feel as isolated when abroad nor does the company view their global experience as irrelevant when they return.

Effectiveness: Who Is and Who Isn't Effective At Re-entry?

Are returnees effective during their initial period back in the home organization? Yes and no. As shown in Figures 8-3 and 8-4, returnees and their bosses do not agree: the bosses see returnees as more effective than the returnees see themselves. Historically, returnees described themselves as initially ineffective followed by increasing effectiveness. By contrast, home-country bosses and colleagues describe the same returnees as initially effective followed by increasingly higher effectiveness. Home-country bosses, especially in companies with multidomestic strategies, tend to compare expatriates' performance at re-entry with their prior predeparture performance without realizing that the expatriates have developed professionally while abroad and can therefore manage higher levels of complexity and responsibility than they could previously. By contrast, returnees generally see themselves as accomplishing relatively little during their first few months back in comparison with the greater breadth and challenge of their work abroad. This pattern of consistently underutilizing returnees leads to ineffectiveness within the organization and dissatisfaction among returnees, which in turn causes many returning expatriates to leave the firm (8;12).

The Xenophobic Response

In addition to disagreeing about returnees' overall effectiveness, reenterers and their bosses also disagree about which returnees are most effective. Returnees who see themselves as highly effective are rarely seen as such by their bosses; similarly, returnees who see themselves as ineffective

FIGURE 8-3 How Effective Are Returnees? The Returnees' Perspective

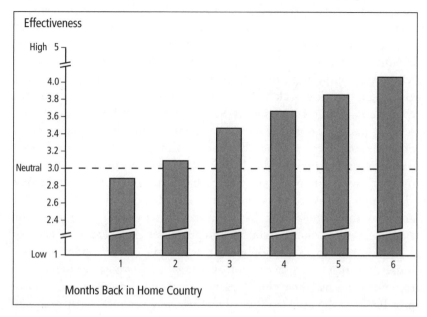

FIGURE 8-4 How Effective Are Returnees? Home-Country Bosses'
and Colleagues' Perspective

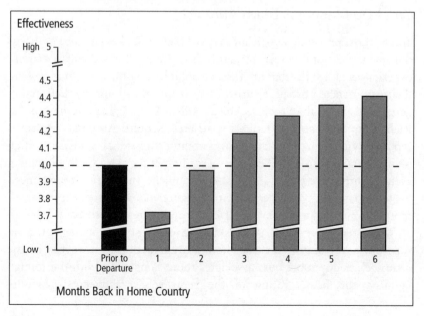

are infrequently rated as such by their bosses. Home-country bosses and colleagues generally assess those returnees who appear "least foreign" as most effective—that is, those returnees who do not know or use foreign languages, do not have foreign friends, and were not born in a foreign country. Similarly, they have historically ranked as most effective those returnees who did not explicitly use the skills and learnings gained while abroad on their job back home. This *xenophobic response*—bosses' and colleagues' fear and rejection of behaviors associated with foreigners—severely handicaps organizations that want to learn from the experience of their employees around the world. Although multidomestic firms competing primarily in individual domestic markets may have tolerated this response, it is no longer acceptable in today's highly competitive global markets. As experts have said, business today is a learning race and only those companies that learn from their clients, colleagues, and employees worldwide will survive and prosper in the twenty-first century.

In contrast to the xenophobic assessments of their home-country bosses, returnees themselves rank as most effective those reenterers who recognize and use their global learning and skills to the greatest extent possible and who are least limited by their home culture. Returnees who speak foreign languages, have friends around the world, and know about other cultures rate themselves more highly than do their less globally knowledgeable and involved colleagues.

What Do Managers Learn Abroad?

Today, most returning expatriates regard their global experience as essential for a successful career, primarily because it allows them to acquire experiences and skills that are rarely available at home (76). In reviewing their experiences abroad, returnees report that they improve their managerial skills more than their technical skills. As highlighted in the Box "A Rich Time of Learning: Skills Expatriates Acquire Abroad," returnees report having enhanced many important professional skills, including many of those seen as critical for succeeding in today's rapidly changing, highly competitive global business environment. In addition to enhanced professional skills, returnees often recognize many personal learnings—most commonly, an improved self-image and increased self-confidence.

When recognized and used, skills acquired abroad increase the returnee's contribution to the home organization. However, if the returnee's xenophobic boss associates these same skills with the foreign country, the boss's rating of the returnee's effectiveness generally

A RICH TIME OF LEARNING:
SKILLS EXPATRIATES ACQUIRE ABROAD[2]

Managerial Skills, Not Technical Skills

Working abroad makes you more knowledgeable about the questions to ask than about the answers.

I learned how to work in two cultures . . . to compromise, not to be a dictator. It's similar to two domestic cultures . . . like marketing and engineering.

I am more open-minded . . . more able to deal with a wider range of people . . . because I ran into many other points of view.

Tolerance for Ambiguity

Because I only understood a fraction of what was really going on abroad, maybe 50 percent, I had to make decisions on a fraction of the necessary information. Now I can tolerate nonclosure and ambiguity much better.

Things you never thought you would put up with, you learn to put up with . . . I always thought I was right, until I went abroad.

Multiple Perspectives

I learned what it feels like to be a foreigner . . . I could see things from their perspective.

I learned to anticipate . . . it's the role of a diplomat.

Ability to Work with and Manage Others

I increased my tolerance for other people. For the first time, I was the underdog, the minority.

I became a soft-headed screamer. I am definitely better now at working with others.

I used to be more ruthless than I am now . . . I was the All-American manager. Now, I stop and realize the human impact. I see others as resources. I do more communicating with others in the organization.

decreases. While both unfortunate and counterproductive, the boss's response is not surprising, given that until recently most firms operated as domestic or multidomestic organizations and transferred employees abroad primarily to get a job done, rather than to develop either the worldwide organization or the expatriate's career—as is often the primary goal in today's more globally networked multinational and transnational organizations. The multidomestic's narrow definition of the expatriate's role, combined with its inherently parochial belief that "our home-country's way of working is the best way"—often labeled as the *not-invented-here syndrome*—severely diminished the perceived value of returnees to most home organizations.

Transition Strategies

The strategies returnees use to fit back into their formerly familiar home country and home organization vary markedly (66). As shown in Table 8-2, some returnees become resocialized, some alienated, and others proactive.

Resocialized Returnees

Resocialized returnees are most common among expatriates who work for multidomestic firms that lack a global orientation. As shown in Table 8-2, resocialized returnees neither recognize nor use their globally acquired skills and learnings. They try to fit back into the domestic organizational structure and culture, that is, to act like managers who have never been away. In treating their experience abroad as nontransferable, they negate the possibility that it could enhance their home-country effectiveness, either at work or at home. Historically, because few home-organization bosses (especially in multidomestic companies) appreciated returnees' increased potential contribution, they often felt satisfied with resocialized returnees' fit-back-in strategy (43). The resocialized mode precludes both the individual and the organization gaining very much from the expatriate experience. This lack of individual and organizational learning is particularly unfortunate today when global firms need continual worldwide learning just to compete, let alone succeed.

Alienated Returnees

These returnees are more common among employees who have had a series of global assignments than those who have had a single such

TABLE 8-2 Coping Strategies: Approaches to Returning Home

ORIENTED TOWARD HOME COUNTRY

Resocialized Returnees attempt to fit back in when they return home. They do not recognize that they have learned skills abroad that they could use at home. In general, they are neither aware of changes in themselves nor in their environment. They are rated as highly effective by their bosses and themselves and feel quite satisfied with their reentry positions and performance. Most resocialized returnees distance themselves from their global experience. Similarly, while living abroad, most resocialized returnees *reject the foreign country*. While abroad many lived in expatriate ghettos separate from the host nationals, who frequently labeled them as "Ugly Foreigners."

Proactive Returnees attempt to integrate their global and their home-country experiences. They recognize changes in themselves and their environment, and try to use the skills and learning they acquired abroad. Whereas proactive returnees rate themselves as effective and satisfied with their job, their bosses only rate them as moderately so. Proactive expatriates aim to effectively *integrate the home and foreign cultures'* ways of life; their approach while abroad was to attempt to adapt to living abroad without "going native."

Alienated Returnees often disassociate themselves from the home culture and home organization. Although they recognize that they have acquired skills and learnings while abroad, they see no way to use them at home. Alienated returnees do not see themselves as particularly effective, nor, in general, do their bosses. They receive the least recognition of the three types of returnees. Similarly, as expatriates, they also *rejected the home culture*. Their approach to living abroad was to try to "go native"—to assimilate into the foreign culture.

ORIENTED TOWARD FOREIGN COUNTRY

assignment, more common among spouses than employees, and more common among volunteers (e.g., Peace Corps and Canadian University Students Overseas) than among corporate returnees. While working abroad, alienated returnees often "go native"—they assimilate the values and lifestyle of the foreign culture. When they return, they continue to see the foreign culture as better than their own culture, believing that it offers a richer way of life. They reject their home culture, and in so doing frequently become personally isolated. Alienated returnees, in believing that they cannot fit back in or use their globally acquired skills and learnings in their home environment, often feel professionally unproductive and personally unsatisfied. Similar to resocialized reenterers, alienated reenterers contribute little to the home organization from their global experience. The home organization generally recognizes the alienated returnees' diminished productivity and evaluates them as ineffective.

Proactive Reenterers

These reenterers reject neither their own nor the foreign culture. Rather, they combine aspects of both in creating new approaches to working and to living. Proactive reenterers usually feel optimistic and creative; they recognize and use their globally acquired skills and learnings to contribute within the work environment and to modify their personal lifestyle. Proactive returnees see themselves as more effective and more satisfied with their job than do users of the other reentry strategies. Proactive reenterers develop highly sophisticated skills at perceiving their environment—whether abroad or at home—and at describing situations, rather than simply comparing and evaluating them. They easily identify similarities and differences without needing to classify one as good and the other as bad. Proactive returnees therefore contribute by creating new, synergistic ways of perceiving and working within the home organization based on their experience both at home and abroad. This synergistic approach—the combining of multiple cultures' ways of working—allows returnees to work more effectively with their multicultural colleagues and clients, to make decisions based on a wider range of alternatives, and to act as leaders in the realm of both ideas and action. Proactive returnees' potential for contributing to the organization exceeds that of both domestic employees and other returnees; however, the home organization must be open to using the returnees' potential contributions and not simply attempt to fit them back in.

Managing Reentry

What makes some returnees more proactive than others? What allows some returnees to contribute more than others (see 11;12;13;42;44;45)? Support provided by the company during reentry can dramatically decrease the number of returnees who choose to quit the organization (5; 12;40;48;70). Two primary processes differentiate the returnees who choose more and less effective approaches to re-entry: the level of communication and the extent of validation.

Communication: Do Expatriates Stay in Contact with the Home Organization While Abroad?

How can companies close the gap between what returnees expect and the actual reality of the country and company they return to (72)? The level of communication refers to the extent to which expatriates receive pertinent information and recognize changes while abroad. Expatriates who maintain close contact with the home organization while abroad become more proactive, and as a result, become more effective, and more satisfied in their reentry jobs. Returnees who perform the best recognize both positive and negative changes in themselves, their organization, their industry, and their country. Given the higher levels of integration and interdependence in today's multinational and global companies—especially in comparison to the multidomestic companies of prior decades—and the ease of e-mail and other forms of instant, worldwide cyber contact, today's reenterers are much more likely than their predecessors to receive adequate communication while abroad.

Validation: How Much Recognition Do Returnees Receive?

Validation involves the amount of recognition, including promotions, expatriates receive upon returning home. Returnees who receive more recognition from bosses and colleagues for their work abroad as well as for their potential future contributions do better than do less recognized returnees. Returnees whom the company promotes do better than those not promoted (44). Organizations that treat expatriates and returnees as if they were "out of sight and out of mind," on vacation, or so far behind that they could not possibly contribute usefully, diminish returnees' proactivity and productivity.

Most organizations do not consciously choose to ignore returnees. However, many expatriates return home when they complete their global assignment and not necessarily when the company has another appropriate position available. Historically, few companies have used sophisticated global career-path systems. One returnee, an engineer, explained that his *Fortune 50* company simply gave him a desk and a phone when he returned and told him to find himself a job within the company. Another engineer, even though he had no human resource management experience, was put in charge of designing reentry procedures for future expatriates, because "Clearly we don't know what to do with you or with the others who will be coming back." External validation through recognizing and valuing returnees' global and reentry experiences is one of the most powerful management techniques for increasing returnees' productivity and satisfaction. Equally important, it is one of the most effective ways for global companies to gather an up-to-date understanding of fluctuations in the worldwide business environment.

Returnees can facilitate their own reentry by using skills similar to those they used in adjusting abroad. Perhaps most important, they must recognize the highly stressful nature of the reentry transition and manage it accordingly. Unfortunately, the natural assumption that the home country is familiar often blinds returnees to the reality of the reentry transition and strips them of the very skills that they need and so successfully developed while working abroad. Clearly, managers returning to globally integrated organizations find reentry much easier than do those who work for domestic or multidomestic companies.

UNDERUTILIZED GLOBAL MANAGERS

The global business environment is highly competitive. Success depends on corporate excellence. To compete, today's global companies select the best people and manage them appropriately. Unfortunately, many organizations frequently fail to profit from their employees' global experience. To benefit fully from their investment, organizations and returnees need to better understand the reentry transition. Both must identify competencies acquired or enhanced abroad and systematically find ways to productively use them. The home organization needs to understand the importance of staying in contact with expatriates, planning for their return, and recognizing the value of their worldwide experience. Attitudes of managers who stay at home must change, as must evaluation and reward schemes. Increasing effectiveness at each stage in the expatriate global career cycle is neither easily nor superficially accomplished, but rather takes a major commitment on the part of the company.

Just as predeparture training can assist expatriates in adjusting to living and working abroad (57), reentry debriefings facilitate the transition back into the home organization as well as significantly increasing home organization learning (59). In debriefing sessions, management asks returnees to describe what they learned abroad. Together returnees and home organization personnel integrate the new appreciations and create synergistic approaches to the ongoing management of worldwide operations. Reentry sessions, in addition to identifying what was learned abroad, facilitate the transition back into the home organization and home community. As a part of a reentry session, experts describe both the personal and professional reentry transition and suggest proactive approaches to managing each. By including home-country managers in debriefing and reentry sessions, the organization increases the global sophistication of all its managers and significantly decreases organizational parochialism and xenophobia. Both home-based and expatriate managers learn to transcend their own experience and integrate their perceptions and understandings of the organization on a global basis.

As home organization personnel become more multicultural and their clientele becomes more global, the need for globally skilled managers also increases. Both companies and expatriates need to cultivate their understanding of the entry and reentry transitions and develop organizational strategies that benefit both parties (64). Companies can no longer afford to send any but their best people abroad. Neither the companies nor the individuals can afford to let the best fail.

COACHING WOMEN FOR GLOBAL SUCCESS

Companies often hesitate to send women abroad on global assignments (25;26). According to *Business Week*, "American women seeking to climb the corporate ladder via overseas positions face steep odds. While females account for some 30% of students in MBA programs, they are only 14% of those chosen by corporate America for foreign postings" (56). The reason is that their male counterparts overestimate the problems awaiting women working outside their home country. Executive coaches often help managers who are considering sending their most senior and highest potential women abroad as well as helping the potential women expatriates themselves. As you read "Coaching Global Executives: Women

Succeeding in a World Beyond Here," ask yourself from whom you get your best coaching advice. The following box describes one executive coach's approach to helping companies and women executives separate the facts from the myths in successful global careers.

COACHING GLOBAL EXECUTIVES: WOMEN SUCCEEDING IN A WORLD BEYOND HERE[3]

Executive coaches bring perspective. They offer a context of meaning beyond each manager's and executive's position, organization, and industry. By quietly asking questions that are beyond the bottom line, coaches offer executives opportunities to more consciously consider the types of contributions they make to their company and to choose the kinds of contributions they would like to make more broadly in the world. Such questions as

- What does success mean to you?
- In which ways is your work helping society?
- Why would your daughter be proud to tell her daughter about your accomplishments?

often appear illegitimate when taken out of the privacy of executive coaching dialogues. In the public glare of business-as-usual, such questions frequently fail to appear sufficiently pragmatic to warrant executive attention. And yet the conversations, reflection, and learning that such questions generate often bring soul, along with deep motivation, back into the pragmatism of professionalism. Context, deep meaning, and soul are without counterparts in the pragmatism of successful careers, organizations, lives, and societies.

Is coaching women executives any different from coaching men?[4]

While few people question whether the world of business has gone global, most assumptions about building global careers and succeeding as global executives remain based on the experience of men. Many of the most fundamental assumptions about executive success remain

continued on next page ∎

■ *continued from previous page*

parochial, limited not only to the experience of men, but often to the experience of men working within their own home country. If companies continue to believe current parochial assumptions about business success, few, if any, women will venture into the world beyond their national borders, and even fewer will succeed once there. To succeed in a global economy, both companies and women managers need to go beyond the myths and erroneous assumptions of history.

Because so few women worked as international managers in the twentieth century, let alone as global executives, ignorance and misleading myths abound. Not surprisingly, many women, especially in such Anglo cultures as the United States, believe that they must emulate men to succeed. Fearing to differentiate themselves in any way from their successful male predecessors and contemporaries, many women become reticent to openly challenge the abundant myths about the barriers women supposedly face when attempting to conduct business abroad. Executive coaching allows women managers and executives to ask societally unacceptable, and therefore publicly unaskable, questions, such as.

- "Is it true that as a woman I cannot succeed in the Middle East?"
- "Will I insult their culture if I lead the negotiating team in Saudi Arabia?"
- "Is it true that our company's expansion into South Asia will be jeopardized if I head up the project?"
- "Even if I succeed in getting the CEO to send me to Korea, will I fail once I am there? I've heard that Korean businessmen just ignore women; that they would never take a business woman seriously."
- "Will our German joint venture partners be annoyed when they see that my company has sent me as the lead engineer?"
- "Will men in Latin America really think that my company has sent me as some kind of sexual plaything? What do I need to do to get Latin men to respect me?"

As I listen to women telling their stories and asking their unaskable questions, my most frequent response is "Why?" Why do you think that that might happen to you? What reality do you want to be true for you? How can you go beyond all the negative scenarios of what you

continued on next page ■

■ *continued from previous page*

and others in your company imagine will occur? Why do you think foreigners will exhibit more prejudice against you than do some of the executives you have already successfully dealt with here at home? How can you go beyond history's erroneous assumptions to create your own reality? In the privacy of executive coaching dialogues, we laugh, question, and explore a world that has literally remained foreign to all too many women and companies. In the process, we lay to rest the misleading belief that women cannot succeed abroad, or, if they do succeed, that they must act like men.

MYTH #1: Global experience is not that important

Lisette, an executive in a major consumer products company with two teenagers, recently turned down an assignment in Brussels. Annoyed with her, Lisette's boss tells her that he will not consider her for a senior vice presidency because she is not mobile. He emphasizes that her promising career will plateau if she does not willingly move abroad to take an expatriate assignment. Lisette challenges the importance of global experience. She knows that neither her boss, nor his boss—the CEO— have had much experience abroad beyond regularly boarding airplanes. Given that she is currently the highest ranked woman in the company, the requirement that she gain global experience looks suspiciously like the latest hurdle her boss is putting in the way of her career progress, the latest hurdle defining the glass ceiling.

My response to Lisette's angry phone call is a resounding, "No!" Business has gone global. Requiring global experience reflects neither sexism nor a new variant of the glass ceiling. "Your boss is right. If you choose not to gain global experience, it is *you* who are choosing to remain well below the glass ceiling. No man or woman should be promoted into the executive ranks of a major twenty-first century company without having acquired a deep understanding and appreciation of global business dynamics. Your boss and the CEO grew their careers in another era, an era dominated by domestic or, at most, multidomestic business. Unless your aim is to progress backward through history and to attempt to have a parochial nineteenth- or twentieth-century career, you would not dare consider limiting your experience to domestic stay-at-home assignments."

continued on next page ■

■ *continued from previous page*

Lisette doesn't like hearing what I am saying, but she believes me. She knows that as an executive coach, I am an outsider and that therefore I am on her side and I will tell her the truth, even if it is an inconvenient truth that she would rather not hear. Recognizing the truth, however, does not imply resignation to a career stopped by a seemingly impenetrable global glass ceiling. The outwardly paradoxical question I raise with Lisette is "How can you get significant international experience *and* keep your commitment to not moving during your children's formative high school years?" Asking paradoxical questions—such as "How can you both move abroad and not move abroad?"—and then helping executives resolve them is a significant aspect executive coaching.

MYTH #2: Given my family commitments, I cannot take a global assignment

In reflecting on her situation, Lisette realized that expatriation, while a powerful way to gain global experience, was not the only option open to her. As we brainstormed alternatives, Lisette discovered that she could significantly increase her global experience in a number of innovative ways. She suggested participating on more global task forces and increasing her international business travel. Her most creative idea was to take short two-month assignments in Europe and Asia while her two teenagers were away each summer at camp. For Lisette, as well as for many other executive women, the problem is the form in which global experience has traditionally been offered (multiyear expatriate assignments), not the requirement for global experience itself. The trap for Lisette would have been to reject global experience because it was "packaged" in its traditional, and to her unacceptable, form, such as a three- to five-year expatriate assignment. The trap for me as a coach would have been to accept her boss's definitions of reality rather than to help Lisette to think beyond the mythology surrounding the corporation's increasingly anachronistic requirements. As Lisette's subsequent discussions with the CEO revealed, expatriation, as a developmental strategy, was a better fit for the company's needs in the past when business strategy required key executives to only have an in-depth knowledge of a single foreign culture. By contrast, today's globally integrated

continued on next page ■

■ *continued from previous page*

business strategies require key executives to understand multiple cultures and their interaction. The option that Lisette was suggesting for herself—shorter exposure to multiple countries—is actually preferable in many cases to the company's traditional emphasis on single-culture learning gained from a multiyear expatriate assignment.

MYTH #3: For global managers, being a woman is a disadvantage

This pervasive and erroneous myth seems to find its way into the thinking of the vast majority of today's executives, both male and female. Valana, a senior financial analyst for a major pharmaceutical company, was offered a regional vice-presidency in Japan. Given the company's new start-up operations in Pakistan, the position in Japan would involve considerable travel to this Islamic country. Valana felt simultaneously excited and cautious. Would she, as a woman, be able to succeed in Japan and Pakistan, both countries reputed to be hostile to women managers and executives? She worried that if she openly raised her fears with her boss, he would change his mind; that, once again, the company would assume that it could not send women abroad. To make sure that she did not ruin the opportunity to work abroad for herself, or for other women, she chose not to raise her concerns inside the company but rather relied on the confidentiality inherent in the executive coaching relationship.

MYTH #4: Certain cultures make it impossible for woman executives to succeed

Valana's initial fear was that no woman could succeed in Japan or Pakistan. Her real fear was that if she accepted the position, she would be setting herself up for failure. When I asked her why she believed she would fail in either of these two Asian countries, she immediately cited the cultural limitations placed on most women in Japan as well as in most Islamic countries: "The scarcity of Japanese and Pakistani women executives says it all. Even with all your travelling, how many Japanese or Pakistani women executives do you know? Not many!" Unconsciously, yet understandably, Valana had fallen into the *Gaijin Trap*. She had assumed that, as a woman, she would be treated similarly to the

continued on next page ■

■ *continued from previous page*

local Japanese and Pakistani women, few of whom are given the cultural latitude to succeed in major multinational companies. Her mistake was not in her statistics: both countries have extremely few women executives. Rather, her mistake was in overemphasizing the salience of being a woman. Based on the actual experience of women executives who have worked abroad, we know that women from outside a particular region are treated as foreigners who happen to be women. They are not treated in the same way as local women. While both the Japanese and Pakistanis limit the roles that local women can take in business, neither culture confuses foreign women with local women. Valana's freedom to succeed lies in the fact that she is visibly foreign. The trap for Valana would be to assume that the Japanese could not tell that she is not Japanese (or that the Pakistanis could not tell that she not Pakistani); they can. To get accurate tips on how to succeed in such cultures, I suggested that Valana restrict her advice-gathering to conversations with other North American and European women who had worked for major multinationals in Japan or Pakistan. From them she could learn the nuances of showing respect for each culture without limiting her potential success. I strongly advised that she disregard suggestions made by both men and women who had not had direct experience with women working in the particular countries in which she would be working. Without direct experience, even the best-intentioned colleagues unconsciously pass on myths disguised as advice. The only thing that eradicates the myth that women cannot succeed abroad—and, simultaneously, the fear that such myths engender in both women executives and the companies that consider sending women on global assignments—is learning about the actual experience of foreign women executives who have worked abroad, the majority of whom unquestionably succeed.[5]

In the next couple weeks, Valana talked with many expatriate women executives, coming back to me frequently to question whether their suggestions would really be advisable for her. Among her many questions, Valana asked if it was true that women executives did not have to stay up drinking until late into the night in order to do business with Japanese firms. My answer, "Absolutely true." Whereas behavior among men in Japan is fairly codified and almost always includes a lot

continued on next page ■

■ *continued from previous page*

of business entertainment and drinking, the newness of women conducting significant business in Japan means that male/female business behavior has yet to become codified. Given the ambiguity, women at this point in history have more latitude than do men to conduct business in ways that feel most comfortable to them. As one highly successful American woman executive, who had been based in Tokyo for years, laughingly related to me, "Among all of my male colleagues, I am the only one who has consistently maintained relationships with Japanese clients without needing to put my liver in jeopardy! I can get away with conducting business over lunch and a Perrier; the men can't."

MYTH #5: Public is public, and private is private: To be taken seriously, a woman executive must hide her role as a wife and mother

The myth, albeit false, is that foreigners will not take a businesswoman seriously unless she focuses 100 percent on work. American women, who come from one of the most task-oriented cultures in the world, often fall into the trap of emulating American businessmen. They try to focus almost exclusively on business, to the detriment of both their worldwide business success and their private life. Perhaps one particularly successful businesswoman's experience says it all. On a business trip to Hong Kong, Katia, a marketing vice president for a global telecommunications firm, was negotiating her first major contract with a consortium of Chinese, Malaysian, and Thai companies. The negotiations were not going well and seemed in jeopardy of failure. At a very tense moment in the deliberations, Katia glanced at her watch, stood up, and apologized for needing to take a 10-minute break. While receiving quizzical looks from the group of businessmen, she explained that it was bedtime for her seven-year-old daughter back home in Chicago, and that she always called to say goodnight to her daughter no matter where she was in the world.

Returning 10 minutes later, Katia was surprised to discover that the tension around the negotiating table had melted. As she entered the room, the Thai executive asked how her daughter was doing. Then the lead Chinese negotiator asked Katia if she had a picture of her daughter. Other negotiators expressed how difficult they imagined it must be

continued on next page ■

■ *continued from previous page*

for a mother to be so far away from her daughter. After this brief exchange of warm interest and concern, the negotiations continued, now clearly with a focus on efficiently finding a mutually beneficial agreement. At noon the following day, the negotiation that had appeared irreversibly stuck came to a successful conclusion.

Most women from Anglo-Saxon cultures, especially those from the United States, have been coached by their colleagues to separate their private life from their professional life. To succeed abroad, however, these same women need to unlearn the advice that their Anglo-Saxon colleagues have given them. Unlike the task-orientation of Anglo-Saxon countries, most other cultures emphasize relationship building. In countries such as China, Malaysia, and Thailand, people will only conduct business with people whom they know, like, and trust. Revealing who you are as a whole person, including unmasking some aspects of your private life, allows colleagues from relationship-building cultures to get to know you and, therefore, to want to do business with you. It is not that people from relationship-oriented cultures are not concerned about getting the task accomplished; they are. It is just that relationship must precede task. Katia's relationship with her daughter added the dimension of wholeness that she needed to succeed.

Today Katia laughs at the number of her women friends who are also global executives who carry pictures of their children very visibly in their business-card cases. Why? Because from the first moment of contact, clients know that they are a whole person—a wife, mother, and businesswoman. As Katia's story spread, rumors began circulating that even single women were borrowing pictures of Katia's children to ensure their success abroad.

Executive Coaching: Reaching Beyond the Myths of History

For both women and men, coaching dialogues foster a depth of questioning that allows executives to escape the bounded thinking of their own professional, organizational, and national cultures. For women, coaching sessions encourage exploring alternatives that reach beyond the accepted "wisdom" gained by successful men working worldwide with other men. At their best, coaching sessions provide the time, space, and learning opportunities that allow executives to offer profound and wise counsel to themselves.

SUMMARY

Transitions are a part of a global manager's career path. Expatriate, in-patriate, and transpatriate managers are sent to other countries, and returned home again after they have completed one or a series of global assignments. Transitions, whether entry or reentry, involve managing the stress that accompanies moving into an unfamiliar environment. In moving abroad, culture shock causes stress. In moving back home, unmet expectations and a lack of validation cause stress. Returning expatriates need to identify what they have learned abroad and how it can benefit the organization. They need to integrate their global perspective with the home-country perspective in proactive ways that enhance successful global careers. Organizations need to focus on what they can learn from expatriates as well as from returnees.

9

A Portable Life:
The Expatriate Spouse

We shall not cease from explorations
And the end of all our exploring
Will be to arrive where we started
And know the place for the first time.

T. S. ELIOT (16)

IN GLOBAL TRANSFERS, the spouse has the most difficult role of any family member. Whereas employees have the organization and job structure that continue from the home to the new country, and children have the continuity and routine of school, spouses often leave behind many of the most important aspects of their lives, including friends, relatives, and meaningful activities. More frequently today, spouses must also leave or restructure a job or career in order to follow their partners abroad. Spouses often lose both the structure and the continuity in their lives (11;25;28). The spouse's dissatisfaction, which often leads to early return, is the single most frequently reported reason for failure on a global assignment—nearly half of 300 surveyed companies have brought families home early due to the reported unwillingness or inability of the spouse to adapt. The average cost to the company of repatriating an executive and family exceeds $100,000 (6).

The experience of global managers differs markedly from that of their spouses (3;7;8;9;23;27). The spouse generally becomes more immersed in the new culture than does the employee; the challenges to adjusting successfully are therefore both different and greater. This chapter begins by

257

reviewing the most common situation historically faced by spouses in single-career families: that of a wife following her employee husband abroad without having a job or career of her own outside the family. The reason is not that all spouses are wives; they are not. However, to date, companies have sent few married women abroad and even fewer whose husbands accompanied them (2;4;19). The chapter then shifts focus and reviews the situation faced by dual-career couples, a newer and yet increasingly important subset of expatriates. Because the dynamics of single- and dual-career families differ markedly, each is discussed separately.

SINGLE-CAREER COUPLES: THE TRADITIONAL EXPATRIATE'S WIFE

Traditionally, wives have moved from country to country in order to follow their husbands' global careers. What challenges does the wife face in living abroad? How does she adapt to each new culture? How does she create a meaningful, "portable" life for herself—one that proves satisfying in whatever situation she encounters? This section discusses the traditional wife's expatriate cycle: her initial reaction to the global move, her arrival in the foreign country, her approach to creating a new lifestyle, and her return to her home country. Although this cycle takes place concurrently with the employee's global career cycle, its dynamics frequently remain unrecognized by both the couple and the organization.

In a major research study, 197 wives of managers sent abroad by North American corporations and by the Canadian International Development Agency described their experiences of moving and living abroad (1;3). The women accompanied their expatriate husbands to Asia, Africa, Europe, and Latin America. Some lived abroad in urban centers while others lived in rural areas; some in economically developed countries and others in extremely poor regions; some in areas linguistically similar to their home countries and others in areas in which the language spoken was totally new to them. Their ages and family situations also varied. Although the diversity of their backgrounds and the international environments in which they lived are noteworthy, the challenges they faced in managing the expatriate transitions and creating meaningful portable lives abroad are strikingly similar.

Moving Abroad: Premade Decisions

Companies' involvement in global operations takes many forms, including exporting, subsidiary management, joint ventures, and strategic alliances.

Companies therefore transfer employees for a wide variety of reasons (5;12; 13;14;15;22;24;30). By contrast, a wife generally moves abroad because the company has transferred her husband (29). Until offered the global assignment, many couples are unaware of the possibility that they might move abroad. Some wives therefore react initially with surprise or shock.

Argentina

I just didn't have any idea what it would be like. I was thoroughly settled in Toronto [Canada]. We were going to live there the rest of our lives. Our family and friends were all around us and everything was very comfortable. . . . I just didn't have any idea of what was ahead of me. I looked South America up on the map and I knew it was an awful long way from Toronto. I remembered a little bit from school about Argentina, that Buenos Aires was the capital. But beyond that, it was just like stepping into oblivion. I had no idea what to expect.

Can a wife turn down an expatriate transfer? Although the company and employee usually believe that the wife has a role in deciding whether to move abroad, she rarely does. By the time the company identifies the employee who it wants to transfer and announces its decision, it has generally made a large investment in his acceptance. Subtle pressure discourages open discussion of the pros and cons of the international move. The employee often feels he would disappoint the company if he did not accept; his wife feels she would disappoint her husband if she refused to go. The employee often feels he would hinder his career by saying no; his wife feels reluctant to disagree. The couple fails to mention concerns they could easily have discussed and resolved prior to departure. At a time when communication is critical, open communication is often absent.

Venezuela

Bill came home in November and asked me what I thought about moving . . . [abroad]. I was silent. Then he told me about what a big promotion it would be and what it would mean for the rest of his career. I told him that I was delighted. The company told us about the things to take and the name of an international school. And we were made busy with the preparations. We left.

"Deciding to Move Abroad: The Carpenter Family's Story" presents the conflicting pressures and dilemmas faced by an American couple when offered the opportunity of a first expatriate assignment. As you read the case, which is based on a true story, ask yourself whether Tom, the manager, should accept the global assignment being offered to him.

Should the family move from the United States to Argentina? If the couple chooses to move, what could Tom, his wife Jane, his boss Mr. Abbott, and the company do to increase the chances of the family succeeding?

DECIDING TO MOVE ABROAD: THE CARPENTER FAMILY'S STORY[1]

Tom and Jane Carpenter are a young couple living comfortably in a New England town in the United States. They have three children, Mary, 11, Jerry, 6, and Ann, 3.

Tom works in the headquarters of a major manufacturing company as an executive in the engineering department. He has an excellent salary and up until now has been satisfied with his job. A quiet, handsome man about 36 years old, he is intelligent, sensitive, ambitious, and known as "a good family man." He has the respect of his colleagues and subordinates. The upper echelons of management regard him as a promising candidate for senior management in this company. They consider Tom a practical man, able to take the changes in life with a basic optimism and adaptability that appear to give him a maturity beyond his years. He likes the material wealth and comfort his years of conscientious work have produced. He enjoys the status of his company, which has an excellent name in its field, being considered one of the most progressive and future-minded of global companies.

If Tom is the practical member of the family, Jane is the "dreamer." She is a pretty, energetic woman of 30, a good wife and mother and an active member of several committees and volunteer groups. She is strongly attached to both her family and her parents, who are in their early sixties and live in a nearby town. She is sincerely interested in many good causes and always finds the time and energy to devote to them. While she is not a very practical woman, her enthusiasm for her projects is admired by her many friends.

Tom and Jane married early and struggled together for several years until they were able to achieve the comfortable life they now enjoy. Their marital life has been happy and more or less undisturbed, and through the struggle of their earlier years they developed a rewarding relationship. Although they have traveled to several parts of the United

continued on next page ■

■ *continued from previous page*

States with and without the children, neither Tom nor Jane had traveled abroad until two years ago. At that time, the company sent Tom, together with three other executives, to Latin America to explore the possibilities of setting up four new plants in four different countries.

Both Tom and Jane have been feeling more and more relaxed in the past years, since they have realized many of their dreams. They have a good family, financial security, and many friends. They feel especially proud of their new home, recently finished. Jane has worked hard to find the furniture and the internal decorations they wanted and now her dream house seems completed. They have both been, so far, generally satisfied with their children, who are well adjusted to their present environment. They have experienced certain problems with Mary, who is a very sensitive and shy girl, and with Jerry, who has had some difficulties adapting in school. But these were very minor problems that have not seriously disturbed the otherwise happy family life. Despite their seemingly very satisfactory family life, there have recently been more occasions when Tom and Jane have felt (each one without admitting it to the other) that something is "missing."

Tom believes his life has fallen into a too comfortable routine. The new tasks the company gives him seem to have less challenge and adventure. For a long while he had been satisfied that his career has had a steady development through the years. The time of anxiety and uncertainty has passed, but along with it the sense of excitement and inner feeling of searching and moving. He had begun to feel that he needed a change and it was at that time that the company sent him for four months to Latin America. Tom felt this trip was one of the most interesting and rewarding experiences of his whole life. Being away for the first time from his family for such a long period, he missed them and was disappointed that wives were not allowed to accompany their husbands on that trip. At the same time, Tom found the prospects of building up the company in Latin America attractive. He discovered that he liked to travel, to meet new people, to become acquainted with different ways of living, to be more a part of the world and of events outside his hometown. The three other executives who traveled with him felt about the same as he did. Each seemed to be a little weary of being "a little fish" at headquarters. The possibility of becoming a pioneer in the new Latin America divi-

continued on next page ■

■ continued from previous page

sion was an exciting prospect. Tom somehow felt reluctant to communicate to Jane his thoughts about that trip and especially his satisfaction. He felt particularly reluctant to tell her how much he was hoping the company would choose him from among the four executives to set up the plants in Latin America.

In a different way, but with the same feeling of restlessness and discontent, Jane also feels that their pleasant, well-organized life lacks the excitement of unpredictability. She divides her time among many activities, but finds herself at times dreaming about the world outside her hometown. Like Tom, she sometimes wonders whether their life has not become too settled, an almost unaltered routine, but unlike Tom, she checks herself by asking the simple question that, after all, isn't this what life really is?

When Tom came home with the news that Mr. Abbott, the president of the company, had offered him the key position in Latin America, she felt pleased to hear of the high esteem his superiors had for Tom. Actually, Jane too had been wondering for some time what would be the result of Tom's trip to Latin America.

Although she would have enjoyed traveling with Tom on his first trip to Latin America, the idea that they would have had to leave the children for such a long time forced her to exclude absolutely the possibility of her going, even if the wives of executives had been allowed to accompany their husbands. After her trip, she used to wonder whether the company would choose Tom, if the decision to establish the plants was made. At that time the idea of having to move to a new environment was not unpleasant.

Now that the offer was firm, with a high salary, cost of living expenses, and opportunity for travel throughout Latin America, she began to have some fears. As Tom talked excitedly about the challenging tasks he would have, her fears grew. She increasingly felt that neither their family nor their life had much to gain from this experience. It would represent a big step forward in Tom's career, to be sure, but Jane felt that Tom would succeed wherever he worked. On his present job, Tom and Jane shared so much time together, while in the new job, as she understood it, Tom would have to travel a great deal. She felt unhappy and ashamed about her fears as opposed to Tom's enthusiasm and obvious willingness to venture ahead.

One evening she tried to sit down by herself and figure out why this

continued on next page ■

■ *continued from previous page*

new job was not so attractive. There was some urgency for Tom to make up his mind within a week, and she felt the need to understand what this decision to move abroad really meant for her and for her family.

She tried to be honest with herself. She naturally had fears about moving to a new environment which was strange and where people spoke another language. She knew that the climate was very different and she believed that the living conditions were likely to offer fewer comforts. She would live far from her friends and her parents. Their furniture would have to be stored, and their new house rented or sold, since it was not clear how many years Tom would need to establish the four new plants.

She feared she would remain isolated because she did not believe she could have close contact with the local people for a long time. Everything she had heard so far about the personality of Latin Americans made her fear that close friendships would be difficult to achieve, at least for some time, because she had the impression that they were rather temperamental and unstable. Although she admitted to herself that she was basing her impression on hearsay and fiction, she somehow could not avoid believing it. She had also heard that there was a great deal of anti-American feeling in the country where they would initially live. She also worried that the sanitary conditions would be dangerous to the health of the children. The company had little experience in Latin America, so it would be likely that they would have to find their own way and learn, probably by hard experience, how to get along in these countries. She realized that what disturbed her more than anything else was that Tom was going to travel a lot. She would have to face most of the problems of their adaptation alone, while up until now they had always shared whatever problems they had to face, and had supported each other in finding solutions. Tom's position also meant that he would see more places, meet more people, and in general enjoy himself more and probably get more satisfaction out of the whole experience than would she and the children. She was distressed to realize that she already resented him for that and felt angry because she could sense that, although he was discussing the decision with her, he had already made up his mind. Jane kept her fears more or less to herself, but she did communicate to Tom her reluctance to go and gave as one of her main reasons her worry about the effect this move would have on the education of their children and their health.

continued on next page ■

■ *continued from previous page*

Tom sensed most of Jane's fears and he reacted to her expressed doubts by attempting to assure her that he thought that the children could adapt after a while and that the experience would be very good for them. They could learn a new language and make new friends. As for themselves, he had the best of memories from his own trip and he believed that they were both going to find this new experience enriching and rewarding. He did not underestimate the difficulties involved, but he expressed his belief that they were capable of overcoming them, while enjoying all the advantages that living abroad would offer. Inwardly Tom felt disappointed with Jane's negative reactions and the difficulties she seemed to be having. He had always believed her to be a woman of courage, endowed with curiosity and interest for the world outside. In previous times of crisis in their life, she had always proven strong and supportive and she had always shown a spirit of adventure and willingness to go ahead. It was a painful surprise for him to realize that this spirit would operate only in the security of the familiar environment, while a more profound change seemed to appear to Jane as a great threat to herself and her family. He had hoped that she would back him in this decision that was so important to his career. Nevertheless, he maintained his confidence in her and he believed she would change her mind in time. He called a nearby language school and made plans for both of them to take Spanish lessons.

When Jane's parents came to visit, Jane told them of the company's offer to Tom. Her father, who had been ailing for some time, was visibly depressed by the news. Her mother said that this was going to be a great experience for them, "a chance of a lifetime," as she put it. Jane knew that her mother had always regretted not being able to travel abroad. Now she was thrilled that the children were given the opportunity and she promised to come and visit them in Latin America if Tom accepted the position.

Dinner with Mr. Abbott

A few days later, Tom's boss, Mr. Abbott, invited Tom and Jane for dinner, saying that he always talked over a new job abroad with both husband and wife, because he felt that it was very important to take into consideration the wife's feelings. Jane had many fears about this dinner. First, she resented being "looked over" by Mr. Abbott who, until

continued on next page ■

■ *continued from previous page*

now, had not spent much time with them socially. Second, she did not want to reveal her doubts to Tom's boss, who had a reputation for making quick judgments about people, often not very favorable.

This dinner turned out to be a very pleasant one. Mrs. Abbott helped to put everyone at ease throughout the dinner, talking about her pleasant experience abroad when Mr. Abbott was managing director of a subsidiary in Europe. Mrs. Abbott had enjoyed Paris and Rome, but admitted she knew little about life in cities like Buenos Aires and Rio.

Mr. Abbott finally turned to Jane and said: "Well, we are very glad you are taking the news of this new assignment for Tom so well. I know you realize what an opportunity this job will be for him. It is a real challenge for him, far greater than what he can get here, you know." Tom hurriedly answered for Jane, who was about to reply to Mr. Abbott: "Jane is really a born traveler. I know that she is looking forward to living in Argentina. She has already found out how she can take Spanish lessons." Mr. Abbott seemed pleased. He said: "That is really fine. You know, Tom, that our firm is rapidly becoming a global company. There will be few opportunities at headquarters for executives whose international experience is limited. Our policy is to create a management team that can base its decisions on actual experience abroad. Of course, having the kind of wife who is willing to take the risk of going off to the jungle is quite an asset. You are a lucky man, Tom."

While Jane joined in the laughter, she was inwardly very angry. That night, she and Tom had a quarrel that continued for the next few days. Jane resented that the whole discussion was conducted as though Tom had already accepted the job, as well as the fact that she was not given a chance to talk about Tom's work with Mr. Abbott. Tom insisted that Mr. Abbott was not the kind of man to whom one could reveal any doubts about a company decision. Discussing the problem the next day with the children confused Tom and Jane even more, because the children's reactions were not clear. Mary was unwilling to go; Jerry and Ann seemed excited, but it was more because of the thrill they felt than because they really understood the issue. By now Jane was finding it difficult to sleep, and Tom said that the company required a formal decision by the following Monday.

Tom and Jane had a long weekend to think over the decision and give a final answer to Mr. Abbott on Monday.

Cross-Cultural Transitions

Expatriates not only experience a grueling physical move abroad, they must also adjust to the new culture and create a meaningful life abroad. Companies generally give considerable attention to the logistics of the transfer itself: what expatriates should pack, which shipper to use, where to stay upon arrival, and so on. They pay much less attention to the skills necessary for adjusting to the new country: good language training; a knowledge of the culture and its people; and an awareness of culturally based differences in values, attitudes, and behaviors. Least attention is paid to assisting the spouse in creating a meaningful portable life abroad. Although rarely recognized as a potent issue by either the employee or the children, the structureless role of the spouse demands explicit attention: if she is to have a fulfilling life abroad, she must create it. The following section reviews the transition itself and the initial adjustment issues confronting the spouse; it then discusses the broader and more fundamental issue of creating a meaningful life abroad.

It Is Harder for the Spouse

As mentioned previously, when a wife moves abroad, she comes into more direct contact with the "foreignness" of the new culture than does her husband. The husband, as an expatriate manager, generally works in the most internationally cosmopolitan strata of society: he meets people who speak English and have met foreigners before. His wife meets people who are much less cosmopolitan. In caring for her family's daily living needs, she often meets people who do not speak English and have rarely met foreigners. Whereas a global manager often has a secretary and colleagues to translate the language and explain local customs, his wife must depend on her own skills and ingenuity. Whereas a global manager works in an office filled with other expatriates to answer his questions and share his frustrations, his wife often finds herself isolated in her world at home. She must confront the differences on her own.

Many wives feel unprepared for their move. They know little about the country, culture, or specific location. Their expectations and the foreign reality have little in common. Upon arrival, they often react with surprise and excitement mixed with bewilderment and fear. In the following comment, two expatriate wives describe their arrival in Africa:

Africa

Well, my expectations were very, how would I say, very large. For me, Africa was . . . totally unknown . . . except that I could equate it with wild animals, missionaries, nice black people, and a very different way of life than in Canada. . . . I didn't question anything. I was very young, just married, and very happy to discover a new country. I could imagine that they had modern cities, that Conakry would be a modern city with all the amenities; I asked no questions and just left.

Finally I arrived at . . . this hazy airport. . . . I got off the plane, and there were . . . all of these black faces that I wasn't really used to in such mass. So I said, "It's so good to be here and I am so looking forward to getting into the house." . . . [My husband] didn't know how to tell me, but he said, "But we don't have a house." So I burst into tears. I guess it was just the whole stress of thinking that finally I was going to be in a house, and the jet lag, and just being in a completely different culture and a completely different color.

Culture Shock: Challenges of the Initial Period Abroad

Culture shock, as described in Chapter 8, is the reaction of expatriates to entering a new, unpredictable, and therefore uncertain environment. During the first few months in a new culture, expatriates often find that other people's behavior does not make sense, and even more disconcerting, that their own behavior fails to produce expected results. Wives, being in more direct contact with the foreign culture than employees, describe some of their initial reactions as surprise, bewilderment, and disorientation:

Guinea

Well, then we went into our building, a very modern building. We were on the ninth floor, and the building had no elevators. So we had to walk the nine floors. And then we arrived in this beautiful, huge apartment, with three bathrooms and no water.

Argentina

Everything I was comfortable with in a North American suburban setting, like my shopping, and the schools, and my daily routine, just was drastically different in Argentina. Perhaps the thing that struck me the most was when I set out to do my grocery shopping (which is something that we take for granted with our big supermarkets [in Canada]). I found myself in the biggest supermarket [in Argentina] . . . which was just a filthy little dump really, and as I looked around to fill my grocery cart, the only thing I recognized was a box of Quaker Oats. Everything was packaged differently, everything had Spanish names on it, and I couldn't tell salt from icing sugar.

Hong Kong

Before I went to Hong Kong, I'd read a lot of books. I expected the Chinese to be dignified and very courteous. The Cantonese in Hong Kong are the opposite of that. They are very noisy and . . . very pushy. In Argentina, I expected the romantic Latin. Instead, I was annoyed at the "macho-ness" of the men. The reality . . . was disappointing.

Frustration. The first few months in a foreign culture are rarely easy. The constant frustration of not understanding and not being able to get simple things done follows the initial surprise.

> It's the constant minor frustrations . . . the phone never works, the electric power is variable, and, oh yes, filling the water bottles at 4 A.M., just to be sure that we'd have some water.

> I had my new Electrolux vacuum cleaner and I tried to show the help how to use it. . . . The next thing I knew they were vacuuming the patio and the grass. They just had no concept of what this [vacuum] was.

> We were not aware of the fact that everything seems to be done through a bribe. We were insulted when it was suggested. I think we just didn't understand the culture. So we waited from January until May before our furniture was sprung from customs.

> Things can be very difficult . . . [say] you have to put on a dinner party: dinner parties are very important because there is not very much entertainment, so you have to make your own entertainment. You have 10 people coming, and there is no electricity, and you have just put the roast in the oven. Right, what do you do? And it's pouring with rain outside so you can't make a barbecue. So you raid the cupboard and find a tin of ham, and you find some tomatoes, and then you find this and that, and you all have a good giggle. You know, really, there is no other way of doing it. You can't get depressed about these things.

I like it . . . but things don't work and it's frustrating. I didn't expect things not to work in Europe. In a developing country, yes, but not in Europe.

While the newness of the environment in large part causes the difficulties, insufficient language competence, loneliness, boredom, and a sense of meaninglessness exacerbate the problems.

Foreign Language Illiteracy. Whereas most employees have less immediate need for foreign language competence than do their wives, many organizations offer language training only to employees. They expect the wife to enroll on her own in language courses, if she so desires, and often not at the company's expense. Consequently, many wives never become fluent in the local language and therefore have little possibility of becoming fully comfortable living in the new culture.

Italy

I think the most difficult thing when you arrive in a country is not being able to communicate. You feel very isolated because you don't speak the language. So everything becomes very difficult; all small details, everyday life is difficult because you don't know how to communicate.

Mexico

The only foreign language I learned is Spanish . . . and I didn't find it easy. I was embarrassed to speak in case I didn't have it right, and this became a big problem. . . . I would pretend I hadn't been there very long, even when I had been there several months. And I'd have the children speaking for me in the taxi because they could speak far better Spanish than I could.

Argentina

I think the thing that bothered me the most was just my inability to express myself in Spanish. It was a while before I was able to take lessons, and I never did become fluent in the language. I could get by in English in most situations, but it was a little disappointing to see my husband learning Spanish through the office and my children learning it in school and yet I just could never seem to find the time or the concentration to sit down and master this thing.

Loneliness. The lack of intimate friendships causes a major part of the difficulty during the initial period abroad. Most wives leave their family and friends at home and experience a void upon arrival abroad. The loneliness expresses itself in a number of ways:

I spent more time alone than anywhere ever. . . . It's hard to spend so much time alone.

We had a lot of acquaintances, few good friends. . . . You can't make friends until you've learned the language.

Loneliness is the biggest problem with all the moves. I can remember moving from Mexico to the United States very worried about what we would find there. Looking down at the little family that was in just a shack in Mexico City and envying them because they had the whole family with them. And I thought, they are better off than I am.

. . . In Hong Kong, not long after we arrived, our daughters were going back to school, my husband was going back with them on a business trip, and I felt, well, this is ridiculous. I am the only one here, and the rest of the family is on the other side of the world.

. . . I think that every country and every move has its low point and then you start going up. . . . I think loneliness is probably the low point.

When you live abroad and you suffer loneliness, you have to . . . be your own best friend.

So I was very alone, very lonely, and my husband was not going through the same problems as I. . . . And I felt more lonely because I couldn't share my problems with him. It was very difficult for . . . at least a year or a year and a half.

Boredom and Meaninglessness. Many wives describe themselves as having hours and hours on their hands with nothing to do. They describe themselves as living in a gilded cage: they have nice homes and servants to do the work but they do not have a meaningful role to fulfill. They no longer feel needed to perform many of the duties that they had previously fulfilled for their families. In addition, many are barred, often by legal restrictions, from working or continuing careers outside of the home.

I was like a prisoner in my own apartment. I had nothing to do. I had no books with me, except for one or two and that's very quickly gone through. . . . I had absolutely nothing to do. So I started to write letters. That was my only contact with the outside world; and I don't like writing letters!

I felt useless. I was a fifth wheel. There was the maid to do the work and no children who needed my attention.

I was going to be a nurse, but I had to have a work permit . . . so I threw myself into the women's club . . . bridge and golf, empty activities, but they filled my time.

Time . . . trying to find things to do with my time. I spent time sewing and I hate to sew. . . . We got together to crochet and talk. Blah!

After the novelty wears off, you have to find something to do with your time. I worked in a hospital, cooked, gardened. . . . I want to work again.

Separation and a Lack of Support

The expatriate employee's frequent absence compounds the difficulties in adjusting to the new environment. Having just started a new job, a global manager often works long hours. Exacerbating the situation further, many global assignments include regional or worldwide responsibilities and a great amount of travel. Whereas the wife has just given up her friends, activities, and in many cases a job or career to follow her husband and family abroad, her husband continues and often increases his major involvement in work, often to the near exclusion of his wife. Separation and lack of support cause numerous complaints:

My husband wasn't there to help me. He did nothing on the move. He works and travels.

My husband was always away; never available. The men are so busy and the women have nothing to do.

Well, I expected him to travel a little, but I didn't expect it to be so long or so often.

My husband, as well as most of the men in the company, was away probably two weeks out of four. We knew before we left that there was going to be a lot of traveling, but it didn't really make its impact until he was actually doing it.

As shown in Figure 9-1, the husband's work often leaves him least

FIGURE 9-1 Need Versus Availability Gap

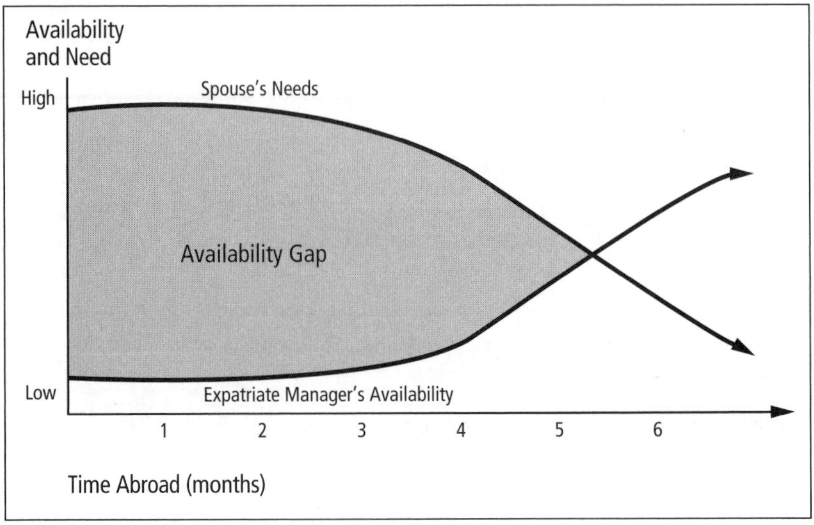

available during the first few months abroad, exactly when his wife needs him the most to help with the logistics of settling in and to provide companionship and support. Unfortunately, the pattern of absent husbands and isolated wives reinforces itself in a vicious cycle. As more problems build up at home, many global managers feel less desire to spend time at home. By their own admission, many spend more time in the office and traveling than the job actually requires. As the wife's situation becomes more difficult, her husband, often feeling guilty at the realization that his career caused the situation in the first place, increasingly avoids home.

Creating a Meaningful Portable Life

Following the initial period of adjustment, the wife faces the hardest task of all: creating a meaningful life abroad. She must identify what she wants to do and find a way to do it in the foreign country. For women who follow their husbands from country to country, it becomes the search for a meaningful portable life.

Being a transient, I tried to develop those things because . . . it is very difficult for me to have a career. And luckily, I am not a particularly career-minded person. I want to take experiences and opportunities as they come. I want to learn different things, and I want to try different things. I mean, I only have one life. So a career and stepping up the ladder isn't important to me personally, it isn't. But it is important for me to take skills that are portable because, being a transient, you have to have something that you can grasp hold of, that you can take with you, that can be a certain continuity.

Creating a meaningful life abroad remains the most neglected aspect of the spouse's experience abroad. People talk about the initial culture shock, learning a foreign language, and adjusting to the new culture. But adjustment is only half of the challenge; it brings a potentially negative situation to neutral, not to positive. Adjustment only brings the wife to the point where the foreign environment no longer constantly frustrates her; it does not provide motivation, direction, and meaning to daily life abroad. Introspection and life planning are necessary for the spouse to answer the questions, "What do I really want to do?" "What would I be happiest having accomplished during my years abroad?" "How can I continue doing the things that I find most satisfying and important even while I no longer live at home?" The answers to these questions vary. One woman becomes an artist, another a counselor to expatriate families, a third teaches English to immigrant children, a fourth does extensive volunteer work, and a fifth starts her own business. Many simultaneously remain very involved in raising a family. One French Canadian woman, who focused on learning the history, literature, and culture of each country in which she lived, described her growing sense of purpose.

You start to understand the people around you. . . . They are different, but very often the difference is not so evident. But slowly, you go into knowing these differences, and it is a new world that opens up to you . . . . You discover the arts, and the folklore, and how the folklore is lived in the modern world. It is not so evident but there is always something that stays from these roots. You start to see all the small differences that you wouldn't notice if you were just a tourist for a month or so in the country. When you live there, slowly you get to know the people much more, the civilization, how they are and why they are like that, and then I think it is very enjoyable. You are gaining something, it is not just giving.

More frequently today the questions center on identifying ways for the spouse to continue a career while living abroad.

Returning Home

Expatriates often remember their home country as a more wonderful and perfect place than it actually is. As things get tough abroad and they experience culture shock and difficulties in adjusting to another culture, they dream about how easy and good life will be when they return home. In reality, however, reentry often presents more challenges than the initial move abroad. Two women, who had lived in a number of countries, capture the difficulty and the disillusionment of returning home.

Canada

Coming back was . . . the most difficult move of all. Why was it so difficult? Because . . . you change, the country changes, the people change. You are expecting . . . that you are coming back to your place and that you will feel good right away. . . . It is not true. You come back and you feel like a foreigner in your own country. . . . People deal with you as if . . . you are different. Even your way of speaking the language. So you feel cut off completely and it is your own country. The roots that you were not really conscious of, but somehow, dreaming with. You know everybody needs some kind of roots and you come back to these roots and you don't feel well [sic] with them.

England

I was in England recently. I was sitting in the train and I watched two English mums coming from the corner shop, standing and talking. And I said to my husband, "I know exactly what they are going to do, they are going to go home, have a little lunch, have a little sleep, and then they will watch a little bit of telly [television] and maybe do some ironing, then they will get dinner." It is a pity that I am not able to do that anymore. I'm wanting more from life. I am pleased that I have changed, that I have matured, that I have developed, but sometimes it would be easier if I had stayed content with that life. We don't feel we can go back to England. We have been gone too long. . . . They have changed and we have changed.

Recommendations for Single-Career Couples

Expatriate wives offer a range of suggestions for coping with cross-cultural transitions and creating a meaningful portable life abroad, including knowing yourself and what you want out of life and taking responsibility for creating the type of life you want to live. They recommend treating the move as permanent, no matter how temporary; persevering and being patient. Whereas some recommendations focus on what wives must do for themselves, most recommendations work best if all three—the organization, employee, and spouse—commit themselves to making the global experience successful. Spouses, for example, must ask themselves what they really want out of the time abroad; the company needs to include spouses in predeparture site visits and, if possible, in selecting a home; and employees, to the extent possible, need to limit their travel during the first three months abroad.

Many companies now interview both the employee and spouse prior to offering the employee a global assignment (18;20;21). They screen out couples with a high probability of failure, including those with excessive alcohol or drug use; indications of rigid and inflexible personalities or lifestyles; lack of communication among the husband, wife, and children; and inappropriate or inadequate coping and stress management mechanisms. Research has shown that the worlds of work and family overlap (10;26). Companies that screen couples recognize that the quality of home life affects the employee's ability to work, and similarly, that the very nature of an expatriate assignment strongly influences the family's daily life.

LIVING GLOBALLY: DUAL-CAREER COUPLES

Over the past decade, the number of couples in which both partners have significant careers outside the home has increased dramatically. As discussed in the prior section, most companies, when filling global assignments, have historically selected men whose wives either did not work outside of the home or who worked in jobs that they were willing to give up in order to follow their husband abroad. This situation is no longer true today. Companies today select both women and men for global assignments and, in both cases, their spouses often have careers of their own (17). Given the recent increase in companies selecting women executives for global assignments, many of whom are in dual-career marriages, this section—in a reversal of the prior section—refers to the employee as "she" and to the spouse, her husband, as "he." Needless to say, the labels would be reversed for companies offering a man the global assignment and having his wife follow him abroad as a *trailing spouse*.

When offered a global assignment, dual-career couples must decide for themselves the conditions under which they would accept. The couple, and especially the trailing spouse, often considers a number of options:

- Simply *turning down the global assignment*, although this option usually results in negative career consequences.
- Finding the trailing spouse a *position in the foreign country*. Ideally, both partners are able to move abroad at the same time, although they more commonly move at different times—with the timing for each move determined by the separate needs of her and his careers.
- Finding the trailing spouse *a position in the region*, thus becoming a shorter-distance commuting couple.
- Having the trailing spouse *remain at home in his current position*, thus becoming a longer-distance commuting couple.
- Having the trailing spouse *take a sabbatical*—a career break that allows him to accompany his wife while she works abroad even though he is unable to continue his own career in the particular country.
- Having the trailing spouse accompany his wife on the global assignment while continuing his own career. This is possible if *the trailing spouse has a portable career*, which the e-business revolution has made increasingly likely.
- *Creating other options* that work for the particular couple and family.

REGIONAL COMMUTING: FROM BEIJING TO OSAKA

A major American manufacturing firm transferred a senior engineer to Beijing for a three-year assignment. When her husband discovered that there were no positions available for his specialty in the Chinese capital, he accepted an excellent position in Osaka, Japan. Although the couple could not live together, their commute between Beijing and Osaka was more reasonable than it would have been if he had remained in Chicago.

Leading companies today increase the chances of dual-career couples finding acceptable options by offering them services and benefits that traditional single-career couples neither need nor find valuable. Leading companies, for example, offer trailing spouses career counseling and global executive-search services. In so doing the company shares responsibility with the couple for finding an appropriate solution. The career counselor initially helps the couple determine whether they would find a commuter lifestyle acceptable. Then the counselor helps the trailing spouse decide whether he wants to continue his current career or change careers. After lifestyle flexibility and career aspirations are established, the executive search firm searches for professional positions in the same city or region as the employee's global assignment. They then coach the trailing spouse on effective ways to meet and interview with potential employers in the particular country or countries. Simultaneously, most leading companies, rather than explaining why it is impossible to secure a work permit for the trailing spouse in the particular country (as has been so common in the past), take responsibility for securing a work permit (often based on the trailing spouse's own newfound position in the foreign country rather than based on the expatriate employee's position).

A PLANNED SABBATICAL: A SWEDISH HUSBAND IN HONG KONG

When a New York bank decided to transfer an American woman to a vice president's position in Hong Kong, they told her Swedish economist husband that Hong Kong would not give spouses work permits. After some reflection, the Swedish economist decided to support his wife's career by taking a sabbatical and following her to Hong Kong without a job. As he thought about his upcoming time in Asia, he looked forward to learning about the Chinese culture and economy and having time to improve his tennis game.

One week after arriving in Hong Kong, the Swedish economist began spending his mornings playing tennis with the other expatriate spouses—the wives of the bank's other executives. Suddenly, to the surprise and amusement of the couple, the bank called and told the Swedish economist that they had found him an ideal position and, based on it, they could obtain a work permit for him.

Whereas the motivation of the bank could certainly be questioned, the outcome benefited all trailing spouses—men and women—who now publicly recognized that the bank could, when motivated, find both appropriate positions and work permits as needed.

Once the couple identifies an acceptable lifestyle and the trailing spouse selects or creates an appropriate position, leading companies support the couple's decisions by offering them a flexible expatriate benefits package tailored to their particular needs. The company, for example, might pay for extra plane fares and telephone bills—"staying connected costs"—for commuting couples.

INTERCONTINENTAL COMMUTING: MONTREAL TO LONDON

A major telecommunications company transferred a Montreal executive to London for four years. Although her husband, a professor, was able to accompany her to England for the first two years while he wrote his book, he had to return to Montreal to continue teaching at the university for the third and fourth years. To continue spending time with each other during the last two years of the assignment, the couple chose to commute every three weeks between London and Montreal. The telecommunications company supported the decision by allowing the couple to spend less of their expatriate-benefits allowance on housing and more on the additional intercontinental airline tickets.

Whereas many companies still falsely believe that transferring dual-career couples poses great obstacles, even more companies erroneously believe that the challenges to sending dual-career couples with children on global assignments remain insurmountable. They are wrong. Many couples report that it is easier, not harder, to maintain the three time-consuming roles of parent, spouse, and manager while abroad on a global assignment than it is at home.

Do all dual-career expatriate couples find good solutions? Unfortunately, no. Husbands who decide to accompany their wives on global assignments without having positions of their own, for example, often find that the cultural dynamics of the local community make it very difficult for them to succeed. Few communities in the world offer social support to a man who chooses to become the primary homemaker or parent in the family. In many communities, such men are both disparaged and isolated. For most couples, however, acceptable solutions can be

BOTH CAREERS TRANSFERRED TO SAME CITY: BANGKOK, WITH A HUSBAND AND CHILDREN

When a major oil company transferred a geologist to Bangkok, her husband, a diplomat, arranged a transfer to the same city. In describing their global lifestyle, the geologist explained that the availability of household help—including a driver, a nanny for their two small children, and a housekeeper—made it much easier for her to balance her three extremely time-consuming roles of mother, wife, and geologist in a way that would be financially impossible for her to achieve in the United States. "Even though everyone thought it would be completely impossible, the expatriate assignment has made my life easier, not more difficult. Time is my scarcest resource, and the household help available in Thailand gives me the time I need to be a good mother, a good wife, and a good manager."

found if both the company and the couple actively work to create them, rather than attempting to fit dual-career couples into the lifestyles of their single-career predecessors.

"The O'Connors' Story" is the true story of a dual-career couple faced with making their fourth international move. If you were the couple, what would you do? If you were the company, what would you offer the couple to make certain that the global assignment succeeded? What could Michael and Kelly each do to increase the chances of success on their move to Hong Kong?

LIVING ABROAD: THE O'CONNORS' STORY[2]

Kelly O'Connor sat in her upstairs study of the Southern California home she shared with her husband Michael and their two children, Kate, age 6, and James, age 4. The computer screen in front of her reminded her that she had only four hours to complete a mid-term analysis of downsizing and present it at her seminar at UCLA, an hour away. If the return traffic wasn't bad, she would have 15 minutes to change and straighten

continued on next page ■

■ continued from previous page

the house before Michael arrived for dinner with his law firm's managing partner from New York. She turned away from the computer, reflecting on the decision she and Michael needed to make. Should they move back to Hong Kong?

Early History: The First Seven Years in Hong Kong

Kelly and Michael had begun their global careers in Hong Kong nearly a decade earlier, one year after their marriage in New York. After graduating from Harvard Law School, Michael had gone to work for a New York law firm. A few years later, bored with domestic work, he joined Fishbeck, Rhodes and Goncourt (FR&G) to take a position in Hong Kong.

The early years at FR&G in Hong Kong were thrilling and Michael showed real talent both for handling complex cross-border financing and for working with difficult clients. In addition, he enjoyed the family feeling the firm cultivated by celebrating American and local holidays with the entire staff at a partner's home, sharing practices, and pinch-hitting for each other. The firm recognized Michael's talent by electing him partner two months before Kate was born, and by giving him responsibility for managing the Hong Kong office, making him the youngest partner ever to be entrusted with line management in the 50-year-history of the firm. Under Michael's leadership, the office achieved its best financial year ever.

Kelly's career also progressed in Hong Kong. The major British company she had joined as marketing administrator promoted her to vice president before her thirtieth birthday.

The Next Two Years in Japan

Recognizing Michael's success at managing the Hong Kong office and concerned about mounting problems in Tokyo, FR&G asked Michael to transfer to Japan. The position they offered him involved managing a start-up operation currently headed by a senior partner whose excesses the firm needed to control. Fortunately, Kelly was able to negotiate a lateral transfer to Tokyo, even though increasing Japanization of her British firm's Tokyo office had created a difficult working climate for expatriates.

As the family prepared to move to Japan, Kelly discovered that she was pregnant again. At the same time, Michael learned that new Japa-

continued on next page ■

■ *continued from previous page*

nese regulations would delay his work permit, thus preventing the family from accompanying him in dependent status. For the family to continue to live together, Kelly therefore needed to acquire a work permit through her own company and to bring in the children and housekeeper as her dependents. The permit problems forced Kelly to remain in Hong Kong for the first nine months while Michael commuted to and from Tokyo. Kelly remembers this period as painful and lonely:

> *After seven years in Hong Kong, most of my expatriate friends had come and gone. I became a lame duck in the Hong Kong office, since everyone knew I was leaving for Tokyo. And shuttling back and forth between Tokyo and Hong Kong satisfied no one.*
>
> *Fortunately, my second pregnancy was relatively easy, although I almost miscarried on a business trip to Perth and, later, the extra weight made me so clumsy that I tripped and broke a toe coming through immigration at Tokyo's Narita Airport, which left me hobbling around for the week of meetings. All the travel and stress finally resulted in the premature birth of my son.*
>
> *As soon as the hospital let us bring the baby home, Michael had to return to Japan. James was so tiny he had to be fed every two hours. I became so exhausted I feared I would sleep through his cries, which were only as loud as a kitten mewing. People from the office sent flowers, but no one visited. My parents flew in from the United States to help. Despite my investment in relationships with colleagues, the only people I felt I could count on were family.*

The family finally moved to Tokyo. Unfortunately, however, neither Michael's nor Kelly's professional situations turned out to be particularly satisfying, and each day brought new annoyances. For example, after having initiated, designed, and analyzed an important market research study, Kelly discovered that a male Japanese colleague planned to present it. When she suggested that this was unfair, her Japanese colleague told her that she could only attend the presentation if she took charge of visual aids.

> *At that point, I considered walking out, but I knew I couldn't. Michael still didn't have a residential working permit, so we would have been asked to leave Japan.*

continued on next page ■

■ *continued from previous page*

Ultimately the Japanese Ministry informed Michael that they had denied his visa application, and that he could accept "trainee" status or leave the country within a year. Although Kelly initially felt disappointed, believing that a longer stay in Japan would have offered them extremely useful international experience, she agreed with Michael that "trainee" status was untenable both for practical and "face saving" reasons

When they had originally agreed to move to Japan, FR&G had promised Michael that he could return to the U.S. office of his choice. As the situation in Japan deteriorated, Kelly and Michael decided to return to Los Angeles and use it as a base for building a new practice. Several months later, however, while dodging the half-full packing boxes on the floor of their Japanese home, Michael received a conference call from the Los Angeles managing partner asking him either not to come to Los Angeles or to delay his arrival. Michael explained that it was too late to change the previously agreed-to plans. A month later Michael left Tokyo having turned the operating revenue from a loss to a profit and having brought in the firm's third largest transaction of the year. As they left, Kelly and Michael felt particularly satisfied that they had helped build office morale in Tokyo by introducing family social events similar to those they had pioneered in Hong Kong.

The Los Angeles Years

Soon after returning to the United States, Michael passed the California State Bar Exam. Kelly settled the children into a rental house, supervised the restoration of their new home, and hunted for a job. The North American headquarters of her British company had originally agreed to transfer her to Los Angeles, but the L.A. office now nixed the idea. As a consequence, Kelly sent out more than 300 résumés, which resulted in more than 75 interviews. To her surprise, American firms did not seem to understand or to appreciate her international experience. Few prospective employers had heard of her prior employer—which is one of Britain's largest companies—nor did they seem to understand the British system of titles and responsibility levels used on her résumé. Kelly's salary requirements frequently intimidated potential employers as well. Kelly sought FR&G's help for introductions, but none were forthcoming. In fact, Kelly was rather surprised that after four months in Los Angeles, which included a holiday season,

continued on next page ■

■ *continued from previous page*
only one couple from the L.A. office had invited them to their home.

> *I guess I shouldn't have been so surprised, but I felt like a foreigner in my own country. I didn't know how things worked. With the exception of my family, it was almost as though we had never existed in the U.S. After nine years in Asia, we had no domestic credit record, which even made buying a car difficult. Our Asian credit histories didn't come with us, nor our driving records. We returned to the U.S. with no debt and tax returns showing more than $400,000 in annual income, and yet no one wanted to issue us a credit card. The language, parochialism, and obsessions with cars and breakfast cereals all made me feel like an alien in disguise.*

For years, Kelly had wanted to return to school for an MBA. Given the dismal employment situation she faced in Southern California, she chose to enter UCLA's Executive MBA (EMBA) Program. The two-year program, designed for executives with 10 or more years of experience, met on alternate weekends, allowing the participants to continue their careers while getting their MBAs.

The Offer to Return to Hong Kong

Shortly after Kelly's initial EMBA session, FR&G's Hong Kong office offered Michael the managing partner position for Hong Kong, China, and Thailand. Michael's initial instinct was to say no, but he had encountered major political and practice problems in the L.A. office for which he saw no easy solution. The L.A. managing partner, who was very senior within the firm, used a *laissez-faire* style of management that created strong competition and practice fiefdoms within the office. There was evidence, for example, that the banking partner with whom Michael thought he shared a practice, was blocking faxes and other business referral communiqués intended for him. Oddly enough, a *feng shui* expert* hired by Michael to advise him on the disposition of his new L.A. office indicated that his good fortune was being blocked in the west. As it happened, the other banking partner held the western office.

*Feng shui (Chinese) translates as "wind water" and is a form of ancient Chinese geomancy for determining the proper positioning of buildings, rooms, and furnishings in relation to the four directions, bodies of water, and other topographic criteria, with the ultimate aim of ensuring the inhabitants' good fortune.

continued on next page ■

■ continued from previous page

In addition, Michael found the practice in L.A. less intellectually challenging than his work in Asia. A further consideration was the hint of a recession on the economic horizon. Michael recognized that his two most promising L.A. clients no longer offered much potential due to internal restructuring and a bankruptcy.

Kelly became concerned that the firm's actions were seriously eroding Michael's self-confidence.

> *Michael claims that he could have happily stayed in L.A. in a secondary role in the firm, but I am not so sure. He forgets how depressed he had become. After his success in Hong Kong and Tokyo, Michael expected the firm to reward him. Instead, they held his salary steady the first year he was back, while raising others' salaries. He would come home at night with this hangdog look and absolutely anything to do with the office became a taboo subject. This hurt. By contrast, the people who originally asked him to go back to Asia were close friends, godparents to our children, and people who shared our sense that work could be exciting and rewarding without the backbiting and private empire building. I encouraged Michael to seriously consider Hong Kong because I wanted him to enjoy what he was doing again.*

While Michael and Kelly considered the Hong Kong offer, the L.A. managing partner announced his transfer to Sydney. He left a triumvirate in charge, including the banking partner with the western office. Prompted by other partners who lacked confidence in the new management team, Michael put forward his name for managing partner in the L.A. office, but the New York managing partner rejected it because the firm wanted Michael to go to Hong Kong.

That spring, Kelly watched several people in her EMBA class lose their jobs while Michael continued to have limited success developing an independent practice. As the national recession hit Southern California, Michael and Kelly began to seriously consider moving back to Hong Kong. Kelly, however, made three stipulations: she wanted an option to return to the United States in three years, to finish her degree within the normal time frame, and to keep their home. She also encouraged Michael to review the Hong Kong office's finances before making a final decision and to begin by commuting to ensure his involvement in any major decisions that might affect them later.

continued on next page ■

■ *continued from previous page*

At this point, in order to graduate with her class, Kelly dropped her outside activities and began doubling up on her course load. Michael began commuting to Hong Kong on a "two-weeks on" and "two-weeks off" basis. Kate and James went to a local preschool during the day and stayed with a baby-sitter in the evenings until Kelly could get home.

Second Thoughts

After four months of commuting, Michael came home one evening and reported that the firm had told an L.A. partner, whom it had sent to Tokyo for a two-year assignment and who now wished to return, that he was unwelcome. Another partner with a young family, who had opened the Moscow office, was told his compensation would be penalized if he returned according to the originally agreed-upon timetable. The firm penalized another expatriate partner at the annual compensation meeting for supposedly treating himself to excessive housing.

> *The more Michael told me about the schism in the firm between international and domestic, the more irritated I became. There is something odd about people's inability to recognize that when you live abroad you still have a right to a private life. Visitors from other offices often expect you to personally pick them up at the airport and to provide personal attention during their entire stay. They seem to expect this as fair recompense for firm-subsidized housing. Perhaps the partners see expatriates' housing as coming directly out of their pockets. Ultimately, as someone who has now lived and worked both abroad and in the United States, I can tell you the lifestyle is better in the United States.*

When Michael finally reviewed the Hong Kong office's financial statements, he discovered that it no longer had a banking practice and that the office would probably earn a mere $1.1 million in operating profits in the current fiscal year, before allocating funds to compensate the five partners. This represented $1 million less than in the prior year. Not surprisingly, morale was very low.

In addition, Michael discovered that the firm's new managing partner had reorganized Asia as the first region to operate with a consolidated P&L. The Asia region would be run jointly by the managing partners in Singapore and Japan, with the prospective managing part-

continued on next page ■

■ *continued from previous page*

ner of Hong Kong and China (Michael) thus being relegated to a mere consultative role.

At the same time, FR&G's new executive committee formally decided that the firm was compensating expatriates excessively both in housing and in other benefits. As a consequence, the committee lowered both the cost-of-living index and the allowable rent scale for Hong Kong. As part of their cost-cutting, they decided that the Hong Kong office was top-heavy and made contingency plans to lay off two partners.

Kelly became increasingly concerned that not only would the move to Hong Kong entail the usual transition costs in terms of emotions and time, but also that their standard of living would come under heavy pressure from the New York partners who no longer supported FR&G's global expansion in Asia:

> *During our previous time in Hong Kong, FR&G gave partners firm-sponsored club memberships and expense accounts for documentable home business entertaining. These were considered routine costs of doing business, as apartment buildings typically had no recreational facilities and most business entertaining was done at home. When Michael had been managing partner in Hong Kong, we had hosted 6 to 12 people for business-related dinners at least once a week. If anything, FR&G's housing subsidies and expatriate benefits were less generous than those of most other American law firms operating in Hong Kong.*

Weighing the Evidence

Kelly couldn't concentrate on her MBA mid-term. Michael had left the final Hong Kong decision up to her, although there was certainly little evidence that he was building a case to stay in Los Angeles.

Both Michael's FR&G experience and her own experience with the British company had convinced Kelly that she had had enough of working for others and of being under their thumbs. She therefore began to think about starting a business, although she wasn't sure what type. She knew she had access to start-up capital and felt confident that over time she could create a business that would serve some of her social goals. The last year had filled her with an almost missionary zeal to make the United States more globally competitive; to

continued on next page ■

■ *continued from previous page*

enjoin business to help in providing better public education for the communities from which they drew their workers; to discover a way to motivate businesses to see the possible synergies in Southern California's increasing cultural diversity rather than just seeing the problems; and to build something her children might inherit, to give them a cultural and family anchor in this rapidly changing world. She audited a class on entrepreneurship, discussed ideas with her business school classmates, and began investigating franchise possibilities.

The years in Hong Kong and Japan had led her to believe in the importance of family taking care of family. Not only did she want to be able to help Kate and James finance college and graduate school, but she also wanted to live near her parents in their senior years. If she said yes to Hong Kong, would the firm really allow them to return in three years?

How much energy would she have at 40? Enough to start again from scratch? Did it make sense to move away from all her UCLA contacts that might help her get a new business off the ground? Did Hong Kong's return to the People's Republic of China pose major political risks for expatriates and foreign businesses in Hong Kong? If she left Los Angeles, what could she build that she could bring back?

Michael was so bright. Couldn't he sidestep the political obstacles at FR&G and build a practice in Los Angeles if he tried? Or find something else? She was tired of the high transition costs of moving: the emotional upheaval, the cultural adjustments, and the long distances from family and friends. She felt weary from trying to build a new life every two or three years, seeing it swept away, and being forced to start over once again.

Kelly worried about moving two small children accustomed to lots of space in their California home back into one of Hong Kong's high rise apartment buildings. Luckily she knew the schools in Hong Kong were good.

Telephone calls poured in nearly every night from friends in Hong Kong and Michael's colleagues trying to convince her to move. Last week, the managing partner in Japan had stopped in L.A. on just such a mission.

"Analysis paralysis," Kelly said aloud, turning back to her computer. She glanced at her watch and resolved to put these thoughts to rest: the mid-term deadline was more imminent. Besides, there was an hour commute to UCLA and at least an hour back to decide on the next three years and the rest of her life.

SUMMARY

Today, companies transfer women and men abroad; they transfer both single-career and dual-career couples. In a single-career couple, the spouse's role is the most difficult of all family members'. The spouse—most often the wife—must adjust to the new culture and create a meaningful life for herself abroad. Her adjustment is made more difficult because she interacts with the least internationally sophisticated strata of society. Her ability to lead a meaningful life is challenged by the lack of structure in her life abroad and compounded by all of the activities, friends, and oftentimes a job or career that she has had to leave behind in her home country. Successfully managing the transition and creating a meaningful life abroad demand the involvement of the expatriate manager, the company, and the spouse.

Increasingly today, companies transfer people abroad who are in dual-career marriages. Leading companies assist such couples in identifying options for the trailing spouse, helping him or her find an appropriate position abroad, and supporting the couple's new lifestyle, especially when it involves global commuting. Assuming joint responsibility and using creativity lead dual-career couples to succeed in living and working abroad; the inappropriate application of procedures and benefits packages designed primarily for single-career couples does not lead to dual-career success.

FILM NOTE

Material in the section on single-career couples is presented in the video program, *A Portable Life*, which highlights the role of the spouse from the perspectives of four wives of global executives working for the Montreal-based multinational, Alcan Aluminum Ltd. (see reference 1 in References). *A Portable Life* is available from McGill University, Instructional Communication Centre, 550 Sherbrooke Street West, Suite 400, Montreal, Quebec, Canada H3A 2K6 (telephone: 1-514-398-7200; fax: 1-514-398-7339; e-mail: peggyg@550sherb.lan.mcgill.ca; web site: *http://www.mcgill.ca/icc*).

10

Global Careers

Ideally, . . . [a global manager] should have the stamina of an Olympic runner, the mental agility of an Einstein, the conversational skill of a professor of languages, the detachment of a judge, the tact of a diplomat, and the perseverance of an Egyptian pyramid builder. [And] that's not all. If they are going to measure up to the demands of living and working in a foreign country, they should also have a feeling for the culture; their moral judgment should not be too rigid; they should be able to merge with the local environment with chameleon-like ease; and they should show no signs of prejudice.[1]

— THOMAS AITKEN (18)

As GLOBALIZATION EVOLVED from a buzzword to a pervasive reality, demand increased for executives sophisticated in managing the complexities of global business. Government and corporate managers need to be able to think globally. They need to be able to work domestically on global projects as well as abroad on expatriate assignments and business travel. Global business has become so important that companies can no longer afford to consider candidates for executive positions unless they have had global experience (27;49;51).

According to Colby Chandler (39), the former CEO of Eastman Kodak Company, "These days there is not a discussion or a decision that does not have an international dimension. We would have to be blind not to see how critically important international experience is." The *Wall Street Journal* claims that "intensifying international competition will make the home-grown chief executive obsolete" (25). Duane Kullberg, Arthur Andersen and Company's former chief executive, agrees that future American CEOs "will be . . . [people] with experience outside the borders of the U.S. . . . If you go back 20 years, you could be pretty insular and still survive. Today, that's not possible" (25).

WHAT IT TAKES TO REACH THE TOP

North American companies compete with British, Chinese, French, German, Korean, and Scandinavian companies, among others, for global executives to manage their worldwide operations. Yet what it takes to reach the top of a company differs from one country to the next; companies view managerial success through their own cultural blinders (37;38;61). American managers, for example, view ambition and drive as the most important characteristic for success; French managers must be labeled as having high potential (61); German managers view creativity as essential for career success (61); and their British colleagues see creating the right image and getting noticed for what they do as essential (61).

Similarly, whereas Swiss and German companies respect technical creativity and competence, French and British companies often view managers with such qualities as "mere technicians" (37). Likewise, U.S. companies highly value entrepreneurs, while their British and French counterparts often view entrepreneurial behavior as disruptive (37). Similarly, whereas only half of Dutch managers see "skills in interpersonal relations and communication" as critical to career success, almost 90 percent of their British colleagues do so (38).

Global management expert André Laurent (61) describes German, British, and French managers' careers as follows (37:10):

> German managers, more than others, believe that creativity is essential for career success. In their minds, successful managers must have the right individual characteristics. German managers' outlook is rational: they view the organization as a coordinated network of individuals who make appropriate decisions based on their professional competence and knowledge.
>
> British managers hold a more interpersonal and subjective view of the organizational world. According to them, the ability to create the right image and to get noticed for what they do is essential for career success. British managers view organizations primarily as a network of relationships among individuals who get things done by influencing each other using communication and negotiation.
>
> French managers look at organizations as an authority network where the power to organize and control members stems from their position in the hierarchy. French managers focus on the organization as a pyramid of differenti-

ated levels of power to be acquired or dealt with. They perceive the ability to manage power relationships effectively and to "work the system" as critical to their career success.

As companies integrate their operations globally, these multiple national realities send conflicting messages to success-oriented managers. Affiliates in different countries operate differently and reward different behaviors based on their unique cultural perspectives (38). Regardless of what headquarters desires or designs, no single best way exists to perform or to achieve global career success (38). The challenge for today's global companies is to recognize local differences, while at the same time creating globally integrated career paths for their most senior executives.

Expatriate assignments form a key part of most global managers' careers. Traditionally, North American managers were attracted to working abroad by the financial rewards, increased responsibility, challenge, and independence as well as the unique lifestyle it afforded. Yet during the 1970s, a weakened U.S. dollar, inflation, and additional taxes reduced the attractiveness of financial packages. By the 1980s, dual-career marriages complicated transfer decisions as well as exacerbating their financial situation; expatriate salary increases rarely made up for reducing a two-income family to a single salary. Stories of prior expatriates whose careers had been sidetracked while abroad also made many managers hesitant to follow a global career path (8;47;51;55;68;80).

Yet today it is no secret that business faces an environment radically changed from that of even a few years ago, the result of increasingly networked and integrated global competition. The new global environment demands more, not fewer, globally competent managers (12). Rather than sidetracking a manager's career, global experience has rapidly become the only route to the top. According to the *New York Times* (39), hands-on global experience has slowly but surely moved out of the "nice but not necessary" category and into the "must have" slot for those on the corporate fast track. Given the increasing demand and potentially diminishing interest in global assignments, what can we predict for the twenty-first century? Will global organizations remain capable of attracting sufficient numbers of young managers? Are today's young managers interested in global work? What do they see as the advantages and disadvantages of global assignments?

As you read this chapter, ask yourself how prepared you are to work globally. What are your strengths and weaknesses as a global manager? How competitive is your company in offering managers the right incentives to pursue global careers?

IS THE TRADITIONAL EXPATRIATE MANAGER EXTINCT?

Traditionally, who was the global executive? According to a study of 1,161 expatriates working in 40 countries (47), the typical global executive from the United States was about 31 years old when he first went abroad, stayed at least three years on each international assignment, and had three such assignments during his career. Expatriate executives were significantly younger than their domestic counterparts; with few exceptions, they were men. Twenty-one percent married foreign women. Global executives came from a higher socioeconomic background than their domestic counterparts. Typically, expatriates stayed longer with one company: 41 percent worked for only one firm during their careers, 25 percent for only two firms, and 87 percent remained with the same firm after accepting their first international assignment. Global executives were better educated than their domestic counterparts: 81 percent graduated from college, compared with less than 70 percent of domestic executives. Global executives' education was less specialized than that of domestic executives, with more graduating in liberal arts and fewer in business and engineering.

Today the portrait of the global executive is changing. First, given the increasing importance of global business, more executives manage global projects and work with people from around the world, even if they never leave home. They work for companies from other countries, buy from suppliers in other countries, sell to clients worldwide, and, most significantly, create global strategies with colleagues from many different nations. Second, more fast-track managers are using expatriate assignments to gain the global experience necessary to rise to the top of major, global companies (15). Third, the number of women seeking global assignments, although still small, is rising (11;16;17;56), with their overwhelming success beginning to break down the men-only barrier (7).

To date, female expatriate managers have been fairly junior within their organizations and careers. Unlike their male counterparts, their average age when they first go abroad is under 30 years old. Also dissimilar to male expatriates, nearly half of the women expatriates are single; few have children. Similar to male expatriates, the female expatriates are very well educated and quite internationally experienced. Almost all hold graduate degrees, an MBA the most common. Over three-quarters of the women have had extensive international interests and experience prior to their companies sending them abroad. More than three-quarters have traveled internationally and almost two-thirds had an international focus in their studies prior to joining the company. Women who become expatriate managers generally speak two or three languages, with some speaking as many as six. In addition, most women selected for global assignments demonstrate excellent interpersonal and social skills (7).

TODAY'S GLOBAL CAREERS

Why would today's young managers accept global assignments: for the job challenge, the adventure, the status? Why would they turn down a global assignment? We conducted a survey to discover why young managers might accept or reject international assignments and global careers.[2] More than 1,000 graduating MBA students from seven top schools in Canada, Europe, and the United States described their level of interest in global careers, their reasons for accepting or rejecting international assignments, and their assessment of global versus domestic opportunities.

Who Are the Future Global Managers?

The backgrounds of the MBAs from the seven schools showed more similarity than difference.[3] Although 41 percent had an international focus in their MBA, few had extensive global work experience. More than 80 percent had traveled abroad; few of their friends, however, were from other countries. As might be expected, European and Canadian MBAs had more international experience than did their American counterparts.

Do Future Managers Want Global Careers?

The future managers showed strong interest in pursuing the global aspects of their careers.[4] More than four out of five wanted an international assignment at some time during their career. Slightly fewer than half seriously considered pursuing a global career, including accepting a series of international assignments. More than a third of the future managers wanted to travel extensively for their jobs. Yet, only one-third wanted an international assignment as their first job after graduation. Clearly, most young managers show an interest in global management, but many fewer would like an international assignment "right now."

How interested are you in global management and a global career? The "Careers in Global Management Questionnaire" (see box) provides a way to assess your own interest in international assignments and a global career.

CAREERS IN GLOBAL
MANAGEMENT QUESTIONNAIRE

Given the substantial increases in global business over the last decade, it has become increasingly important for managers and companies to understand the global career aspirations of their managers and executives. This questionnaire allows you to increase your understanding of your own career aspirations, and those of your colleagues and subordinates.

Background: How Prepared Are You?

1. Including your native language, which languages do you speak fluently?

   _____

2. How many years have you studied outside of your country of origin?
   _____ total number of years in _____
                                                  (COUNTRY/COUNTRIES)

3. How many months outside your country of origin have you traveled, lived, or worked? ____

4. Did either of your parents travel internationally for their work? ____
   How many of your friends are neither from your country of citizenship nor from the country in which you are currently living?
   _____ none _____ a few _____ about half _____ most _____ all

What Are Your Career Plans?

In the following section:

   Home Country refers to your country of citizenship.

   An International Assignment refers to an expatriate assignment in which the company sends an employee for a single assignment of a year or more to another country.

   A Global Career refers to a series of international assignments in various countries.

   International Travel refers to a business trip to another country without the employee moving abroad.

   An Expatriate refers to an employee who is sent by the company to live and work in another country.

continued on next page ■

■ *continued from previous page*

How true is each of the following statements for you?   TRUE/FALSE

1. I am seriously considering pursuing a global career.   _____

2. I would like my next job to be in another country.   _____

3. If offered an equivalent position in my home country or in the foreign country of my choice, I would rather work at home.   _____

4. While continuing to live in my home country, I would like to travel internationally more than 40 percent (approximately 20 weeks/year) of my time.   _____

5. I would like to have an international assignment at some time during my career.   _____

6. I would like to follow a global career path in which I had a series of international assignments.   _____

7. I never thought about taking an international assignment until I read this questionnaire.   _____

For many reasons, people may choose not to pursue a global career. Which of the following would discourage *you* from pursuing a global career or taking an international assignment?

8. I like living in my home country.   _____

9. I do not want to learn another language.   _____

10. I do not want to adjust to another culture.   _____

11. My spouse would not want to move to another country.   _____

12. It is not good to move children.   _____

13. I want my children to be educated in my home country.   _____

14. I do not want to live in:
    a. any country except my home country   _____
    b. Africa   _____
    c. Asia   _____
    d. Europe   _____
    e. Latin or South America   _____
    f. the Middle East   _____
    g. North America   _____
    h. my home country   _____
    i. other (specify)   _____

continued on next page ■

■ continued from previous page

15. International jobs involve too much travel.   _____

16. If I live in a another country, my children will not gain
    a sense of national identity.   _____

17. My spouse would not want to interrupt his or her career.   _____

18. I would lose my sense of identity, my roots.   _____

19. International assignments put too much strain on
    a marriage.   _____

20. When you are on an international assignment you
    become "invisible" to the company and tend to be
    forgotten for promotions.   _____

21. It would be difficult to come back home after having
    lived and worked for a long time in another country.   _____

22. I do not want to be exposed to the political instability
    experienced by some parts of the world.   _____

23. I would be too socially isolated and lonely in
    another country.   _____

24. I would be exposed to too much personal danger
    in another country.   _____

In comparing potential domestic and global careers, which do you think
could give you the greatest professional opportunities?

	DOMESTIC CAREER	ABOUT SAME	GLOBAL CAREER
25. I could succeed faster in	_____	_____	_____
26. I could earn a higher salary in	_____	_____	_____
27. I could have greater status in	_____	_____	_____
28. I could be more recognized for my work in	_____	_____	_____
29. I could have a more interesting professional life in	_____	_____	_____
30. I could have a more satisfying personal life in	_____	_____	_____

continued on next page ■

■ *continued from previous page*

In comparing women and men, who do you think has a greater chance of being

	WOMEN	EQUAL CHANCES	MEN
31. Selected for an international assignment?	____	____	____
32. Effective on an international assignment?	____	____	____
33. Successful in advancing in a global career?	____	____	____
34. Effective on domestic assignments?	____	____	____
35. Successful in advancing in a domestic career?	____	____	____
36. Socially isolated and lonely in another country?	____	____	____
37. Exposed to personal danger in another country?	____	____	____

In Your Opinion

1. What are the main reasons that would encourage you to accept an international assignment?

   a. _____

   b. _____

   c. _____

2. What are the main reasons why you would turn down an international assignment?

   a. _____

   b. _____

   c. _____

3. What barriers might block women, but not men, from successfully pursuing global careers that include international assignments?

   a. _____

   b. _____

   c. _____

Why Managers Accept Global Assignments

Managers accept global assignments for a multitude of reasons (30;86). As shown in Table 10-1, opportunity for cross-cultural and personal growth experiences is the most common reason for accepting a global assignment. More than half of future managers want to see other cultures, travel, learn new languages, and gain a greater understanding of another way of life; that is, they want to expand their horizons. Having a learning orientation is a good predictor of success on a global assignment (74). The second most important reason for accepting a global assignment is the job itself. Forty percent of future managers see global positions—as compared with available domestic positions—as providing more interesting and challenging work, allowing for more autonomy, power, status, and responsibility, and as providing opportunities for more meaningful contributions to the company and society. The third reason for accepting a global assignment is money. More than a quarter of young managers believe they would earn a higher salary and more benefits in a global than in a domestic position.

The fourth reason for accepting a global assignment is career advancement. One future manager in five sees an expatriate assignment as increasing company-wide exposure and thus the potential for promotion. The fifth reason is a good location. Almost 16 percent express more willingness to accept a global assignment in a politically stable country with a good climate, good social and living conditions, few threats to personal safety, and with an English-speaking population. Young managers are most attracted to countries that are more similar to their own country and more economically developed. The sixth reason to accept an international assignment is the more satisfying life abroad. Eleven percent look forward to a change—less routine, more fun, more adventure, more excitement, more variety, more personal freedom, and a higher quality of life than they imagine having in their home country.

When future managers compare the advantages of global versus domestic careers, they see the primary benefits of a global assignment as greater challenge and responsibility, more interesting work, and better financial rewards. By contrast, they see domestic careers as offering slightly greater status, a more satisfying personal life, more rapid career advancement, and greater recognition for their work than would a global career.

TABLE 10-1 Why Managers Accept Global Assignments

Percent of Future Managers Citing Reason	Reasons for Accepting a Global Assignment
52	*Cross-Cultural Experience and Personal Growth* Seeing other cultures Learning new languages Gaining greater understanding of another way of life Personal growth: expanding horizons, broadening background
40	*Job* More interesting and challenging More opportunities, responsibilities, and chances for useful work More power, autonomy, and status
28	*Money* Higher salary, more benefits, and more savings
21	*Career Advancement* Increased exposure Increased opportunities Better future domestic promotion
16	*Good Location* Politically stable country Good climate Good social and living conditions Safe English-speaking or speaking language similar to home country
11	*Satisfying Life* Greater personal freedom More fun, excitement, and adventure More variety, less routine, a change Higher quality of life
4	*Spouse and Family* Good job or career opportunities for spouse Good situation for family (education, health facilities) Spouse willing to go
3	*Short Term; Other* No domestic jobs available Women managers respected by local nationals Personal business opportunities available in foreign country Single

NOTE: 1,129 graduating MBAs cited 1,867 reasons for accepting global assignments; the most frequently cited reasons are given here. Listed numbers are the percent of MBAs citing the particular reason. Because each MBA listed more than one reason, the total percentage exceeds 100%.

Why Managers Reject Global Assignments

The future managers gave seven major reasons for turning down a global assignment. As shown in Table 10-2, the most frequently mentioned reason is a bad location. More than half the young managers would reject an expatriate assignment if the host country appeared too politically unstable, "uncivilized," dangerous, hostile towards expatriates, or to have a high potential for war and public violence. The second reason they gave for rejecting a global assignment is the job itself and the potentially negative impact on their careers. One third of the young managers would turn down a global assignment if the job appeared unchallenging or boring. Similarly, one third see global assignments as a bad long-term career strategy. They fear the higher risk of job failure abroad and the possible damage to their careers caused by extended isolation from the company's headquarters. They fear being "lost" at reentry and forgotten at times of promotion.

The third reason, also mentioned by one third of the future managers, focuses on their concerns about spouses and families. Young managers view problems confronting dual-career couples as major, especially if the spouse cannot find a suitable position abroad. They also fear the increased marital strain as well as the potentially inadequate educational and medical facilities for children. The fourth reason is money. Nearly one quarter of the young managers would reject an assignment if the salary and benefits package inadequately compensated them for the disruption and additional problems caused by moving and living in another country. Young managers cite potentially unpleasant cross-cultural differences as their fifth reason. Nearly 20 percent reject introducing too much change into their lives, learning new languages, adjusting to new cultures, and subjecting themselves to the isolation, loneliness, fear, and uncertainty associated with living abroad. One young manager in seven rejects disrupting his or her current, enjoyable home-country lifestyle. Other reasons mentioned by some of the young managers include the contract being too long, fear that local nationals would not accept women managers, the assignment requiring too much travel, or unacceptable home company policies toward the host country.

Future managers consistently rate global work as offering greater job satisfaction, while they perceive domestic work as offering greater organizational recognition and a more satisfying private life. Young managers would accept positions in other countries for the cross-cultural experience and opportunity for personal growth, the job itself, and the higher salary

TABLE 10-2 Why Managers Reject Global Assignments

Percent of Future Managers Citing Reason	Reasons for Rejecting a Global Assignment
59	*Poor Location* Politically unstable "Uncivilized" Dangerous Hostility toward expatriates Extreme poverty High potential for war or violence
35	*Negative Impact Job and Career* Boring, unchallenging, professionally uninteresting Not good long-term career strategy Higher risk of job failure Isolation from company headquarters Displacement from company's hierarchy: forgotten at time of promotion, "lost" at reentry
33	*Negative Impact on Spouse and Family* Inadequate medical or educational facilities Children wrong age to move (especially teenagers) Problems confronting dual-career couples Spouse unwilling to move Spouse unable to find a suitable position to further career
23	*Inadequate Compensation* Salary and benefits package inadequate
19	*Unpleasant Life Abroad* Unwillingness to learn new language or to adjust to new culture Isolation, loneliness, fear, uncertainty Restrictions on personal life: lack of physical and intellectual freedom, restricted access to people
14	*Disruption to Home Country Life* Disruption to personal and social life Reneging on commitments to family, parents, friends
6	*Contract Too Long; Other* Women not accepted as managers Existing good domestic position Opposition to company's global policies, product, or marketing strategy Too much travel

NOTE: 1,129 graduating MBAs cited 2,308 reasons for rejecting global assignments; the most frequently cited reasons are given here. Listed numbers are the percent of MBAs citing the particular reason. Because each MBA listed more than one reason, the total percentage exceeds 100%.

and financial benefits. They would reject global assignments due to the negative impact on spouses and families, the personal danger and inconvenience of living in a "bad" location, and the potentially detrimental effect on career advancement both while abroad and when returning home.

Young managers' perceptions of the advantages and disadvantages of living and working abroad reflect those of many managers. Experienced expatriates frequently describe such advantages as increased personal growth opportunities and the inherently more interesting, challenging, and responsible work abroad, as well as traditionally generous salaries and benefit packages. Today's young managers show a greater awareness than their predecessors of the detrimental effects of expatriate positions on their private lives and careers. Research has shown that the major cause of failure on global assignments, often leading to early return, is dissatisfaction on the part of the spouse (83; see Chapter 9). Nearly half of 300 surveyed companies have brought families home early due to the spouse's inability to adapt (21). With the increasing prevalence of dual-career couples, the impact of global assignments on the spouse and family will increase, not decrease (see Chapter 9). Young managers appear well aware of these problems.

Potentially negative impacts of global assignments on employees' careers have also become more widely recognized. In the past, most expatriates believed that global assignments would help their careers; the majority returned to discover the opposite was true (8). Returning employees have all too frequently discovered that home-country jobs were at substantially lower levels of responsibility and authority than were their expatriate positions or, more dramatically, that no jobs at all were available to return to (see Chapter 8). Meanwhile, returnees found that domestic colleagues had been promoted while their own careers had plateaued.

Today's young managers appear considerably more aware of the hazards of moving abroad and successfully returning home than were the managers of five, 10, or 15 years ago. Future managers consequently are less likely to accept global assignments that could jeopardize their careers. Luckily, with increasing globalization and the parallel rise in importance of global experience, the risks of derailing one's career by going abroad are diminishing just as young managers' interest is increasing.

GLOBAL MANAGERS AND LEADERS: NO LONGER MEN ALONE

Are women and men equally interested in global careers (16;53)? Yes. Although less than 15 percent of current expatriate managers are women

(1;11;27;28;86), male and female future managers express an equal interest in accepting global assignments and pursuing global careers (10).

Women Becoming Global Managers

Although equally interested, both young male and female future managers believe that companies offer fewer opportunities to women than to men to pursue careers in global management (32). Similarly, both believe that companies offer fewer opportunities for women in global than in domestic management. The young managers are right. In a survey of 60 major North American companies with operations around the world, more than half expressed reluctance to select women managers for global assignments (1;3;7;35). The two primary concerns, expressed by three-quarters of the companies, are their beliefs that foreigners are so prejudiced against women managers that they could not succeed, and that the difficulties faced by dual-career couples in moving abroad are insurmountable. Even with the barriers and hesitance, almost three-quarters of the companies believe that the number of women working globally will continue to increase (3).

Similar to the companies, more than 80 percent of the future managers themselves believe that foreigners' prejudice against women managers poses the primary barrier to women's success (2;10). More than 70 percent label the home company's reluctance to select women for global assignments and the difficulties faced by global dual-career couples as the second and third most important barriers (10;31;50;70). Whereas young managers correctly see companies' current selection processes as creating barriers, neither they nor the companies correctly understand what they perceive to be "foreigners' prejudice." A major study of North American women working in countries around the world showed that expatriate women managers are highly successful (7;17;56). As one woman expatriate accurately summarized, "The most difficult job is getting sent, not succeeding once sent" (7).

Why do women succeed as global managers? They succeed because they are seen as *foreigners who happen to be women*, not as women who happen to be foreigners. Although the difference may appear subtle, the effect is huge. Countries such as Japan, Korea, and Saudi Arabia, which promote few of their own women into significant managerial positions, treat foreign women with the respect they accord male expatriate managers. As one woman who works successfully in Hong Kong explained, "It doesn't make any difference if you are blue, green, purple, or a frog; if you have the best product at the best price, the Chinese will buy"

(7). In some countries—Japan, for example—being a foreign woman is actually an advantage (16). In essence, global business pragmatism wins out over prejudice.

Although more barriers may exist for women than men, today's organizations clearly can select global managers from equally interested groups of male and female managers. When considering a woman for a global position, companies would be wise not to assume (a) that she does not want to go—she probably does; (b) that foreigners are so prejudiced that such assignments would be bad for both the company and the woman's career; and (c) that dual-career issues are insolvable. As discussed in Chapter 9, many North American women expatriates actually find it easier to balance the time-consuming and seemingly conflicting roles of professional, wife, and mother while on a global assignment than at home, because global assignments often provide them with the luxury of a higher level of household help than they have access to at home. Luckily, just at the time when the intensity of global competition demands that companies use nothing but their best managers, both the companies and the women are discovering that success is both possible and probable.

Women and Global Companies[5]

Given the increasing importance of global corporations, it is encouraging that their impact on women in management, to date, has been primarily positive. Global companies include women in ways that domestic, multidomestic, and multinational firms did not and do not. First, the extremely competitive business environment forces global firms to select the best people available. The opportunity cost of prejudice—of rejecting women and limiting selection to men—is much higher than in previous economic environments. As *Fortune* magazine succinctly reported, "The best reason for believing that more women will be in charge before long is that in a ferociously competitive global economy, no company can afford to waste valuable brainpower simply because it's wearing a skirt" (43:55).

Second, whereas domestic and multidomestic companies hire primarily local nationals and, therefore, must closely adhere to local norms relating to hiring—or not hiring—women managers, global companies are not similarly limited. Because the corporate culture of global firms is not coincident with the local culture of any particular country, global firms have greater flexibility in defining selection and promotion criteria that best fit their needs rather than those that most closely mimic the historical patterns of a particular country. Said simply, global companies can and do hire local women managers even in countries in which the local companies rarely do so.

U.S.–based global companies, for example, have often hired local women managers when local firms would not. This dynamic has been particularly pronounced in Japan, where non-Japanese companies have had difficulty attracting top-ranked male applicants (60). American firms, for example, have led the way in hiring well-qualified Japanese women, whereas Japanese firms are still extremely reluctant to hire them (81). Following the same pattern, Japanese companies operating in the United States hire more women managers in their American affiliates than they do in their home-country operations (77).

By hiring women, global companies act as role models for firms in many countries that have not seriously considered promoting significant numbers of women into managerial positions. The greater the number of expatriates involved in foreign affiliates, the less likely they are to follow local human resource practices, including being less likely to restrict the number of women mangers (77). The firm's global character allows it organizational freedoms and imposes competitive demands not present in domestic or multidomestic environments.

Third, as discussed previously, global companies send women abroad as expatriate managers (11). Because global firms use expatriate and local managers, they can benefit from the greater flexibility that many cultures afford foreign women. As has been described, most countries do not hold foreign women to the same professionally limiting roles that restrict local women (7;56). The outstanding success of the initial group of women expatriate managers in all geographical areas—Africa, the Americas, Asia, Europe, and the Middle East—is encouraging firms both to continue sending women abroad (7;69) and to begin promoting more local women into management (56).

Fourth, whereas domestic, multidomestic, and multinational firms have been characterized by structural hierarchies, global companies are increasingly characterized by networks of equals. Research suggests that women work particularly well in such networks:

> . . . women . . . are countering the values of the hierarchy with those of the web . . . when describing their roles in their organizations, women usually refer . . . to themselves as being in the middle of things. . . . Insepara-ble from their sense of themselves as being in the middle . . . [is] women's notion of being connected to those around them (52:45–46,51).

Not surprisingly, global firms see women managers as bringing needed collaborative and participative skills to the workplace (72).

Fifth, leading management scholars have identified innovation as a key factor in global competitiveness (22;48;75). An inherent source of innovation is well-managed diversity (1). Women bring diversity to global companies that have heretofore primarily hired men.

Global companies thus include more women than their predecessors could (or would) and benefit organizationally from their professional contributions in new ways. They benefit both from women's increased representation at all levels of the organization as well as from their unique ways of contributing to the organization, which complement those of men.[6]

Women in Global Leadership

Are women strictly becoming managers or are they assuming senior leadership positions (34)? For the first time in history, countries and companies are selecting women to lead them. More than 80 percent of women who have led their country as president or prime minister have come into office in just the last decade. Similarly, the proportion of CEOs leading major global firms who are women is increasing dramatically. The box, *Global Leadership: A Dialogue with Future History*, describes this rapid shift from male-dominated global leadership to leadership that includes both men and women. It tells the story of women who are global leaders through the eyes of Charity Ngilu, the first woman to run for president in Kenya.

GLOBAL LEADERSHIP: A DIALOGUE WITH FUTURE HISTORY[7]

Did you hear?
On July 9th, 1997 Charity Ngilu declared her candidacy to run for president of Kenya. If she had succeeded, Ngilu would have become the first woman ever to become president of Kenya.[8]

Ngilu's candidacy puts her in good company. Thirty-one of the 47 women who have held their country's highest leadership position have come into office since 1990.[9] Forty of the 47 women are the first women their country has ever selected. Whereas no women became

continued on next page ■

■ *continued from previous page*

president or prime minister in the 1950s, only three came into office in the 1960s, five in the 1970s, and eight in the 1980s; yet 31 came into office in the 1990s. More than the total of all the women who have ever previously achieved their country's highest leadership position came to power in just the last five years. It does not take a statistical genius to notice that there is a trend, and that that trend is toward an increasing number of women in the world's most senior leadership positions.

According to leadership scholar Michael Genovese, "Studies of . . . leadership have been remarkably non-gender specific" . . . "This is due primarily to a tacit assumption . . . that leaders are men!" . . . "Historically, there is of course a good deal of validity to this assumption—almost all . . . leaders have been men" (45). Referring "to a generic head of state as 'him' may . . . be understandable," even if, as we enter the twenty-first century, it has become wholly inaccurate" (45).

Why might Charity Ngilu have become the world's next woman president? Does she come from a politically prominent family? Did she grow up with wealth and privilege? Is she a lawyer with a degree from one of the world's most prestigious law schools? Did she serve for years in increasingly important positions in one of her country's dominant political parties?

Well, no, not quite.

Did you hear? Charity Ngilu, the daughter of a local Christian minister, the ninth of 13 children, announced her candidacy to run for president of Kenya. While she did go to high school, after graduation she became a secretary, not a lawyer. And only after she married did she go on to college where she earned her degree in business administration and then became an entrepreneur, not a politician.

So how did Ngilu come to be considered as a serious candidate for her nation's foremost leadership position? Had Charity dreamed of becoming a national leader from the time she was a child, or at least from the time she was in college? Since her own family comes from a very modest background, did at least her husband come from a politically prominent family? Did her party rally around her and eagerly nominate Ngilu for the presidency of Kenya?

continued on next page ■

■ *continued from previous page*

Well, no, not quite.

Did you hear? Charity Ngilu, candidate for the presidency of Kenya, entered politics only five years ago. On that day, a group of women, each with leafy branches in their hands, none with briefcases, came to her backdoor in Kitui, 75 miles away from cosmopolitan Nairobi.[10] *Charity knew the women; most belonged to a local women's association with which Charity had worked for years to build both health clinics and better water-supply systems. One of the women knocked on Charity's door. Charity came out, drying her hands on her apron. The women asked Charity to run for parliament in Kenya's first multiparty elections. Charity's response? "You are joking! You are crazy, obviously!"*

Clearly not the power-hungry response of the all too typical twentieth-century status- and ego-driven aspiring politician.

Is Charity atypical?

Yes. But only if viewed through the career paths of most of history's recognized world leaders.[11] Former U.S. president Bill Clinton is typical. Bill Clinton dreamed of becoming president from the time he was a little boy. At age 16, after having just shaken the hand of then-president John F. Kennedy, Clinton announced that he would like Kennedy's job, that he too would like to become president of the United States of America. To date, as children, none of the women presidents or prime ministers have dreamed about becoming their country's leader. You see, for most women who become leaders, it is not the desire for the position nor for power per se that motivates them to seek the highest leadership positions, rather it is their commitment to a compelling vision of what society could be, of what society must be.[12]

Charity was an outsider to politics. Is Charity atypical?

Yes again. But only when viewed from the perspective of most men's paths to political and corporate power. Most women who become leaders do not work their way up through the company or political party power hierarchy. Rather, they laterally transfer into the most senior position (4). Ngilu was an entrepreneur; five years

continued on next page ■

■ *continued from previous page*

later people considered her as possibly the next president of Kenya. Tansu Çiller served as an economics professor in Istanbul; three years later she became prime minister of Turkey. Gro Harlem Brundtland, a medical doctor, became Norway's first woman prime minister just six years after accepting her first government position.

Is the pattern similar among business leaders? To a large extent, yes. Most women who become business leaders do not work their way up through the company to its most senior position; rather they laterally transfer into the top position of one company after having built a career in another organization (4). As a double outsider, Marjorie Scardino, the only woman CEO to lead a *Financial Times* (FT-SE) 100 firm, provides a good example. Not only was she brought in from the *Economist* to assume the leadership of Pearson Plc, but as an American, she was the first non-English executive to hold a senior executive position in this esteemed British firm (73). Laterally transferring into senior leadership calls into question our image of the glass ceiling. Perhaps the route to the top is not to follow men's paths and attempt to break through the glass ceiling, but rather to simply go around the glass ceiling. Why else do we see so many more women CEOs in entrepreneurial enterprises than in major publicly held corporations? And one must ask, why should today's senior women follow the same paths to leadership in the twenty-first century that men followed in the twentieth century? Not surprisingly, such mimicry serves neither society's nor women's best interests.

Charity initially rejected her women friends' suggestion that she run for parliament. Is Charity atypical?

Yes, but once again, only if we believe that women should try to copy men's twentieth-century paths to power. Typical of women, but not of men, many of the world's women leaders decline senior leadership positions when they are originally offered (4). Golda Meir, for example, initially told her party "no" when offered the Israeli prime ministership. Corazon Aquino's first response to running for president of the Philippines was also "no." Maria Liberia Peters told her party "no" when they first offered to nominate her for prime minister of the Netherlands-Antilles. Her party then went on to unanimously nominate her, without her consent![13]

continued on next page ■

■ *continued from previous page*

Luckily for Kenya, and the world, the group of women at Ngilu's kitchen door convinced Charity to take them seriously. She ran. And, with what the press described as unusually strong grass-roots support, she beat the governing party's incumbent. Today many of the traditional, male, party-supported legislators—most of whom ignored Ngilu previously— fervently wish that the women at Charity's kitchen door had failed to convince Ngilu to run. For you see, Charity Ngilu did not just win, but rather she went on to become "a stubborn thorn in the side of both President Daniel arap Moi and his ministers, upbraiding them on a regular basis for doing little or nothing for the poor, [and] especially [little for poor] women."

From the perspective of traditional politicians, the "problem" with Charity Ngilu is that she does not want power for power's sake; she really does want to change Kenya; she really does want to make her country a better place.

Years ago, Ngilu had been shocked that Kenyans were dying of treatable diseases while traditional government politicians continued to spend large sums of money on the trappings of power. It was Ngilu's outrage at the indignities of poverty that led her to run for Parliament in 1992, and, in 1997 to declare her candidacy for the presidency. Ngilu, along with an increasingly vocal number of Kenyans, had become outraged at President Moi spending the "colossal sum of $60 million to buy himself a presidential jet [and spending] . . . another $70 million to build an airport in his hometown. Then [as Ngilu incredulously observed] Moi has the audacity to go in front of women [and] say, 'Please vote for me.' The women he is telling that to are walking naked . . . carrying sick children on their back[s], and their homes have holes in them that you can see through, because of poverty."

Charity Ngilu has a vision, a vision for the people of Kenya. It is her burning desire to achieve her vision that drove her to seek the presidency. She wanted the office to accomplish her vision; she did not need or want the office itself.

Did you hear? Charity Ngilu became a candidate for president. But how did she get to be a presidential candidate? Yes, she's appalled at the

continued on next page ■

■ *continued from previous page*

*poverty and equally appalled at President Moi's abuses of power. But
how did she become a candidate? When did her party nominate her?
Why her? Why then?*

Good questions. But once again, such traditional questions do
not lead us to understand at all how the story unfolded. Ngilu's
party did not nominate her. Ngilu defected from the Kikuyu-domi-
nated Democratic Party when it became clear that it would not
nominate her. Ngilu did not run as a candidate of the Democratic
party: she ran as a candidate of the much smaller Social Democratic
Party.

Strange? Well, no, not really.

Hierarchical power structures, whether political or corporate,
often fail to support women as candidates for senior leadership positions. Most women draw their support directly from the people—
whether via the ballot box or the marketplace—rather than from
either political or corporate hierarchical power structures (4). Mary
Robinson, for example, before becoming president of Ireland, visited
more small communities than any politician before her. The opposition now admits that they did not take her candidacy seriously until
it was too late (42). Similarly, former prime minister Benazir Bhutto
visited more communities in Pakistan than any politician before her.
She was only taken seriously as a candidate when "far more people
[turned out upon her return to Pakistan in 1986] than anyone—
politicians, diplomats, and analysts—had foreseen. Many people had
doubted that Benazir Bhutto, a woman, could receive the kind of
support from the people that her father had enjoyed, but her
triumphant return proved them all wrong" (20). Likewise, former
President Corazon Aquino held rallies in more than 1,000 Filipino
communities while her opponent, Ferdinand Marcos, campaigned in
only 34. Her victory was labeled the People's Revolution (33). Is not
this, at its most fundamental level, what we call democracy? Broadly
based community support which has not been orchestrated by a
political or societal power elite? Is not this what we increasingly
recognize as twenty-first-century networked power as opposed to
the hierarchic power that dominated the twentieth century? Is not

continued on next page ■

■ *continued from previous page*

this what management scholars refer to as power-with ("empower-ment") rather than power-over?[14]

It certainly does not surprise anyone who has been observing women in organizations that the strongest evidence for a difference in the way women and men lead is in women's tendency to adopt more democratic, participative styles, while men tend to use more autocratic, directive styles. In more than 90 percent of the almost 400 studies comparing male and female leaders' behavior, women exhibit more democratic behavior than do men (40).

Unlike many political parties in Kenya, the one that Ngilu chose has no particular ethnic allegiance. That she chose this party is not in the least bit surprising. Ngilu ran, in part, on a unity platform. For you see, "Ngilu sees herself not only as a champion of women and the poor, but [also] as someone who can heal the ethnic rifts that have divided Kenya since independence." As Ngilu says, "This is a wounded nation. . . . There is open hostility and hatred between different tribes. Some neutral person, somebody with a difference, must sit down and moderate. . . . I don't have a score to settle with anyone."

For many Kenyans, "Ngilu represent[s] a complete break with [the] divisive tribal politics of the past." As one Kenyan observed during the election campaign, "Charity is talking about unity, and this unity will unite both men and women. . . . If we vote for a man, there will be no change. With a woman, there will have to be a [very] big change."

Is Kenya unique? Is there something particular about Charity Ngilu's personality or behavior that leads Kenyans to believe that both change and unity are possible? From the details of Charity's story, one might be tempted to conclude that her story is unique. Certainly the rich history of behavioral and trait theories of leadership would suggest that it is something special in Charity Ngilu that allows Kenyans to hope for unity and to believe in change.[15] But enlarging our perspective beyond the male leaders on which almost all leader-ship theories have been based, changes our perspective (5). Through-out the world, among political, business, and societal leaders, women bring with them the symbolic possibility of fundamental societal and organizational change. The combination of women being outsiders at senior leadership levels previously completely dominated by men

continued on next page ■

■ *continued from previous page*

and of beating the odds to become the first woman to lead her particular country or company produces powerful public imagery about the
possibility of other fundamental changes (4).

If a woman can be chosen to be president, prime minister, or CEO
when no other woman has held such an office and when few people
thought that she could possibly be selected, then other major
changes become believably possible (4). Mary Robinson's presidential
acceptance speech captured the coupling of the unique event of a
woman being elected president of Ireland with the possibility of
national change and unity: "I was elected by men and women of all
parties and none, by many with great moral courage who stepped
out from behind the faded flags of Civil War and voted for a new
Ireland. And above all by the women of Ireland . . . who instead of
rocking the cradle rocked the system, and who came out massively to
make their mark on the ballot paper, and on a new Ireland."[16]

The pattern of women leaders symbolizing change and unity is
overwhelming. Both Nicaragua's first woman president, Violeta
Chamorro, and the Philippines' first woman president, Corazon
Aquino, became symbols of national unity in their strife-torn countries. Chamorro even claimed "to have no ideology beyond national
'reconciliation'" (24). Chamorro's ability to bring all the members of
her family together for Sunday dinner each week achieved near
legendary status in Nicaragua. Why? Because, of Chamorro's four
adult children, two were prominent Sandinistas while the other
two equally prominently opposed the Sandinistas, not an unusual
split in war-torn Nicaragua. As the ". . . matriarch who can still hold
[her] family together, Chamorro gives symbolic hope to the nation
that it too can find peace, based on a unity, that can bring together
all Nicaraguans" (79). Are these isolated examples? No, Corazon
Aquino, although widely condemned in the press for supposed
naiveté, invited members of both her own party and the opposition
party into her cabinet, a conscious strategy to attempt to reunify
her deeply divided country (33). In an attempt to bring peace and
unity to Sri Lanka, Executive President Chandrika Kumaratunga
chose to meet directly with the Tamil separatists, even though her
husband is widely believed to have been murdered by the Tamils
and such a unity strategy breaks directly with the policies of her
father and her mother, both of whom had previously served as

continued on next page ■

■ *continued from previous page*

prime minister of Sri Lanka before Kumaratunga.

Given that women leaders symbolize unity and the possibility for change, it is not surprising that a woman business leader, Rebecca Mark, when she was chief executive of Enron Development Corporation, and not a male executive, became the first person to successfully negotiate a major commercial transaction following the Middle East peace accords. Mark brought the Israelis and the Jordanians together to build a natural gas power generation station.[17]

Perhaps the best-known woman symbolizing hope for the type of significant change that could bring peace is the elected prime minister of Burma, Nobel Peace Prize Laureate Aung San Suu Kyi (9). Even after the military denied her the opportunity to take office and placed her under house arrest for six years, Suu Kyi still chose to meet directly with the military opposition leaders.

Perhaps the least recognized woman symbolizing the potential for change and unity is Rwanda's former prime minister Agatha Uwilingiyimana. Uwilingiyimana was brought in as Rwanda's prime minister only after it was decided that the war had to be ended and a peace treaty had to be signed. The former prime minister—a man—refused to have anything to do with signing the peace agreement as did the majority of his male colleagues. Uwilingiyimana became prime minister knowing that she was risking her life to do so. She paid the ultimate price; she was killed, not by the opposition, but by members of her own people who could not move beyond the tribal animosity of war (54;78).

What does the future portend? Did Charity Ngilu stand a chance of winning the election? The odds were against her. President Moi had been in power for nearly two decades. Even the chairwoman of one of the major opposition parties thought that Ngilu did not stand a chance ". . . not because [Charity was] not a good candidate, but because . . . sexism is still too deeply embedded in Kenya. . . . [Kenya] is not stable . . . , and it will take these men time to accept being ruled by a woman."

Some political strategists disagreed, believing that Ngilu had a fighting chance of winning. They observed that "hundreds [of men] in a mostly male audience cheered [Ngilu] . . . when she rose to speak" at political rallies. Some men "said [that] they were ready to vote for . . . Ngilu." They said "they were weary of the usual cast of opposition

continued on next page ■

■ *continued from previous page*

politicians, many of whom [had] served in Moi's government at one time or another."

Would she make it? No one knew. No one could predict the next election, let alone the twenty-first century, neither for Kenya nor for the rest of the world. Change comes at a price, yet continuing on our current path might well extract an even higher price—the extinction of civilization as we know it. Leaders become lightning rods for the dissension within society. Charity Ngilu was not an exception.

On Saturday, July 12th, only three days after Charity declared her candidacy for president, thugs with machetes attacked her after she spoke at a rally.[18] "The government [of course] denies that its agents orchestrated the attack, but [Charity] . . . , who was wounded, maintains . . . [that her] assailants were from the youth wing of the governing party". As Charity explained, ". . . I received a threatening telephone call, [then] the man [on the phone] said, 'So, you are still running for [president,] . . . after what happened [to you] on Saturday?'".
Her answer was "Yes!"

Societal change is not a game for cowards. Global leadership is not a game played by cowards. Charity Ngilu has a vision—a vision for a peaceful, democratic Kenya in which all citizens, rich and poor, female and male, from all backgrounds can live in dignity. It is a vision worthy of the world, not just of Kenya. It is a vision more strongly supported by the people than by the current political and economic power elite. It is a vision that requires not only a shift in how we see society but also a shift in how we act within society: Ngilu's vision is based on unity, rather than any form of divisive tribalism; on broadly based networked power, rather than any form of hierarchic centralized power; and on broadly based access to economic and social well-being, rather than on extreme advantage reserved only for those at the top of a hierarchic, predominantly male pyramid.

Societal change has never come without powerful symbols of change. Women leaders symbolize change. But societal change does not come through symbols alone. To achieve the type of society in the twenty-first century that we might envision, the women and

continued on next page ■

■ *continued from previous page*

men who lead must be vision-driven, globally inclusive, and multiculturally persuasive. Such leaders must combine courage with humility.

What makes these women global leaders, rather than national leaders? Partially, it is the dynamics of twenty-first-century society that challenges us all, women and men, to think and to act within a global context. But for women, it is also the intersecting dynamics of time and place. Because the women who become leaders are unique, the media chooses to tell their story.[19] The *New York Times* reported Charity Ngilu's candidacy and spread the story throughout the world on the major wire services. Rightly or wrongly, the world press probably would not have picked up the story had one of the smaller political parties in Africa nominated a man. Women leaders are global leaders because society is going global and because the world press makes them globally visible. And their global visibility allows them to act in ways that would be much more difficult, if not impossible, for less visible male leaders. All too many countries have been known to silence or to eliminate opposition politicians. Charity was placed under house arrest in 1992 after running for parliament. She was attacked with machetes after declaring her candidacy for president. It is much less likely that Charity will "disappear" while the world is watching than were the world to remain oblivious. Global visibility supports courageous action.

Global Leadership

To become leaders, do women need to fit into the predominantly male history of leadership theory? The answer is a resounding no; women neither fit nor do they need to fit. Neither men nor women leaders in the twenty-first century need to fit the patterns of twentieth century leadership.

Charity's story is our story, the story of civilization at a crucial transition as it either accelerates its demise or celebrates its transformation. Charity's story is our story, the story of leadership—whether by women or men—that transcends history to establish new directions worthy of civilization. As Madeleine Albright, former U.S. Secretary of State reminds us, "We have a responsibility in our time, as others have had in theirs, not to be prisoners of history, but to shape history (19)."

continued on next page ■

■ *continued from previous page*

Afterword

In early January 1998, former president Daniel arap Moi was reelected as president of Kenya. All sides claim that there was extensive fraud in the election (among many others, see 36;62;63;64;65;88).

SUMMARY

Do young managers want global careers? Yes, under certain conditions. Whereas some young male and female managers still see more advantages from domestic than global careers, more than 80 percent would like a global assignment at some time during their careers. Are women as interested as men in pursuing global careers? Yes, and both women and men are highly successful once sent abroad and in leadership positions. Increased competition is forcing global companies to select the most talented employees for managerial and professional positions, without regard to their nationality or gender.

Epilogue

There are good reasons for suggesting that the modern age has ended. Many things indicate that we are going through a transitional period, when it seems that something is on the way out and something else is painfully being born. It is as if something were crumbling, decaying and exhausting itself, while something else, still indistinct, were arising from the rubble. . . . This state of affairs has its social and political consequences. The planetary civilization to which we all belong confronts us with global challenges. We stand helpless before them because our civilization has essentially globalized only the surface of our lives. . . .

[World leaders] . . . are rightly worried by the problem of finding the key to insure the survival of a civilization that is global and multicultural. . . . The central . . . task . . . [for the twenty-first] century, then, is the creation of a new model of co-existence among the various cultures, peoples, races, and religious spheres within a single interconnected civilization.

— VACLAV HAVEL, *president of the Czech Republic*[1]

V ACLAV HAVEL'S APPRECIATION of the transition that the world is now experiencing is certainly important to each of us as human beings. Equally importantly, his appreciation of the world situation challenges us as managers and leaders.

The world *has* gotten smaller. Global business now dominates world business. Managers worldwide are becoming more internationally sophisticated. It is only as we recognize the extent to which we are culture bound that we can go beyond the limitations of our own necessarily narrow perspectives. It is only as we work globally that we can recognize and benefit from a world economy. We have entered an era in which global organizations, companies, and alliances determine our economic and social well-being. To the extent that organizations respect individual cultural differences, they allow us to contribute based on our uniqueness. To the extent they transcend national boundaries, they encourage a world, fraught with wars and animosities, to collaborate and to cooperate. If we fail to recognize cultural differences and choose to maintain ethnocentric domestic approaches, we condemn the world to divisiveness and its own demise.

In the past, multinational corporations have not been celebrated for their contributions to world peace or understanding. Perhaps it is only today, as we recognize that worldwide understanding and cooperation have become critical for our very survival, that the function of global companies becomes apparent. Governments reflect national boundaries; global companies go beyond national boundaries and national defini-tions. Global companies can use their transnational status, their creative public-private partnerships, and their ever-expanding networks of alliances in ways that benefit and enrich their worldwide constituencies or in ways that impoverish us all. The challenge is immense. The impor-tance is inestimable.

Notes

CHAPTER 1

1. Blaise Pascal Pensées, 60 (294), as cited in Geert Hofstede's *Culture's Consequences* (Beverly Hills, Sage Publications, 1980).
2. Unless otherwise stated, all dollar figures are in U.S. dollars.
3. Arguments for both the pessimistic and optimistic appreciations of shifting world business dynamic summarized by Professor Arshad Ahmad, Concordia University, Montreal, Canada.
4. Adapted from material originally appearing in the Preface by Nancy J. Adler of Henry W. Lane and Joseph J. diStefano's *International Management Behavior*, 4th edition (Toronto: Nelson Canada, 2000, pp. xiii–xvi).
5. Although the term American literally refers to all peoples from North and South America, it is used in this book as a shorthand way to refer to citizens of the United States of America.
6. Domestic multiculturalism refers to multiple cultures within a particular country. Multiculturalism, as it is used in this book, refers to international multiculturalism; that is, many cultures represented from multiple countries.
7. As conducted and cited by Jim Cornell et al., "Cultural Aspects Influencing Advertising Messages Aimed at French Canadians" (Working Paper, McGill University), interview with Jacques Grenier of Publi Plus, Inc., March 10, 1982.

8. Kluckhohn and Strodbeck reflect a North American perspective in their work. Their framework is therefore most accurate in describing Western cultures.
9. Stig-Eric Gruman, BCom, McGill University.
10. Anne H. Whetham, MBA, McGill University.
11. For an excellent review of the literature on individualism and collectivisim, see Earley and Gibson (1998) and Triandis (1995).
12. Ismail Elkhaby, MBA, McGill University.
13. Matts Franck, MBA, McGill University.
14. Yuk Tsui Grace Seto, BCom, McGill University.
15. John Clancy, BCom, McGill University.

CHAPTER 2

1. Ken Dang, MBA, McGill University.
2. Hofstede (1980) originally labeled this dimension as masculinity/femininity. However, since the dimension does not correspond with contemporary understandings of masculinity and femininity, Adler changed the labels to more accurately reflect their underlying meanings. It should be noted that Hofstede never intended to suggest that today's male and female students or managers possess or lack certain attributes that would make one a better manager than the other.
3. Shigeki Iwashita, MBA, McGill University.
4. Jennifer Oakes, MBA, McGill University.
5. Anne H. Whetham, MBA, McGill University.
6. See note 2.
7. Matts Franck, MBA, McGill University.

CHAPTER 3

1. From Michael Miles, *Adaptation to a Foreign Government*, Canadian International Development Agency. Reprinted by permission of the author.
2. The Anti-Defamation League Rumor Clinic designed the sessions to show how rumors operate and how to distinguish rumors from gossip.
3. Anglophone Québecois are native English speakers living in the predominantly French-speaking province of Quebec, Canada.
4. From John P. Feig and G. Blair, *There Is a Difference: Survival Kit for Overseas Living*, 1979. Reprinted by permission of Robert Kohls, Washington International Center, Washington, DC.
5. From John P. Feig and G. Blair, *There Is a Difference: Survival Kit for Overseas Living*, 1979. Reprinted by permission of Intercultural Press, Inc. Adapted by Adler, 2002.
6. From Nancy J. Adler and Moses N. Kiggundu, "Awareness at the Crossroad: Designing Translator Based Training Programs," in D. Landis and R. Brislin, *Handbook of Intercultural Training*, Vol. II. Copyright © 1983 Pergamon Press.
7. This is the true experience of a Scottish executive as described to his

colleagues in the *Managerial Skills for International Business* executive seminar at INSEAD, in Fontainebleau, France.

CHAPTER 4

1. The term *groupthink* was first coined by I. L. Janis. From Irving L. Janis, *Groupthink*, 2d ed. Copyright © 1982 Houghton Mifflin Company. Reprinted by permission. See Chapter 5 for a more in-depth discussion of the topic.
2. Clifford Clarke, president, Clarke Consulting Group, was instrumental in interpreting the cross-cultural air freight situation. His insight and creativity in creating cultural synergy with Japanese organizations continues to advance our global insight and practice.
3. According to Islamic tradition, a man may take up to four wives if he can support each of them and their children.

CHAPTER 5

1. The film *Going International,* Part 2, by Copeland Griggs Productions, San Francisco, dramatizes a similar situation between an Indian and an American manager.
2. The film *The Heart of the Bull,* produced by V. P. Human Resources David Dotlich, documents the different working styles of French and American managers at the French computer company Groupe Bull.
3. Based on an incident described by a European manager attending the "Managerial Skills for International Business" executive seminar at INSEAD in Fontainebleau, France.
4. See Note 3.

CHAPTER 6

1. University of Pennsylvania Professor Robert House and his worldwide research team have conducted a major multidomestic study of leadership to define leadership practices in countries around the world (74;75;76;77).
2. Such classic theories as Likert's "System 4" Management (100;101) and Blake and Mouton's "Managerial Grid" (28;29) make assumptions similar to Theory Y; that is, that high concern for people and high productivity go together.
3. For an excellent review of current international cross-cultural leadership research see (44). For other reviews and current research on leadership, see references 19, 21, 36, 37, 47, 51, 57, 60, 81, 114, 132, 133, 134, 135, 136, 155, 156.
4. Although Maslow's hierarchy has been questioned within the United States, it has become one of the accepted bases for explaining and understanding behavior within organizations. Generalizing from this U.S.–based acceptance to worldwide applicability is questioned in this chapter.
5. Hofstede (72) originally labeled this dimension masculinity/femininity. To

better reflect its underlying meaning, it has been relabeled in this book as career success/quality of life. For a more in-depth discussion of this dimension, see Chapter 2.

6. The quotation is from the play *Man of La Mancha* (as found in Otis L. Guernsey, Jr., New York: Dodd, Mead, 1966, p. 214), which is based on the book *Don Quixote* by Miguel Cervantes.

7. From George W. Renwick and Robert T. Moran, *Basic Responsibility and International Business Ethics (BRIBE)*, January 1982, American Graduate School of International Management, Glendale, AZ, Reprinted by permission.

CHAPTER 7

1. From Dr. George Renwick, *Malays and Americans: Definite Differences, Unique Opportunities.* Copyright © 1985. Intercultural Press. Reprinted by permission of the author.

2. Example provided by Prof. John L. Graham, Graduate School of Management, University of California, Irvine.

CHAPTER 8

1. The research and quotations on reentry, unless otherwise cited, are based on Nancy J. Adler, *Re-entry: A Study of the Dynamic Coping Processes Used by Repatriated Employees to Enhance Effectiveness in the Organization and Personal Learning During the Transition Back into the Home Country*, Graduate School of Management, University of California at Los Angeles (UCLA), 1980; as summarized in Nancy J. Adler, "Reentry: Managing Cross-Cultural Transitions" (3).

2. Based on Nancy J. Adler, "Reentry: Managing Cross-Cultural Transitions" (3).

3. Adapted from Nancy J. Adler's "Coaching Global Executives: Women Succeeding in a World Beyond Here" (1). Copyright © 2000. This material is used by permission of Jossey-Bass, Inc., a subsidiary of John Wiley & Sons, Inc.

4. For a more in-depth discussion of women's global leadership and international management careers, see Nancy J. Adler and Dafna N. Izraeli, eds. *Competitive Frontiers: Women Managers in a Global Economy* (Cambridge, MA: Blackwell Publishing, 1994), and Nancy J. Adler's "Global Leaders: A Dialogue with Future History," *International Management,* vol. 1, no. 2 (1997), pp. 21–33.

5. For research documenting expatriate women managers success abroad, see Adler's "Competitive Frontiers: Women Managing Across Borders" (2). Also see Caligiuri and her colleagues' re-search (25;26;29;30;32).

CHAPTER 9

1. Copyright © by Foulie Psalidas-Perlmutter, Ph.D. Reprinted by permission.

2. Copyright © Katherine D'Arcy. The author drew the material for this case from life experience and framed the issues during an organizational behavior

course that focused on the importance of cultural understanding. Reprinted by permission.

CHAPTER 10

1. The pronoun "he" has been changed in the quote to "they" to include male and female global managers.

2. This chapter is based, in part, on the study reported in N. J. Adler, "Do MBAs Want International Careers?" *International Journal of Intercultural Relations,* vol. 10, no. 3 (1986), pp. 277–300. The research was supported by a grant from the Social Sciences and Humanities Research Council of Canada.

3. The surveyed MBAs were young (average age 27 years), most were single (68%), approximately a third were women (32%), and most were studying for their MBAs in the country in which they were born, held citizenship, and had received their undergraduate education. The most common undergraduate degrees were business and economics (34%) and engineering (11%), while the most common MBA concentrations were finance (44%) and marketing (29%). Although 38 percent had no work experience, the majority had worked for a short time (approximately two years) prior to entering the MBA program. More than one third (36%) had never lived abroad. Few of the MBAs' parents had worked internationally. See Table 1 in Adler (2).

4. See Table 2 in Adler (2).

5. This section is adapted from N. J. Adler's "Competitive Frontiers: Women Managing Across Borders" (1:22–23).

6. For a discussion of how one company's CEO chose to increase the number of women from around the world at the highest levels of executive leadership, see references 13;14;69.

7. Adapted from "Did You Hear? Global Leadership in Charity's World," in *Journal of Management Inquiry,* Vol. 7, No. 2, pp. 135–143. Copyright © 1998 Sage Publications. Reprinted by permission of Sage Publications. Adapted and updated by Adler, 2002.

8. Facts about Charity Ngilu's life are as documented in J. C. McKinley Jr.'s *New York Times* (World late edition) article, "A Woman to Run Kenya? One Says, 'Why Not?'" (August 3, 1997), Section 1, p. 3, column 1.

9. See Adler's "Global Leadership: Women Leaders" (5) for a complete list of the women presidents and prime ministers, 1950 to the present.

10. In Kenya, carrying and waving leafy branches symbolizes change and peace.

11. See Adler's "Global Leaders: A Dialogue with Future History" (4) for a description of women leaders' aspirations and paths to power.

12. See Adler's "Global Women Political Leaders: An Invisible History, An Increasingly Important Future," (6) for a description of the visions motivating women's leadership.

13. Author's personal interview with Maria Liberia-Peters in Curacao, June 2, 1997.

14. For an excellent discussion of the increasing overlap of the managerial and

feminist literatures, both of which now refer to "power with," see Fondas (44).

15. For an excellent review of the leadership literature, including, but not limited to, behavioral and trait theories, see Yukl (89).

16. Mary Robinson's presidential acceptance speech, RDS, Dublin, 9 November 1990 as reported by Finlay (42).

17. See "Amman. Joint Jordan-Israeli Energy Project promises a flying start to cooperation" *(http://arabia.com/star/951228/bus1.html)*.

18. For a description of the attack, see "Attack on Presidential Candidate Motivated," Agence France-Press, 14 July 1997. For a description of an earlier attack on Ngilu's home, see "Kenyan Opposition MPs Protest Police Brutality," Agence France-Press, 15 April 1997.

19. Ngilu's opposition complains that "she is always covered [by the local and international media] when she speaks" (58).

EPILOGUE

1. Quote from Vaclav Havel: Copyright © 1983/94 by The New York Times Company. Reprinted by permission.

References

CHAPTER 1

1. Adler, N. J. "Cross-Cultural Management Research: The Ostrich and the Trend," *Academy of Management Review*, vol. 8, no. 2 (1983), pp. 226–232.
2. Adler, N. J. "Do MBAs Want International Careers?" *International Journal of Intercultural Relations,* vol. 10, no. 3 (1986), pp. 277–300.
3. Adler, N. J. "Women as Androgynous Managers: A Conceptualization of the Potential for American Women in International Management." Reprinted with permission from *International Journal of Intercultural Relations*, vol. 3, no. 6 (1979), p. 411.
4. Adler, N. J., and Bartholomew, Susan. "Academic and Professional Communities of Discourse: Generating Knowledge on Transnational Human Resource Management," *Journal of International Business Studies*, vol. 23, no. 3 (1992), pp. 551–569.
5. Adler, N. J., and Ghadar, F. "International Strategy from the Perspective of People and Culture: The North American Context," in A. M. Rugman, ed., *Research in Global Strategic Management: Intercultural Business Research for the Twenty-First Century: Canada's New Research Agenda*, vol. 1 (Greenwich, CT: JAI Press, 1990), pp. 179–205.
6. Ball, D. A., and McCulloch, W. H. *International Business: Introduction and Essentials* (Plano, TX: Business Publications, 1982).

7. Barnouw, V. *Culture and Personality* (Homewood, IL: Dorsey Press, 1963).

8. Bartlett, Chris A., and Ghoshal, Sumantra. *Managing Across Borders: The Transnational Solution,* 2d ed. (Boston: Harvard Business School Press, 1998).

9. Bartlett, Chris A., and Ghoshal, Sumantra. "Matrix Management: Not a Structure, a Frame of Mind," *Harvard Business Review*, (July–August, 1990), pp. 138–145.

10. Beechler, Schon; Taylor, Sully; Boyacigiller, Nakiye A.; and Levy, Orly. "Building global mind set for competitive advantage: A conceptual integration of global mindset, international human resource management, and organizational performance in multinational corporations," paper presented at the Academy of Management Annual Meeting, Chicago (August 1999).

11. Bennis, Warren, and Slater, P. *The Temporary Society* (New York: Harper & Row, 1968), p. 124.

12. Black, Stuart; Gregersen, Hal; and Mendenhall, Mark. *Global Assignments* (San Francisco: Jossey-Bass, 1992).

13. Boyacigiller, Nakiye; Kleinberg, M. Jill; Phillips, Margaret E.; and Sackman, Sonja. "Conceptualizing Culture" in B. J. Punnett and O. Shenkar, (eds.), *Handbook for International Management Research*. (Cambridge: Blackwell, 1996), pp. 157–208.

14. Brown, L. K. "For Women in Business, No Room in the Middle," *New York Times* (December 28, 1981), p. B18.

15. Brown, M. A. "Values—A Necessary but Neglected Ingredient of Motivation on the Job," *Academy of Management Review,* vol. 1 (1976), pp. 15–23.

16. *Business and International Education* (Washington, DC: American Council of Education, 1977), pp. 9–10.

17. Calori, R.; Johnson, G.; and Sarnin, P. "CEO's Cognitive Maps and the Scope of the Organization," *Strategic Management Journal,* vol. 15 (1994) pp. 435–457.

18. Caproni, Paula J.; Lenway, Stephanie A.; and Murtha, Thomas P. "Multinational Mind Sets: Sense Making Capabilities as Strategic Resources in Multinational Firms," Working paper #679, Division of Research, School of Business Administration, The University of Michigan (1992).

19. Carrol, M. P. "Culture," in J. Freedman, ed., *Introduction to Sociology: A Canadian Focus* (Scarborough, Ontario: Prentice-Hall, 1982), pp. 19–40.

20. Chandler, C. H., as quoted in C. H. Deutsch, "Losing Innocence Abroad: American Companies Are Trying to Shake Their Provincialism by Shipping Executives Overseas," *New York Times* (July 10, l988), Business, pp. 1, 2.

21. *Chicago Tribune* (February 4, 1981), as cited in S. H. Kim, *International Business Finance* (Richmond, VA: Robert F. Dame, Inc. 1983).

22. "Corporate Scoreboard," *Business Week* (July 21, 1980), p. 118; and *1980 World Bank Atlas* (Washington, DC: The World Bank, 1981).

23. Daniels, John D.; Ogram, E. W.; and Radebaugh, Lee H. *International Business Environments and Operations,* 3d ed. (Reading, MA: Addison-Wesley, 1982).

24. Dhawan, K. C.; Etemad, Hamid; and Wright, Richard W. *International Business: A Canadian Perspective.* (Reading, MA.: Addison-Wesley, 1981).

25. diStefano, Joseph J. "A Conceptual Framework for Understanding Cross-Cultural Management Problems" (London, Ontario: School of Business Administration, University of Western Ontario, 1972). Also see H. W. Lane and J. diStefano, *International Management Behavior,* 4th ed. (Cambridge: Blackwell, 2000).

26. Dowling, Peter; Welch, D.; and Schuler, Randall, *International HumanResource Management,* 3d ed. (Cincinnati, OH: South-Western, 1999).

27. Dun & Bradstreet, Canada, Ltd. *Canadian Book of Corporate Management, 1980* (Toronto: Dun & Bradstreet, Canada, Ltd., 1980).

28. Earley, Christopher, and Gibson, Christina. "Taking Stock in Our Progress on Individualism-Collectivism: 100 Years of Solidarity and Community," *Journal of Management,* vol. 24, no. 3 (1998), pp. 265–304.

29. *Economic Outlook* (Washington, DC: International Monetary Fund, October 1998).

30. Eiteman, David K., and Stonehill, Art I. *Multinational Business Finance,* 2d ed. (Reading, MA.: Addison-Wesley, 1979).

31. England, George W. *The Manager and His Values: An International Perspective* (Cambridge, MA.: Ballinger, 1975).

32. Erez, Miriam, and Earley, P. Chris. *Culture, Self-Identity, & Work* (New York: Oxford University Press, 1993).

33. "The Global Economy," *The Economist* (October 1, 1994), pp. 3–4, 14.

34. "Global Strategist," *U.S. News & World Report* (March 7, 1988), p. 50.

35. Godkin, L.; Braye, C. E.; and Caunch, C. L. "U.S.-Based Cross-Cultural Management Research in the Eighties," *Journal of Business and Economic Perspectives,* vol. 15, no. 2 (1989), pp. 37–45.

36. Govindarajan, V., and Gupta, A. "Success Is All in the Mindset," *Financial Times* (London, February 27, 1998), pp. 2–3.

37. Guth, William D., and Taguiri, R. "Personal Values and Corporate Strategies," *Harvard Business Review,* vol. 43 (1965), pp. 123–132.

38. Hambrick, Don C.; Korn, Lester B; Frederickson, J. W.; and Ferry, R. M. *21st Century Report: Reinventing the CEO* (New York: Korn/Ferry and Columbia University's Graduate School of Business, 1989), pp. 1–94.

39. Hampden-Turner, Charles, and Trompenaars, Fons. *The Seven Cultures of Capitalism: Value Systems for Creating Wealth in the United States, Britain, Japan, Germany, France, Sweden, and the Netherlands.* (New York: Doubleday, 1993).

40. Hamrin, R. D. *Managing Growth in the 1980s* (New York: Praeger, l980).

41. Hannerz, U. "Cosmopolitans and Locals in World Culture," in U. Hannerz, ed., *Transnational Connections: Culture, People, Places* (London: Routlege, 1996), pp. 102–111; originally published in *Theory, Culture and Society,* vol. 7 (1991), pp. 237–251.

42. Hannerz, U. *Transnational Connections: Culture, People, Places* (London: Routlege, 1996).

43. Hofstede, Geert. "Attitudes, Values and Organizational Culture: Disentangling the Concepts," *Organizational Studies*, vol 19, no. 3 (1998), pp. 477–492.

44. Hofstede, Geert. *Cultures and Organizations: Software of the Mind* (London: McGraw-Hill, 1991).

45. Hofstede, Geert. *Culture's Consequences: International Differences in Work-Related Values* (Beverly Hills, CA: Sage, 1980), p. 25.

46. International Monetary Fund and ACLI International, Inc. *Wall Street Journal* (May 28, 1981), p. 50.

47. International Monetary Fund, International Financial Statistics, United Nations Monthly Bulletin of Statistics, and national statistics as cited in *International Trade*, 1982/83. Contracting Parties to the General Agreement on Tariffs and Trade, Geneva, 1983, Ap-pendix Table A4.

48. Jelinek, Mariann, and Adler, N. J. "Women: World Class Managers for Global Competition," *Academy of Management Executive,* vol. 2, no. 1 (1988), pp. 11–19.

49. Kanter, Rosabeth Moss. "Afterward: What 'Thinking Globally' Really Means," in R. S. Barnwik and R. M. Kanter, eds., *Global Strategies* (Boston: Harvard Business School Press, 1994), pp. 227–232.

50. Kanter, Rosabeth Moss. *"World Class: Thriving Locally in the Global Economy"* (New York: Simon and Schuster, 1995).

51. Kim, S. H. *International Business Finance* (Richmond, VA: Robert F. Dame, 1983).

52. Kluckhohn, F., and Strodbeck, F. L. *Variations in Value Orientations* (Evanston, IL: Row, Peterson, 1961).

53. Kobrin, Steve J. "Is There a Relationship Between a Geocentric Mind-Set and Multinational Strategy?" *Journal of International Business Studies* (Third Quarter 1994), pp. 493–511.

54. Korn, Lester B. "How the Next CEO Will Be Different," *Fortune* (May 22, 1989), pp. 157–158.

55. Kroeber, A. L., and Kluckhohn, F. *Culture: A Critical Review of Concepts and Definitions,* Peabody Museum Papers, vol. 47, no. 1 (Cambridge, MA: Harvard University, 1952), p. 181. Reprinted with permission of the Peabody Museum of Archaeology and Ethnology, Harvard University.

56. Krugman, P. "Does Third World Growth Hurt First World Prosperity?" *Harvard Business Review* (July–August 1994), pp. 113–121.

57. Lane, Harry W., and diStefano, Joseph J. *International Management Behavior: From Policy to Practice,* 4th ed. (Cambridge: Blackwell, 2000).

58. Levy, Orly; Beechler, Schon; Taylor, Sully; and Boyacigiller, Nakiye "What We Talk About When We Talk About 'Global Mindset,' " paper presented at the Academy of Management Annual Meeting (Chicago, August 1999).

59. Lyles, Marjorie. "A Research Agenda for Strategic Management in the 1990s," *Journal of Management,* vol. 27, no. 4 (1990), pp. 363–375.

60. McCain, M. "Résumés: Separating Fact from Fiction," *American Way* (December 1983), p. 85.

61. McEvoy, G. M., and Buller, P. F. "International Human Resource Management Publications: Even in the Eighties and Needs for the Nineties," Utah State University (1992), pp. 1–21.

62. Mankoff, A. W. "Values—Not Attitudes—Are the Real Key to Motivation," *Management Review,* vol. 63, no. 12 (1979), pp. 23–29.

63. Mathews, J., and Mathews, L. *One Billion: A China Chronicle* (New York: Ballantine Books, 1983).

64. Merton, R. K. "Patterns of Influence: Local and Cosmopolitan Influentials." in R. K. Merton, *Social Theory and Social Structure* (Glencoe, IL: Free Press, 1957), pp. 368–380.

65. Mitroff, Ian I. *Business Not As Usual* (San Francisco: Jossey-Bass, 1987).

66. Murtha, Thomas P; Lenway, Stephanie A.; and Bagozzi, Rick P. "Global Mind-Sets and Cognitive Shift in a Complex Multinational Corporation," *Strategic Management Journal,* vol. 19, no. 2 (1998), pp. 97–114.

67. Parry, T. G. "Foreign Direct Investment and the Multinational Corporation," in Ingo Walter, ed., *Handbook of International Business* (New York: Wiley, 1982), Chapter 16, pp. 4–5.

68. Peng, T. K.; Peterson, Mark F.; and Shri, Y. P. "Quantitative Methods in Cross-National Management Research: Trends and Equivalence Issues," *Journal of Organization Behavior,* vol. 12, no. 1 (1990), pp. 87–107.

69. Peters, T. "Competition and Compassion," *California Management Review,* vol. 28, no. 4 (1986), pp. 11–26.

70. Porter, Michael E. *The Competitive Advantage of Nations* (New York: The Free Press, 1990).

71. Posner, Barry Z., and Munson, J. M. "The Importance of Values in Understanding Organizational Behavior," *Human Resource Management,* vol. 18 (1979), pp. 9–14.

72. Prahalad, C. K., and Doz, Yves L. *The Multinational Mission: Balancing Local Demands and Global Vision* (New York: The Free Press, 1987).

73. Pucik, Vladimir. "Globalization and Human Resource Management," in V. Pucik, N. Tichy, and C. Barnett, (eds.), *Globalization Management: Creating and Leading the Competitive Organization.* (New York: John Wiley & Sons, 1992), pp. 61–84.

74. Redding, S. Gordon, and Martyn-Johns, T. A. "Paradigm Differences and their Relation to Management with Reference to South-East Asia," in George W. England, Anant R. Negandhi, and B. Wilpert, eds., *Organizational Functioning in a Cross-Cultural Perspective* (Kent, OH: Kent State University Press, 1979).

75. Rhinesmith, Stephen H. *Cultural Organizational Analysis: The Interrelationship of Value Orientations and Managerial Behavior* (Cambridge, MA: McBer Publication Series Number 5, 1970).

76. Rhinesmith, Stephen H. "Global Mindsets for Global Managers," *Training and Development,* vol. 46, no. 10 (1992), pp. 63–69.

77. Rhinesmith, Stephen H. *A Manager's Guide to Globalization: Six Keys to*

Success in a Changing World (Homewood, IL: Business One Irwin, 1993).

78. Rhinesmith, Stephen H. "Open the Door to a Global Mindset," *Training and Development*, vol. 49, no. 5 (1995), pp. 35–43.

79. Rhinesmith, Stephen H., and Renwick, G. W. *Cultural Managerial Analysis Questionnaire* (New York: Moran, Stahl and Boyer, 1982).

80. Rugman, Alan M., and Verbeke, A. "Strategic Responses to Free Trade," in M. Farrow and A. M. Rugman, eds., *Business Strategies and Free Trade, Policy Study No. 5* (Toronto: C.D. Howe Institute, 1988), pp. 13–29.

81. Sackman, Sonia. *Cultural Knowledge in Organizations: Exploring the Collective Mind* (Newbury Park, CA: Sage, 1991).

82. Scarangello, A., ed. *American Education Through Foreign Eyes* (New York: Hobbs, Dorman, 1967). Examples contributed by Robert Kohls.

83. Schneider, Susan C., and Barsoux, Jean-Louis. *Managing Across Cultures* (New York: Prentice Hall, 1997).

84. Schwab, K., and Smadja, C. "The New Rules of the Game in a World of Many Players," *Harvard Business Review* (July–August 1994), pp. 40–44, 46, 50.

85. Shapiro, A. C. *Multicultural Financial Management*, 4th ed. (Needham Heights, MA: Allyn & Bacon, 1992), p. 5.

86. Simon, P. *The Tongue-Tied American: Confronting the Foreign Language Crisis* (New York: Continuum Publishing Corp., 1980).

87. Symington, J. W. "Learn Latin America's Culture," *New York Times* (September 23, 1983). Copyright © 1983/94 by The New York Times Company. Reprinted by permission.

88. Taylor, E. B. *Primitive Culture: Researches into the Development of Mythology, Philosophy, Religion, Language, Arts and Customs*, vol. 1 (New York: Henry Holt, 1977), p. 1.

89. Tichy, Noel M.; Brimm, Michael Ian; Charan, R.; and Takeuchi, H. "Leadership Development as a Lever for Global Transformation," in V. Pucik, N. M, Tichy, and C. K. Barnett, eds., *Globalizing Management: Creating and Leading the Competitive Organization* (New York: John Wiley, 1992), pp. 47–60.

90. Tichy, Noel, and Sherman, S. *Control Your Destiny or Someone Else Will: How Jack Welch Is Making General Electric the World's Most Competitive Company* (New York: Currency/Doubleday, 1993).

91. Tinsley, R. L., as quoted in V. V. Merchant's book review of *The Tongue-Tied American: Confronting the Foreign Language Crisis*, in *International Psychologist*, vol. 25, no. 1 (1983).

92. Triandis, Harry C. *Individualism and Collectivism* (Boulder, CO: Westview Press, 1995).

93. Trompenaars, Fons, and Hampden-Turner, Charles. *Riding the Waves of Culture: Understanding Cultural Diversity in Business*, 2d ed. (New York: McGraw-Hill, 1998).

94. U.S. Department of Commerce. *Survey of Business* (February 1977).

95. U.S. Department of Labor, "Hourly Compensation Costs in the U.S. Dollars." Table 1 (Washington DC: U.S. Department of Labor, Bureau of Labor Statistics, September 1998).

96. Vernon, Raymond. "International Investment and International Trade in the Product Cycle," *Quarterly Journal of Economics,* vol. 8, no. 2 (1966), pp. 129–144.

97. *1999 World Development Indicators* (Washington, DC: The World Bank, 1999).

98. Yip, George S.; Johansson, Johny K.; and Roos, Johan. "Effects of Nationality on Global Strategy," *Management International Review,* vol. 37, no. 4 (1997), pp. 365–385.

CHAPTER 2

1. Adler, N. J., and Jelinek, S. Mariann. "Is 'Organization Culture' Culture Bound?" *Human Resource Management,* vol. 25, no. 1 (1986), pp. 73–90.

2. Boyacigiller, Nayike; Kleinberg, M. Jill; Phillips, Margaret E.; and Sackman, Sonja. "Conceptualizing Culture" in B. J. Punnett and O. Shenkar (eds.), *Handbook for International Management Research* (Cambridge: Blackwell, 1996), pp. 157–208.

3. Burke, Warner, ed. "Special Issue on Organizational Culture," *Organizational Dynamics* (Autumn 1983).

4. Child, John. "Culture, Contingency and Capitalism in the Cross-National Study of Organizations," in L. L. Cummings and B. M. Staw, eds., *Research in Organizational Behavior,* vol. 3 (Greenwich, CT: JAI Press, 1981), pp. 303–356.

5. Chinese Culture Connection. "Chinese Values and the Search for Culture-Free Dimensions of Culture," *Journal of Cross-Cultural Psychology,* vol. 18, no. 2 (1987), pp. 143–164.

6. Earley, Christopher, and Gibson, Christina. "Taking Stock in Our Progress on Individualism/Collectivism: 100 Years of Solidarity and Community," *Journal of Management,* vol. 24, no. 3 (1998), pp. 265–305.

7. Hall, Edward T. *Beyond Culture.* Copyright © 1976, 1981 by Edward T. Hall. Used by permission of Doubleday, a division of Bantam Doubleday Dell Publishing Group, Inc., New York.

8. Hampden-Turner, Charles. *Charting the Corporate Mind* (Oxford, England: Blackwell, 1991).

9. Hofstede, Geert. *Cultures and Organizations: Software of the Mind* (London: McGraw-Hill, 1991).

10. Hofstede, Geert. *Culture's Consequences: International Differences in Work-Related Values* (Beverly Hills: Sage, 1980).

11. Hofstede, Geert. "Motivation, Leadership, and Organizations: Do American Theories Apply Abroad?" *Organizational Dynamics* (Summer 1980), pp. 42–63.

12. Hofstede, Geert, and Bond, Michael H. "The Confucius Connection: From

Cultural Roots to Economic Growth," *Organizational Dynamics*, vol. 16, no. 4 (1988), pp. 4–21.

13. Jelinek, Mariann; Smircich, Linda; and Hirsch, Paul, eds. "Organizational Culture" (Special Issue), *Administrative Science Quarterly*, vol. 28 (September 1983), p. 3.

14. Laurent, André. "The Cultural Diversity of Western Conceptions of Management," *International Studies of Management and Organization*, vol. 13, no. 1–2 (1983), pp. 75–96.

15. Lubatkin, M.; Calori, R.; Very, Philippe; and Veiga, J. "Managing Mergers Across Borders: A Two-Nation Exploration of a Nationally Bound Administrative Heritage," *Organization Science*, vol. 9, no. 6 (1998), pp. 670–684.

16. McGregor, Douglas M. *The Human Side of Enterprise*, 25th anniversary edition (New York: McGraw-Hill, 1985).

17. Muna, F. A. *The Arab Executive* (New York: Macmillan, 1980), Table 6.2.

18. Nasierowski, Wojciek, and Mikula, Bogusz. "Culture Dimensions of Polish Managers: Hofstede's Indices," *Organizational Studies*, vol. 19, no. 3 (1998), pp. 495–509.

19. Schneider, Susan. "National vs. Corporate Culture: Implications for Human Resource Management," *Human Resource Management*, vol. 27, no. 2 (1988), pp. 231–246.

20. Trompenaars, Fons, and Hampden-Turner, Charles. *Riding the Waves of Culture: Understanding Cultural Diversity in Business*, 2d ed. (New York: McGraw-Hill, 1998).

21. Uttal, B. "The Corporate Culture Vultures," *Fortune*, vol. 108, no. 8 (1983), pp. 66–72.

CHAPTER 3

1. Aksenova, Olga, and Beadle, Mary. "America and Russia in International Communication," *Journal of Language for International Business*, vol. 10, no. 1 (1999), pp. 8–23.

2. Anti-Defamation League Rumor Clinic.

3. Asch, Solomon. "Forming Impressions of Persons," *Journal of Abnormal and Social Psychology*, vol. 40 (1946), pp. 258–290.

4. Bagby, J. W. "Dominance in Binocular Rivalry in Mexico and the United States," in I. Al-Issa and W. Dennis, eds., *Cross-Cultural Studies of Behavior* (New York: Holt, Rinehart and Winston, 1970), pp. 49–56. Originally in *Journal of Abnormal and Social Psychology*, vol. 54 (1957), pp. 331–334.

5. Berry, John; Kalin, R.; and Taylor, Donald. *Multiculturalism and Ethnic Attitudes in Canada* (Ottawa: Minister of Supply and Services, 1977).

6. Burger, P., and Bass, Bernard M. *Assessment of Managers: An International Comparison* (New York: Free Press, 1979).

7. Carney, Carmen V., and Franciulli, Matilde. "Stereotypes of Latin Americans Among Graduate Students of International Management: Determining Cultural Needs of the U.S.-Trained Business Professional," *Journal of*

Language for International Business, vol. 10, no. 2 (1999), pp. 29–45.

8. Gancel, C., and Ratiu, Indre. Internal document, Inter Cultural Management Associates, Paris, France, 1984.

9. Gundling, Ernest. "How to Communicate Globally" *Training and Development Journal,* vol. 53, no. 6 (1999), pp. 28–31.

10. Hall, Edward T. *Beyond Culture* (Garden City, NY: Anchor Press/ Doubleday, 1976). Also see Edward T. Hall's *The Silent Language* (Doubleday, 1959, and Anchor Books, 1973); and *The Hidden Dimension* (Doubleday, 1966, and Anchor Books, 1969).

11. Ho, A. "Unlucky Numbers Are Locked out of the Chamber," *South China Morning Post* (December 26, 1988), p. 1.

12. Kanungo, Rabindra N. *Biculturalism and Management* (Ontario: Butterworth, 1980).

13. Lau, J. B., and Jelinek, Mariann. "Perception and Management," in *Behavior in Organizations: An Experiential Approach* (Homewood, IL: Irwin, 1984), pp. 213–220.

14. Maruyama, M. "Paradigms and Communication," *Technological Forecasting and Social Change,* vol. 6 (1974), pp. 3–32.

15. Prekel, Truda. "Multi-Cultural Communication: A Challenge to Managers," paper delivered at the International Convention of the American Business Communication Association, New York, November 21, 1983.

16. Ratiu, Indre. "Thinking Internationally: A Comparison of How International Executives Learn," *International Studies of Management and Organization,* vol. 13, nos. 1–2 (1983), pp. 139–150. Reprinted by permission of publisher, M. E. Sharpe, Inc., Armonk, New York.

17. Singer, Marshall. "Culture: A Perceptual Approach," in L. A. Samovar and R. E. Porter, eds., *Intercultural Communication: A Reader* (Belmont, CA: Wadsworth, 1976), pp. 110–119.

18. Snyder, M. "Self-Fulfilling Stereotypes," *Psychology Today* (July 1982), pp. 60–68.

19. *South China Morning Post,* "Mystery Man Gives a Fortune for Lucky '7'" (January 22, 1989), p. 3; and "Lucky '7' to Go on Sale" (January 4, 1989), p. 4.

20. Taylor, Donald. "American Tradition," in R. G. Gardner and R. Kalin, eds., *A Canadian Social Psychology of Ethnic Relations* (Toronto: Methuen Press, 1980).

21. U.S. Office of Education. *On Teaching the Vietnamese* (Washington, DC: General Printing Office, 1976).

CHAPTER 4

1. Adler, N. J. "Cross-Cultural Management: Issues to Be Faced," *International Studies of Management and Organization,* vol. 13, no. 1–2 (1983), pp. 7–45.

2. Adler, N. J. "Cross-Cultural Management Research: The Ostrich and the Trend," *Academy of Management Review,* vol. 8, no. 2 (1983), pp. 226–232.

3. Adler, N. J. "Cultural Synergy: The Management of Cross-Cultural Organi-

zations," in W. W. Burke and L. D. Goodstein, eds., *Trends and Issues in OD: Current Theory and Practice* (San Diego, CA: University Associates, 1980), pp. 163–184.

4. Adler, N. J. "Domestic Multiculturalism: Cross-Cultural Management in the Public Sector," in W. Eddy, ed., *Handbook on Public Organization Management* (New York: Marcel Dekker, 1983), pp. 481–499.

5. Adler, N. J. "Organizational Development in a Multicultural Environment," *Journal of Applied Behavioral Science,* vol. 19, no. 3 (1983), pp. 349–365.

6. Adler, N. J., and Bartholomew, Susan. "Academic and Professional Communities of Discourse: Generating Knowledge on Transnational Human Resource Management," *Journal of International Business Studies,* vol. 23, no. 3 (1992), pp. 551–569.

7. Adler, N. J., and Boyacigiller, Nakiye. "Global Organizational Behavior: Going Beyond Tradition," *Journal of International Management,* vol. 1, no. 1 (1995), pp. 73–86.

8. Adler, N. J., and Laurent, André. Unpublished results from the Cultural Synergy Survey collected at INSEAD in 1980–1983 and in 1982 at major American and Canadian multinationals ($n = 145$).

9. Boyacigiller, Nakiye, and Adler, N. J. "Insiders and Outsiders: Bridging the Worlds of Organizational Behavior and International Management," in Brian Toyne and Doug Nigh, eds., *International Business Inquiry: An Emerging Vision* (Columbia, SC: University of South Carolina Press, 1997), pp. 396–416.

10. Boyacigiller, Nakiye, and Adler, N. J. "The Parochial Dinosaur: The Organizational Sciences in a Global Context," *Academy of Management Review,* vol. 16, no. 2 (1991), pp. 262–290.

11. Dumaine, B. "What the Leaders of Tomorrow See," *Fortune* (July 3, 1989), pp. 48–62.

12. Fuller, R. Buckminster. *Critical Path* (Washington, DC: St. Martin's Press/ World Future Society, 1981).

13. Godkin, L.; Braye, C. E.; and Cauch, C. L. "U.S.–Based Cross-Cultural Management Research in the Eighties," *Journal of Business and Economic Perspectives,* vol. 15, no. 2 (1989), pp. 37–45.

14. Hayles, Robert. "Costs and Benefits of Integrating Persons from Diverse Cultures in Organization," paper presented at the 20th International Congress of Applied Psychology, Edinburgh, Scotland, July 25–31, 1982.

15. Hofstede, Geert. *Culture's Consequences: International Differences in Work-Related Values* (Beverly Hills, CA: Sage, 1980).

16. Laurent, André. "The Cultural Diversity of Western Conceptions of Management," *International Studies of Management and Organization,* vol. 13, no. 1–2 (1983), pp. 75–96.

17. Laurent, André, and Adler, N. J. "Managerial Skills for International Business," executive seminars held at INSEAD in Fontainebleau, France, August, 1981–1983.

18. McEvoy, G. M., and Buller, P. F. "International Human Resource Management Publications: Even in the Eighties and Needs for the Nineties," Working Paper. Utah State University, 1992, pp. 1–21.

19. Moran, Robert T., and Harris, Philip R. *Managing Cultural Synergy*, 3d ed. (Houston, TX: Gulf Publishing Company, 1983), Chapter 15, p. 303.

20. Peng, T. K.; Peterson, Mark F.; and Shyi, Y. P. "Quantitative Methods in Cross-National Management Research: Trend and Equivalence Is-sues. *Journal of Organizational Behavior,* vol. 12, no. 1 (1990), pp. 87–107.

21. Prekel, Truda. "Multicultural Communication: A Challenge to Managers," paper delivered at the International Convention of the American Business Communication Association, New York, November 21, 1983, p. 11.

22. Ricks, David A. *Blunders in International Business*, 3d ed. (Cambridge, MA: Blackwell, 1998).

23. Stewart, Edward C. *American Cultural Patterns: A Cross-Cultural Perspective* (Chicago: IL: Intercultural Press, 1979).

24. Trompenaars, Fons, and Hampden-Turner, Charles. *Riding the Waves of Culture: Understanding Cultural Diversity in Business*, 2d ed. (New York: McGraw-Hill Book Company, 1998).

25. Ziller, R. C. "Homogeneity and Heterogeneity of Group Membership," in C. G. McClintock, ed., *Experimental Social Psychology* (New York: Holt, Rinehart, and Winston, 1972), pp. 385–411.

CHAPTER 5

1. Abramson, F. "Factors Influencing the Entry of Canadian Software Manufacturers into the United States Market." Ph.D. dissertation, The University of Western Ontario, 1992.

2. Adler, N. J. "Domestic Multiculturalism: Cross-Cultural Management in the Public Sector," in W. Eddy, ed., *Handbook of Organization Management* (New York: Marcel Dekker, 1983), pp. 481–499.

3. Adler, N. J., and Ghadar, F. "International Strategy from the Perspective of People and Culture: The North American Context," in A. M. Rugman, ed., *Research in Global Strategic Management: International Business Research for the Twenty-First Century; Canada's New Research Agenda*, vol. 1 (Greenwich, CT: JAI Press, 1990), pp. 179–205.

4. Allport, G. W. *The Nature of Prejudice* (Reading, MA: Addison-Wesley, 1954), p. 281.

5. Amir, Y. "Contact Hypothesis in Ethnic Relations," *Psychological Bulletin*, vol. 71 (1969), pp. 319–342; and Amir, Y. "The Role of Intergroup Contact in Change of Prejudice and Ethnic Relations," in P. A. Katz, ed., *Toward the Elimination of Racism* (New York: Pergamon, 1976).

6. Anderson, K. "The New Ellis Island," *Time* (June 13, 1983), pp. 16–23.

7. Anderson, L. R. "Leader Behavior, Member Attitudes and Task Performance of Intercultural Discussion Groups," *Journal of Social Psychology*, vol. 69 (1966), pp. 305–319.

8. Anderson, L. R. "Management of the Mixed-Cultural Work Group," *Organizational Behavior and Human Performance*, vol. 31, no. 3 (1983), pp. 303–330.

9. Bass, Bernard M. "A Plan to Use Programmed Group Exercises to Study Cross-Cultural Differences in Management Behavior," *International Journal of Psychology*, vol. 1, no. 4 (1966), pp. 315–322.

10. Blakar, R. M. *Communication: A Social Perspective on Clinical Issues* (Oslo: Universitetsforlaget, 1984).

11. Blakar, R. M. "Toward a Theory of Communication in Terms of Preconditions: A Conceptual Framework and Some Empirical Explorations," in H. Giles and R. N. St. Clair, eds., *Recent Advances in Language, Communication, and Social Psychology* (London: Lawrence Erlbaum Associates, 1985).

12. Brislin, R. W. *Cross-Cultural Encounters* (New York: Pergamon, 1981).

13. Canney Davison, S. F. 1995. Intercultural Processes in Multinational Teams. Unpublished doctoral dissertation, London Business School.

14. Chemers, M. M.; Fiedler, F. E.; Lekhyananda, D.; and Stolurow, L. M. "Some Effects of Cultural Training on Leadership in Heterocultural Task Groups," *International Journal of Psychology*, vol. 1, no. 4 (1966), pp. 301–314.

15. Chen, Chao C.; Chen, Xiao-Ping; and Meindl, James R. "How Can Cooperation Be Fostered? The Cultural Effects of Individualism-Collectivism," *Academy of Management Review,* vol. 23, no. 2 (1998), pp. 285–304.

16. Cox, T. H.; Lobel, S. A.; and McLeod, P. L. "Effects of Ethnic Group Cultural Differences on Cooperative and Competitive Behavior on a Group Task," *Academy of Management Journal,* vol. 34, no. 4 (1991), pp. 827–847.

17. Davidson, W. H. "Small Group Activity at Musashi Semiconductor Works," *Sloan Management Review*, vol. 23, no. 3 (1982), pp. 3–14.

18. Delgado, M. "Hispanic Cultural Values: Implications for Groups," *Small Group Behavior*, vol. 12, no. 1 (1981), pp. 69–80.

19. Devonshire, C., and Kremer, J. W. *Toward a Person-Centered Resolution of Intercultural Conflicts* (La Jolla, CA: Center for the Whole Person).

20. Diab, L. "A Study of Intragroup and Intergroup Competition Among Experimentally Produced Small Groups," *Genetic Psychology Monographs*, vol. 82 (1970), pp. 325–332.

21. Earley, P. Christopher. "East Meets West Meets Mideast: Further Explorations of Collectivistic and Individualistic Work Groups," *Academy of Management Journal,* vol. 36, no. 2 (1993), pp. 319–348.

22. Earley, P. Christopher. "Social Loafing and Collectivism: A Comparison of the United States and the People's Republic of China," *Administrative Science Quarterly*, vol. 34, no. 4 (1989), pp. 565–581.

23. Earley, P. Christopher, and Mosakowski, Elaine. "Creating Hybrid Team Cultures: An Empirical Test of Transnational Team Functioning," *Academy of Management Journal,* vol. 43, no. 1 (2000).

24. Ferrari, S. "Human Behavior in International Groups," *Management International Review*, vol. XII, no. 6 (1972), pp. 31–35.

25. Fiedler, F. E. "The Effect of Leadership and Cultural Heterogeneity on Group Performance: A Test of the Contingency Model," *Journal of Experimental Social Psychology*, vol. 2 (1966), pp. 237–264.

26. Fiedler, F. E.; Meuwese, W. A. T.; and Oonk, S. "Performance on Laboratory Tasks Requiring Group Creativity," *Acta Psychology*, vol. 18 (1961), pp. 110–119.

27. Hackman, J. R. "The Design of Work Teams," in J. W. Lorsch, ed., *Handbook of Organizational Behavior* (New York: Prentice Hall, 1987), pp. 315–341.

28. Hare, A. P. "Cultural Differences in Performances in Communication Networks in Africa, United States and the Philippines," *Sociology and Social Research*, vol. 54, no. 1 (1969), pp. 25–41.

29. Hare, A. P. *Handbook of Small Group Research* (New York: Free Press, 1976).

30. Harrison, D. A.; Price, K. H.; and Bell, M. P. "Beyond Relational Demography: Time and the Effects of Surface- and Deep-Level Diversity on Work Group Cohesion," *Academy of Management Journal*, vol. 41, no. 1 (1998), pp. 96–107.

31. Hayles, R. "Costs and Benefits of Integrating Persons from Diverse Cultures into Organizations." Paper presented at the 21st International Congress of Applied Psychology, Edinburgh, Scotland, July 1982.

32. Hitt, Michael A.; Tyler, Beverly B.; Hardee, Camilla; and Park, Daewoo. "Understanding Strategic Intent in the Global Marketplace," *Academy of Management Executive*, vol. 9, no. 2 (1995), pp. 12–19.

33. Hoefer, H. J. *Hawaii*, 4th ed. (Hong Kong: APA Productions, 1983).

34. Hoffman, L. R. "Homogeneity of Member Personality and Its Effect on Group Problem-Solving," *Journal of Abnormal Psychology*, vol. 58 (1959), pp. 27–32.

35. Hoffman, L. R., and Maier, N. R. F. "Quality and Acceptance of Problem Solutions by Members of Homogeneous and Heterogeneous Groups," *Journal of Abnormal Psychology*, vol. 62, no. 2 (1961), pp. 401–407.

36. Hurst, D. K., Rush, J. C.; and White, R. E. "Top Management Teams and Organizational Renewal," *Strategic Management Journal* (1989), vol. 10 (Special Issue), pp. 87–105.

37. "It's Your Turn in the Sun: Now 19 Million and Growing Fast, Hispanics Are Becoming a Power," *Time*, vol. 112, no. 16 (1978), pp. 48–61.

38. Jackson, S. E.; May, K. E.; and Whitney, K. "Understanding the Dynamics of Diversity," In R. A. Guzzo, E. Salas, and Associates, eds., *Team Effectiveness and Decision Making in Organizations* (San Francisco: Jossey-Bass, 1995).

39. Janis, I. L. *Groupthink*, 2d ed. (New York: Houghton Mifflin Company, 1982). Copyright © 1982 Houghton Mifflin Company. Reprinted by permission.

40. Jewell, L. N., and Reitz, H. J. *Group Effectiveness in Organizations* (Glenview, IL: Scott, Foresman, 1981).

41. Katz, J.; Goldston, J.; and Benjamin, L. "Behavior and Productivity in Biracial Work Groups," *Human Relations*, vol. 11 (1958), pp. 123–151.
42. Kirsch, J. (citing former Lieutenant Governor M. Cymally of California) "Chicano Power," *New West*, vol. 3, no. 19 (1978), pp. 35–46.
43. Kirschmeyer, C., and Cohen, A. "Multicultural Groups: Their Performance and Reactions with Constructive Conflict," *Group and Organization Management*, vol. 17, no. 2 (1992), pp. 153–170.
44. Kovach, C. Based on observations of 800 second-year MBAs in field study teams at UCLA. Evaluation of teams was conducted by corporate executives and business professors in Los Angeles, California, 1980. Original model based on Kovach's paper, "Some Notes for Observing Group Process in Small Task-Oriented Groups," Graduate School of Management, University of California at Los Angeles, 1976.
45. Kumar, K.; Subramanian, R.; and Nonis, S. A. "Cultural Diversity's Impact on Group Process and Performance: Comparing Culturally Homogeneous and Culturally Diverse Work Groups Engaged in Problem-Solving Tasks," *Southern Management Association Proceedings* (1991).
46. Lattimer, Robert L. "The Case for Diversity in Global Business, and the Impact of Diversity on Team Performance," *Competitiveness Review*, vol. 8, no. 2 (1998), pp. 3–17.
47. Lattimer, Robert L. *Managing Diversity for Strategic and Competitive Advantage* (New York: Doubleday Books, 2000).
48. Lau, D. C., and Murnighan, J. K. "Demographic Diversity and Faultlines: The Compositional Dynamics of Organizational Groups," *Academy of Management Review*, vol. 23, no. 2 (1998), pp. 325–340.
49. Levine, R. A., and Campbell, D. T. *Ethnocentrism* (New York: Wiley, 1972).
50. Likert, R. "The Nature of Highly Effective Groups," in *New Patterns of Management* (New York: McGraw-Hill, 1961).
51. McDermott, Lynda; Waite, Bill; and Brawley, Nolan. "Putting Together a World-Class Team," *Training and Development*, vol. 53, no. 1 (1999), pp. 46–51.
52. McGrath, J. E. *Groups: Interaction and Performance* (Upper Saddle River, NJ: Prentice Hall, 1984).
53. McLeod, P. L. and Lobe, S. A. "The Effects of Ethnic Diversity on Idea Generation in Small Groups," *Academy of Management Best Paper Proceedings* (1992), pp. 227–231.
54. Maier, N. R. F., and Hoffman, L. R. "Group Decision in England and the United States," *Personnel Psychology*, vol. 15, no. 2 (1962), pp. 75–87.
55. Mann, L. "Cross-Cultural Studies of Small Groups," in H. Triandis, ed., *Handbook of Cross-Cultural Psychology*, vol. 5 (Boston: Allyn & Bacon, 1980).
56. Maznevski, M. L. "Process and Performance in Multicultural Teams." Working paper. London, Ontario, Canada: The University of Western Ontario, School of Business, 1995, p. 49.

57. Maznevski, M. L. "Understanding Our Differences: Performance in Decision-Making Groups with Diverse Members," *Human Relations*, vol. 47, no. 5 (1994), pp. 531–552.

58. Maznevski, M. L., and diStefano, Joseph J. "Synergistic Performance in Multicultural Management Teams: A Communications Perspective," paper presented at the Academy of International Business Annual Meeting, Brussels, 1992.

59. Meade, R. "An Experimental Study of Leadership in India," *Journal of Social Psychology*, vol. 72 (1967), pp. 35–43.

60. Meade, R. "Leadership Studies of Chinese and Chinese-Americans," *Journal of Cross-Cultural Psychology*, vol. 1 (1970), pp. 325–332.

61. Milliken, F. J., and Martins, L. L. "Searching for Common Threads: Understanding the Multiple Effects of Diversity in Organizational Groups," *Academy of Management Review,* vol. 21, no. 2 (1996), pp. 402–433.

62. Misumi, J. "Experimental Studies on Group Dynamics in Japan," *Psychologia*, vol. 2 (1959), pp. 229–235.

63. Mitchell, R. "Team Building by Disclosure of Internal Frames of Reference," *Journal of Applied Behavioral Science,* vol. 22, no. 1 (1986), pp. 15–28.

64. Novack, M. *The Rise of the Unmeltable Ethnics* (New York: Macmillan, 1972).

65. "Over the Rainbow," *Economist* (November 22, 1997), p. 76.

66. Probst, Tahira M.; Carnevale, Peter J.; and Triandis, Harry C. "Cultural Values in Intergroup and Single-Group Social Dilemmas," *Organizational Behavior and Human Decision Processes*, vol. 77, no. 3 (1999), pp. 171–191.

67. Punnett, Betty Jane, and Clemens, Jason. "Cross-National Diversity: Implications for International Expansion Decisions," *Journal of World Business*, vol. 34, no. 2 (1999), pp. 128–138.

68. Rombauts, J. "Gedrag en Groepsbeleving in Etnisch-Homogene en Etnisch-Heterogene Groepen," *Tijdschrift Voor Opvoedkunde*, no. 1 (1962–1963).

69. Ruhe, J., and Eastman, J. "Effects of Racial Composition on Small Work Groups," *Small Group Behavior*, vol. 8, no. 4 (1977), pp. 479–486.

70. "The Samoans Among Us," *The Los Angeles Times* (January 2, 1979), p. 1.

71. Sherif, M.; Harvey, O.; White, B.; Hood, W.; and Sherif, C. *Inter-Group Conflict and Cooperation: The Robbers Cave Experiment* (Norman, OK: Institute of Group Relations, 1961).

72. Shuter, R. "Cross-Cultural Small Group Research: A Review, an Analysis, and a Theory," *International Journal of Intercultural Relations*, vol. 1, no. 1 (1977), pp. 90–104.

73. Simard, L. M., and Taylor, D. M. "The Potential for Bicultural Communication in a Dyadic Situation," *Canadian Journal of Behavioral Science*, vol. 5 (1973), pp. 211–225.

74. Snow, C. C.; Snell, S. A.; Canney Davidson, S.; and Hambrick, D. C. "Use Transnational Teams to Globalize Your Company," *Organizational Dynamics*, vol. 24, no. 4 (1996), pp. 50–67.

75. Steiner, I. D. *Group Process and Productivity* (New York: Academic Press, 1972).
76. Toffler, A. *The Third Wave* (New York: William Morrow, 1980).
77. Triandis, H. C.; Hall, E. R.; and Ewen, R. B. "Some Cognitive Factors Affecting Group Creativity," *Human Relations*, vol. 18, no. 1 (1965), pp. 33–35.
78. U. S. Office of Immigration. Personal conversation with immigration official (Los Angeles, CA, November 1979).
79. Walsh, J. P.; Henderson, C. M.; and Deighton, J. "Negotiated Belief Structures and Decision Performance: An Empirical Investigation," *Organizational Behavior and Human Decision Processes,* vol. 42, no. 2 (1988), pp. 194–216.
80. Watson, W. E., and Kumar, K. "Differences in Decision-Making Regarding Risk-Taking: A Comparison of Culturally Diverse and Culturally Homogeneous Task Groups," *International Journal of Intercultural Relations*, vol. 16, no. 1 (1992), pp. 53–66.
81. Watson, W. E.; Kumar, K.; and Michaelson, L. K. "Cultural Diversity's Impact on Interaction Process and Performance: Comparing Homogeneous and Diverse Task Groups," *Academy of Management Journal*, vol. 36, no. 3 (1993), pp. 590–602.
82. Watson, W. E., and Michaelson, L. K. "Group Interaction Behaviors That Affect Group Performance on an Intellective Task," *Group and Organization Studies*, vol. 13, no. 4 (1988), pp. 495–516.
83. Ziegler, S. "The Effectiveness of Cooperative Learning Teams for Increasing Cross-Ethnic Friendship: Additional Evidence," *Human Organization: The Journal of the Society for Applied Anthropology*, vol. 40, no. 3 (1981), pp. 264–268.
84. Ziller, R. C. "Homogeneity and Heterogeneity of Group Membership," in C. G. McClintock, ed., *Experimental Social Psychology* (New York: Holt, Rinehart and Winston, 1972), pp. 385–411.

CHAPTER 6

1. Abramson, Neil R.; Keating, Robert J.; and Lane, Henry W. "Cross-National Cognitive Process Differences: A Comparison of Canadian, American, and Japanese Managers," *Management International Review*, vol. 36, no. 2 (1996), pp. 123–147.
2. Adler, N. J. "Cross-Cultural Management Research: The Ostrich and the Trend," *Academy of Management Review*, vol. 8, no. 2 (1983), pp. 226–232.
3. Adler, N. J. "Did You Hear? Global Leadership in Charity's World," *Journal of Management Inquiry*, vol. 7, no. 2 (1998), pp. 21–33.
4. Adler, N. J. "Global Entrepreneurs: Women, Myths, and History," *Global Focus*, vol. 1, no. 4 (1999), pp. 125–134.
5. Adler, N. J. "Global Leaders: A Dialogue with Future History," *International Management*, vol. 1, no. 2 (1997), pp. 21–33.
6. Adler, N. J. "Global Leaders: Women of Influence," in Gary Powell, ed.,

Handbook of Gender in Organizations (Thousand Oaks, CA: Sage, 1999), pp. 239–261.

7. Adler, N. J. "Global Leadership: No Longer Men Alone" in Martin J. Gannon and Karen L. Newman (eds.) *Handbook of Cross-Cultural Management* (Oxford, England: Blackwell, 2001).

8. Adler, N. J. "Global Leadership: Women Leaders," *Management International Review*, 37 (Special Issue 1, 1997), pp. 135–143.

9. Adler, N. J. "Global Women Political Leaders: An Invisible History, An Increasingly Important Future," *Leadership Quarterly*, vol. 7, no. 1 (1996), pp. 133–161.

10. Adler, N. J. "Societal Leadership: The Wisdom of Peace," in Suresh Srivastva, ed., *Executive Wisdom and Organizational Change* (San Francisco: Jossey-Bass, 1998), pp. 243–337.

11. Adler, N. J. "Twenty-First Century Leadership: Reality Beyond the Myths" in Richard Wright, volume ed., *Research in Global Strategic Management*, Vol. 7: *International Entrepreneurship: Globalization of Emerging Business* (Greenwich, CT: JAI Press, 1999), pp. 173–190.

12. Adler, N. J., and Bartholomew, Susan. "Academic and Professional Communities of Discourse: Generating Knowledge on Transnational Human Resource Management," *Journal of International Business Studies*, vol. 23, no. 3 (1992), pp. 551–569.

13. Adler, N. J., and Boyacigiller, Nakiye. "Global Management and the 21st Century," in B. J. Punnett and O. Shenkar, eds. *Handbook of International Management Research* (Cambridge, MA: Blackwell, 1996), pp. 537–555.

14. Adler, N. J., and Boyacigiller, Nakiye. "Global Organizational Behavior: Going Beyond Tradition," *Journal of International Management*, vol. 1, no. 3 (1995), pp. 73–86.

15. Adler, N. J., and Boyacigiller, Nakiye. "Going Beyond Traditional HRM Scholarship," in R. N. Kanungo and D. M. Saunders, eds. *New Approaches to Employee Management*. vol. 3, *Employee Management Issues in Developing Countries* (Greenwich, CT: JAI Press, 1995), pp. 1–13.

16. Adler, N. J.; Brody, Laura W.; and Osland, Joyce S. "Advances in Global Leadership: The Women's Global Leadership Forum," in William H. Mobley, ed., *Advances in Global Leadership*, vol. 2 (Greenwich, CT: JAI Press, 2001), pp. 351–383.

17. Adler, N. J.; Brody, Laura W.; and Osland, Joyce S. "The Women's Global Leadership Forum: Enhancing One Company's Global Leadership Capability," *Human Resource Management*, vol. 39, nos. 2 and 3 (2000), pp. 209–225.

18. Albright, Madeleine K. *Harvard University Commencement Address* as reported in the *New York Times,* June 6, 1997, p. A8.

19. Al-Gratton, A. A. "Test of the Path-Goal Theory of Leadership in the Multinational Domain," *Group and Organizational Studies*, vol. 10, no. 4 (1985), pp. 429–445.

20. Allen, Douglas B.; Miller, E. L.; and Nath, R. "North America," in R. Nath, ed., *Comparative Management* (Cambridge, MA: Ballinger, 1988), pp. 23–54.

21. Ayman, R. "Leadership Perception: The Role of Gender and Culture," *Leadership Theory and Research* (San Diego: Academic Press, 1993), pp. 137–166.

22. Badawy, M. K. "Managerial Attitudes and Need Orientations of Mideastern Executives: An Empirical Cross-Cultural Analysis," *Academy of Management Proceedings*, vol. 39 (1979), pp. 293–297.

23. Badawy, M. K. "Styles of Mideastern Managers," *California Management Review*, vol. 22, no. 3 (1980), pp. 51–59.

24. Bass, Bernard M. *Leadership and Performance Beyond Expectations* (New York: Free Press, 1985).

25. Bass, Bernard M., and Stogdill, R. M. *The Handbook of Leadership*, 3d ed. (New York: Free Press, 1989).

26. Bennis, Warren. *Why Leaders Can't Lead: The Unconscious Conspiracy Continues* (San Francisco: Jossey-Bass, 1989).

27. Bennis, Warren, and Nanus, Burt. *Leaders: Strategies for Taking Charge* (New York: Harper & Row, 1985).

28. Blake, R. R., and Mouton, J. S. *The Managerial Grid* (Houston, TX: Gulf Publishing,1964).

29. Blake, R. R., and Mouton, J. S. "Motivating Human Productivity in the People's Republic of China," *Group and Organization Studies*, vol. 4, no. 2 (1979), pp. 159–169.

30. Bluntt, P., and Jones, M. L. *Managing African Organizations*. (Berlin: Walter de Gruyter, 1992).

31. Bolman, L., and Deal, T. *Leading with Soul* (San Francisco: Jossey-Bass, 1995).

32. Boyacigiller, Nakiye, and Adler, N. J. "Insiders and Outsiders: Bridging the Worlds of Organizational Behavior and International Management," in Brian Toyne and Doug Nigh, eds., *International Business Inquiry: An Emerging Vision* (Columbia, SC: University of South Carolina Press, 1996), pp. 22–102.

33. Boyacigiller, Nakiye, and Adler, N. J. "The Parochial Dinosaur: The Organizational Sciences in a Global Context," *Academy of Management Review*, vol. 16, no. 2 (1991), pp. 262–290.

34. Brenner, S. N., and Molander, E. A. "Is the Ethics of Business Changing?" *Harvard Business Review* (January–February 1977), pp. 70–71.

35. Buera, A., and Glueck, W. "Need Satisfaction of Libyan Managers," *Management International Review*, vol. 19, no. 1 (1979), pp. 113–123.

36. Chemers, M. M., "A Theoretical Framework for Examining the Effects of Cultural Differences on Leadership." Paper presented at the 23rd International Congress of Applied Psychology, Madrid, Spain, 1994.

37. Chemers, M. M., and Ayman, R. "Directions for Leadership Research," *Leadership Theory and Research* (San Diego: Academic Press, 1993), pp. 321–332.

38. Chu, P. C.; Spires, Eric E.; and Sueyoshi, Toshiyuki. "Cross-Cultural Differ-

ences in Choice Behavior and Use of Decision Aids: A Comparison of Japan and the United States," *Organizational Behavior & Human Decision Processes*, vol. 77, no. 2 (1999), pp. 147–170.

39. Chung, K. H.; Lee, H. C.; and Jung, K. H. *Korean Management: Global Strategy and Cultural Transformation* (Berlin: Walter de Gruyter, 1997).

40. Conger, J. A. *The Charismatic Leader: Behind the Mystique of Exceptional Leadership* (San Francisco: Jossey-Bass, 1989).

41. Conger, J. A., and Kanungo, R. N., eds., *Charismatic Leadership* (San Francisco: Jossey-Bass, 1988).

42. Crabbs, R. A. "Work Motivation in the Culturally Complex Panama Canal Company," *Academy of Management Proceedings* (1973), pp. 119–126.

43. Dewey, J. *How We Think* (Boston: D.C. Heath, 1933).

44. Dorfman, P. W. "International and Cross-Cultural Leadership," in B. J. Punnett and O. Shenkar, eds., *Handbook for International Management Research* (Cambridge, MA: Blackwell, l996), pp. 267–349.

45. Dorfman, P. W., and Howell, J. P. "Dimensions of National Culture and Effective Leadership Patterns: Hofstede Revisited," *Advances in International Comparative Management*, vol. 3 (Greenwich, CT: JAI Press, 1988), pp. 127–150.

46. Dorfman, P. W., Howell, J. P., Hibino, S., Lee, J. K., Tate, U., and Bautista, A. "Leadership in Western and Asian Countries: Commonalties and Differences in Effective Leadership Processes Across Cultures," *Leadership Quarterly*, vol. 8 (1997), pp. 233–274.

47. Dorfman, P. W., and Ronen, S. "The Universality of Leadership Theories: Challenges and Paradoxes." Paper presented at the National Academy of Management annual meeting, Miami, Florida, 1991.

48. Driver, M. J. "Individual Decision Making and Creativity," in S. Kerr, ed., *Organizational Behavior* (Columbus, OH: Grid Publishing, 1979), pp. 59–91.

49. Drucker, P. F. "What We Can Learn from Japanese Management," *Harvard Business Review* (March–April 1971), pp. 110–122.

50. Elenkov, D. S. "Can American Management Concepts Work in Russia? A Cross-Cultural Comparative Study," *California Management Review*, vol. 40, no. 4 (1998), pp. 133–157.

51. Erez, M., and Earley, P. Christopher. *Culture, Self-Identity and Work* (New York: Oxford University Press, 1993).

52. Fiorina, Carly. "Anytime You Have a Fiercely Competitive Business," *Nortel World* (November 1999), p. 8.

53. Foy, N., and Gadon, H. "Worker Participation Contrasts in Three Countries," *Harvard Business Review* (May–June 1976), pp. 71–84.

54. Friedman, Thomas L. *The Lexus and the Olive Tree* (New York: Farrar, Straus, Giroux, 1999).

55. Gardner, Howard. *Leading Minds: An Anatomy of Leadership* (New York: Basic Books, 1995).

56. Gardner, John W. *Gardner on Leadership* (New York: The Free Press, 1989).

57. Gerstner, C. R., and Day, D. D. "Cross-Cultural Comparison of Leadership Prototypes," *Leadership Quarterly*, vol. 5, no. 1 (1994), pp. 121–134.

58. Goleman, Daniel. *Emotional Intelligence* (New York: Bantam, 1995).

59. Goleman, Daniel. "What Makes a Leader," *Harvard Business Review* (November–December 1998), pp. 92–102. Also see Goleman, Daniel. "Leadership That Gets Results," *Harvard Business Review* (March–April 2000), pp. 78–90; and Goleman, Daniel. *Emotional Intelligence at Work* (New York: Bantam, 1998).

60. Graen, G. B., and Wakabayashi, M. "Cross-Cultural Leadership Makings: Bridging American and Japanese Diversity for Team Advantage," *Handbook of Industrial and Organizational Psychology*, vol. 4, 2d ed. (Palo Alto, CA: Consulting Psychologists Press, 1994), pp. 415–446.

61. Grauman, C. F., and Moscovici, S. *Changing Conceptions of Leadership* (New York: Springer-Verlag, 1986).

62. Gyllenhammer, P. G. "How Volvo Adapts Work to People," *Harvard Business Review*, vol. 55, no. 4 (1977), pp. 102–113.

63. Haire, M.; Ghiselli, E. E.; and Porter, L. W. "Cultural Patterns in the Role of the Manager," *Industrial Relations*, vol. 2, no. 2 (1963), pp. 95–117.

64. Hammer, W. C. "Motivation Theories and Work Applications," in S. Kerr, ed., *Organizational Behavior* (Columbus, OH: Grid Publishing, 1979), pp. 41–58.

65. Hendry, John. "Universalizability and Reciprocity in International Business Ethics," *Business Ethics Quarterly*, vol. 9, no. 3 (1999), pp. 405–420.

66. Herzberg, F. "One More Time: How Do You Motivate Employees?" *Harvard Business Review* (January–February 1968), pp. 54–62.

67. Herzberg, F.; Mausner, B.; and Snyderman, B. *The Motivation to Work*, 2d ed. (New York: Wiley, 1959).

68. Hessling, P., and Keenen, E. E. "Culture and Subculture in a Decision Making Exercise," *Human Relations*, vol. 22 (1969), pp. 31–51.

69. Hines, G. H. "Achievement, Motivation, Occupations and Labor Turnover in New Zealand," *Journal of Applied Psychology*, vol. 58, no. 3 (1973), pp. 313–317.

70. Hines, G. H. "Cross-Cultural Differences in Two-Factor Theory," *Journal of Applied Psychology*, vol. 58, no. 5 (1973), pp. 375–377.

71. Hofstede, Geert. *Cultures and Organizations: Software of the Mind* (London: McGraw-Hill, 1991).

72. Hofstede, Geert. *Culture's Consequences: International Differences in Work-Related Values* (Beverly Hills, CA: Sage, 1980).

73. Hofstede, Geert. "Motivation, Leadership and Organization: Do American Theories Apply Abroad?" *Organizational Dynamics*, vol. 9, no. 1 (1980), pp. 42–63.

74. House, Robert J. "GLOBE: The Global Leadership and Organizational Behavior Effectiveness Research Program," *Polish Psychological Bulletin*, vol. 28, no. 3 (1997), pp. 215–254.

75. House, Robert J., and Aditya, R. N. "The Social Scientific Study of Leadership: Quo Vadis?" *Journal of Management,* vol. 23, no. 3 (1997), pp. 409–473.

76. House, Robert J.; Hanges, Paul J.; Ruiz-Quintanilla, S. Antonio; Dorfman, Peter W.; Javidan, Mansour; Dickson, Marcus; Gupta, Vipin; and GLOBE Country Co-Investigators. "Cultural Influences on Leadership and Organizations: Project Globe," in William H. Mobley, M. Jocelyne Gessner, and Val Arnold, eds., *Advances in Global Leadership,* vol. 1 (1999), pp. 171–233.

77. House, Robert J.; Wright, N. S. and Aditya, R. N. "Cross-Cultural Research on Organizational Leadership: A Critical Analysis and a Proposed Theory," in P. C. Earley and M. Erez, eds., *New Perspectives in International Industrial/Organizational Psychology* (San Francisco: New Lexington, 1997), pp. 535–625.

78. Howell, J. P; Dorfman, P. W.; Hibino, S.; Lee, J. K; and Tate, U. "Leadership in Western and Asian Countries: Commonalities and Differences in Effective Leadership Processes and Substitutes Across Cultures." Center for Business Research, New Mexico State University, 1994.

79. Howell, P.; Strauss, J.; and Sorensen, P. F. "Research Note: Cultural and Situational Determinants of Job Satisfaction Among Management in Liberia," *Journal of Management Studies* (May 1975), pp. 225–227.

80. Hundal, P. S. "A Study of Entrepreneurial Motivation: Comparison of Fast- and Slow-Progressing Small Scale Industrial Entrepreneurs in Punjab, India," *Journal of Applied Psychology,* vol. 55, no. 4 (1971), pp. 317–323.

81. Hunt, J. W. *Leadership: A New Synthesis* (Newbury Park, CA: Sage, 1991).

82. Iacocca, L., and Novak, W. *Iacocca* (New York: Bantam, 1984).

83. Illman, P. E. "Motivating the Overseas Work Force," in *Developing Overseas Managers and Managers Overseas* (New York: AMACOM, 1980), pp. 83–106.

84. Jaeger, A. M., and Kanungo, R. N., eds., *Management in Developing Countries* (London: Routledge, 1990).

85. Jaggi, B. "Need Importance of Indian Managers," *Management International Review,* vol. 19, no. 1 (1979), pp. 107–113.

86. Jain, C. H., and Kanungo, R. *Behavioral Issues in Management: The Canadian Context* (Toronto: McGraw-Hill Ryerson, 1977), pp. 85–99.

87. Jennings, E. *The Anatomy of Leadership.* (New York: Harper and Row, 1960).

88. Kakar, S. "Authority Patterns and Subordinate Behavior in Indian Organizations," *Administrative Science Quarterly,* vol. 16, no. 3 (1971), pp. 298–308.

89. Kanter, Rosabeth Moss. Comments on Nancy A. Nichols' *Reach for the Top: Women and the Changing Facts of Work Life.* Boston: Harvard Business School Press, as cited in the book review by John R. Hook in *The Academy of Management Executive,* vol. 8, no. 2 (1994), pp. 87–89.

90. Kaufman, F. "Decision Making—Eastern and Western Style," *Business Horizons,* vol. 13, no. 6 (1970), pp. 81–86.

91. Kavcic, B.; Rus, V.; and Tannenbaum, A. S. "Control, Participation, and

Effectiveness in Four Yugoslavian Industrial Organizations," *Administrative Science Quarterly*, vol. 16, no. 1 (1971), pp. 74–86.

92. Keizan, W. "Decision Making by Socialist Managers in Complex Organizations," *International Studies of Management and Organization*, vol. 9, no. 4 (1979), pp. 63–77.

93. Koch, M.; Nam, S. H.; and Steers, R. M. "Human Resource Management in South Korea," In L. Moore and D. Jennings, eds., *Human Resource Management on the Pacific Rim* (Berlin: Walter de Gruyter, 1995), pp. 217–242.

94. Kotter, J. *The Leadership Factor* (New York: Free Press, 1988).

95. Kuchinke, K. Peter. "Leadership and Culture: Work-Related Values and Leadership Styles Among One Company's U.S. and German Telecommunication Employees," *Human Resource Development Quarterly*, vol. 10, no. 2 (1999), pp. 135–154.

96. Laurent, André. "The Cultural Diversity of Western Conceptions of Management," *International Studies of Management and Organization*, vol. 13, nos. 1–2 (1983), pp. 75–96.

97. Lawler, E. E., III. "Job Design and Employee Motivation," *Personnel Psychology*, vol. 22 (1969), pp. 426–435.

98. Lawler, E. E., III. *Pay and Organizational Effectiveness: A Psychological View* (New York: McGraw-Hill, 1971).

99. Reprinted by permission of the publishers from *Executive* by Harry Levinson, Cambridge, MA: Harvard University Press. Copyright © 1968, 1981 by the President and Fellows of Harvard College. As cited in R. H. Mason and R. S. Spich, *Management: An International Perspective* (Homewood, IL: Irwin, 1987), pp. 190–191.

100. Likert, R. *The Human Organization* (New York: McGraw-Hill, 1967).

101. Likert, R. *New Patterns of Management* (New York: McGraw-Hill, 1961).

102. McClelland, D. C. *The Achieving Society* (Princeton, NJ: Van Nostrand, 1961).

103. McClelland, D. C.; Atkinson, J. W.; Clark, R. A.; and Lowell, E. L. *The Achievement Motive* (New York: Appleton-Century-Crofts, 1953).

104. McClelland, D. C., and Burnham, D. H. "Power Is the Great Motivator," *Harvard Business Review*, vol. 54, no. 1 (1976), pp. 100–110.

105. McGregor, D. *The Human Side of Enterprise* (New York: McGraw-Hill, 1960).

106. Maslow, A. H. *Motivation and Personality* (New York: Harper & Row, 1954).

107. Maslow, A. H. "A Theory of Human Motivation," *Psychology Review* (July 1943), pp. 370–396.

108. Maslow, A. H. *Toward a Psychology of Being* (Princeton, NJ: Van Nostrand, 1962).

109. Matsui, T., and Terai, I. "A Cross-Cultural Study of the Validity of the Expectancy Theory of Work Motivation," *Journal of Applied Psychology*, vol. 60, no. 2 (1979), pp. 263–265.

110. Miller, J. J., and Kilpatrick, J. A. *Issues for Managers: An International Perspective* (Homewood, IL: Irwin, 1987).

111. Mitroff, I. I. *Business Not as Usual* (San Francisco: Jossey-Bass, 1987).

112. Mutiso, G. C. M. *Socio-Political Thought in African Literature: Weusi* (New York: Barnes and Noble, 1974).

113. Nath, R., and Narayanan, V. K. "A Comparative Study of Managerial Support, Trust, Openness, Decision-Making, and Job Enrichment," *Academy of Management Proceedings*, vol. 40 (1980), pp. 48–52.

114. Oh, T. K. "Theory Y in the People's Republic of China," *California Management Review*, vol. 19, no. 2 (1976), pp. 77–84.

115. Ohmae, K. *Beyond National Borders* (Homewood, IL: Dow Jones-Irwin, 1987).

116. O'Reilly, C. A., and Roberts, K. H. "Job Satisfaction Among Whites and Nonwhites," *Journal of Applied Psychology*, vol. 57, no. 3 (1973), pp. 295–299.

117. Pascale, R. T. "Communication and Decision Making Across Cultures: Japanese and American Comparisons," *Administrative Science Quarterly*, vol. 23 (March 1978), pp. 91–110.

118. Pfeffer, J. *Organizations and Organization Theory* (Boston: Pitman, 1982).

119. Punnett, B. J. "Language, Cultural Values and Preferred Leadership Styles: A Comparison of Anglophones and Francophones in Ottawa," *Canadian Journal of Behavioral Sciences*, vol. 23, no. 2 (1991), pp. 241–244.

120. Reitz, H. J. "The Relative Importance of Five Categories of Needs Among Industrial Workers in Eight Countries," *Academy of Management Proceedings* (1975), pp 270–273.

121. Reitz, J., and Grof, G. *Similarities and Differences Among Mexican Workers, in Attitudes to Worker Motivation* (Bloomington, IN: Indiana University, 1973).

122. Robertson, Chris, and Fadil, Paul A. "Ethical Decision Making in Multinational Organizations: A Culture-Based Model," *Journal of Business Ethics*, vol. 19, no. 4, Part 1 (1999), pp. 385–392.

123. Roddick, Anita. *Body and Soul* (New York: Crown, 1991).

124. Sagie, A.; Elizur, D.; and Yamauchi, H. "The Structure and Strength of Achievement Motivation: A Cross-Cultural Comparison," *Journal of Organizational Behavior*, vol. 17, no. 5 (1996), pp. 431–444.

125. Sampson, E. D. "Psychology and the American Ideal," *Journal of Personality and Social Psychology*, vol. 35, no. 11 (November 1977), pp. 767–782.

126. Schlesinger, A. M., Jr. *A Thousand Days* (Boston: Houghton Mifflin, 1965).

127. Shelton, A. J. "Behavior and Cultural Value in West African Stories," *Literary Sources for the Study of Culture Contact*, Africa, vol. 34 (1964), pp. 353–359.

128. Shenkar, Oded; Ronen, Simcha. Shefy, Erella; and Chow, Irene Hau Siu.

"The Role Structure of Chinese Managers," *Human Relations*, vol. 51, no.1 (1998), pp. 51–72.

129. Simon, Herbert A. *Administrative Behavior* (New York: The Free Press, 1957).

130. Simon, Herbert A. *The New Science of Management Decision* (New York: Harper & Row, 1960).

131. Sirota, D., and Greenwood, M. J. "Understanding Your Overseas Workforce," *Harvard Business Review*, vol. 14 (January–February 1971), pp. 53–60.

132. Smith, P. B.; Misumi, S.; Tayeb, M.; Peterson, M.; and Bond, M. "On the Generality of Leadership Style Measures Across Cultures," *Journal of Occupational Psychology*, vol. 62, no. 2 (1989), pp. 97–109.

133. Smith, P. B., and Peterson, M. F. "Leadership as Event Management: A Cross-Cultural Survey Based upon Middle Managers from 25 Nations." Paper presented in the symposium on Cross-Cultural Studies of Event Management at the 23rd International Congress of Applied Psychology, Madrid, Spain, 1994.

134. Smith, P. B., and Peterson, M. F. *Leadership, Organizations and Culture* (London: Sage, 1988).

135. Smith, P. B.; Peterson, M. F.; Misumi, J.; and Bond, M. "A Cross-Cultural Test of Japanese PM Leadership Theory," *Applied Psychology: An International Review*, vol. 41, no. 1 (1992), pp. 5–19.

136. Smith, P. B.; Peterson, M. F.; Misumi, J.; and Tayeb, M. "Testing Leadership Theory Cross-Culturally," *Recent Advances in Social Psychology: An International Perspective* (Amsterdam: North-Holland, 1989), pp. 383–391.

137. Staw, B. M. "Organizational Behavior: A Review and Reformulation of the Field's Outcome Variables," *Annual Review of Psychology*, vol. 35 (1984), pp. 627–666.

138. Staw, B. M. "Rationality and Justification in Organizational Life," in B. M. Staw and L. L. Cummings, eds., *Research in Organizational Behavior*, vol. 2 (Greenwich, CT: JAI Press, 1980), pp. 45–80.

139. Steers, R. M., and Porter, L. W., eds., *Motivation and Work Behavior* (New York: McGraw-Hill, 1975).

140. Steers, Richard M., and Sanchez-Runde, Carlos. "Culture, Motivation, and Work Behavior," in Martin J. Gannon and Karen L. Newman, eds., *Handbook of Cross-Cultural Management* (London: Basil Blackwell, 2001, in press).

141. Stephens, D.; Kedia, B.; and Ezell, D. "Managerial Need Structures in U.S. and Peruvian Industries," *Management International Review*, vol. 19 (1979), pp. 27–39.

142. Stogdill, R. M. "Personal Factors Associated with Leadership: A Survey of the Literature," *Journal of Psychology*, vol. 25 (1948), pp. 37–71.

143. Tadepalli, Raghu; Moreno, Abel; and Trevino, Salvador. "Do American and Mexican Purchasing Managers Perceive Ethical Situations Differently?"

Industrial Marketing Management, vol. 28, no. 4 (1999), pp. 369–380.

144. Takamiya, S. "Group Decision Making in Japanese Management," *International Studies of Management and Organization*, vol. 2, no. 2 (1972), pp.183–196.

145. Theobald, Robert. "Management of Complex Systems: A Growing Societal Challenge," in F. Feather, ed., *Through the 80s: Thinking Globally, Acting Locally* (Washington, DC: World Future Society, 1980), pp. 42–51.

146. Triandis, H. C. "Dimensions of Cultural Variations as Parameters of Organizational Theories," *International Studies of Management and Organization*, vol. 12, no. 4 (1983), pp. 139–169.

147. Trompenaars, Fons. *Riding the Waves of Culture* (London: The Economist Books, 1993).

148. Tscheulin, D. "Leader Behavior Measurement in German Industry," *Journal of Applied Psychology*, vol. 57 (1973), pp. 28–31.

149. Tzu, Lao. *The Way of Lao Tzu (Tao-Te Ching): Translated with Introductory Essays, Comments and Notes by Wing-Tsit Chan* (Indianapolis, IN: Bobbs-Merrill, 1963). As cited in "Lao Leader Behaviors," *Management International Review*, vol. 19 (1979), p. 214. (Lao Tzu wrote in the sixth century B.C.)

150. Van Fleet, D., and Al-Tuhaih, S. "A Cross-Cultural Analysis of Perceived Leader Behaviors," *Management International Review*, vol. 19 (April 1979), pp. 81–88.

151. Vardi, Y.; Shrom, A.; and Jacobson, D. "A Study of Leadership Beliefs of Israeli Managers," *Academy of Management Journal*, vol. 23, no. 2 (1980), pp. 367–374.

152. Vroom, V. H. *Work and Motivation* (New York: Wiley, 1964).

153. Vroom, V. H., and Yetton, P. W. *Leadership and Decision Making* (Pittsburgh, PA: University of Pittsburgh Press, 1973).

154. Williams, L. K.; Whyte, W. F.; and Green, C. S. "Do Cultural Differences Affect Workers' Attitudes?" *Industrial Relations*, vol. 5 (1966), pp. 105–117.

155. Xu, L. C. "A Cross-Cultural Study of the Leadership Behavior of Chinese and Japanese Executives," *Asia Pacific Journal of Management*, vol. 4, no. 3 (1987), pp. 203–209.

156. Yukl, Gary A. *Leadership in Organizations*, 3d ed. (Upper Saddle River, NJ: Prentice Hall, 1994).

CHAPTER 7

1. Adair, Wendy L. "Exploring the Norm of Reciprocity in the Global Market: U.S. and Japanese Intra- and Inter-Cultural Negotiations" in S. J. Havlovic, ed., *59th Annual Meeting of The Academy of Management Proceedings*, 1999.

2. Adler, N. J., and Graham, John L. "Business Negotiations: Canadians Are Not Just Like Americans," *Canadian Journal of Administrative Sciences*, vol. 4, no. 3 (1987), pp. 211–238.

3. Adler, N. J., and Graham, John L. "Cross-Cultural Interaction: The International Comparison Fallacy," *Journal of International Business Studies*, vol. 20, no. 3 (1989), pp. 515–537.

4. Adler, N. J.; Graham John L.; and Brahm, R. "Strategy Implementation: A Comparison of Face-to-Face Negotiations in The People's Republic of China," *Strategic Management Journal*, vol. 13, no. 7 (1992), pp. 449–466.

5. Adler, N. J.; Schwartz, T; and Graham, John L. "Business Negotiations in Canada (French and English Speakers), Mexico, and the United States," *Journal of Business Research*, vol. 15, no. 4 (1987), pp. 411–429.

6. Al-Ghamdi, Salem M. "Success and Failure in Saudi-American Negotiations: American Views," *International Negotiation*, vol. 4, no. 1 (1999), pp. 23–36.

7. Beliaev, E.; Mullen, T.; and Punnett, B. J. "Understanding the Cultural Environment: U.S.A.-U.S.S.R. Trade Negotiation," *California Management Review*, vol. 27, no. 2 (1985), pp. 100–112.

8. Blaker, M. *Japanese International Negotiating Style* (New York: Columbia University Press, 1977).

9. Brett, Jeanne M.; Adair, Wendy L.; Lempereur, A.; Okumura, T.; Tinsley, Catherine; and Lytle, A. "Culture and Joint Gains in Negotiation," *Negotiation Journal*, vol. 14, no. 1 (1998), pp. 61–86.

10. Brett, Jeanne M. and Okumura, Tetsushi. "Inter- and Intracultural Negotiation: U.S. and Japanese Negotiators," *Academy of Management Journal*, vol. 41, no. 5 (1998), pp. 495–510.

11. Campbell, N.; Graham, J. L.; Jolibert, A.; and Meissner, H. "Marketing Negotiations in France, Germany, the United Kingdom, and the United States," *Journal of Marketing*, vol. 52, no. 2 (1988), pp. 49–62.

12. Casse, Pierre. *Training for the Cross-Cultural Mind*, 2d ed. (Washington, DC: Society for Intercultural Education, Training, and Research, 1981).

13. Cohen, H. *You Can Negotiate Anything* (Secaucus, NJ: Lyle Stuart, 1980).

14. Dupont, C. *La Négociation: Conduite, Théorie, Applications* (Paris: Dalloz, 1982).

15. Fayweather, John, and Kapoor, A. "Simulated International Business Negotiations," *Journal of International Business Studies*, vol. 3 (Spring 1972), pp. 19–31.

16. Fayweather, John, and Kapoor, A. *Strategy and Negotiation for the International Corporation* (Cambridge, MA: Ballinger, 1976), pp. 29–50.

17. Fisher, Glenn. *International Negotiations: A Cross-Cultural Perspective* (Chicago: Intercultural Press, 1980).

18. Fisher, R., and Ury, W. *Getting to Yes* (Boston: Houghton Mifflin, and New York: Penguin, 1981).

19. George, Jennifer M.; Jones Gareth R.; and Gonzalez, Jorge A. "The Role of Affect in Cross-Cultural Negotiations," *Journal of International Business Studies*, vol. 29, no. 4 (1998), pp. 749–772.

20. Glenn, E. S.; Witmeyer, D.; and Stevenson, K. A. "Cultural Styles of Persuasion," *International Journal of Intercultural Relations*, vol. 1, no. 3 (1977), pp. 52–66.

21. Graham, John L. "Brazilian, Japanese, and American Business Negotiations," *Journal of International Business Studies,* vol. 14, no. 1 (1983), pp. 47–61.

22. Graham, John L. "Deference Given the Buyer: Variations Across Twelve Cultures," in P. Lorange and F. Contractor, eds., *Cooperative Strategies in International Business* (Lexington, MA: Lexington Books, 1987).

23. Graham, John L. "An Exploratory Study of the Process of Marketing Negotiations Using a Cross-Cultural Perspective," in R. Scarcella, E. Andersen, and S. Krashen, eds., *Developing Communicative Competence in a Second Language* (Rowley, MA: Newbury House Publishers, 1989).

24. Graham, John L. "A Hidden Cause of America's Trade Deficit with Japan," *Columbia Journal of World Business* (Fall 1981), pp. 5–15.

25. Graham, John L. "The Influence of Culture on the Process of Business Negotiations," *Journal of International Business Studies,* vol. 16, no. 1 (1985), pp. 81–96.

26. Graham, John L. "The Problem-Solving Approach to Interorganizational Negotiations: A Laboratory Test," *Journal of Business Research,* vol. 14 (1986), pp. 271–286.

27. Graham, John L., and Herberger, R. A., Jr. "Negotiators Abroad—Don't Shoot from the Hip," *Harvard Business Review* (July–August 1983), pp. 160–168.

28. Graham, John L.; Kim, D. K.; Lin, C. Y.; and Robinson, M. "Buyer-Seller Negotiations Around the Pacific Rim: Differences in Fundamental Exchange Process," *Journal of Consumer Research,* vol. 15 (June 1988), pp. 48–54.

29. Graham, John L., and Sano, Y. *Smart Bargaining: Doing Business with the Japanese* (Cambridge, MA: Ballinger, 1984).

30. Harnett, O. L., and Cummings, L. L. *Bargaining Behavior: An International Study* (Houston, TX: Dane Publications, 1980).

31. Hofstede, Geert, and Bond, Michael H. "Confucius and Economic Growth: New Trends into Culture's Consequences," *Organizational Dynamics,* vol. 16, no. 4 (1988), pp. 4–21.

32. Ikle, F. C. *How Nations Negotiate* (New York: Harper & Row, 1964), pp. 225–255.

33. Jastram, R. W. "The Nakado Negotiators," *California Management Review,* vol. 17, no. 2 (1974), pp. 88–90.

34. Jehn, Karen, and Weigelt, Keith. "Chinese Thought, Game Theory, and Strategic International Negotiations," *International Negotiation,* vol. 4, no. 1 (1999), pp. 79–93.

35. Jensen, L. "Soviet-American Behavior in Disarmament Negotiations," in I. W. Zartman, ed., *The 50 Percent Solution* (New York: Anchor, 1976).

36. Kapoor, A. "MNC Negotiations: Characteristics and Planning Implications," *Columbia Journal of World Business* (Winter 1974), pp. 121–130.

37. Kapoor, A. "Negotiation Strategies in International Business-Government Relations: A Study in India," *Journal of International Business Studies,* vol. 1–2 (Summer 1970), pp. 21–42.

38. Kennedy, John F. Address given at American University, Washington, DC, June 10, 1963.

39. Kirkbride, P. S.; Tang, Sara F. Y.; and Westwood, R. I. "Chinese Conflict Preferences and Negotiating Behaviour: Cultural and Psychological Influences," *Organizational Studies,* vol. 12, no. 3 (1991), pp. 365–386.

40. Komorita, S. S., and Brenner, A. R. "Bargaining and Concession-Making Under Bilateral Monopoly," *Journal of Personality and Social Psychology,* vol. 9 (1968), pp. 15–20.

41. Krauthammer, C. "Deep Down, We're All Alike, Right? Wrong," *Time* (August 15, 1983), p. 30.

42. Kumar, Rajesh. "Communicative Conflict in Intercultural Negotiations: The Case of American and Japanese Business Negotiations," *International Negotiation,* vol. 4, no. 1 (1999), pp. 63–78.

43. Lall, A. *How Communist China Negotiates* (New York: Columbia University Press, 1966).

44. Lewicki, Roy J.; Weiss, Stephen E.; and Lewin, D. "Models of Conflict, Negotiation and Third Party Intervention: A Review and Synthesis," *Journal of Organizational Behavior,* vol. 13 (1992), pp. 209–252.

45. Mehrabian, A., and Ferris, S. R. "Inference of Attitudes from Nonverbal Communication in Two Channels," *Journal of Consulting Psychology,* vol. 31, no. 3 (1967), pp. 248–252. Also see Mehrabian, A. "Communicating Without Words," *Psychology Today* (September 1968), p. 53.

46. Muna, F. A. *The Arab Mind* (New York: Scribners, 1973).

47. Perlmutter, Howard. "More Than 50 Percent of International Managers' Time Is Spent in Negotiating—in Interpersonal Transaction Time Influencing Other Managers," statement made at Academy of Management Meetings, Dallas, Texas, August 1983, and at The Wharton School, University of Pennsylvania, 1984.

48. Plantey, A. *La Négociation Internationale: Principes et Méthodes* (Paris: Editions du Centre National de la Recherche Scientifique, 1980).

49. Pye, Lucian. *Chinese Commercial Negotiating Style* (Cambridge, MA: Oelgeschlager, Gunn and Hain, Publishers, 1982).

50. Raider, Ellen. *International Negotiations: A Training Program for Corporate Executives and Diplomats* (Brooklyn, NY: Ellen Raider International, Inc.; and Plymouth, MA: Situation Management Systems, Inc., 1982); and Berlew, D.; Moore, A.; and Harrison, R. *Positive Negotiation Programs* (Plymouth, MA: Situation Management Systems, Inc., 1978, 1980, and 1983). Reprinted by permission.

51. Roemer, Christina; Garb, Paula; Neu, Joyce; and Graham, John L. "A Comparison of American and Russian Patterns of Behavior in Buyer-Seller Negotiations Using Observational Measures," *International Negotiation,* vol. 4, no. 1 (1999), pp. 37–61.

52. Rubin, J. Z., and Brown, B. R. *The Social Psychology of Bargaining and Negotiation* (New York: Academic Press, 1976).

53. Sawyer, J., and Guetzkow, H. "Bargaining and Negotiation in International Relations," in H. C. Kelman, ed., *International Behavior: A Social Psychological Analysis* (New York: Holt, Rinehart and Winston, 1965), pp. 464–520.

54. Tang, Sara F. Y., and Kirkbride, Paul S. "Developing Conflict Management Skills in Hong Kong: An Analysis of Some Cross-Cultural Implications," *Management Education and Development,* vol. 17, part 3 (1986), pp. 287–301.

55. Terasawa, Y. "The Japanese Perspective in International Business Negotiations." Paper presented at the Academy of Management Meetings, Dallas, Texas, August 16, 1983.

56. Tinsley, Catherine H. "Models of Conflict Resolution in Japanese, German and American Cultures," *Journal of Applied Psychology*, vol. 83 (1998), pp. 316–323.

57. Tinsley, Catherine H., and Weiss, Stephen E. "Examining International Business Negotiations and Directions for the Future," *International Negotiation,* vol. 4, no. 1 (1999), pp. 95–97.

58. Tung, Rosalie L. *Business Negotiations with the Japanese* (Lexington, MA: Lexington Books, 1984).

59. Tung, Rosalie L. "How to Negotiate with the Japanese," *California Management Review,* vol. 26, no. 4 (1984), pp. 62–77.

60. Tung, Rosalie L. "U.S.-China Trade Negotiations: Practices, Procedures and Outcomes," *Journal of International Business Studies*, vol. 13 (1982), pp. 25–38.

61. Van Zandt, H. F. "How to Negotiate in Japan," *Harvard Business Review* (November–December 1977), pp. 72–80.

62. Volkema, Roger J. "Ethnicality in Negotiations: An Analysis of Perceptual Similarities and Differences Between Brazil and the United States," *Journal of Business Research*, vol. 45, no. 1 (1999), pp. 59–67.

63. Weiss, Stephen E. "Analysis of Complex Negotiations in International Business: The RBC Perspective," *Organization Science,* vol. 4, no. 2 (1993), pp. 269–300.

64. Weiss, Stephen E. "Creating the GM-Toyota Joint Venture: A Case in Complex Negotiation," *Columbia Journal of World Business,* vol. 22, no. 2 (1987), pp. 23–37.

65. Weiss, Stephen E. "International Negotiations: Bricks, Mortar, and Prospects," in B. J. Punnett and O. Shenkar, eds., *Handbook for International Management Research* (Cambridge, MA: Blackwell, 1996), pp. 209–265.

66. Weiss, Stephen E. "The Long Path to the IBM-Mexico Agreement: An Analysis of the Microcomputer Investment Negotiations, 1983–1985," *Journal of International Business Studies*, vol. 21, no. 4 (1990), pp. 565–596.

67. Weiss, Stephen E. "Negotiating with 'Romans'—Part 1," *Sloan Management Review* (Winter 1994), pp. 51–62.

68. Weiss, Stephen E. "Negotiating with 'Romans'—Part 2," *Sloan Management Review* (Spring 1994), pp. 85–100.

69. Weiss, Stephen E., and Strip, W. G. "Negotiating with Foreign Business

Persons." Working paper # 85–86, New York University, New York, 1985.

70. Weiss-Wik, S., "Enhancing Negotiators' Successfulness," *Journal of Conflict Resolution,* vol. 27, no. 4 (1983), pp. 706–739.

71. Wells, L. T. "Negotiating with Third World Governments," *Harvard Business Review* (January–February 1977), pp. 72–80.

72. Wright, P. "Doing Business in Islamic Markets," *Harvard Business Review,* vol. 59, no. 1 (1981), pp. 34ff.

CHAPTER 8 REFERENCES

1. Adler, N. J. "Coaching Global Executives: Women Succeeding in a World Beyond Here" in Marshall Goldsmith, Lawrence Lyons, and Alyssa Freas, eds., *Coaching for Leadership* (San Francisco: Jossey-Bass, 2000), pp. 347–356.

2. Adler, Nancy J. "Competitive Frontiers: Women Managing Across Borders," in Adler, N. J. and Izraeli, Dafna N., eds. *Competitive Frontiers: Women Managers in a Global Economy* (Cambridge, MA: Blackwell Publishing, 1994), pp. 22–40.

3. Adler, N. J. "Reentry: Managing Cross-Culture Transitions," *Group and Organization Studies,* vol. 6, no. 3 (1981), pp. 341–356. Copyright 1981. Reprinted by permission of Sage Publications, Inc.

4. Adler, N. J., and Ghadar, F. "Strategic Human Resource Management: A Global Perspective," in Rudiger Pieper, ed., *Human Resource Management in International Comparison* (Berlin: de Gruyter, 1990), pp. 235–260.

5. Allen, Douglas, and Alvarez, Sharon. "Empowering Expatriates and Organizations to Improve Repatriation Effectiveness, "*Human Resource Planning,* vol. 21, no. 4 (1998), pp. 29–39.

6. Austin, C. N. *Cross-Cultural Reentry: An Annotated Bibliography* (Abilene, TX: Abilene Christian University Press, 1983).

7. Barham, K., and Antal, A. B. "Competences for the Pan-European Manager," in P. Kirkbride, ed., *Human Resource Management in Europe* (London: Routledge, 1995), pp. 221–241.

8. Baughn, C. "Personal and Organizational Factors Associated with Effective Repatriation," in Jan Selmer, ed., *Expatriate Management: New Ideas for International Business* (Westport, CT: Quorum Books, 1995), pp. 215–230.

9. Black, J. Stuart. "Locus of Control, Social Support, Stress, and Adjustment in International Assignments," *Asia-Pacific Journal of Management,* vol. 7 (1990), pp. 1–29.

10. Black, J. Stuart, and Gregersen, Hal B. "The Right Way to Manage Expatriates," *Harvard Business Review* (March–April 1999), pp. 52–62.

11. Black, J. Stuart, and Gregersen, Hal B. "When Yankee Comes Home: Factors Related to Expatriate and Spouse Repatriation Adjustment," *Journal of International Business Studies,* vol. 22, no. 4 (1991), pp. 671–695.

12. Black, J. Stuart; Gregersen, Hal B.; and Mendenhall, Mark E. *Global Assignments: Successfully Expatriating and Repatriating International Managers* (San Francisco: Jossey-Bass, 1992).

13. Black, J. Stuart; Gregersen, Hal B.; and Mendenhall, Mark E. "Toward a Theoretical Framework of Repatriation Adjustment," *Journal of International Business Studies,* vol. 23, no. 4 (1992), pp. 737–760.

14. Black, J. Stuart; Gregersen, Hal B.; Mendenhall, Mark E.; and Stroh, L. K. *Global Assignments* (New York: Addison-Wesley, 1999).

15. Black, J. Stuart, and Mendenhall, Mark E. "Cross-Cultural Training Effectiveness: A Review and Theoretical Framework for Future Research," *Academy of Management Review,* vol. 15 (1990), pp. 113–136.

16. Black, J. Stuart; Mendenhall, Mark E.; and Oddou, G. "Toward a Comprehensive Model of International Adjustment: An Integration of Multiple Theoretical Perspectives," *Academy of Management Review,* vol. 16 (1991), pp. 291–317.

17. Black, J. Stuart, and Stephens, G. K. "The Influence of the Spouses on American Expatriate Adjustment in Overseas Assignments," *Journal of Management,* vol. 15 (1989), pp. 529–544.

18. Borg, M. *International Transfers of Managers in Multinational Corporations* (Uppsala, Sweden: Acta Universitatis Upsaliensis, Studia Oeconomiae Negotiorum, no. 27, 1988).

19. Boyacigiller, Nakiye. "The Role of Expatriates in the Management of Interdependence, Complexity and Risk in Multinational Corporations," *Journal of International Business Studies,* vol. 21, no. 3 (1990), pp. 357–381.

20. Brewster, C. "Current Issues in Expatriation," *International Studies of Management and Organization,* vol. 24, no. 3 (1994).

21. Brewster, C. *The Management of Expatriates* (London: Kogan Page, 1991).

22. Brislin, R. W., and Van Buren, H. "Can They Go Home Again?" *International Educational and Cultural Exchange,* vol. 1, no. 4 (1974), pp. 19–24.

23. Business International Corporation. "Successful Repatriation Demands Attention, Care, and a Dash of Ingenuity," *Business International,* vol. 25, no. 9 (1978), pp. 57–65.

24. Caligiuri, P. M. "Performance Measurement in a Cross-National Context: Evaluating the Success of Global Assignments," in W. Bennett, D. Woehr, and C. Lance, eds., *Performance Measurement: Current Perspectives and Future Challenges* (Lawrence Erlbaum, 2001), in press.

25. Caligiuri, P. M., and Cascio, W. "Can We Send Her There? Maximizing the Success of Western Women on Global Assignments, "*Journal of World Business,* vol. 33, no. 4 (1998), pp. 394–416.

26. Caligiuri, P. M., and Cascio, W. "Sending Women on Global Assignments: Challenges, Myths and Solutions," *World at Work Journal,* vol. 9, no. 2 (2000), pp. 34–41.

27. Caligiuri, P. M., Hyland, M., and Joshi, A. "Families on Global Assignments: Applying Work/Family Theories Abroad," in A. Rahim, ed., *Current Topics in Management* (Greenwich, CT: JAI Press, vol. 3, 1998), pp. 313–328.

28. Caligiuri, P. M., Hyland, M., Joshi, A., and Bross, A. "A Theoretical Framework for Examining the Relationship Between Family Adjustment and Expa-

triate Adjustment to Working in the Host Country," *Journal of Applied Psychology,* vol. 83, no. 4 (1998), pp. 598–614.

29. Caligiuri, P. M., Joshi, A., and Lazarova, M. "Factors Influencing the Adjustsment of Women on Global Assignments," *International Journal of Human Resource Management,* vol. 10, no. 2 (1999), pp. 163–179.

30. Caligiuri, P. M., and Lazarova, M. "The Influence of Social Interaction and Social Support on Female Expatriates' Cross-Cultural Adjustment," *International Journal of Human Resource Management* (2001, in press).

31. Caligiuri, P. M., and Lazarova, M. "Strategic Repartition Policies to Enhance Global Leadership Development," in Mendenhall, T. Kuehlmann, and G. Stahl, eds., *Developing Global Business Leaders: Policies, Process, and Innovations (*Westport, CT: Quorum Books, 2001).

32. Caligiuri, P. M. and Tung, R. L. "Male and Female Expatriates' Success in Masculine and Feminine Countries," *International Journal of Human Resource Management,* vol. 10, no. 2 (1999), pp. 763–782.

33. Copeland, L., and Griggs, L. *Going International* (New York: Random House, 1985).

34. Coyle, W. *On the Move: Minimising the Stress and Maximising the Benefits of Relocation* (Sydney, Australia: Hampden Press, 1988).

35. DeCieri, Helen, and Dowling, P. J. " Strategic Human Resource Management in Multinational Enterprises: Theoretical and Empirical Developments," in P. M. Wright, L. D. Dyer, J. W. Boudreau, and G. T. Milkovich, eds., *Research in Personnel and Human Resources Management: Strategic Human Resources Management in the Twenty-First Century,* Supplement 4 (Stamford, CT: JAI Press, 1999), pp. 305–327.

36. Derr, C. B., and Oddou, G. "Are U.S. Multinationals Adequately Preparing Future American Leaders for Global Competition?" *International Journal of Human Resource Management,* vol. 2, no. 2 (1991), pp. 227–244.

37. Dowling, Peter J. "Human Resource Issues in International Business," *Syracuse Journal of International Law and Commerce,* vol. 13, no. 2 (1986), pp. 255–271.

38. Dowling, Peter J.; Welch, D. E.; and Schuler, Randall S. *International Human Resource Management: Managing People in a Multinational Context,* 3d ed. (Cincinnati, OH: South-Western, 1998).

39. Fayerweather, John. *The Executive Overseas* (Syracuse, NY: Syracuse University Press, l959).

40. Feldman, D. C.; and Thompson, H. B. "Expatriation, Repatriation, Domestic Geographical Relocation: An Empirical Investigation of Adjustment to New Job Assignments," *Journal of International Business Studies,* vol. 24 (1993), pp. 507–529.

41. Greengard, Samuel. "Technology Is Changing Expatriate Training," *Workforce,* vol. 78, no 12 (1999), pp. 106–108.

42. Gregersen, H. B. "Commitment to a Parent Company and a Local Work Unit During Repatriation," *Personnel Psychology,* vol. 45 (1992), pp. 29–54.

43. Gregersen, H. B., and Black, J. S. "Antecedents to Commitment to a Parent Company and a Foreign Operation," *Academy of Management Journal,* vol. 35, no. 1 (1992), pp. 65–90.

44. Gregersen, H. B., and Black, J. S. "Keeping High Performers After International Assignments: A Key to Global Executive Development," *Journal of International Management,* vol. 1, no. 1 (1995), pp. 3–31.

45. Gregersen, H. B., and Black, J. S. "A Multifaceted Approach to Expatriate Retention in International Assignments," *Group and Organization Studies,* vol. 15 (1990), pp. 461–485.

46. Gullahorn, J. T., and Gullahorn, J. E. "An Extension of the U-Curve Hypothesis," *Journal of Social Sciences,* vol. 19, no. 3 (1963), pp. 33–47.

47. Harvey, M. G. "The Other Side of Foreign Assignments: Dealing with the Repatriation Dilemma," *Columbia Journal of World Business,* vol. 17, no. 1 (1982), pp. 53–59.

48. Harvey, M. G. "Repatriation of Corporate Executives: An Empirical Study," *Journal of International Business Studies,* vol. 20 (1989), pp. 131–144.

49. Hazzard, M. S. *Study of the Repatriation of the American International Executive* (New York: Korn/Ferry International, 1981).

50. Howard, C. "The Returning Overseas Executive: Culture Shock in Reverse," *Human Resources Management,* vol. 13, no. 2 (1974), pp. 22–26.

51. "How to Ease Reentry After Overseas Duty," *Business Week* (June 11, 1979), pp. 82–84.

52. Inkson, K.; Arthur, M. B.; Pringle, J.; and Barry, S. "Expatriate Assignment Versus Overseas Experience: Contrasting Models of International Human Resource Development," *Journal of World Business,* vol. 32 (1997), pp. 351–368.

53. Kendall, D. W. "Repatriation: An Ending and a Beginning," *Business Horizons* (November–December 1981), pp. 21–25.

54. Kobrin, Steve J. "Expatriate Reduction and Strategic Control in American Multinational Corporations," *Human Resource Management,* vol. 27 (1988), pp. 63–75.

55. Kobrin, Steve J. "Is There a Relationship Between a Geocentric Mind-Set and Multinational Strategy?" *Journal of International Business Studies,* vol. 25 (1994), pp. 493–511.

56. Koretz, Gene. "A Woman's Place Is . . ." *Business Week* (September 28, 1999), p. 13.

57. Lein, Janet D., and Sisco, Nichole L. "Language and Cross-Cultural Training for Expatriate Employees: A Comparison Between the U.S. and Germany," *Journal of Language of International Business,* vol. 10, no. 2 (1999), pp. 47–59.

58. Mendenhall, Mark E.; Dunbar, E.; and Oddou, G. R. "Expatriate Selection, Training and Career-Pathing: A Review and Critique," *Human Resource Management,* vol. 26, no. 3 (1987), pp. 331–345.

59. Mendenhall, Mark E., and Oddou, G. R. "Acculturation Profiles of Expa-

triate Managers: Implications for Cross-Cultural Training Programs," *Columbia Journal of World Business* (Winter 1986), pp. 73–79.

60. Mendenhall, Mark E., and Oddou, G. R. "The Dimensions of Expatriate Acculturation: A Review," *Academy of Management Review,* vol. 10, no. 1 (1985), pp. 39–47.

61. Mendenhall, Mark; Kuhlmann, T.; and Stahl, G. *Developing Global Business Leaders: Policies, Processes, and Innovations* (Westport, CT: Quorum Books, 2000).

62. Murray, J. A. "International Personnel Repatriation: Cultural Shock in Reverse," *MSU Business Topic,* vol. 21, no. 2 (1973), pp. 59–66.

63. Noer, D. M. "Integrating Foreign Service Employees to Home Organization: The Godfather Approach," *Personnel Journal* (January 1974), pp. 45–51.

64. Osland, J. S. *The Adventure of Working Abroad: Hero Tales from the Global Frontier* (San Francisco: Jossey-Bass, 1995).

65. Ratiu, Indre. "Thinking Internationally: A Comparison of How International Executives Learn," *International Studies of Management and Organization,* vol. 13, nos. 1–2 (1983), pp. 139–150.

66. Selmer, Jan. "Effects of Coping Strategies on Sociocultural and Psychological Adjustment of Western Expatriate Managers in the PRC, *Journal of World Business,* vol. 34, no. 1 (1999), pp. 41–51.

67. Selmer, Jan, ed. *Expatriate Management: New Ideas for International Business* (Westport, CT: Quorum Books, 1995).

68. Shaffer, Margaret A.; Harrison, David A; Gilley, K. Matthew. "Dimensions, Determinants, and Differences in the Expatriate Adjustment Process," *Journal of International Business Studies,* vol. 30, no. 3 (1999), pp. 557–581.

69. Smith, L. "The Hazards of Coming Home," *Dun's Review* (October 1975), pp. 71–73.

70. Stroh, L. K. "Predicting Turnover Among Repatriates: Can Organizations Affect Retention Rates?" *International Journal of Human Resource Management,* vol. 6 (1995), pp. 443–456.

71. Stroh, L. K., and Caligiuri, P. M. "Strategic Human Resources: A New Source for Competitive Advantage in the Global Arena," *International Journal of Human Resource Management,* vol. 9 (1998), pp. 1–17.

72. Stroh, L. K.; Gregersen, H. B.; and Black, J. S. "Closing the Gap: Expectations Versus Reality Among Repatriates," *Journal of World Business,* vol. 33 (1998), pp. 111–124.

73. Taylor, S.; Beechler, S.; Najjar, M.; and Ghosh, B. C. "A Partial Test of a Model of Stragic International Human Resource Management," in J. L. C. Cheng and R. B. Peterson, eds., *Advances in International and Comparative Management,* vol. 12 (Stamford, CT: JAI Press, 1998), pp. 207–236.

74. Theoret, R.; Adler, N. J.; Kealey, D.; and Hawes, F. *Reentry: A Guide to Returning Home* (Hull, Quebec: Canadian International Development Agency, 1979).

75. Torbiorn, I. *Living Abroad: Personal Adjustment and Personnel Policy in Overseas Setting* (New York: Wiley, 1982).

76. Tung, Rosalie. "American Expatriates Abroad: From Neophytes to Cosmopolitans," *Journal of World Business,* vol. 33 (1998), pp. 125–144.

77. Tung, Rosalie L. "Career Issues in International Assignments," *Academy of Management Executive,* vol. 2, no. 3 (1988), pp. 241–244.

78. Tung, Rosalie L. "Expatriate Assignments: Enhancing Success and Minimizing Failure," *Academy of Management Executive,* vol. 1, no. 2 (1987), pp. 117–126.

79. Tung, Rosalie L. *The New Expatriates: Managing Human Resources Abroad* (Cambridge, MA: Ballinger, 1988).

80. Tung, Rosalie L. "Selection and Training Procedures of U.S., European, and Japanese Multinationals," *California Management Review,* vol. 25, no. 1 (1982), pp. 57–71.

81. Werkman, S. L. "Coming Home: Adjustment of Americans to the United States After Living Abroad," in G. V. Coelho and P. I. Ahmed, eds., *Uprooting and Development: Dilemmas of Coping with Modernization* (New York: Plenum Press, 1980).

82. "Workers Sent Overseas Have Adjustment Problems, a New Study Shows," *Wall Street Journal* (June 19, 1984), p. 1, col. 5.

CHAPTER 9

1. Adler, N. J. *Managing International Transitions* (Montreal: Alcan Aluminum Limited, 1980).

2. Adler, N. J. "Pacific Basin Managers; A Gaijin, Not a Woman," *Human Resource Management,* vol. 26, no. 2 (1987), pp. 169–192.

3. Adler, N. J. *Reentry: A Study of the Dynamic Coping Processes Used by Repatriated Employees to Enhance Effectiveness in the Organization and Personal Learning During the Transition Back into the Home Country.* Ph.D. dissertation, University of California, Los Angeles, June 1980.

4. Adler, N. J. "Women in International Management: Where Are They?" *California Management Review,* vol. 26, no. 4 (1984), pp. 122–132.

5. Adler, N. J., and Ghadar, F. "International Strategy from the Perspective of People and Culture: The North American Context," in A. M. Rugman, ed., *Research in Global Strategic Management: International Business Research for the Twenty-First Century: Canada's New Research Agenda,* vol. 1 (Greenwich, CT: JAI Press, 1990), pp. 179–205.

6. Baker, J. C. "An Analysis of How the U.S. Multinational Company Considers the Wives of American Expatriate Managers," *Academy of Management Proceedings,* vol. 35 (1975), pp. 258–260.

7. Black, J. Stuart, and Gregersen, Hal B. "When Yankee Comes Home: Factors Related to Expatriate and Spouse Repatriation Adjustment," *Journal of International Business Studies,* vol. 22, no. 4 (1991), pp. 671–695.

8. Black, J. Stuart; Gregersen, Hal B.; and Mendenhall, Mark E. *Global Assignments: Successfully Expatriating and Repatriating International Managers* (San Francisco: Jossey-Bass, 1992).

9. Black, J. Stuart, and Stephens, G. K. "The Influence of the Spouses on Amer-

ican Expatriate Adjustment in Overseas Assignments," *Journal of Management,* vol. 15 (1989), pp. 529–544.

10. Culbert, Sam, and Renshaw, Jean. "Coping with the Stresses of Travels as an Opportunity for Improving the Quality of Work and Family Life," *Family Process,* vol. 11, no. 3 (1972), pp. 321–337.

11. D'Orazio, N. "Foreign Executives' Wives in Tokyo," *Institute of Comparative Culture Business Series,* Bulletin No. 82 (Tokyo: Sophia University, 1981).

12. Edstrom, A., and Galbraith, Jay R. "Alternative Policies for International Transfer of Managers," *Management International Review,* vol. 17, no. 2 (1977), pp. 11–22.

13. Edstrom, A., and Galbraith, Jay R. "International Transfer of Managers: Some Important Policy Considerations," *Columbia Journal of World Business,* vol. 11 (1976), pp. 100–112.

14. Edstrom, A., and Galbraith, Jay. "Transfer of Managers as Coordination and Control Strategy in Multinational Organizations," *Administrative Science Quarterly,* vol. 22 (June 1977), pp. 248–263.

15. Edstrom, A., and Lorange, Peter. "Matching Strategy and Human Resources in Multinational Corporations," *Journal of International Business Studies,* vol. 15 (1984), pp. 125–137.

16. Excerpted from "Little Gidding," from *Four Quartets,* copyright 1942 by T. S. Eliot and renewed 1970 by Esme Valerie Eliot, reprinted by permission of Harcourt, Inc.

17. Frazee, Valerie. "Expert Help for Dual-Career Spouses," *Workforce,* vol. 4, no. 2 (1999), pp. 18–20.

18. "Gauging a Family's Suitability for a Stint Overseas," *Business Week* (April 16, 1979), pp. 127–130.

19. Jelinek, Mariann, and Adler, N. J. "Women: World Class Managers for Global Competition," *Academy of Management Executive,* vol. 2, no. 1 (1988), pp. 11–19.

20. Karras, E. J., and McMillan, R. F. "Interviewing for a Cultural Match," *Personnel Journal* (April 1971), p. 276.

21. Labovitz, G. "Managing the Personal Side of the Personnel Move Abroad," *Advanced Management Journal,* vol. 42, no. 3 (1977), pp. 26–39.

22. Ondrack, Dan A. "International Transfers of Managers in North American and European MNEs," *Journal of International Business Studies,* vol. 16 (1985), pp. 1–19.

23. Osland, Joyce S. *The Adventure of Working Abroad: Hero Tales from the Global Frontier* (San Francisco: Jossey-Bass, 1995).

24. Pazy, A., and Zeira, Yoram. "Training of Parent-Country Professionals in Host Country Organizations," *Academy of Management Review,* vol. 8, no. 2 (1983), pp. 262–272.

25. Priestoff, N. "The Gaijin Executive's Wife," *The Conference Board Record,* vol. 13, no. 5 (1976), pp. 51–64.

26. Renshaw, Jean R. "An Exploration of the Dynamics of the Overlapping Worlds of Work and Family," *Family Process*, vol. 15, no. 1 (1976), pp. 143–165.

27. Selmer, Jan, ed. *Expatriate Management: New Ideas for International Business* (Westport, CT: Quorum Books, 1995).

28. Thompson, A. "Australian Expatriate Wives and Business Success in Southeast Asia," *Euro-Asia Business Review*, vol. 5, no. 2 (1986), pp. 14–18.

29. Wederspahn, Gary M. "The Overseas Wife: Excess Baggage," *The Bridge*, vol. 5, no. 4 (1980), p. 16.

30. Zeira, Yoram, and Harrari, E. "Genuine Multinational Staffing Policy: Expectations and Realities," *Academy of Management Journal*, vol. 20, no. 2 (1979), pp. 327–333.

CHAPTER 10

1. Adler, N. J. "Competitive Frontiers: Women Managing Across Borders," in N. J. Adler and D. N. Izraeli, eds., *Competitive Frontiers: Women Managers in a Global Economy* (Cambridge, MA: Blackwell, 1994), pp. 22–44.

2. Adler, N. J. "Do MBAs Want International Careers?" *International Journal of Intercultural Relations*, vol. 10, no. 3 (1986), pp. 277–300.

3. Adler, N. J. "Expecting International Success: Female Managers Overseas," *Columbia Journal of World Business*, vol. 19, no. 3 (1984), pp. 79–85.

4. Adler, N. J. "Global Leaders: A Dialogue with Future History," *International Management*, vol. 1, no. 2 (1997), pp. 21–33.

5. Adler, N. J. "Global Leadership: Women Leaders," *Management International Review*, Special Issue 1, vol. 37 (1997), pp. 171–196.

6. Adler, N. J. "Global Women Political Leaders: An Invisible History, An Increasingly Important Future," *Leadership Quarterly*, vol. 7, no. 1 (1996), pp. 133–161.

7. Adler, N. J. "Pacific Basin Managers: A Gaijin, Not a Woman," *Human Resource Management*, vol. 26, no. 2 (1987), pp. 169–191.

8. Adler, N. J. "Re-Entry: Managing Cross-Cultural Transitions," *Group and Organization Studies*, vol. 6, no. 3 (1981), pp. 341–356.

9. Adler, N. J. "Societal Leadership: The Wisdom of Peace," in Suresh Srivastva, ed., *Executive Wisdom and Organizational Change* (San Francisco: Jossey-Bass, 1998), pp. 205–221.

10. Adler, N. J. "Women Do Not Want International Careers: And Other Myths About International Management," *Organizational Dynamics*, vol. 13, no. 2 (1984), pp. 66–79.

11. Adler, N. J. "Women in International Management: Where Are They?" *California Management Review*, vol. 26, no. 4 (1984), pp. 78–89.

12. Adler, N. J., and Bartholomew, Susan. "Managing Globally Competent People," *Academy of Management Executive*, vol. 6, no. 3 (1992), pp. 52–65.

13. Adler, N. J., with Brody, Laura W., and Osland, Joyce S. "Advances in Global Leadership: The Women's Global Leadership Forum," in William H. Mobley, ed., *Advances in Global Leadership,* vol. 2 (Greenwich, CT: JAI Press, 2001), pp. 351–383.

14. Adler, N. J., with Brody, Laura W. and Osland, Joyce S. "The Women's Global Leadership Forum: Enhancing One Company's Leadership Capability," *Human Resource Management,* vol. 39, no. 2 & 3 (2000), pp. 209–225.

15. Adler, N. J., and Ghadar, F. "Globalization and Human Resource Management," in Alan M. Rugman, ed., *Research in Global Strategic Management: A Canadian Perspective,* vol. 1 (Greenwich, CT: JAI Press, 1989), pp. 179–205.

16. Adler, N. J., and Izraeli, D. N. *Competitive Frontiers: Women Managers in a Global Economy* (Cambridge, MA: Blackwell, 1994).

17. Adler, N. J., and Izraeli, D. N. *Women in Management Worldwide* (Armonk, NY: M. E. Sharpe, 1988).

18. Aitken, T. "What It Takes to Work Abroad," in T. Aitken, *The Multinational Man: The Role of the Manager Abroad* (New York: Halstead Press, 1973).

19. Albright, Madeleine K. Commencement address. Harvard University, Cambridge, Massachusetts, June 5, 1997.

20. Anderson, Nancy Fix. "Benazir Bhutto and Dynastic Politics: Her Father's Daughter, Her People's Sister," in Michael A. Genovese, ed., *Women as National Leaders* (Newbury Park, CA: Sage, 1993), pp. 41–69.

21. Baker, J. C. "An Analysis of How the U.S. Multinational Company Considers the Wife of American Expatriate Managers," *Academy of Management Proceedings,* vol. 35 (1975), pp. 258–260.

22. Bartlett, Chris A., and Ghoshal, Sumantra. *Managing Across Borders: The Transnational Solution* (Boston: Harvard Business School Press, 1989).

23. Bass, Bernard. *Bass & Stogdill's Handbook of Leadership,* 3d ed. (New York: The Free Press, 1991).

24. Benn, Melissa. "Women Who Rule the World," *Cosmopolitan* (February 1995).

25. Bennett, A. "Going Global: The Chief Executives in Year 2000 Will Be Experienced Abroad," *Wall Street Journal* (February 27, 1989), pp. A1, A9.

26. Bennis, Warren, and Nanus, Burt. *Leaders: Strategies of Taking Charge* (New York: Harper & Row, 1985), p. 4.

27. Black, J. Stuart, and Gregersen, Hal B. "The Right Way to Manage Expatriates," *Harvard Business Review* (March–April 1999), pp. 52–62.

28. Black, J. Stuart; Gregersen, Hal B.; Mendenhall, Mark E.; and Stroh, L. K. *Global Assignments* (New York: Addison-Wesley 1999).

29. Bowman, L., and Deal, Terrance. *Leading with Soul* (San Francisco: Jossey-Bass, 1995).

30. Brett, Jeanne M., and Stroh, Linda K. "Willingness to Relocate Internationally," *Human Resource Management,* vol. 35, no. 3 (1995), pp. 405–424.

31. Carter, Nancy. "Solve the Dual-Career Challenge," *Workforce,* vol. 2 (Global Workforce Supplement) (1997), pp. 21–22.

32. Chusmir, L. H., and Frontczak, N. T. "International Management Opportu-

nities for Women: Women and Men Paint Different Pictures," *International Journal of Management*, vol. 7, no. 3 (1990), pp. 295–301.

33. Col, Jeanne-Marie. "Managing Softly in Turbulent Times: Corazon C. Aquino, President of the Philippines," in M. A. Genovese, ed., *Women as National Leaders* (Newbury Park, CA: Sage, 1993), pp. 13–40.

34. Daily, C. M.; Certo, S. T.; and Dalton, D. R. "A Decade of Corporate Women: Some Progress in the Boardroom, None in the Executive Suite," *Strategic Management Journal*, vol. 20 (1999), pp. 3–99.

35. Davidson, E. D., and Punnett, B. J. "International Assignments: Is There a Role for Gender and Race in Decisions?" *International Journal of Human Resource Management*, vol. 6, no. 2 (1995), pp. 411–438.

36. Davies, Karen. "Delays Extend Kenya Election to 2nd Day," *Chicago Sun-Times* (December 30, 1997), p. 21.

37. Derr, C. Brooke. *Managing the New Careerists* (San Francisco: Jossey-Bass, 1986).

38. Derr, C. Brooke, and Laurent, André. "The Internal and External Careers: A Theoretical and Cross-Cultural Perspective," in M. Arthur, D. T. Hall, and B. S. Lawrence, eds., *The Handbook of Career Theory* (Cambridge, England: Cambridge University Press, 1989).

39. Deutsch, C. H. "Losing Innocence, Abroad," *New York Times* (July 10, 1988), Business section, pp. 1, 26.

40. Eagly, Alice H., and Johnson, Blair T. "Gender and Leadership Style: A Meta-analysis" *Psychological Bulletin*, vol. 8, no. 2 (1990), pp. 233–256, as cited in Vinnicombe, Susan and Colwill, Nina. *The Essence of Women in Management* (London: Prentice Hall, 1995), p. 32.

41. Eisler, Riane. *The Chalice and the Blade: Our History, Our Future* (San Francisco: Harper & Row, 1987).

42. Finlay, Fergus. *Mary Robinson: A President with a Purpose* (Dublin, Ireland: The O'Brien Press, 1990).

43. Fisher, Anne B. "When Will Women Get to the Top?" *Fortune* (September 21, 1992), pp. 44–56.

44. Fondas, Nanette. "The Origins of Feminization," *Academy of Management Review*, vol. 22 (1997), pp. 257–282.

45. Genovese, Michael. *Women as National Leaders* (Newbury Park, CA: Sage, 1993), p. ix.

46. Gimbutas, Marija. *The Civilization of the Goddess: The World of Old Europe* (San Francisco: Harper San Francisco 1991).

47. Gonzales, R. F., and Neghandi, Anatute R. *The United States Overseas Executive: His Orientations and Career Patterns* (East Lansing, MI: Graduate School of Business Administration, Michigan State University, 1967).

48. Hammond, Val, and Holton, V. "The Scenario for Women Managers in Britain in the 1990s," in N. J. Adler and D. N. Izraeli, eds. *Competitive Frontiers: Women Managers in a Global Economy* (Cambridge, MA Blackwell, 1994), pp. 224–242.

49. Harris, H. "Organizational Influences on Women's Career Opportunities in International Management," *Women in Management Review*, vol. 10 (1995), pp. 26–31.

50. Harvey, Michael. "Addressing the Dual-Career Expatriation Dilemma," *Human Resource Planning*, vol. 19 (1996), pp. 18–39.

51. Heenan, D. "The Corporate Expatriate: Assignment to Ambiguity," *Columbia Journal of World Business*, vol. 5 (1970), pp. 49–54.

52. Helgesen, Sally. *The Female Advantage: Women's Ways of Leadership* (New York: Doubleday 1990).

53. Hill, C. J., and Tillery, K. R. "What Do Male/Female Perceptions of an International Business Career Suggest About Recruitment Policies?" *SAM Advanced Management Journal* (Autumn 1992), pp. 10–14.

54. Hill, K. "Agathe Uwilingiyimana (1953–1994)," *http://www.fiu.edu*, in R. Salokar and M. Volcansek, *Women and the Law* (Westport, CT: Greenwood Press, 1996).

55. Howard, C. "The Returning Overseas Executive: Culture Shock in Reverse," *Human Resources Management*, vol. 13, no. 2 (1974), pp. 22–26.

56. Jelinek, Mariann, and Adler, N. J. "Women: World Class Managers for Global Competition," *Academy of Management Executive*, vol. 2, no. 1 (1988), pp. 11–19.

57. Jennings, E. *The Anatomy of Leadership* (New York: Harper & Row, 1960).

58. "Kalonzo Tells Ngilu to Bow Out of Race," *The Nation*, Africa News Service: Africa on line (August 12, 1997).

59. "Kenyan Opposition MPs Protest Police Brutality," Agence France-Press (April 15, 1997).

60. Lansing, P., and Ready, K. "Hiring Women Managers in Japan: An Alternative for Foreign Employers," *California Management Review*, vol. 30, no. 3 (1988), pp. 112–127.

61. Laurent, André. "The Cross-Cultural Puzzle of International Human Resource Management," *Human Resource Management*, vol. 25, no. 1 (1986), pp. 91–102. Copyright 1986 John Wiley & Sons, Inc.

62. Lovgren, Stephan. "Kenya: No Surprise: The 'Big Man' Wins," *U.S. News & World Report*, (January 12, 1998), p. 36.

63. McKinley, James C. "All Sides in Kenya Cry Fraud in Election," *New York Times* (December 31, 1997), p. A4.

64. McKinley, James C. "Chaos in Kenya Voting Sets Off Accusations of Fraud," *New York Times International* (December 30, 1997), p. A6.

65. McKinley, James C. "Kenya's President Takes Lead as Ballot Counting Drags On," *New York Times* (January 1, 1998), p. A4.

66. McKinley, James C. "A Woman to Run Kenya? One Says, 'Why Not?'" *New York Times* (August 3, 1997); Section 1, page 3, column 1.

67. Moran, Stahl, and Boyer, Inc. *Status of American Female Expatriate Employees: Survey Results* (Boulder, CO: International Division, 1988).

68. Murray, Alex. "International Personnel Repatriation: Cultural Shock in Reverse," *MSU Business Topics*, vol. 21, no. 2 (1973), pp. 59–66.

69. Osland, Joyce S.; Adler, N. J.; and Brody, Laura W. "Women and Global Leadership at Bestfoods," in Joyce S. Osland, David Kolb, and Irwin Rubin, eds., *Organizational Behavior: An Experimental Approach* (Upper Saddle River, NJ: Prentice Hall, 2001), pp. 533–555.

70. Pellico, M. T. and Stroh, Linda K. "Spousal Assistance Program: An Integral Component of the International Assignment," *New Approaches to Employee Management*, vol. 4 (1997), pp. 225–241.

71. Perham, J. C. "The Boom in Executive Jobs," *Dun's Review*, vol. 110, no. 5 (1977), pp. 80–81.

72. Perry, N. J. "If You Can't Join 'em, Beat 'em," *Fortune* (September 21, 1992), pp. 58–59.

73. Pogrebin, Robin. "Pearson Picks an American as Executive," *New York Times* (October 18, 1996), p. D7.

74. Porter, Gayle, and Tansky, Judith W. "Expatriate Success May Depend on a "Learning Orientation: Considerations for Selection and Training," *Human Resource Management*, vol. 38, no. 1 (1999), pp. 47–60.

75. Porter, Michael. *The Competitive Advantage of Nations* (New York: Free Press, 1990).

76. Roddick, Anita. *Body and Soul* (New York: Crown, 1991), p. 226.

77. Rosenzweig, P. M., and Nohria, N. "Influences on Human Resource Management Practices in Multinational Corporations," *Journal of International Business Studies,* 2nd quarter (1994), pp. 229–251.

78. "Rwanda: First Woman Premier Dies," Inter-Press Service Newswire (April 8, 1994).

79. Saint-Germain, Michelle A. "Women in Power in Nicaragua: Myth and Reality," in M. A. Genovese, ed., *Women as National* Leaders (Newbury Park, CA: Sage, 1993), pp. 70–102.

80. Smith, L. "The Hazards of Coming Home," *Dun's Review* (October 1975), pp. 71–73.

81. Steinhoff, P. G., and Tanaka, K. "Women Managers in Japan," in N. J. Adler and D. N. Izraeli, eds., *Competitive Frontiers: Women Managers in a Global Economy* (Cambridge, MA: Blackwell, 1994), pp. 79–100.

82. Steinhoff, P. G., and Tanaka, K. "Women Managers in Japan," in N. J. Adler and D. N. Izraeli, eds. *Women in Management Worldwide* (Armonk, NY: M.E. Sharpe, 1988), pp. 103–121.

83. Stogdill, R. *Handbook of Leadership* (New York: The Free Press, 1974).

84. Tung, Rosalie L. "American Expatriates Abroad: From Neophytes to Cosmopolitans," *Journal of World Business*, vol. 33 (1998), pp. 125–144.

85. Tung, Rosalie L. "Canadian Expatriates in Asia-Pacific: An Analysis of Their Attitude Toward and Experience in International Assignments," Paper presented at the meeting of the Society for Industrial and Organizational Psychology, St. Louis, MO (1997).

86. Tung, Rosalie L. "U.S. Multinationals: A Study of Their Selection and Training for Overseas Assignments," *Academy of Management Proceedings*, vol. 39 (1979), pp. 298–301.

87. Vinnicombe, Susan, and Colwill, Nina. *The Essence of Women in Management* (London: Prentice Hall, 1995).
88. "Vote Fraud Charges Fly in Kenya Election," *Chicago Sun-Times* (December 31, 1997), p. 28.
89. Yukl, Gary. *Leadership in Organizations,* 4th ed. (Upper Saddle River, NJ: Prentice Hall, 1998).

Index

V

W

About the Author

Nancy J. Adler is a professor of International Management in the Faculty of Management of McGill University in Montreal, Canada. She received her B.A. in economics, M.B.A., and Ph.D. in management from the University of California at Los Angeles (UCLA).

Dr. Adler conducts research and consults on strategic international human resource management, global leadership, women in international management, international negotiating, expatriation, developing culturally synergistic approaches to problem solving, and international organization development. She has authored more than 100 articles, produced the film *A Portable Life*, and published the books *International Dimensions of Organizational Behavior*, *Women in Management Worldwide*, and *Competitive Frontiers: Women Managers in a Global Economy*.

Dr. Adler consults to private corporations and government organizations on projects in Asia, Europe, North and South America, and the Middle East. She has taught Chinese executives in the People's Republic of China, held the Citicorp Visiting Doctoral Professorship at the University of Hong Kong, and taught executive seminars at INSEAD in France, Bocconi University in Italy, and Oxford University in England. She has twice received McGill University's Distinguished Teaching Award in Management.

Dr. Adler has served on the Board of Governors of the American Society for Training and Development (ASTD), the Canadian Social Science Advisory Committee to UNESCO, the Strategic Grants Committee of the Social Sciences and Humanities Research Council, the Executive Committees of the Pacific Asian Consortium for International Business, Education and Research, the International Personnel Association, and the Society for Human Resource Management's International Institute, as well as having held leadership positions in the Academy of International Business (AIB), the Society for Intercultural Education, Training, and Research (SIETAR), and the Academy of Management. Dr. Adler received ASTD's International Leadership Award, SIETAR's Outstanding Senior Interculturalist Award, the Sage Award for Outstanding Contributions to Management Research, and the YWCA's Femme de Mérite (Woman of Distinction) Award. She was selected as a 3M Teaching Fellow honoring her as one of Canada's top university professors, and elected to the Fellows of both the Academy of International Business and the Academy of Management. Dr. Adler has also served as an artist in residence at the Banff Centre for the Arts.